A/ wk
11

The French Revolution of 1789 and Its Impact

Recent Titles in
Contributions to the Study of World History

Christopher Columbus and the Portuguese, 1476–1498
Rebecca Catz

Clinging to Grandeur: British Attitudes and Foreign Policy in the
Aftermath of the Second World War
Michael Blackwell

The Legend of the Mutilated Victory: Italy, the Great War, and
the Paris Peace Conference, 1915–1919
H. James Burgwyn

Spain in the Nineteenth-Century World: Essays on Spanish
Diplomacy, 1789–1898
James W. Cortada, editor

The Entangling Alliance: The United States and European Security,
1950–1993
Ronald E. Powaski

Kings of Celtic Scotland
Benjamin T. Hudson

America's Feeble Weapon: Funding the Marshall Plan in France and
Italy, 1948–1950
Chiarella Esposito

The Jews of Medieval France: The Community of Champagne
Emily Taitz

Royalist Political Thought During the French Revolution
James L. Osen

Theatre in the Third Reich, the Prewar Years: Essays on Theatre
in Nazi Germany
Glen Gadberry

Between Ideology and *Realpolitik*: Woodrow Wilson and the Russian
Revolution, 1917–1921
Georg Schild

Stanley K. Hornbeck and the Open Door Policy, 1919–1937
Shizhang Hu

The French Revolution of 1789 and Its Impact

Edited by
Gail M. Schwab
and John R. Jeanneney

Prepared under the auspices
of Hofstra University

Contributions to the Study of World History, Number 44

Greenwood Press
Westport, Connecticut • London

Library of Congress Cataloging-in-Publication Data

The French Revolution of 1789 and its impact / edited by Gail M.
  Schwab and John R. Jeanneney.
        p.   cm.— (Contributions to the study of world history ; ISSN
  0885–9159 no. 44)
    Includes bibliographical references and index.
    ISBN 0–313–29339–2
    1. France—History—Revolution, 1789–1799—Influence—Congresses.
  2. Social change—Congresses.   3. Arts and revolutions—Congresses.
  4. Civilization, Modern—French influences—Congresses.   5. France—
  Relations—Foreign countries—Congresses.   I. Schwab, Gail M.
  II. Jeanneney, John R.   III. Series.
  DC158.8.F695   1995
  944.04—dc20   94–4795

British Library Cataloguing in Publication Data is available.

Library of Congress Catalog Card Number: 94–4795
ISBN: 0–313–29339–2
ISSN: 0885–9159

First published in 1995

Greenwood Press, 88 Post Road West, Westport, CT 06881
An imprint of Greenwood Publishing Group, Inc.

Printed in the United States of America

The paper used in this book complies with the
Permanent Paper Standard issued by the National
Information Standards Organization (Z39.48–1984).

10 9 8 7 6 5 4 3 2 1

Contents

Acknowledgments

The editors would like to express their thanks to Hofstra University without whose financial support the Conference, **The French Revolution of 1789 and Its Impact**, would never have taken place. We also thank the Cultural Service of the French Embassy in New York for its financial assistance.

Our heartfelt appreciation goes to the co-directors of the Hofstra University Cultural Center, Natalie Datlof and Alexej Ugrinsky, and the Conference coordinator, Athelene A. Collins, and to Judith M. D'Angio, who painstakingly and with infinite patience prepared the manuscript.

Introduction

Gail M. Schwab and John R. Jeanneney

All discourse is an attempt to impose a certain politicized order on the chaos of the universe. That particular discourse known as history, which makes sense out of the nonsense of the past, is no exception, and can only theoretically be differentiated from more obviously literary, or artistic, forms of discourse. The following essays from The French Revolution of 1789 and Its Impact, a conference held in October of 1989, attempt to come to terms, often from conflicting points of view, with the complex relationship between events past and present and their representations.

How did the lived experience that eventually became known as the French Revolution come to be organized? In the permanent and necessary absence of any monolithic narrative explanation, we are left with the efforts of different individuals to piece together a legible text. Where did the pieces come from? We might compare them to a patchwork, where old swatches of discourse, previously serving an entirely different ideological purpose, are appropriated for the new quilt, all taking on new qualities of texture, tone and color in relation to surrounding patches.

Erica Joy Mannucci shows masterfully in her "Providence for the Revolutionary People" how old Christian concepts, which had been systematically voided by the critical work of the Enlightenment, came to be recharged with a new revolutionary content. The term *providence* came to signify, not the working of God's will through time, but the inevitable secular triumph of the Revolution. Professor Mannucci also shows in great detail how the traditional Christian concepts of Hell, the Last Judgment, and martyrdom, secularized and carnivalized, helped the "Revolutionary People" come to terms with their situation.

Tom Conner's "Writing Revolution: Michelet's *History of the French Revolution*" deals with a similar theme, revealing Michelet's struggles to "rewrite and replace the sacred masterplot of Providential Christian history," with a different masterplot--that of "the progressive triumph of freedom." The old theological-monarchical concepts of grace and justice are rendered meaningless and then reendowed with significance through Michelet's efforts to "render strange the familiar" and "familiar the strange"--an operation which is, as Professor Conner shows, metaphorical, that is, literary and rhetorical.

Jeanne Fuchs's "Sexual Politics: Marivaux's *La Colonie*" demonstrates the same metaphorical transformations in three little-known works of the eighteenth-century playwright Marivaux. Many years before Michelet haunted the National Archives and even before the Revolutionary People took providence into their own hands, Marivaux had carnivalized the sexual politics of his society. In a world as topsy-turvy as the one discussed by Professor Mannucci, Marivaux's female heroines declare their independence from men and claim their right to equality. However, as Professor Fuchs concludes, no literal transformation results from Marivaux's metaphors. Nevertheless, although his sexual revolution had yet to be conceived on the political stage, some of its underlying motivations were represented on the comic stage, demonstrating the extreme complexity of the relationship between discourse and events. Are events not representations of discourse, just as discourse is representation of events? (Jeffrey Mehlman's essay takes up this paradoxical problem in Chapter 14).

Claudine Hunting, in "Cazotte and the Counterrevolution, or the Art of Losing One's Head," and Gislinde Seybert, in "The Concept of Virtue in Literature and Politics During the French Revolution of 1789: Sade and Robespierre," also examine traditional prerevolutionary structures as they are appropriated and changed to deal with revolutionary realities. Jacques Cazotte, in his quasi-delirious counterrevolutionary apologies, reads the French Revolution through the Book of Revelations, and casts himself in the role of the prophet Eleazar and the executed king in the role of the crucified Christ. Events can only signify through preexisting texts--through old language--and Professor Seybert shows both how revolutionaries like Robespierre strove to make use of old language, in this case the Christian and antique concepts of virtue, to establish and exercise totalitarian political control, and how a "subversive" like Sade articulated and undercut the revolutionaries' ideological program in his "Libertine's" carnivalizations of virtue.

Women played a role in revolutionary politics, and it is further illustration of the highly politicized nature of historical representations that their role in the making of the Revolution and in the inscribing of it in discourse, has all but been effaced, and is only just now being re-created as history by writers such as Susan Tenenbaum, Mary Trouille, and Catherine Montfort. Susan Tenenbaum, in "Mme. de Staël: Comparative Politics as Revolutionary Practice," demonstrates Mme. de Staël's mastery of the Montesquieuian system of comparative politics, and shows how in her hands it became a "revolutionary practice," alternately a sharp propaganda technique deployed against Napoleonic hegemony in Europe and a constructive agenda for the advancement of democracy among all European peoples. Mary Trouille, in "Revolution in the Boudoir: Mme. Roland's Subversion of Rousseau's Feminine Ideals," shows how a different Enlightenment discourse shaped the life and the writings of Mme. Roland. This extraordinary woman, who was to welcome death on the guillotine because it permitted her to die both in love and virtuous like Rousseau's divine Julie, played a key role in the Girondist period both as a writer and as a behind-the-scenes political activist.

These were activities Julie would never have embraced and would in fact have rejected as highly improper for the female sex, but as Professor Trouille proves, Mme. Roland, like all revolutionaries, appropriated a preexisting discourse to her own personal, political and ideological agenda.

In "French Women Writers and the Revolution: Preliminary Thoughts," Catherine R. Montfort addresses the question of the effacement of women from history, and of the distortion of both women's activity and their writing for political purposes. Professor Trouille had shown that Mme. Roland was condemned to the scaffold less for her subversive political ideals than for her subversive "unfeminine" behavior, and for daring to write in a male literary world. Professor Montfort's chapter further shows how Mme. de Staël's sexual behavior was subjected to the same scrutiny, criticism and ridicule, while the unquestionably excessive passion of Mme. de Sévigné for her daughter was glossed over, "normalized," and held up as an example of maternal devotion by a regime striving to force women to return to their traditional roles, after the Revolution had begun to effect some changes in their status. The dominant political discourse of the Napoleonic era, totalitarian and imperialist, created a Madonna-like Mme. de Sévigné according to the image of womanhood it was attempting to propagate, and a diabolical Mme. de Staël, the brilliant, independent woman who was the antithesis of this image. Paradoxically, the writings of both women, as well as their reputations, suffered distortion from the postrevolutionary political agenda.

The vicissitudes of politics and historical events affected the reputations of men as well as women. In "The Sublimity of Speech as Action: The Myth of Mirabeau, 1792−1848," Patricia A. Ward shows how the changing political climate in France after Mirabeau's death elevated him into a monumental and legendary hero, only to reject and ultimately forget him in the 1840s. Historical figures are created and re-created according to the different political needs of changing times and governments. They are functions not only of their own times but also of all succeeding moments.

The public nature of the dramatic genre would seem to make it particularly subject to the political pressures of rapidly changing times. Mario Hamlet-Metz's "French Theater and Revolution: The Eve and the Aftermath" shows how the revolutionary years, the Napoleonic era, and the Restoration period shaped the development of French theater, which was struggling to renew itself aesthetically despite governmental censorship, jingoism and popular demands. Barbara T. Cooper, in "Rewriting the Revolutionary Past in *Les Prussiens en Lorraine*," shows how the image of the Revolution itself became a tool of propaganda in the France of the July Monarchy. We see from Professor Cooper's analysis of Gustave Lemoine's and Prosper-Parfait Goubaux's 1840 play *Les Prussiens en Lorraine* how the violent class struggles of the 1789 Revolution are mitigated and softened to the point of effacement, so that the political ideals of 1840, national unity, and bourgeois and liberal aristocratic domination, become the principal motivating elements of the Revolution.

Evlyn Gould, in "Prosper Mérimée Is Thinking the Revolution," also focuses on a text of the late July Monarchy, Mérimée's *Carmen*. In a wonderfully playful and insightful equation of the Bohemian life of Carmen the *gitane* with the revolutionary ideals of *liberté, égalité, fraternité*, Professor Gould, concentrating on the complex and often ignored narrative frame of the Carmen story, shows Mérimée questioning the scientific status of historical discourse. She claims that Carmen "must be read as an exploration into the aesthetic problems confronted by the writer of history, that writer who sets out to relate objective, impersonal facts about the past but whose objectivity is undermined by personal fascinations and choices about chronology, value, point of view, and identity." Mérimée demonstrates, long before Freud, the working of desire through the text.

Both Jeffrey Mehlman in "Georges Sorel and the 'Dreyfusard Revolution,'" and Gail M. Schwab in "Revolution in the *Education sentimentale*: Structure, Theory and History," deal with writers of the late nineteenth century. Both also attempt to come to terms with postmodernist critical theory and its relationship to history. Professor Mehlman, like Professor Gould, opens the question of the historian's "personal fascinations," as he develops what he calls the Sorelian "myth" of the "counterrevolutionary revolution," or the "revolution played out in the decadent mode." He further plays one historian's personal myth off against another's, ending up with what he calls a "double chiasmus," or the ultimate undecidability of historical discourse which, as interpretation, is subject to all the contradictions of hermeneutics.

Professor Schwab, in her reading of Gustave Flaubert's 1869 *Education sentimentale*, both embraces ahistorical, structural interpretations of this novel and moves beyond them to reopen the question of history in the text. The relationship between literature and history is articulated at the level of dialogue in a Bakhtinian synthesis. Events, values, ideas, morals and historical figures exist only in language, and it is only in language that they become history.

Writers working within the academic discipline of history have also carried on their own ever-changing dialogue with the French Revolution and its many ramifications. Charles Tilly in "Cities, Bourgeois and the French Revolution" analyzes the French Revolution as an extension of the state's direct rule, down to the most local, rural levels where prerevolutionary administration had been indirect and left in the hands of nobles and priests. For Tilly, the revolutionary empowerment of the bourgeoisie in the capital was paralleled by their newly achieved role as guarantors and administrators of state power in the provinces. In a year when it is not fashionable to do so, Professor Tilly restates the thesis that the French Revolution was a social revolution in an administrative sense as well. This is one of the reasons why state centralization was so abhorrent to counterrevolutionaries.

The question of noble decline during the French Revolution is examined from an economic perspective by John Dunne. His analysis, "The Nobility's New Clothes: Revisionism and the Survival of the Nobility During the French Revolution," examines the research and arguments supporting and opposing the thesis that the nobility suffered significant losses of land; he concludes that all is still inconclusive. More fundamental evidence is needed, and he points out directions for further research.

Malcolm Crook and Melvin Edelstein both investigate the new era of popular national elections. Professor Crook's "The Rights of Man and the Right to Vote: The Franchise Question During the French Revolution" compares revolutionary theories of the franchise with the actuality of voter participation. Professor Crook maintains that the primary barrier to democracy was the multilevel system of indirect elections. The concept of passive citizen and the restrictions on the rights of males to vote were less significant.

In "Aux Urnes Citoyens! The Transformation of French Electoral Participation (1789—1870)," Melvin Edelstein shows that the comparatively low rates of voter participation described by Malcolm Crook did not change dramatically until 1848. Edelstein concludes by advancing his own explanation for successful nationalization of mass politics under the Second Republic and the Second Empire.

The French Revolution had a greater impact on England than any domestic political event in that nation. Marilyn Morris presents "The Impact of the French Revolution on London Reform Societies," demonstrating how the members were first stimulated and then somewhat inhibited by the course of events across the Channel. Her analysis of the minutes of the London Corresponding Society, a workingman's organization, suggests that although these members drew back from the French revolutionary governments, they modified rather than abandoned their own democratic, Paineite aspirations.

Richard Herr argues in "The French Revolution and Spain" that the impact of the French Revolution has been overstated. Spain had its own Enlightenment and its own enlightened despot in Carlos III. He believes that "one can find precedents in the reforms of the 18th century for almost every measure that they [the Spanish liberals of 1812] enacted." The discrediting of the Spanish Bourbons came more from a personal rejection of Carlos IV and his entourage than from any French example. Similarly, the physical impact of the revolutionary wars had a greater impact on Spain than any ideas from France.

Professor Herr's mode of analysis for Spain in the era of the French Revolution is avowedly "counterfactual." Uffe Ostergaard follows a similar approach in exploring an alternative to the French Revolution in his native Denmark. Professor Ostergaard's "Republican Revolution or Absolutist Reform?" discusses how the Danish monarchy, under Crown Prince Frederick and his advisers, imposed an enduring social and economic revolution from above shortly before the Revolution broke out in France. By liberating the more substantial peasant landholders and giving the bourgeoisie entry into politics and administration, Denmark was rendered proof against violent political and social upheavals. Professor Ostergaard finds that the "Danish *ancien régime* developed rather smoothly into capitalist modernity whereas republican France took a much more cumbersome path."

As the storm of the French Revolution swelled on the Continent, repercussions were felt across the Atlantic in the Spanish Empire. Gregory Ludlow's "The French Revolution of 1789 and its Impact on Spanish-American Independence" takes a broad hemispheric overview of the hispanic domains, and Julia Ortiz Griffin's "Waves Breaking on a Distant Shore: Puerto Rico in the Era of the French Revolution" is more narrowly focused.

Professor Ludlow stresses the role of a Spanish Enlightenment in the Americas somewhat less than does Professor Herr in dealing with Spain. The ideas of Rousseau were certainly more useful than any to come from Spain when it came to justifying nineteenth-century independence movements, but once independence was achieved, a general conservative shift took place in the ruling circles of the new states. In any case, ideology was not enough to bring about change. The sorry spectacle of Carlos IV and the Bonapartist policy of encouraging the colonies toward independence or equality with the Iberian provinces were also major factors.

Professor Ortiz Griffin's narrative of Puerto Rico during the revolutionary era demonstrates that a Spanish island in the Caribbean could be an exception to many of the generalizations applied by Professor Ludlow to Spanish America as a whole. Puerto Rico remained an unyielding bastion of loyalty to the Spanish crown long after the wave of revolutionary independence had swept the mainland of Latin America. Professor Ortiz Griffin explains that a certain national consciousness was raised during these years of revolution elsewhere, but Puerto Rico remained essentially a garrison island, the staging area for the unsuccessful Spanish attempts to maintain authority to the west and south.

As we turn from the nineteenth to the twentieth century, two chapters on the Russian Revolution of 1917 reveal that it, too, was profoundly conditioned by interpretations of the Revolution of 1789. George Jackson's "The Influence of the French Revolution on Lenin's Conception of the Russian Revolution" discusses how Lenin used the French Revolution as an analytical model and a starting point for planning and interpreting his own revolution. To be sure, Lenin did revise the scenario at critical junctures, but he identified similar interplays of social forces, and he adapted the revolutionary taxonomy of 1789 — 1794 to his own needs and purposes.

In "Uses of the Past: Bolshevism and the French Revolutionary Tradition," Gabriel Schoenfeld exhibits a broader focus on the same subject. Using illustrative examples, Schoenfeld identifies characteristic ways in which the Bolsheviks and their successors have used history in their revolutionary thinking, such as in defining the political environment through comparison with past historical situations, or in assessing the effectiveness of different strategies. Homages to the French Revolution as touchstone are still in evidence among Russians of many political persuasions, although the frequency and sincerity of these cultural reverences have certainly diminished.

The French Revolution gave legal emancipation to the Jews, but the authors of two chapters pointed out that this was one principle that was questioned or disregarded even after the consolidation of the Third Republic.

Willa E. Silverman in "Marianne Revisited: Anti-Republican Political
Caricature, 1880—1900" presents and analyzes increasingly scurrilous
renditions of the republicon icon Marianne which reveal the growing
viciousness and anti-Semitism of the anti-republican right.

Sondra M. Rubenstein expands on the theme of postrevolutionary anti-
Semitism in France in "The Lost Legacy of the French Revolution and the
Persecution of French Jewry in Vichy France." Professor Rubenstein reviews
the emancipating legislation that grew out of the French Revolution, traces
the persistence of anti-Semitism, and assesses the reluctance of Jews,
particularly the more recent immigrants from Eastern Europe, to assimilate
themselves into French culture. Her chapter concludes with an account of the
fate of the Jews under the French State of Vichy.

The essays presented in this volume clearly show that the French
Revolution was more than a series of political events that took place in one
European country at the end of the eighteenth century. The French Revolution
was a transhistorical, multinational, and multicultural discourse. It served
finally not only as a point of reference by which and through which a complex
of cultural values and styles could be defined, but also as a model or a
negative model for the elaboration of ideologies, and of political and
administrative strategies for bureaucracies around the world.

The French Revolution
of 1789 and Its Impact

1

Providence for the Revolutionary People

Erica Joy Mannucci

Generally speaking, we can say that in the revolutionary debates and decisions on religious issues we can recognize the accomplishment of the classic Enlightenment critique of clerical religion. Secularization and a drastic reduction of the material and moral power of the clergy are, indeed, among the major political questions of the French Revolution. In different ways, different political leaders tend toward a reorganization of the religious apparatus, concepts and sentiments.

In the Gironde circles there were nonbelievers--heirs to encyclopedism and to a certain skeptical tradition--like Condorcet or Brissot, who wanted for the New France a constitutional Catholic Church, which in their opinion, would have contributed to political stability. And there are Catholics, like Bishop Fauchet, one of the founders of the *Cercle Social* in the early years of the Revolution, who tempered his traditional faith with a certain amount of both tolerance and sentimentalism. In the inaugural address for the *Confédération Universelle des Amis de la Vérité* (Universal Confederation of the Friends of Truth), Fauchet, saluting "this era of regeneration, better, of veritable creation, where the moral universe is finally to emerge from the chaos of dissension, hatred and discord, to enter, after the upsetting that necessarily goes with the conquest of the rights of nature, into the eternal order of amity, union and harmony, "exclaimed: "Homage to Providence! She has long prepared the means; the revolution was needed to use them."[1]

Among the Jacobins, Robespierre is heir to the tradition of "natural religion," a nonclerical religion of the Supreme Being, guaranteed by the idea of the immortality of the soul. Robespierre knowingly renounces the interiority of this faith to make it into a constitutional article.[2] For him, as well, France cannot do without a God linked to a public cult. Robespierre sees faith in the Supreme Being as the faith of the oppressed, and he proclaims himself morally and politically opposed to what he calls "atheism."[3] He speaks about providence as well, using a notion of it that is purified of the dogmatism of revealed religion: "To invoke the name of Providence," he says in March 1792 at the Jacobin Club "and to express the idea of a Supreme Being guiding the destinies of nations and seemingly keeping most particular vigil over the French Revolution is to voice (. . .) a sentiment that comes from my heart and is for me of the utmost importance."[4]

But another tradition--which I have elsewhere examined at some length and called the "other enlightenment"[5]--whose long history antedates that of the Enlightenment, arrives at its culmination in the revolutionary period, whether directly or through mediation, whether combined with Enlightenment thought or not. This tradition, which over centuries had gathered complex elements, from heresy to heterodox mysticism, from utopianism to millennialism and esoterism as well, helps us to become aware of certain questions of historical interpretation. The history of the clash between orthodoxy in power and heterodoxy; between an unfathomable God of priests and a different God, humanized to the point of becoming a non-God; between a providence projected exclusively into the next world, and another that aims at liberation in this world, suggests to us that the concept of atheism itself is a historical problem. (In the political thought of revolutionary leaders it is a given category, often meaningful only in a negative sense--absence of belief in any God--or as an ideological accusation). One starting point in our examination of this problem can be the question of whether the theoretical and political break runs between religious belief and atheism, or whether it is more accurate from a historical and political point of view to say that the split runs between the religion of authority, and concrete and combative forms of hope, which turn even the meaning of originally theological ideas upside-down, to the point where they are no longer necessary.[6]

I want to give two examples of an extremely heterodox use of religious concepts and images, and in particular of the idea of providence, in the context of revolutionary thought. I choose two quite different figures, who experience the same events but from different theoretical points of view. They both had links with the *Cercle Social*, but their ideas were not those of the Gironde;[7] they are the most important Illuminist of the period, Louis-Claude de Saint-Martin, and the atheist writer Sylvain Maréchal, the journalist of *Révolutions de Paris*, author of the *Manifesto of Equals*, heir to the tradition of eighteenth century free-thinkers, but also to a utopianism that has its point of reference in the myth of the golden age.

PROVIDENCE AND REVOLUTION IN SAINT-MARTIN

Saint-Martin was a member of the poor provincial nobility, born in 1743. In his twenties he was a member of the *Elus Coens*, a heterodox masonic group of theosophists who practiced theurgy, the same group with which Cazotte had links.[8] Saint-Martin later denied both masonry and theurgy, but maintained the fundamental ideas of theosophy, a mystical vision that is Christian but heterodox, anticlerical and opposed by the Church.[9] This cultural atmosphere was not rare among the European upper classes in the second half of the eighteenth century, although different political implications were attached to it. It implied confidence in the possibility of human regeneration, of a reintegration of the original harmony with divinity for a humanity that is only temporarily degraded and confused, but still has potentialities of wisdom and perfection. It aims at a regeneration defined in spiritual and moral (but nonetheless historical) terms, to be attained as soon as possible, in this world. This vision has contact points with apocalyptic hopes, and these we find developed in Saint-Martin's writings, influenced by the reality of the French Revolution, of which the theosophist heartily approved, and in which he participated, even if he cannot strictly be called a political activist.

In his *Lettre à un ami sur la Révolution française*, written toward the end of the Terror but published in the year III, we again find the idea that providence guides the Revolution.[10] If Fauchet's providence was Catholic and Robespierre's deist, Saint-Martin's is both theosophic and apocalyptic, and it has a central position in his discourse. He declares that he has a total confidence in the French Revolution, "abridged image of the Last Judgment," because it is the work of providence: "I believe that its equitable hand had the object of destroying all the abuses which infected the old government of France on all sides."

For Saint-Martin, providence intended to make humanity break away from the apathy that was its daily guilt. If the French people were to become the people of the "new law," a period of "strong and violent action" was necessary, and that action he called human-divine. With this action, that is, Revolution, providence started a radical change of all existing structures, punishing with "vengeful hand" the aristocracy, "this monstrous growth among individuals who are equal by nature," and more importantly, the clergy, the guiltiest party, "enjoying all their artificial rights and temporal usurpations" and "indirect cause of the crimes of kings," because it was they who had arrogated the right to legitimize the kings. The clergy, covering religion with mystery because often they were not even able to demonstrate the existence of their God, sought power, and first of all power over consciences, making "their sacred books only a tariff to be extorted on the faith of souls . . . with the aid of terror."

Providence struck down the French monarch as well, and with him the entire institution of monarchy, which concentrated "a whole nation in one man and his supporters, whereas all men of a State should forget themselves, to devote themselves and recognize themselves exclusively in the Nation." After Louis XVI, providence will punish all monarchs, as a guilty "class of men." Saint-Martin writes that "Our enemies" cannot understand that the Revolution has brought irreversible changes; they are incapable of raising their eyes high enough to see the ultimate meaning of what is happening, which "could be called the revolution of mankind." The "devil's puppets"[11] think that they can treat "a great Nation, free and watching over her own interests by herself, as they had done in former times with a ministerial cabinet," that is, with those contingent political or ministerial changes that had been called "revolutions" in the *ancien régime*.

What he saw in the Revolution was that the oppressed "as if by supernatural power," had taken back their usurped rights, which for him were spiritual and political as a consequence. Revolution had opened the way to the moral regeneration of French society and hence of all humanity. We find this idea, with different nuances, in revolutionary militants, among them Maréchal himself.   But their utopic vein is secular and characterized by socioeconomic and political projects, whereas Saint-Martin always remains first and foremost a spiritualist, even when he condemns private property.[12] For him the first goal is the regaining of harmony between man and God.

But concepts like man, God, or the relationship between man and God, have different political implications depending on the definitions they are assigned. Saint-Martin's divinity is luminous and good, and man should feel only love and spontaneous admiration for it: this sentiment ought not to be called "religion," he says, because this word has acquired a "somber" character. And man has "sweet virtues," "loving and effusive qualities" that he had developed in the free fraternal society before the fall, when he was "glorious" and in harmony with the divine.

Thus, the relationship between man and God, as it shows itself in the relation providence-revolution, human-divine action, tends to be one of consonance. In Saint-Martin's spiritualism there is no radical distance between the divine and the human and no unfathomably punishing God. We are in a conceptual universe far different from that of a God whose providence avenges the oppressed people. In this universe man is not a metaphysically evil being over whom God lords it like a despot. The latter premises are, rather, those of De Maistre's political thought, and his negative apocalyptic vision of the revolution.

If, on the other hand, we compare Saint-Martin's man with Fauchet's man of natural rights, or with the militant man-citizen who identifies with the political chorus of the "nation" or the "*patrie*"--an image that we can symbolically associate with Robespierre--the man in Saint-Martin's utopia, member of that society without coercive authority, based on the free development of potentialities and always open to "perfectibility," as we see him in the *Eclair sur l'association humaine* of year V, is a man who goes beyond even the necessity of being represented and governed. This is because he is *l'homme-esprit*, a divine man. Perhaps Saint-Martin's utopia is similar to that hypothetical society of gods, the only one where a pure democracy would be possible for Rousseau, an author he admired.

Coming back to the problem of the historical meaning of religiousness and atheism, it is legitimate to reflect on the idea that in the concept of a divine man lies the first step toward the idea of God as a product of human self-alienation. Certainly, Saint-Martin would have refused this perspective. But his human-divine providence may be seen as a theoretical bridge toward a vision in which humanity, seeking in the liberation from repressive institutions the way to reach its best potentialities, recognizes itself as the maker of its own destiny.

ATHEISM AND CARNIVAL IN MARÉCHAL'S THEATER

In Maréchal's *The Last Judgment of Kings: Prophecy in One Act*, we can see how a declaredly atheist author builds on these themes a didactic political play.[13] His is a new theater, different in style even from that of the first revolutionary period, for example, Chénier's *Charles IX*.[14] Written in October 1793, just after Marie-Antoinette's execution, it addresses itself especially to the *sans-culottes* audience, with a subject designed to receive unanimous applause, as in fact it did in its numerous performances in Paris and other cities. The Committee of Public Safety had thousands of copies printed to send to the front and even provided the gunpowder, sorely needed at the front, to repeat the final eruption of the volcano every night at the Théâtre de la République.

It is a new theater, but the title itself shows us that the author uses the strength of a long tradition, securely established in the expectations of the audience, to break with tradition, filling well-known themes and images with new content and form. The theme of the Last Judgment had been used for didactic purposes since the Middle Ages, in the theater, in frescoes, in stained-glass windows. In Maréchal's revolutionary play, the images that belong to the religious apocalyptic tradition are turned upside-down and at the same time are brought to the extreme consequences of popular heretic interpretation, because the responsibility for historical events belongs solely to the European peoples. Moreover, not only are the Last Judgment and prophecy secular in character, but also the atmosphere of the play is rather gay and sometimes comic. The 1793 audiences laughed, cheered, and made merry; this play really spoke to the sans-culottes, because it was the work of a cultured man from a semipopular background, who knew how to use not only high but popular culture as well, presenting it transformed but understandable to the members of his audience.

The prophecy is that of the extension of the Revolution to all Europe and of the dethronement and punishment of all monarchs (as we have seen, a prophecy found in Saint-Martin's *Lettre* as well). Maréchal had already written this prophecy, just before the Revolution, in the *Apologues modernes à l'usage du dauphin*.[15] A passage that is reprinted at the beginning of the text of the *Last Judgment* represents a visionary dream that all the peoples of the earth, on the day of Saturnalia, get hold by previous mutual consent of their monarchs. They gather them all together and bring them to a desert island, where they have to make do without their retinue, and where they will not be able to live peacefully together, but will eventually destroy each other.

After the French Revolution this is no longer seen as a dream, but rather as a historical possibility. In the *Last Judgment* the visionary is transformed into an aged Robinson Crusoe, exiled by the French monarchic system to a volcanic desert island because twenty years before he had dared try to snatch his young daughter from the clutches of rapist aristocrats. He is an *ante-litteram* sans-culotte punished by the corrupt ancien régime for his moral dignity. At the entrance of the cave where he lives, he has carved the motto "It is better to have a volcano for a neighbor than a king. Liberty, Equality," a motto combining political choice with irony. The representatives of the European sans-culottes, along with the former monarchs, land one day on the island. The sans-culottes recognize the old man as a "martyr" of the old regime, who might have died without knowing that his country and Europe had been liberated, though, as the "sacred words" in his motto show, he had been able to conceive of it.

The sans-culottes tell him the story of the liberation of the oppressed peoples brought about by the people themselves. The old man is enthusiastic. He had never dared hope for such a revolution, though "I had always believed that the people, who are as powerful as the God preached to them, had only to desire." Here there is no longer a divine or human-divine providence, as in Saint-Martin; the revolutionary people replace it with their own will. Thus, the sans-culottes tell the old man how they came to the decision to rise up simultaneously all over Europe. They tell him how a "Convention européenne" had decided to deport all kings to an island rather than execute them. And the old man assures them that the island is suitable for their purpose, especially since the volcano seems on the point of erupting.

Let us stop here before the tyrants are brought ashore. Certain elements stand out in this text, although their presence must not be seen as a logical chain, an orderly discourse that "stands" on its own. Every symbol has several interpretations that do not necessarily "agree" and may not always be deliberate. Nor could it be otherwise; the new must arise from the disarrangement of many traditional symbols, the Last Judgment, for example. This Christian theme recurs throughout the play, turned upside-down, of course, because the sans-culottes substitute their will for God's, or, as the Roman sans-culotte later says contemptuously to the Pope, "We want no more prayers from a priest: the sans-culottes' God is liberty, it's equality, it's fraternity." Of particular interest is the insistence on the collective decision for all to rise up together on an established date. This gesture not only generally recalls, in its solemn choral character, the idea of the ritual and the sacred, but it is also an inverted reminder of the insistence of the Gospels, and in particular of Matthew 24, that it is not given to men to know the *exact moment* when the Apocalypse and the Last Judgment will come to *all the nations*. The kings are condemned because they are the persecutors of the poor and the weak, as in the Gospels and Revelation, but they are condemned by the poor and the weak themselves, and no longer by the supreme authority into which they had projected themselves until the Revolution.[16]

The island and the old man himself are also symbols rich in interpretations and antecedents. There are not only classical allusions, but also literary and utopian references, and last but not least, biblical allusions. The biblical references are the most relevant here. This polysemic aspect is especially clear in the figure of the old man. As we have already seen, he may be viewed as a Robinson Crusoe, and *Robinson Crusoe* was the only book Rousseau's Emile was allowed to read in the first stage of his education, because the character represented the free, purely human man. Maréchal was considerably influenced by Rousseau. The old man may also be compared to Maréchal's own utopian patriarch.[17] But he is also defined as "martyr" of the ancien régime, like the martyrs avenged in the Last Judgment; he is presented as a prophet as well, who has forseen the Revolution, and who makes us think of the figure of the "just man" who lived before the age of redemption and is saved in the Christian Last Judgment.

To write for the sans-culottes meant to use more or less deliberately those sacred or profane images that they already knew. With the landing of the tyrants the profane element comes into play. The former kings are brought ashore with the Pope and Catherine II (impersonated in Paris by the comic actor Michot). The sans-culottes from each country enumerate their crimes, and the sovereigns attempt pitiful justifications. (George of England exclaims: "You can't punish a madman! You bring him to hospital!") The sans-culottes invite nature to complete their work with the volcano's fire and they leave the kings alone. A fight breaks out between the Pope and Catherine. Then another fight breaks out when the monarchs discover that the king of Spain has concealed a piece of bread and is trying to eat it. The whole scene is full of comic and grotesque elements.[18] The sans-culottes return and throw the kings a case of hardtack because "they feel pity as well as justice." The riot that follows is brought to an end by the eruption of the volcano. The kings are dashed underground. (The French text says "dans les entrailles de la terre entr' ouverte" — into the half-open bowels of the earth).

In the introductory passage we have seen a reference to the Saturnalia. At the time of the play, the turning upside-down is, or seems, established forever, and is no longer simply realized for a single day as in the tradition of the carnival. This tradition is as strongly rooted in popular culture as that of the Last Judgment, and we see it in revolutionary provincial festivals and other instances. Furthermore, the contents of the two traditions, the sacred and the profane, tend to agree in popular culture.

The comic and the grotesque in the play should be seen in this perspective of carnival. In carnival, for example, the body and bodily functions have a crucial role. In Maréchal's play we find two physical elements. First, and of course not by chance, is the deposed monarchs' greed for food: they fight over it. The second is the scene of the bodily fight between the Pope, a man "in a skirt," and Catherine, a woman who is holding a sceptre, and who is, moreover, interpreted by a man; a woman against whom the only vulgar expression in the play— "Madame de l'enjambée" (Madame Straddle) is used. There is also a nasty pun whose meaning is that she is a whore. Catherine was famous for her sexual license; in anticlerical satire the priest, dressed like a woman, is a hypocrite preaching chastity but acting like a libertine. Thus, the fight has a salacious touch that makes it all the funnier.

The image of the volcano recalls a compulsory part of every carnival, "'hell' . . . represented by a balloon throwing out flames."[19] According to Jacques Proust, the fact that it is nature-volcano that makes the final decision represents a political limitation of the play, because it is a sign of the impotence of the sans-culottes.[20] This may be true in a way,[21] but at the same time this solution to the play follows the logic of popular grotesque comedy; the kings become comic bogeymen, in a "carnivalization" (to borrow an expression of Bakhtin's) of consciousness that accompanies the overturning

of the old, the regenerating, almost sensually liberating eruption.   This is
Maréchal's intelligence; he builds his didactics with moral and sacred emotion
and with laughter, a laughter that defuses the violence in the tyrants' death.
Thus, he proposes a joyous providence of the people, their own providence,
aiming at the attainment of happiness.[22]   His emphasis is not on bloody
regenerations or national wars, but on a fraternal choral action of all the
European peoples without direct violence.[23]

CONCLUSION

A revolution in progress is a time when all former certitudes are put to
the test, and new codes, new ideological patterns, must be created and
established. In other writings Maréchal warned that the Revolution would not
be accomplished as long as its makers remained tied to old ideas, changing
them only superficially. He said that revolutionary France owed its only good
laws to the popular movement, demonstrating in the streets, *and* showing its
freedom of judgment in the theaters. For Maréchal the religious politics of
leaders like the Girondins or Robespierre were not a real solution to the
problem of the relations among religion, ignorance and power. The political
leaders exploited the authority of the fundamental religious ideas--God, the
immortality of the soul--or of a "tamed" clergy to support the new regime.
Maréchal tried a new pattern, using the pathos of liberation of popular religion
and carnival, to create in his audience a new secular confidence in their own
historical and political strength.
If Maréchal's attempt is the beginning of a new ideological pattern, in
Saint-Martin we see the culmination of an old heterodox tradition. It is the
maximum development of the idea of the potentialities for regeneration present
in a spiritual, universal man. This man can become human-divine. Thus,
heterodox spiritualism tends to become a secular philosophy. But it remains
in the realm of philosophy because the figure of the *homme-esprit* cannot be
translated into actual modern political terms. From a political point of view,
Saint-Martin's thought cannot go beyond a version of traditional millennialism
influenced by the reality of the Revolution, while Maréchal's ideas interact
with the social sources of popular culture.

NOTES

1. *Bouche de fer*, III October (1790). All translations from French into
English are mine. The ideas and images concentrated in this passage recur in
many revolutionary texts.

2. Robespierre's religious ideas and politics have not only given rise
to intense historiographic debate, but were also vehemently attacked by some
authors (such as Michelet). A recent nonacademic biography even stresses
religious vision as the key to interpreting this figure. See Henri Guillemin,
Robespierre politique et mystique (Paris, 1987).

3. See in particular Robespierre's well-known *Rapport fait au nom du Comité de salut public* on 18 floréal, year II, where atheism is attacked as an "arid doctrine" linked to a system of conspiracy against the Republic, and an "affectation of zeal against what they call religious prejudices," typical of all the "deserters of the cause of the people," who thus try to compensate their indulgence toward aristocrats and tyrants. On the other hand, there is nothing "resembling atheism so much as the religions [the priests] have made" [Editor's translations]. Moreover, the idea of the mortality of the soul is seen as a "degradation of humanity" [Author's translation].

4. Cited by George Rudé, *Robespierre: Portrait of a Revolutionary Democrat* (London, 1975).

5. See Erica J. Mannucci, *Gli altri lumi: Esoterismo e politica nel Settecento francese* (Palermo, 1988).

6. For a philosophical perspective on these themes, see Ernst Bloch, *Atheismus im Christentum* (Frankfurt, 1968).

7. See Gary Kates, *The "Cercle Social": The Girondins the French Revolution* (Princeton, N.J., 1985).

8. The classic book on the *Elus Coens* is René Le Forestier, *La Franc-Maçonnerie occultiste au XVIIIe siècle et l'ordre des Elus Coens* (Paris, 1928). Theurgy is a sort of magic-mystic art, born in Neoplatonic circles: it is based on the knowledge of the "true essence" of divinity: this knowledge should give the power to influence divinity, forcing it to incarnate itself temporarily, or at least to manifest itself through "agents." Theurgy was adopted by certain occultists in the Renaissance.

9. This is the *voie intime*, in mystic terms: it is the alternative to the "exterior way"--rituals, churches, and so on. It does not imply initiation. The "inner" and the "exterior" ways are two aspects of esoterism, which can often intertwine in individuals. Saint-Martin wrote his own spiritual biography, *Mon Portrait historique et philosophique* (Paris, 1961). There are nineteenth-century books about him which are now quite obsolete). Today two experts on Saint-Martin are Robert Amadou and Nicole Jacques-Chaquin; in addition, Antoine Faivre has written about him in various works.

10. Louis-Claude de Saint-Martin, *Lettre à un ami, ou Considérations politiques, philosophiques et religieuses sur la Révolution Francaise* (Paris, year III [1795]. His other political texts are: *Eclair sur l'association humaine* (Paris, year V [1797]); *Réflexions d'un observateur sur la question: Quelles sont les institutions les plus propres à fonder la morale d'un peuple?* (n.p., [1798] and *Le Crocodile, ou la Guerre du bien et du mal arrivée sous le règne de Louis XV* (Paris, year VII [1799]).

11. In a letter to Liebisdorf Saint-Martin calls the enemies of the Revolution "mannequins" of the devil.

12. Saint-Martin does not accept the idea that property is a natural right and that society was founded to defend it, because this vision implies the exclusion from society of those who have nothing. Private property is considered by Saint-Martin the institution *par excellence* of degraded humanity.

13. Sylvain Maréchal, *Le Jugement dernier des rois: Prophétie en un acte et en prose* (Paris, year II [1793]). On Maréchal, see Maurice Dommanget, *Sylvain Maréchal, l'égalitaire, l'homme sans dieu* (Paris, 1950) and Françoise Aubert, *Sylvain Maréchal* (Pisa, 1975).

14. On French revolutionary theater in general, see Marvin Carlson, *The Theatre of the French Revolution* (Ithaca, N. Y., 1966); Jean Truchet, *Théâtre du XVIIIe siècle*, vol. II (Paris, 1974); Daniel Hamiche, *Le Théâtre et la Révolution* (Paris, 1973); Emmet Kennedy, *A Cultural History of the French Revolution* (New Haven, Conn./London, 1989). More specifically, compare the point of view of this essay with Judith Schlanger's "Théâtre révolutionnaire et représentation du bien," *Poétique: Revue de théorie et d'analogie littéraire* 22 (1975).

15. Sylvain Maréchal, *Apologues modernes à l'usage du dauphin: Premières leçons du fils aîné d'un roi* (Bruxelles, 1788).

16. Jacques Proust has written that Maréchal did not reinterpret the Christian myth with sufficient freedom and irony. But this comment, which is not developed by the author, does not, I think, take into account the delicate transitional moral and political phase in which the audience Maréchal wanted to reach found itself. See "De Sylvain Maréchal à Maiakovski: Contribution à l'étude du théâtre révolutionnaire," *Studies in XVIIIth Century French Literature* (Exeter, 1975).

17. Maréchal developed his patriarchal utopianism in many works before and during the Revolution: see in particular *Correctif à la Révolution* (Paris, year II [1793]).

18. Revolutionary caricature comes to mind: see Antoine de Baecque, *La caricature révolutionnaire* (Paris, 1988), where we read: "Varennes and the arrest of the king in flight mark a profound rupture in the French political imaginary. The image of the king, brutally desacralized, comes to concentrate within itself all negative attributes. . . . With a predilection for the pig, caricature represents the king as obese gourmand, clumsy cuckold, or impenitent drinker" [Editor's translation]. The author goes on to say that revolutionary caricature maintained a largely inherited aesthetics (grotesque,

allegory, etc.), but was at the same time deeply modern, because it inaugurated an important tradition: every person with a political function, no matter how popular he/she is, is subject to the changes of public opinion.

19.   Mikhail Bakhtin, *Rabelais and His World* (Cambridge, Mass., 1968).

20.   Jacques Proust, "Jugement dernier des rois," *Approches des Lumières: Mélanges offerts à Jean Fabre* (Paris, 1974).

21.   In English counterrevolutionary caricature the French Revolution itself is represented at least in one instance as a volcano. I want to thank Pascal Dupuy for showing me the caricature: "The Eruption of the Mountain," July 25, 1794.

22.   In *Théodore Desorgues ou la Désorganisation* (Paris, 1985), Michel Vovelle has raised the following question: "These masquerades of the year II, associating derision, the inversion of sex roles, and transvestism [or disguise], in a pedagogy which follows all the well-worn paths of popular anticlericalism. . . . I have often wondered how the exchange had been able to take place between the language of de-Christianization of the bourgeois elite and that of popular groups. Just like the Sylvain Maréchal of the *Jugement dernier des rois*, Desorgues illustrates this contamination by different currents" [Editor's translation.] See also Vovelle, *La mentalité révolutionnaire* (Paris, 1985).

23.   See his ideas on wars, violence, and the like, in *Correctif à la révolution*. Maréchal's opinions cited in the conclusions below can be found in particular in this work and in *Dame Nature à la barre de l'Assemblée Nationale* (Paris, 1791).

2

Writing Revolution: Michelet's *History of the French Revolution*

Tom Conner

Jules Michelet (1798—1874) today stands out as the Gargantua of French historians. His massive, protean seventeen-volume *Histoire de France*, concluded in 1876, and his earlier *Histoire de la Révolution Française*, published between 1847 and 1853, are brilliant examples of a hybrid discourse commonly known as "romantic history." This history is neither entirely fact nor fiction, at once romance and history, a strange offspring of the romantic aesthetic that produced Quasimodo--what you might call, in homage to Hugo's hunchback in *Notre-Dame de Paris*, "un discours historique à peu prés" (an almost historical discourse), both sublime and grotesque, monstrous yet awesome, inspiring emotions of dread, veneration, and wonder in the reader. On the relationship between history and the novel, the French Romantic poet Alfred de Vigny had this to say, and one cannot help but think of Michelet:

By a sort of fusion which has produced confusion, the work of fiction, or the novel, has borrowed from history the exactitude and the reality of the facts, whereas history, which is the work of memory and of judgement, has taken some of the novel's passion, of its tragic and comic ways, and detailed descriptions.[1]

Some readers distrust Michelet's emotional style and the freedom with which he interprets certain documents, but most admire this odd and at the same time intriguing mixture of genius and patent absurdity, and are quite content to read if not *history* proper (if indeed there is such a thing), then at least *his-story* of the French Revolution. Michelet began researching the subject in 1841 and interrupted his *magnum opus*, the *Histoire de France*, in 1846 to start writing. Only two historians had ever attempted to write on the French Revolution before him (Mignet and Thiers), so Michelet's concern for careful documentation is understandable, although the contemporary reader often wishes that Michelet might have included references to his sources. Actually, Michelet needed less than a year to complete the two first volumes; however, the following volumes dragged on, and the work was not completed until 1853. The *Histoire de la Révolution Française* was not an immediate success with the public and did not become widely read until the Third Republic.

As Hayden White has pointed out in his monumental study on nineteenth-century historiography,[2] Michelet worked at a time when history as an academic discipline was only just emerging and when its theoretical or conceptual basis necessarily remained rather unclear. Was "history" a "science" or an "art"? This was a hotly debated question that was never resolved one way or the other in Michelet's lifetime. As far as Michelet was concerned, "history" should be both a science and an art. On the one hand, the historian must base his narrative on research conducted in historical archives, on authentic documents; and, on the other hand, the historian, the true historian, in order to have maximum effect on his readers, must be both entertaining and moral.[3]

But to return to Michelet's *History of the French Revolution*, hoping to resolve the ontological status of the text once and for all would be pointless. Much has already been said on the related subject of Michelet's rhetoric of style itself, of the metaphorical paradigm underlying the work as a whole. So let us instead explore the idea of narrative desire, and by that I mean the desire to *plot* or *emplot* the telling of the French Revolution in significant narrative form or structure. Plot is, as it were, fundamental to our view of reality and indeed to the meaning we try to give to life. As Peter Brooks writes, "plot is usually conceived as the design and intention of narrative, what shapes a narrative and gives it a certain direction or intent of meaning. Plot is the syntax of a certain type of discourse, one that develops its propositions through temporal sequence and progression.[4]

The idea that life is chaos, a fortuitous flux, in which there is no design whatsoever, is inconceivable to us. It makes sense then to study Michelet in light of, for example, Aristotle's *Poetics*, because plot, the single most important structural ingredient in any one of Michelet's texts, is arguably at the core of all being, real and imaginary, historical and fictional.

As important as our desire *for* plot, which carries us through the text, is the desire *of* plot itself, and by that I mean the seemingly irreversible and irresistible production of textual meaning. In this view, textual desire is like Freud's notion of Eros, a force including sexual desire but larger and more polymorphous, which "seeks to combine organic substances into ever greater unities."[5] Once all the elements of plot are in place, it is transformed into a self-contained signifying or sense-making system. Just like sexual desire at work in dreams, a desire that projects itself from the latent to the manifest, historical meaning, as well as ideology for that matter, is a dynamic force that more often than not expresses itself in an indirect and roundabout way-- vicariously. Plot can seemingly lose its direction; there are numerous detours, pitfalls, and impasses along the way. The work of plot can be both manifest and latent, which throws the reader of historical plot into the awkward position of having constantly to move from the obvious to the hidden. However, the desire of plot always comes through at the end and delivers in what only appears to be an unseemly and untimely climax. Michelet seems to be suggesting that history, too, is a dialectic between different forces that often are misread for something they are not. The ambition to distill yet another, but this time definitive, plot of history makes Michelet's text all the more intriguing and puts the messianic tone of his discourse into another perspective.

In *Michelet's Poetic Vision*, Ed Kaplan provides an original translation of the historian's 1869 Preface to his *Histoire de France*, and argues convincingly that it exposes two central problems that continue to fascinate Michelet scholars: the artistic problems posed by the notion of "historical recreation" or, in Michelet's own language, "resurrection," and the writer's relationship with Catholicism.[6] An equally important preface is the 1847 Introduction to the *Histoire de la Révolution Française*,[7] but, surprisingly, it has gone largely unnoticed. In this essay I would, therefore, like to outline a study of this formidable fifty-five page introduction to Michelet's project as a whole. I will show how Michelet attempts and indeed succeeds in rewriting and replacing the sacred masterplot of providential Christian history, in uncovering another *plot* or rather, masterplot, which asserts itself *otherwise* (that is to say, indirectly and surreptitiously) through Work, in a complex design and logic, in a temporal unfolding, by way of sequence, through complication, peripety, or discovery, and *dénouement*, and imposes itself on the amorphous magma of modern, nonprovidential history. Perhaps it is the loss of a sacred masterplot which accounts for the copious production of both fiction (and especially realist and historical fiction) and history throughout the nineteenth century. To understand the life of an individual, or the evolution of society, suddenly becomes more important when it is no longer possible to look to religion for support and guidance, for a unifying framework. But precisely, Michelet argues that there is still a logic at work in history, and it is the desire for the "progressive triumph of freedom."[8]

Michelet pits the two main protagonists of the historical drama against each other, Christianity and Revolution, and *analyzes* their intercourse, showing how each at times was somehow mistaken for the other. In the end, of course, he forces us to recognize that each is necessarily contained in the other: "What is the old regime, the king and the priest in the old monarchy? Tyranny, in the name of Grace. What is the Revolution? The re-action of equity, the tardy advent of Eternal Justice."[9]

Thus, Michelet's ambition must be double: to render strange the familiar, that is, first and foremost Christianity in its traditional institutional or *unjust* shape, but also the monarchy of the *ancien regime*; and, second, to render familiar the strange, that is the Revolution; to penetrate under the blood and the gore and reveal its true nature as the fulfillment of eternal justice for all.

Michelet has no doubt whatsoever about the authority of his point of view. In the very first line, as a matter of fact, he declares: "I define the Revolution--the advent of the Law, the resurrection of Right, and the reaction of Justice."[10] His story gives new meaning to the term *omniscient narration*, because the historicity of the text confers new authority on the narrator. The first part of this introduction is entitled "On the Religion of the Middle Ages" and it is concerned with the *être* and the *paraître* of Christianity, its reality and appearance. Is Christianity grace or justice? Can it be that one has been mistaken for the other all along? When and how can we recognize which is which? These are the questions with which Michelet is concerned here, not for any personal religious reasons as such, but because grace and justice can be construed as the two mastertropes of not only the history of France, but also of the history of Western civilization as a whole, since France can be said to lead humanity on the road to freedom. "O France, you are saved! O world, you are saved,"[11] Michelet exclaims triumphantly to confirm the significance of 1789.

The history of France, Michelet tells us, consists of "two grand facts, two principles, two actors and two persons, Christianity and the Revolution."[12] Michelet treats both as persons. "I was first to have established France as a person, . . . to perceive her as a soul and as a person,"[13] he writes elsewhere in an attempt to justify this personification and others like it, which can perhaps be explained by the historian's allegorical conception of history and by what Hayden White has identified as the metaphorical principle, which inspired Michelet's conception of the struggle between opposing forces in history. Christianity represents the ancien régime: "All the institutions of the civil order which the Revolution met with, had either emanated from Christianity, or were traced upon its forms, and authorized by it."[14] The Revolution is the "nouveau principe," or "new principle," which "emerged and made room for itself" in history,[15] and the struggle between Christianity and the Revolution can, therefore, be conceived as the eternal struggle between justice and injustice.

"The Revolution continues Christianity, and it contradicts it,"[16] Michelet continues in what at first appears to be both a surprising and contradictory statement. Christianity and the Revolution are related in a general sort of way in that they are inspired by a common sense of human solidarity, "communion" or "fraternité." The main difference, on the other hand, is the creation by medieval Christianity of an elaborate theological superstructure of predestination--that is, grace--which necessarily obscures and obviates human effort, merit and pity--that is, justice. You might say that Christianity (and by Christianity, Michelet means theology in general, as well as the early Christian Church) has done away with that very principle of justice that Christ had both originated and instituted through his suffering and death: justice through faith in God's love for the world, justice through good works. To believe was to be just, to be just was to do good.

What Michelet does here, in other words, is to render strange the familiar understanding of Christianity as first of all a religion of justice, of progress. "Let us consider this grand sight,"[17] Michelet writes, and over the next couple of pages he traces the gradual transformation of Christianity into a system of oppression in the name of justice, that is to say, its tragic *dechéance* or fall, from justice into its opposite--arbitrary, gratuitous grace. At one time the spirit of Christianity and the spirit of the Revolution were one and the same, but centuries of corruption, oblivion, and deliberate perversion of its origins had rendered Christianity unrecognizable and, what is even worse, had rendered the unrecognizable the basis of the recognizable. The illegitimate had become legitimate. The history of France, then, is the history of the slow alienation of justice and of its inevitable return in 1789. "One day

Justice shall return,"[18] Michelet writes confidently in a sentence that sums up quite nicely the work of the historian: to trace the gradual restoration of justice.

The ancien régime, for reasons of good government and public order in general, however, had covered up the perversion of justice, the privilege or grace of the elect few, and sought above all else to maintain the happy myth of the pie in the sky.[19] To displace justice was not hard to do, through "forgetting" and "silence," through "sombre doctrine," ambiguity, and threats.

> To simple confiding persons, to women, to children, whom they keep docile and obedient, they teach the old doctrine which places a terrible arbitrariness in God and in the man of God, and gives up the trembling creature defenseless to the priest. This terror is ever the faith and the law of the latter; the sword ever remains keen-edged for those poor hearts.[20]

Grace is the incarnation of the arbitrary and extends well beyond the realm of theology proper. It is a symbol of society at large: "Arbitrariness reaches, penetrates the developments of the dogma, all the religious institutions which are derived from it; and, lastly, the civil order, which, in the middle ages, is itself derived from those institutions, imitates its forms and is swayed by its spirit."[21]

Thus, "la religion de la grâce" corresponds to a "gouvernement de la grâce" (the religion of grace corresponds to a government of grace). Because he is the head of state, the king is the symbol of grace. But at one time kings too were *just*. Through the early years of the reign of Louis XV, in fact, the people at large, Michelet says, perceived the king to be good; "the king's endeavours to do equal justice to all, to lessen the odious inequality of taxation, gained him the heart of the people."[22]

By the mid-eighteenth century, however, it was no longer possible to be duped, not with the *Livre Rouge* and the Bastille. By then the elements of change are in place. But change, as in Tocqueville's *Ancien Régime*, is more a matter of names than of essence, and thus it is that Michelet's strategy must be double. After rendering strange the familiar, exposing the ancien régime, he now must render familiar the strange and show how the Revolution, in fact, is justice. This operation is metaphor, which seeks "transfers" (in the etymological, Greek, sense of the word), that is, renders *the same but differently*. Michelet goes on to show that revolutionary consciousness dates back six centuries to a time when, precisely, the monarchy joined with the Church to suppress justice in the name of grace. For a long time, justice lay hidden in the deepest oblivion. Not until the eighteenth century, in fact, when Voltaire and the other "docteurs de la révolution" began their undermining work did justice stand a chance. And then everything went like clock-work.[23] The rest is history one might say.

Justice triumphs in 1789, and the historian, who has toiled alone in the archives of France for what seems an eternity, rejoices: "O France, you are saved! O World, you are saved!"[24] Moreover, the triumph of justice is dialectical, or at least a synthesis, insofar as the "new" justice of 1789 incor-

porates the best of both justice and grace. Justice, as it so happens, was
not the only victim of the distortions, to speak euphemistically, of
history. In fact, grace, too, had fallen victim to a perversion of love and pity,
both emblematic of Christianity, into a system of oppression of the many by
the few. "Grand period, sublime moment, . . . when Grace, in whose name
Tyranny had crushed us, is found to be consonant, identical with
Justice. . . . O heavenly Justice of God. For thou art truly Love, and
identical with Grace."[25]

The eschatology of revolution in Michelet, however, is problematic for
a number of reasons. For one thing the French Revolution was much more
than 1789, more than the Declaration of the Rights of Man and the apotheosis
of fraternity and national unity represented by the Festival of the Federations
on July 14, 1790. The events of 1789, as everyone knows, led to the execution
of Louis XVI, which ushered in the Reign of Terror, and such an aberration
could have no place in Michelet's progressive scheme of things. Moreover,
according to Michelet, the Terror paved the way for the Restoration and
certainly inspired the climate of political reaction, which was to have such a
pervasive influence in France throughout the nineteenth century. As Susan
Dunn writes:

Michelet and Lamartine attributed the Restoration to Jacobin pitilessness; however,
they also traced what was for them the real failure--the moral failure--of the
Revolution to the Terror and to the Terror's initial crime and founding act, the
regicide. Politically, Jacobin mercilessness served the royalist cause; morally, it
destroyed the Revolution and discredited republican ideology for decades to come.[26]

Without attempting to resolve this question, which extends well beyond
the limits of this chapter, it should be said in conclusion that toward the end
of his life Michelet became increasingly aware of the naïveté of his understanding of the Revolution as the end of history, as the realization of perfect
societal harmony, as that day of judgment toward which France had been
moving ever since the beginning of time. It would be fair to say that he
realized not only that the French Revolution was only one more stop on the
road to freedom but perhaps also that the triumph of justice and grace, as he
saw it, was a utopian dream of perfect harmony (or "anarchy," as Hayden
White calls this state of natural and spontaneous unity)[27] impossible to realize
fully in an imperfect world. "O Justice, my mother! Right, my father! ye
who are but one with God."[28]

The magic touch in Michelet's style derives less from the use of poetic
metaphor as such than from a dynamics reminiscent of Freudian peripety with
its sudden revelation of an inevitable but perfectly unexpected metamorphosis.
I think here of some apparently innocuous scene in a dream which, of course,
turns out to have quite another, sexual, meaning. Michelet's approach is no
different. In his-story of France, justice is temporarily deformed and distorted
into grace. The historian's voice takes on a prophetic, apocalyptic tone and
assumes a universal authority, because it emphasizes the virtual, not the actual.
Michelet's voice carries a special quality. I mean that quality which Aristotle

says distinguishes the poet from the historian--the ability to describe that which might be (or might have been).

What Michelet has in mind, he says, is the "resurrection of the integral life of the past."[29] Such a philosophy of history is most often associated with the German historian Ranke and his dream of showing "Wie es eigentlich gewesen," or "how it really was." Another German cliché more conducive perhaps to Michelet's Romantic frame of mind would be *Einfühlung* or empathy, that is, "sympathetic understanding" of the past. The historian understands the past by reenacting it in his own mind. Michelet dies to the present, lives with the dead and finally resurrects them by describing what he himself feels. "In the lonely galleries of the Archives nationales," he confides in us, "where I wandered for twenty years, in that deep silence, MURMURS nevertheless would reach my ears."[30] The orphic overtones are anything but fortituous, and the reader must also repeat the poet's quest and descend into the past, and let himself be swallowed up by history. The myth of Orpheus illustrates the dual function of Michelet the historian and Michelet the naturalist, as both teacher and poet: to educate and civilize and at the same time to explain the mysteries of life by revealing the symbols of nature that show the routes ordained for man by God.

Of course, this does not mean that Michelet's story is lacking in objectivity. It is dramatic and metaphorical but at the same time analytical and retains within itself its full lucidity. One of Michelet's original contributions to the discipline of history as such was to have made use of previously unpublished documents that lay buried in archives. Another more important quality was the ability to go beyond the isolated object and situate it in a larger context. Michelet truly fulfills Ernst Cassirer's definition of an historian as someone who embodies "a keen sense for the empirical reality of things combined with the free gift of imagination upon which the true historical synthesis or synopsis depends."[31] Historians are what Cassirer calls "empiricists"; "they are careful observers and investigators of special facts; but they do not lack the 'poetic spirit.'"[32] Modern historians have shown that Michelet's synopsis belongs largely to the realm of visionary poetry, but they continue to read *The History of the French Revolution*, if not for exact historical knowledge (as someone like Fernand Braudel working in the *annales* tradition would define historical objectivity), then at least for inspiration and even moral purpose.

The insistence on plot suggests a poetic temperament through and through, more far-reaching than the romantic-lyrical style in general, an existential anxiety coupled with an imagination so powerful that Michelet, despite a preoccupation with accuracy in historical detail, will forevermore be most closely associated with the great nineteenth-century narrative tradition that expressed itself not only in literature but in many other fields as well, such as history and philosophy, and defined truth as that which was essentially "narratable" through basic narrative structures such as plot. As every-one knows, the nineteenth century in France was nothing less than a Golden Age of narrative, a time when authors and readers alike apparently shared the conviction that plot was the only way to organize and to put into perspective, to understand that larger picture we call reality.

NOTES

1. The English translation is mine, and for this quotation I am indebted to M. G. Hutt and Christophe Campos, eds., "Romanticism and History," in *French Literature and Its Background*, Vol. 4 (London: Oxford University Press, 1969), 97.

2. Hayden White, *Metahistory: The Historical Imagination in Nineteenth-Century Europe* (Baltimore and London: Johns Hopkins University Press, 1973).

3. Ibid., 135-139.

4. Peter Brooks, *Reading for the Plot* (New York: Vintage Books, 1985), xi.

5. Ibid., 37.

6. Edward Kaplan, *Michelet's Poetic Vision: A Romantic Philosophy of Nature, Man and Woman* (Amherst: University of Massachusetts Press, 1977).

7. Jules Michelet, "Introduction," in *Histoire de la Révolution Française*, 2 vols. (Paris: Gallimard, 1952). All subsequent references to this text are to this edition and to the English translation by Charles Cocks.

8. Ibid., 20.

9. Jules Michelet, *History of the French Revolution*, trans. Charles Cocks, ed. Gordon Wright (Chicago and London: University of Chicago Press, 1967), 80.

10. Ibid., 17.

11. Ibid., 79.

12. Ibid., 18.

13. Kaplan, *Michelet's Poetic Vision*, 158.

14. Michelet, *History*, 17.

15. Ibid., 18.

16. Ibid., 22.

17. Ibid., 23.

18. Ibid., 30.

19. "If he remained faithful to the principle that salvation is a gift, and not the reward of Justice, man would have folded his arms, sat down, and waited; for well he knew that his works could have no influence on his lot." Ibid., 25.

20. Ibid., 26.

21. Ibid., 23.

22. Ibid., 42.

23. "Justice, thou who wast lately so feeble, how canst thou grow so fast! If I but turn aside a moment, I know thee no longer. I find thee every hour grown ten cubits higher." Ibid., 32.

24. Ibid., 78.

25. Ibid., 80.

26. Susan Dunn, "Michelet and Lamartine: Regicide, Passion, and Compassion," *History and Theory* (October 1989), 275-276.

27. White, *Metahistory*, 162.

28. Michelet, *History of the French Revolution*, 80.

29. Kaplan, *Michelet's Poetic Vision*, 4.

30. Ibid., 164.

31. Ernst Cassirer, *An Essay on Man* (New Haven, Conn. and London: Yale University Press, 1944), 204-205.

32. Ibid., 204.

3

Sexual Politics: Marivaux's *La Colonie*

Jeanne Fuchs

French women won the right to vote in 1944. How can we reconcile this brutal fact with the celebrated slogan of the French Revolution, "Liberty, Equality, Fraternity?" It would seem that the last word, fraternity, must be interpreted in its most narrow meaning--for it clearly excludes women--and thereby calls into question the validity of the other two words in the phrase, liberty and equality.

Although French women did not attain equal rights in the political arena until long after the 1789 Revolution, they fared better on the literary stage. A case in point is the work of Pierre Carlet de Chamblain de Marivaux whose writings had a major impact on that most revolutionary of writers, Beaumarchais, but whose own works have not usually been considered especially rebellious.

Born in 1688, Marivaux was a contemporary of Montesquieu, and it is fair to say that the philosopher's thought played a key role in Marivaux's own ideas and work.

In French literature, Montesquieu--whose main subject was liberty--remains one of the beacons of freedom for women. His heroine, Roxanne, in the *Persian Letters*, makes a powerful statement of individual liberty and human dignity with her suicide, which represents the ultimate act of liberty and freedom of choice.

With Marivaux we are a long way from such dramatic choices, and although one does not usually think of placing Marivaux with such socially aware and critical authors as Molière, Montesquieu, Voltaire, or Rousseau, to name only the most famous of them, there exists a trio of lesser known plays in which social awareness in terms of liberty and equality for all remains the mainspring of motivation in the plots.

These three plays could well be subtitled "the island plays" since that is the locale of each. They are the *Ile des Esclaves* (1725) (Slave Island), the *Ile de la Raison ou les Petits Hommes* (1727) (The Isle of Reason or the Little Men), and *La Nouvelle Colonie ou la Ligue des Femmes* (1729) (The New Colony or the League of Women), rewritten in 1750 and retitled *La Colonie*.

That Marivaux chose an island as the setting for all three of his socio-philosophical plays is not accidental. The island represents the microcosm and remains a powerful metaphor of a haven or refuge. The island has the possibility of becoming a utopia because it affords an exclusivity that is necessary for change, for a return to a prior state. In a larger sense the island is also the symbol of lost innocence--Eden, the Garden of Paradise--the antithesis of society and the corruption it engenders. For those who long to return to the island, it is perhaps the promise of Paradise regained.

The list of island paradises described in literature is long. Whether one arrives there as a result of shipwreck, mutiny, or kidnapping, whether one is born there, leaves, and is drawn back, the island seems a subject of eternal fascination to writers and readers alike.

To return to Marivaux's islands, I will briefly summarize the plots in each play so that the playwright's overall social concerns will become clear.

In the first play, *Slave Island*, a group of slaves have escaped from Athens and have established a government on an island. There is a shipwreck, and a master and his slave have washed ashore. In previous times, the inhabitants of the island would kill the master and free the slave, but they have since decided to reform the masters--a process that takes three years. This procedure entails complete role reversal (a favorite technique of Marivaux's). The characters change clothes, names, and social position.

The leader on the island, Trivelin, explains that those undergoing "treatment" should not consider themselves "slaves" but rather "*malades*," sick people, who can be "cured." When they are "rehabilitated," they may return to Athens, having learned the moral lesson. The play closes with a ballet in which the slaves cast off their chains.

In the second play, *The Isle of Reason or the Little Men*, Marivaux was inspired by Jonathan Swift's *Gulliver's Travels*. Once again, there is an island with eight Europeans who have become small in stature. They are completely puzzled by their metamorphosis until the islanders, who keep them in cages like cute little animals, inform them that they are small because they lack reason or common sense. As soon as they acquire it, they will return to normal size. A fascinating role reversal on this island is that the women are aggressive and the men are passive in matters of the heart. When one of the Europeans discovers this reversal, he is shocked and asks for an explanation of this strange custom. The governor's assistant gives the following justification:

What will become of love, if the weaker sex is responsible for surmounting advances? What! You place seduction on the men and the necessity of resisting it on the women! And if they succumb, what do you say of them? What strange laws you have concerning love! Really, you children, it is not reason but vice which makes these rules; and vice has its own interests. In a country where one has ruled that women should resist men, one only wants virtue to serve to sharpen passions rather than tame them. (TC: 518)

Again, all's well that ends well, and the Europeans achieve normal stature when they adapt themselves to the islanders' ways and become "reasonable."

The role reversal in sexual customs in *The Isle of Reason* prepares us for the central issue in the third island play, *The New Colony or the League of Women*--equal rights for women. *The New Colony* was a three-act play presented in 1729 at the Théâtre Italien; just as *The Isle of Reason* had been booed at its premiere, so too *The New Colony* failed. Marivaux withdrew the play, and it was never published. No trace of the manuscript has ever been found. It is only thanks to a detailed review of the play that appeared in the *Mercure de France* that we know its subject matter (TC: 1545—1546).

In 1750 Marivaux reworked the play, reduced it to one act, and retitled it *La Colonie*. It appeared in the *Mercure de France* and was played by private groups. *La Colonie* is astonishing for its revolutionary ideas and for its feminist stance. It is not difficult to understand why it failed in its first incarnation, nor why it was not officially performed in its one-act reincarnation. If we consider that the initial version was written just fourteen years after the death of Louis XIV (sixty years *before* the Revolution), and that even the second version predates the Revolution by thirty-nine years, the modernity and audacity of Marivaux's position on women becomes quite striking.

La Colonie describes a group of Europeans who have fled their country to escape political oppression. Installed on an island, the colonists are preparing to form a new government. The men have chosen two representatives, one from the nobility and one from the proletariat, to establish a political system and make laws. As the curtain rises, the women have chosen their own representatives from the second and third estates as they intend to have a voice in all that is proposed and implemented in their new country. This is their golden opportunity to begin anew--*tabula rasa*, at least in the figurative sense.

The women demand equality. They want to vote; they want to take part in judicial and military affairs and in fiscal matters. They want to be included in everything that has to do with the new state. They even plan to abolish marriage, which symbolizes surrender to a life of slavery. They complain that in marriage the men are "masters" and "tyrants" and the women no more than "slaves" and "servants." They want no more of it, and they want freedom immediately.

As usual in Marivaux's universe, the cast divides into couples: there is Arthénice, a noblewoman, and her suitor, Timagène; Mme. Sorbin and her husband represent the workers; and Lina, the Sorbin's daughter, and Persinet her suitor complete the group as the young love interest. The person who represents a kind of arbiter between the various classes is Hermocrate, who at first is taken for a nobleman, but who is actually a bourgeois philosopher. The remainder of the cast is comprised of a group of noble and working-class women.

The note that is struck from the outset between Arthénice and Mme. Sorbin is one of unity. They refer to each other as both "comrade" and "companion," and they agree to act as one. When Arthénice suggests that they need fortitude to rise to this crucial occasion, Mme. Sorbin replies that she cares not a straw for her life, is totally committed to the cause, and would rather live in the "annals of history" than in this "base world." Arthénice exclaims, "I guarantee your name will be immortalized," and her comrade adds, "twenty thousand years from now, we will still be the news of the day" (Gerould 1983: 59).

The problem of love as a possible barrier to their lofty aspirations is introduced from the outset. Mme. Sorbin questions Arthénice about Timagène who has been courting her. The aristocrat assures her ally that there is no cause for alarm because their plan takes precedence over all other considerations. For her part, Mme. Sorbin states raucously that she has no difficulty in dropping M. Sorbin--after all, there is no love in marriage anyway. No big loss.

A drum roll interrupts the women, which signals the beginning of the men's meeting. The women plan to announce their decree of separation from the men with a trumpet blast.

As the men pass and stop only briefly to speak with the women, they react predictably to the women's announcement that they are drawing up their own plans. The men laugh and accuse them of acting silly, of playing a game, and of engaging in nonsense at such a serious moment. Arthénice reminds them with not a little irony that they have had to flee their homeland to escape tyranny and that they should all be equal now. Even though the men have expressed misgivings about their own ability to lead the new community, they scoff at the notion that the women could provide any help at all, much less become equal.

Neither the aristocrat nor the commoner can fathom what the women are getting at, although Timagène, the suitor, is much more anxious about this new turn of events than M. Sorbin, the husband, who dismisses it as foolishness.

As they exit, Arthénice makes the cutting observation: "Not to understand us is a new way of abusing us" (Gerould 1983: 63). So much for Freud's famous question/comment--answered and understood more than one hundred years before he made it. Mme. Sorbin's reply to the remark is equally insightful: "It is their time-honored habit of being arrogant, handed down from father to son, that blocks their mental powers" (Gerould: 63).

Enter Persinet, Lina's would-be lover, eager to ask Mme. Sorbin about a marriage between him and Lina. The poor fellow gets what could only be described as both barrels from the irritated women. They inform him disdainfully that circumstances compel them to break off relations with his "entire species."

Persinet stays to plead his cause; both he and Lina are baffled. He is content to follow the women at a distance, but he is banished until "peace" returns. Still puzzled, he charmingly and romantically comments: "But who shattered the peace? Cursed war, while I wait for it to finish, I shall go off by myself and grieve to my heart's content" (Gerould: 64).

A key passage follows in which the outrage of the mature women is punctuated by the comic innocence and pathos of the young girl in love. It

shows Marivaux at his most effective. The common sense of Arthénice and
Mme. Sorbin makes *no* sense to Lina:

> -Why do you mistreat him mother? Don't you want him to love
> me any more or to marry me?
> -No, daughter, we are in a situation where love is nothing but
> sheer idiocy.
> -Oh, dear me, what a pity!
> -And marriage, such as it has been up until now is nothing more
> than pure enslavement which we are abolishing . . .
> -Abolish marriage! And what will take its place?
> -Nothing.
> -That's giving it short shrift.
> -You know Lina, until now women have always been submissive to
> their husbands.
> -Yes, Madam, but that custom has never prevented anyone from
> falling in love.
> -I forbid you to have anything to do with love.
> -When one is in love, how is it possible to get out?
> I did not choose love, love chose me, and I cannot help
> submitting to it. (Gerould: 64)

Practical moralist that he is, Marivaux must uncover one of the real barriers
to equality facing women: how to deal with romantic love? Marivaux excels
in painting love's awakening and recognition. For his subtle understanding
and analysis of the female heart and mind, he has most often been compared
with Racine. Racine depicted the tragic surprises that love can bring, whereas
Marivaux's surprises are pleasant ones, full of charm, warmth, tenderness, and
sensuality. Lytton Strachey called Marivaux, "Racine by moonlight" (Strachey
1912: 145).
　　　Still another barrier to equality for women is human vanity. This
proves to be too great a hurdle for some of the women in *La Colonie*. As we
know from present-day problems in the struggle for women's rights, large
numbers of women prefer the status quo. On Marivaux's island, the women
join together to take an oath with their leaders. They list their grievances at
the same time.
　　　Just as Mme. Sorbin had stated earlier in the play that men are the way
they are because of learned behavior from father to son, so, too, the women
blame their mothers for their former passivity. "What do you expect?" they
shout. "From the cradle we are told that we are incapable of anything and
that we shouldn't get involved in anything. We should just behave. Our
mothers believed it and repeated it to us. They beat these bad ideas into our
heads" (TC: 653).
　　　The women agree that they have been reduced to objects; their intellect
has been stifled; they have been condemned to spinning, to household management, and to lives of domestic drudgery--in short, to knitting their lives away.
Arthénice sums up their role well when she states: "we're expected to know
how to pass judgement on matters of dress, to entertain them at their evening

dinner parties, to inspire them with pleasurable emotions, to reign in a world
of trifles, and ourselves to be no more than the foremost of all the trifles."
(Gerould: 68-69).

Next, the women condemn poets who flatter them by comparing them
to the stars and the sun and by praising their charms using all sorts of metaphors and hyperbole. They consider all the acclaim, the compliments, and the
sighs of despair with which they are regaled as nothing more than the little
candies that one gives to children (TC: 655). And they realize that they have
been accepting those candies for six thousand years! (TC: 655).

In a passage that presages Rousseau, Arthénice declares that women
have been discounted and demeaned despite the fact that they are responsible
for having civilized men, for having taught them manners, and for having
refined the ferocity of their souls (TC: 654).

The waste of time and intelligence that has been put into coquetry galls
them. With all of that energy and calculation, they could govern two worlds.
Again, Arthénice sums up their deplorable state when she states: "All that
intelligence accomplishes nothing except to turn the heads of small minds who
are easy prey, and winning us some idiotic compliments which their vices and
their giddiness, not their reason, lavish on us; their reason has never offered
us anything else but insults" (Gerould: 69). Dissension occurs when Mme.
Sorbin proposes that they avenge themselves on the men by making themselves
ugly. Some of the women feel that revenge would be more effective if they
were to make themselves more attractive; the men would suffer more. The
wily Mme. Sorbin counters that such a tactic is tantamount to falling into the
same trap again.

The meeting begins to lose its idealistic tone when some women note
that it may be easier for Mme. Sorbin to make herself ugly than it is for them.
After several exchanges of insults, the meeting breaks up with Arthénice
advising moderation.

Finally convinced that the women are serious about their demands, the
men decide that they must restore "order" and put the women back in their
place, which is to be married off as girls and to obey their husbands and take
care of their homes as women. Period.

The men are nonplussed when the women hang an edict up on a tree
listing their demands. The confrontation finally occurs. Arthénice stresses the
importance of education in the formation of attitudes and expectations. She
informs the men that she and the other women can learn how to use the sword
and the pistol, that they have been made "cowards by upbringing" (Gerould:
54). The women continue to parry and thrust at all of the men's objections.
The eloquence and ability to abstract that Arthénice demonstrates are
complemented by the down-to-earth practicality of Mme. Sorbin.
Arthénice remarks coolly:

Sir, I have only one more word to say, take it to heart; there is no nation
that does not complain of the shortcomings of its government; where do these
shortcomings originate? It is because the earth has been denied our intellect in
instituting laws, it is because you make no use of that half of the human mind we

possess, and because you employ only your own, which is the weaker half. (Gerould: 75)

The more economical Mme. Sorbin sums up Arthénice's view: "That's exactly it, for want of cloth, the coat goes short" (Gerould: 75).

During the course of the exchange with the men, Arthénice actually uses the word "republic" in referring to their projected government. The word is particularly noteworthy when we keep in mind the date of the revision--1750.

Perceiving that they are making little progress with the men, the women decide to pack their bags, leave the men to their own devices, and go off to the woods to hunt and fish. The women storm off taking Lina with them. Both Persinet and M. Sorbin burst into tears.

To prevent the women from carrying out their plans, Hermocrate realizes that action is necessary. He sends Persinet after the women and, with the other men, plans to warn them all of an imminent attack by the "savages" that inhabit the island. The ploy works: the women return. When the attack is announced and the women decline to help in the fighting because they do not, as yet, know how to use weapons, it is agreed that they will return to their homes. Hermocrate informs them that he will add their demands to the order he is drawing up. Mme. Sorbin decides that there is only one demand that she wants included: the abolition of the nobility. Since Arthénice cannot agree to this, it is set aside. The noblewoman insists on only one article: that men be treated the same as women regarding infidelity. Women are dishonored by society; men should be too. Mme. Sorbin rejects this article, stating that simple women have no need for such a restriction because they do not change lovers and husbands the way great ladies do. She adds that men are weaker than women in these matters anyway, and that society needs to give them free rein in matters of fidelity.

The play ends on an optimistic note: Timagène announces that they will consider the women's rights and look after them in the rules that they are going to establish.

If we examine what Marivaux has achieved here, it is quite remarkable. He has had his characters recite a litany of issues that underscores the injustice done to women for "six thousand years." He has had these issues articulated by two different types of women, both thoroughly effective in expressing a particular point of view. He has almost allowed them to win. In addition, he has interposed that uncontrollable emotion, love. Lina and Persinet, with their simple and unsullied view of life, become more touching when compared with the already complex circumstances that surround the adults in the play. The primary stumbling blocks to achieving equality are clearly not love but rather vanity and class distinctions. The women's alliance breaks down because they refuse to make themselves unattractive. Even Arthénice, who has spoken so eloquently throughout the play on the importance of equality, refuses to give up her privileged status in society. She wants to keep the advantages she was born with. Mme. Sorbin is clearly the most revolutionary figure in the play. Her idea of abolishing the aristocracy reveals the basis for all inequality.

At first, the men in the play want to maintain their traditional advantage over the women, but they do show some signs of flexibility once they realize that the women are quite determined to be heard. The two extremes are M. Sorbin and Persinet: Sorbin is set in his views and speaks in clichés about being the lord and master and the head of the family, whereas Persinet is so blinded by his love for Lina that he is willing to concede everything to win her.

On the other hand, Timagène and Hermocrate are more reasonable. Timagène concedes that the woman's complaints will be addressed in setting up the new government; Hermocrate breaks the deadlock between the sexes when he drives them together in the face of the imagined mutual enemy. He helps them out of the impasse they have reached.

In addition to being a moralist, Marivaux is a pragmatist. He realizes that customs and habits will not and usually do not change overnight. He follows in the long comedic-philosophical tradition of *castigo ridendo*. When the curtain falls, the world has not changed, but the master rhetorician has presented the women's complaints in detail and with lucidity.

Marivaux's entire *oeuvre* bears witness to his admiration for women. He never treats them as second-class citizens. On the contrary, they are at the center of his theater as well as his novels. Marivaux's heroines display a deep sense of their own worth; they are intelligent and resourceful, and they exhibit unusually independent natures.

Although Marivaux was successful in his own century, his genius and originality were not fully recognized until the nineteenth century. Clearly, his literary descendants are, in the nineteenth century, Musset, and in the twentieth, Giraudoux and Anouilh.

La Colonie illustrates his advanced views on women's rights and places him in the vanguard of French male writers who loved and appreciated women and presented them as many-faceted individuals possessing among other qualities intelligence, integrity, and courage.

NOTE

Marivaux, *Théâtre Complet* (TC), Editions Gallimard, Bibliothèque de la Pléiade, 1949, p. 518. All quotes from this text are my translations.

REFERENCES

Gerould, Daniel. *Gallant and Libertine. Eighteenth Century French Diver-tissements and Parades.* Edited, translated, and with an introduction by D. Gerould. New York: Performing Arts Journal Publications, 1983.

Marivaux, Pierre de Carlet. *Théâtre Complet*. Ed. by Marcel Arland. Paris: Editions Gallimard, Bibliothèque de la Pléiade, 1949.
Strachey, G. Lytton. *Landmarks in French Literature*. New York: Henry Holt & Co., 1912.

4

Cazotte and the Counterrevolution or the Art of Losing One's Head

Claudine Hunting

In a critical letter--first published in 1989 to commemorate the French Revolution Bicentennial in France--the Marquis de Sade, ostensibly an active revolutionary, summed up the political and human situation in December 1793, on the very eve of his arrest and imprisonment, in the following terms: "Liberty? No one has ever been less free; they all look like droves of somnambulists. Equality? There is only equality of those beheaded. Fraternity? Informers have never been so busy."[1] Now thoroughly disenchanted with the Revolution and its empty slogans, Sade lamented: "O Lights, Lights of the Enlightenment were you but a prelude for this Age of Darkness?" (Sade 1989: 20). If revolutionaries themselves were reduced to hiding and were struck by the Terror, what fate could counterrevolutionaries reasonably expect? And what would their own writings express at a time of turmoil and violence, in which they were the primary targets?

Indeed, a year earlier, only two months before his own death on the guillotine, in September 1792, French writer Jacques Cazotte, the object of this study and Sade's contemporary, but on the opposite side of the political and ideological spectrum, had, in his own correspondence, already reached a similar conclusion. He had announced ironically that "Philosophy" and the human progress it had championed would be short-lived in the bloodbath of the French Revolution: "The lights of this century, which have dazzled us, are fading out."[2]

In point of fact, the utopian world of peace, justice, freedom, equality, and fraternal solidarity, of which the French philosophers had dreamed, and the "enlightened" society, which they had envisioned throughout the Enlightenment, did not materialize in the last decade of the eighteenth century that saw the rise and fall of the French Revolution. Events quickly went out of control. Political ideals long advocated by the *philosophes* were soon dismissed during the Revolution. Instead, another kind of despotism replaced that of the *ancien régime*, equally intolerant, but more cruel and barbaric, as the "September Massacres" in French prisons and the scaffold, that year, and henceforth, claimed ever-increasing numbers of victims.

Within such a grim historical context, Jacques Cazotte's case is particularly significant. On the one hand, his personal experience during those troubled times is indicative of the ordeals suffered by many of his compatriots and peers in the reality of their daily lives. On the other hand, the aura of mystery and legend associated with his name--notably in connection with his fight against the Revolution and, initially, with his prophetic visions of it as a Hell on earth--lends his odyssey a distinctive quality, a uniqueness worthy of our investigation, as it propelled to fame, both in the eighteenth and nineteenth centuries, a relatively little-known figure in French literature. Furthermore, his story epitomizes, two hundred years before the Salman Rushdie controversy and *The Satanic Verses* (1988), the fate of dissenting authors threatened with death or executed for their opinions and writings by oppressive societies.

This reference to a recent incident is relevant in more than one way. Cazotte's best known work, *Le Diable amoureux (The Devil in Love)*, published in 1772, also focuses on the demonic and oneiric as allegories for the inherent "evils" he perceived in a dominant ideology.[3] The writers' basic viewpoints, however, are diametrically opposed. The modern Anglo-Indian appears to reject tradition, whereas his French predecessor staunchly defended his religious and cultural heritage threatened by the Revolution.

Cazotte, the author of fables, short stories, and oriental tales, met with considerable success in France when his novel *Le Diable amoureux* was published. His notoriety endured in the next century, first because of his tragic end and the legends and controversies attached to it; and second, and even more importantly, because of his highly innovative approach in that particular work, which was to be recognized and imitated widely by nineteenth-century writers in France, England, and Germany.[4] Modern critics, like Todorov, generally agree that Cazotte introduced a new genre in modern Western literature: that of the "fantastic," which has had, in our times, the vogue we all know.[5] In Cazotte's novel, the fantastic--a skillful blending of "real" and supernatural elements within a tragicomic framework--results in basic uncertainty and anguish for both hero and reader, as they try to interpret a conflicted perception of human experience, while the author weaves his tale with deliberate ambiguity.

Curiously, Cazotte was to cast the latter part of his life in the same fantastic mold. His literary work and his life, then, uncannily appear to correspond, as reality and the supernatural, the rational and irrational, merge at a time of uncertainty and terror. Like Alvare, the fictional hero of *Le Diable amoureux*, the novelist, despite rare flashes of lucidity, demonstrates his inability to discern fact from fiction, reality from illusion, dream and wishful thinking. The new literary genre he has thus introduced seems to fit to perfection the sober, nightmarish mode of his existence during the Revolution.

Our main objective here will be to explore Cazotte's dual perception of the French Revolution as both a "fantastic" and an only-too-real experience. His correspondence with friends and family, which was to play a crucial role in his indictment, and some of his later writings will help us unravel the intricate threads of his emotional and intellectual involvement in historical events, particularly on the mystical and political planes. Archival documents pertaining to his arrest, imprisonment and trial--under infamous public prosecutor Fouquier-Tinville, whose first case was that of Cazotte--also shed some light on a highly charged situation.

Beheaded for his political leanings, Jacques Cazotte ironically had shown little interest in politics most of his life. It was as a moralist and believer in the "true faith" that he naturally became a vocal opponent of the philosophes such as Voltaire, Rousseau, and Diderot. A devout Catholic, he could not tolerate the philosophers' attacks on the Church, nor could he condone their key role in changing traditional morality, based on duty, self-discipline, and restraint. He considered the new ethics of the Enlightenment to be far too permissive, oriented toward self-indulgence and pleasure, and leading to outright perdition. His novel *Le Diable amoureux* has, in fact, often been considered an allegory implicitly depicting "Philosophy" as a beautiful female devil, who tempts and seduces an unwary "hero," and, in what seems to be a dream--but is it?--endangers his very salvation.

To a great extent, the French Revolution was an outcome of the philosophes' battle throughout the eighteenth century, for a better, more liberal society. As Cazotte became acutely aware of their impact on the Revolution, he started getting involved in politics too--a change in attitude also necessitated by what he viewed as a rapidly deteriorating situation in society, notably in political and religious principles and mores. The writer essentially considered departure from tradition and disaffection with religion and the monarchic order to be rebellion and the destruction of everything he valued most highly. In other words, he considered the coming of the new order, brought about by the philosophes, a gradual descent into the reaches of Hell. He was quick, therefore, to lay the blame for all revolutionary excesses on the philosophes and their "beguiling" doctrines. And he clearly accused them of perverting the French, euphemistically designated as "we," in one of his last letters to his friend Pouteau: "Aversion for religious dogma had inclined us to give our trust to what we called 'Philosophy'; and our fondness for the principles this chimerical creature stood for instantly toppled our world and turned it into a living image of Hell" (*Corr.* 214).

From that standpoint, Cazotte's opposition to the French Revolution seems rational and his actions understandable. When we deal with this author, however, we must also be prepared for the irrational and the unexpected. Shortly before the Revolution and, again, in its first year, he indeed fulfills that expectation.

Initially, Cazotte's reputation as a prophet was precariously established by a legend that portrayed him as an awesome soothsayer at an elegant dinner party in January 1788. Claiming that he was a witness to this momentous event, literary critic La Harpe has vividly evoked, in his memoirs, the striking figure of the white-haired old man accurately predicting to his startled host and the other guests the imminent coming of the Revolution and uncannily describing in minute detail the horrifying crimes that would be committed then, in the name of philosophy and reason, against them, the royal family, and himself.[6]

This episode, reported widely by other writers in the nineteenth century, was to contribute significantly to Cazotte's growing notoriety as a visionary, which his writings and personal inclinations had already earned him in his lifetime. An explorer of the supernatural in his best known works and, at one point, a follower of Illuminists Martines de Pasqually and Louis-Claude de Saint-Martin, who founded the Martinist order of Illuminism in France, our author maintained a balance between the rational and the irrational until the Revolution. Then, as the situation became unbearable, the scales tipped and Cazotte took refuge in mysticism.

Before this was to happen, the writer astonishes us, once more, by a turnabout, seemingly at odds with his prior convictions: acceptance, at first, of the French Revolution. On the verge of the Revolution, in January 1789, as the Estates General were about to meet in an effort to resolve the serious economic crisis faced by the government, Cazotte, who had heard the rumors, surprisingly anticipated with joy and hope the social changes he then foresaw. This was such a departure from his previous stand that he showed a certain discretion about it, only confiding in those closest to him. Among them was his wife, to whom he then wrote: "Rejoice; the Third Estate is becoming a body of respectable citizens," adding he could "foresee . . . happy changes" brought about by the new political situation, as the king convened the Estates General (*Corr.* 119-120).[7]

This new stance is symptomatic of the fluctuations and uncertainties also experienced, in that period of transition and confusion, by many of his compatriots.   Furthermore, Cazotte's change in attitude had its own inescapable logic, shared by a number of his contemporaries in his socal class at the time. Although he suffered from inner conflicts on this issue--because of his deep religious feelings and his personal attachment to the king--he was fundamentally a man of the people. He belonged to that Third Estate. His roots were in the middle class, the bourgeoisie, not in the aristocracy. Educated and relatively secure financially, he nevertheless did not share in the special privileges enjoyed by the nobility. All his life he had been conditioned to accept the *status quo*. But now a seemingly quiet "revolution," initiated by the king himself--prompted, in truth, by the Parliament of Paris's call for the convocation of the Estates General six months earlier--brought new hopes. It promised a better present for him and his family, and a rosier future for his children in terms of a promotion for a whole social class. The bourgeoisie, called in by the king, would request equality for everyone on the crucial question of taxes. No more financial privileges should be granted the lords; they must pay taxes too. Bourgeois representatives, aware of their own human value, would also ask for equality of opportunity in seeking professional and political charges and honors, economic fulfillment and personal growth, which should be based solely on merit, not on the virtue of a title and hereditary prerogatives as in the past.

All these aspirations, shared by so many of his compatriots at the time, were ambiguously expressed in the same letter by Cazotte:

It (the Third Estate) has just won its case; inept princes wished to drag it down back into the mud; the king has blamed them; the people have reproved them. From now on, taxes will be equally shared; the odious name of "taille" will disappear; we will easily find comfort in the fact that we are not the sons of . . . , because those who are, paying just like everyone else, will be nothing special, since we will no longer be divided into nobles and commoners on this. The king, weary of his courtiers, and seeing nothing noble in the nobility, will come closer to the industrious part of his Nation (*Corr.* 119).[8]

Robert Darnton focused on that particular aspect of the problem when he pointed to some of the motivations of early French revolutionaries like Brissot and Marat, in his *Mesmerism and the End of the Enlightenment in France* (1968, notably 90-105). Another significant example given by Darnton is that of Nicolas Bergasse. Although he was a rich bourgeois, Bergasse could not achieve his political ambitions in the ancien regime. Thus, he demanded for himself and his fellow mesmerists: "All careers must be opened up to us" (101). Interestingly, Bergasse used, before Cazotte, the same expression in one of his publications, when he referred to the rights of "the industrious class of the nation," which he contrasted with the aristocracy, viewed by him as incompetent, parasitic, and unfairly advantaged.[9]

The economic and social changes, envisioned by contemporaries from his own milieu, thus precipitated Cazotte's political interests and raised his consciousness in terms of an existing class struggle. On the eve of the French Revolution, he shared with them some of their dreams. In brief, we are not dealing with contradiction here, but with evolution--however momentary it might be--a gradual change brought about by external circumstances and conscious acknowledgment of repressed inner yearnings. He admitted that he too desired a better, more just society, which would benefit him, his family, and the Third Estate.

Cazotte was probably also influenced on this matter by his eldest son, Scévole.[10] The young man then held views that were judged too radical by his father. Nevertheless, Jacques could not help but be convinced by the merits of some of his son's beliefs and hopes in a new political and social order that would favor the ambitions and aspirations of the new generation. Cazotte's letters obliquely reflect those family concerns and probable discussions on the subject, notably regarding the future of the young in the context of a fairer, more just society. A year later, for instance, he wrote his cousin, an early revolutionary, also named Jacques Cazotte. In his letter, the author repeated to his cousin the very words he used to comfort his son Scévole, then unhappy in love, with visions of success in his new career:

Your beginnings here are auspicious. Your talents, conduct, and morals are held in high esteem. General opinion and respect gather, as you can see, many people around your poor old father. He will be able to direct back to you the public favor he now enjoys. . . . In two years, you can become a member of our Sovereign Assembly. And as you know the basic principles of calculus, who knows whether you might not become a member of the new Chamber of Accounts . . . and, next, why not its President?

In the career now open to you, my dear Scévole, one can expect anything, when natural talents are combined with dedication. . . . Personal merit now is an asset (*Corr.* 140).

Such expectations, unreasonable in another age, were indeed becoming a reality. Cazotte had just been elected mayor of Pierry, the village where he owned a considerable estate and vineyards. His son now was a lieutenant in the National Guard and had just been elected commanding officer of his unit. Cazotte's positive attitude toward the Revolution would persist for about a year and a half with alternating hope and disappointment.

In view of his well-known feelings toward the philosophes and his earlier misgivings about their "child," the Revolution, we may wonder what deeper motive may have prolonged Cazotte's bittersweet partiality for the new order of things. The answer probably lies in the author's delusion that the new Revolution would bring together the "good" people of France and their "good" king. As suggested in his letter to his wife, already quoted, the writer was dreaming of a close alliance between the Third Estate and the king, at the expense of the aristocracy: "The king, weary of his courtiers and seeing nothing noble in the nobility, will come closer to the industrious part of his Nation" (119).

Although he had many friends among the lords, Cazotte intensely disliked and distrusted the aristocracy as a social class, not only because of the basic inequity of their privileges, to which so many nobles were still desperately clinging, but also, essentially, because of their excessive power and close association with the party of the philosophes. It was, no doubt, in these last two areas that the writer mostly found fault with the nobility. During the Regency of the Duke d'Orléans (1715–1723) and the remaining years of King Louis XV's reign, which lasted until 1774, French aristocrats had regained much of the political and economic power they had lost under Louis XIV. The Sun King had subdued the lords into abject submission, turning them deliberately into his personal domestics and retainers. From the outset, he had sought the support of the bourgeoisie to accomplish this objective, as many of his ancestors had done before him to monopolize power and become absolute monarchs. To a certain extent, Cazotte longed for that earlier "golden age." In his eyes, the perfect harmony between king and church could only inspire a virtuous society of dutiful, gentler, and kinder citizens from the Third Estate.[11] In the final analysis, his dream was as utopian as that of the philosophes.

He deemed the nobles dangerous, not only because of political reasons, but also because they were poor role models. Their moral depravity, apparent to everyone according to Cazotte, since they had seized the reins of power, threatened all strata of society, as he told his wife in the same letter:

How can you be content with present times? Was there ever a time more barbarous than this, if the disorder of ideas and things is indeed the mark of ignorance and barbarity. Courtiers, now the masters of this kingdom, share their spoils with concubines. They trample good morals, commitment, knowlege, and honesty. They keep the king in irons and all good citizens in slavery. In the king's council, they are destroying the laws that governed us and they are now killing us with all sorts of decrees and extravagant edicts (*Corr.* 118-119).

But, essentially, the writer came to view the close ties between nobility and philosophy as a mutually beneficial partnership bent on destroying the world, "his" world. French philosophers had gained growing political support and official acceptance. They were seldom exiled or imprisoned anymore for their opinions and writings. Enlightened aristocrats indeed considered the philosophes, their new ideology, and the emerging Third Estate as stepping stones to personal power and success. In fact, quite a few representatives of the nobility in the Constituent Assembly had allied themselves with the people against the king and his moderate or conservative supporters.

A case in point was Cazotte's *bête noire*, Duke Philippe d'Orléans, a descendant of the previous regent. For the writer, the duke epitomized all that was evil in the privileged class. The author's correspondence resounds with curses at the "Duke of Pikes," as he nicknamed him.[12] He even saw him, pike in hand, as the quintessential instrument of the devil and absolute embodiment of evil. Shortly after Cazotte's death, Philippe-Egalité, as the duke then called himself, voted for the death of his cousin the king, a fact attesting to the validity of the author's perception. Philippe d'Orléans did not fare much better as, a few months later, he shared the same fate; he was also beheaded on the republican scaffold.

Ironically, the efforts of both antagonists to win over the people to their side eventually failed and resulted in the same expeditious and bloody elimination of all parties concerned, as radical representatives from the Third Estate rapidly hardened their positions and rose to undisputed dominance. Cazotte's hope to have the old flame between the king and his people rekindled was thus doomed to failure.

A crucial event was the catalyst that changed the direction of the Revolution and accelerated its extremism: the king's escape and his arrest in Varennes on June 21, 1791. This was also the turning point for Cazotte, for he lost his last illusions for a possible covenant between the king and his people. To rescue the king, Cazotte took his first steps on the dangerous path of counterrevolution. He had no more hope in the French Revolution, as he saw the "good" people of France turning into a mob, a rabble, determined to harm the king and his family, as well as established religion.

From that moment, the writer clearly saw his double duty of patriot and devout Catholic as a defender of Louis XVI, who stood for both monarchy and church. Most of the political problems of the king--a very religious man and representative of God, officially anointed in the traditional coronation cere- mony in the Cathedral of Reims, like all his ancestors--stemmed from his un- willingness to accept the drastic church reforms advocated, and then enforced

by the more radical elements of the Third Estate.[13]   Cazotte, like many of his
compatriots who shared his views, had no other alternative but to engage in
battle, courageously, for his faith and his king. It was a matter of religious
duty and moral obligation in which his whole family became involved. They
were about to be part of history, in that "war" between good and evil which,
all his life, Cazotte had been fighting.

The Varennes incident marked the first direct involvement of the
Cazotte family in historical events. Jacques sent his eldest son, Scévole, to
rescue the king and the royal family and protect them from the mob, as they
were brought back to Paris from Varennes. Scévole Cazotte, as we know, a
captain in the National Guard, was by now deeply disillusioned by the
Revolution and had begun to share his father's views. His efficient and brave
assistance to the king, at a time of turmoil and hardship, is recorded in
history. Louis XVI himself sent words of gratitude to Jacques Cazotte.

This first public gesture, defending the king, was the symbol of
Cazotte's new political engagement against the Revolution. All his writings
and actions, henceforth, would be geared toward the destruction of the
"Beast," a term he used for both the Revolution and Satan. For Cazotte, the
French Revolution and the devil--its "true" instigator--were becoming one and
the same thing.[14]   Counterrevolution, for the writer and mystic, was turning
into a crusade against the forces of evil, a religious war in which the king was
a new Christ, hounded and tortured in the drama and passion of the
Revolution. And Cazotte was his "disciple." "Ah!," he writes Pouteau in
June 1792, consciously confusing king and Christ with the terms "Lord" and
"Savior," which, emphasized in the text by the author, have a dual meaning,
earthly and celestial: "How much we wept in my home when we learnt of the
circumstances of the passion of *our Lord*! But it was with faith in his
resurrection and confidence that he will be the *Savior* of our country, just as
the One, whose very image he is, in every sense, saved all men" (*Corr.* 209).
Politics and religion were merging in the writer's inflamed mind; they had
become one and the same cause.[15]   At a time of chaos and fanaticism, Cazotte
plunged into extremism and mysticism, as the only way to save the king and
help bring about regeneration and redemption to a stricken nation. Soon
regarded by many of his opponents as insane, or as the French say, maybe
aptly within this historical context, "ayant perdu la tête" (having lost his head),
Cazotte gradually entered a world of delusion, where supernatural forces and
spirits gave him a helping hand to destroy evil--a world in which reality and
illusion were becoming indistinguishable.

Cazotte fought the Revolution on all fronts: in his political actions, his
writings and his religious activities. As mayor of his village, Pierry, since
1791, he used his office effectively to influence the people, who respected him,
and to protect the clergy persecuted by the Revolution. When the situation became critical, not only for aristocrats and priests, but also for landowners and
religious believers like himself, he refused to hide or go abroad, as so many
were doing. Emigrating would have meant desertion. Despite his old age, he
felt that his presence and actions, as an "ouvrier de Dieu," a worker or,

better, a soldier of God, were too valuable for him to abandon his post (*Corr.* 210).

The writer also attacked the Revolution through a new and powerful political medium: the newspapers. These were becoming predominant at the time of the French Revolution. Journalists, commonly called *nouvellistes* (newsgivers), were now playing a major role in politics. Cazotte availed himself of that medium to convince a wide public that the Revolution was evil, the work of the devil. Thus, he contributed to a royalist paper directed by his friend Pouteau, *Le Journal à deux liards* (*The Two-cent Newspaper*). His letters to Pouteau are full of anecdotes, ideas and plans for insertion in the paper. His inflammatory rhetoric was effective, even though it was anonymous. Pouteau would use the author's contributions extensively, but would only refer to him as "a virtuous man, whose name I am not disclosing" (*Corr.* 203 n.9).

Cazotte's political activism in that newspaper was discovered, however, when Pouteau disappeared, trying to escape prosecution, and the author's correspondence was seized in his friend's office by the revolutionaries. The revolutionaries methodically searched for and pointed out the similarity of ideas and expressions contained in Cazotte's letters to Pouteau and articles published in the paper, often verbatim reproductions (see *Corr.* 203-205 and notes). As a result, journalists of the republican press were, paradoxically, to recognize Cazotte as a professional colleague. They paid him an indirect tribute--which he certainly would not have appreciated--when they reported his execution in *Le Patriote français* of September 25, 1792, and called him, on that occasion, "le Marat du royalisme" (a royalist Marat)--a curious contradiction in terms.[16]

In his letters to Pouteau and others, at the time, Cazotte essentially comes through as a counterrevolutionary activist. Rumors from abroad, news from émigrés, from the front, and from foreign armies abound in his letters, as do improbable plots, vague plans, and grand designs to overturn the Revolution, mostly the products of the novelist's fertile imagination and wishful thinking, presumably unconnected with actual political intrigue and scheming. But the revolutionaries did not take this lightly. After the writer's arrest, they used it as evidence to condemn him to death, if not for actual deeds, which could not be proven, at least for his subversive opinions.

After all, the republicans saw themselves as "saviors" of humanity, enlightened soldiers of freedom, justice, and equality. They could not take kindly to being portrayed as demagogues, fanatics, rogues, rascals, brigands, ruffians, or worse: repulsive vermin, rabid dogs, monstrous hydras, hordes of assassins, possessed by the devil, and so on, as Cazotte depicted them in his correspondence and newspaper contributions. He could not expect any indulgence from those who had scores of people beheaded for lesser peccadilloes, particularly when the writer called God's wrath upon them and asked for a just retribution for their crimes in this world and the next: retaliation, execution, even rat-poisoning which, in French, is rendered literally by the expression "la mort-aux-rats" (death-to-the-rats). All this came from a man who had been generally recognized, before the advent of the Revolution, as kindly, warm, affectionate and witty, with a perpetual smile on his face. Cazotte's delirium matched his opponents' in those explosive times:

Abominable scoundrels, who have no respect for faith or law, no other rule than your personal interest, short-sighted at that! God gives me a thirst and hunger for vengeance to fall upon you, as it must. . . . I would accept to be crushed in the grinder, so that you may be punished as you deserve . . . I have said about the Duke of Orl . . . . . . he had so defiled crime, that no one else would commit any for another century out of sheer disgust (*Corr.* 208).

The kingdom, defiled by so many crimes, can be cleansed by the blood of those criminals . . . so many guilty men to be punished! (*Corr.* 206-207)

Cazotte's correspondence is very clear. Only a miracle could have saved him from the hands of his irate jailers. Strangely enough, that "miracle" would happen--we will touch upon it shortly--but he would not avail himself of it. His new mystical grand design, which included his personal martyrdom, simply could not be interfered with.

His inner torment, in those brutal times, further intensified his dependence on mysticism and the supernatural, which became a refuge for him and a possible answer to the evils he and so many others were suffering from. His letters then mirror this growing sorrow. More and more they expressed his own moral anguish for living under the yoke of tyranny and terror. He often describes his pain in touching physical terms, as if he had become one of his vine trees, submitting to a violent winter storm: "We are frozen, injured by hail and frost-bite; we will suffer" (*Corr.* 192). And again: "When shall we be able to breathe? I am frost-bitten, hail-potted, injured; I can't even feel, because I suffer too much" (*Corr.* 201). In page after page, Cazotte tells his correspondents of his "extreme suffering" (*Corr.* 205). His traumatic experience, at times, affected him so violently that it induced physical revulsion, states of nausea (*Corr.* 165), and vomiting (*Corr.* 180).

In his mental and physical anguish, prayers and Bible reading were of great solace to Cazotte: "My home is a house of orisons," he would write, adding: "Let us find comfort in *acting* them *out*" (*Corr.* 203, italics added). Indeed, prayers were more than a refuge to him. They became part of his political activism. Religion and politics were definitely interlocked in his "poor head," as he readily admitted (*Corr.* 198). Cazotte was spinning into the world of the supernatural.

He ascribed extremely potent qualities to his prayers. Together with his friend Mme. de la Croix, another Illuminist, who lived on his country estate and whose very name, "of the Cross," seemed to predestine her for such activities, through ritual incantations he invoked spirits to help the nation and protect the king. In a vision, he would perceive around the fallen monarch a spiritual "invisible guard" that replaced the human one withdrawn from him by his tormentors (*Corr.* 206). Cazotte would often mention this "celestial guard" at the king's side, in his letters and daily conversations (*Corr.* 210).

The author's days and nights were now filled with dreams of benevolent and evil spirits who interfered with human actions. These supernatural creatures gradually invaded his waking hours so that, at times, he could no longer differentiate reality from dream and illusion, as demonstrated by his correspondence with Pouteau and confirmed by eyewitnesses, as well as his own writings at the time. One of his last texts, *Mon Songe de la nuit du samedi au dimanche de devant la Saint-Jean 1791* (*My Midsummer Night's Dream . . . 1791*), illustrates an oneiric state, which he believed was also occurring in his real life:

I enter a room where I find a young lady alone. . . . She seems to recognize me and greets me. I soon notice that she is having fits of giddiness. She appears to say sweet nothings to an object facing her. I can see she is in a visionary state addressing a spirit. I command at once the spirit to appear, while I make the sign of the cross on the lady's brow. I now can see a figure, fourteen or fifteen years old, not uncomely, but . . . looking like a rascal. I tie him and he protests that I should do so. Another lady appears, equally obsessed. I do the same to her. Both spirits then shed their pretenses and arrogantly confront me. . . . I put both prisoners in the power of Jesus Christ. . . . I am walking out now when a big man suddenly attacks me right in the middle of a large courtyard, crowded with people. I lay my hand on his brow and tie him in the name of the Holy Trinity and that of Jesus, in whose power I put him. The power of Christ! the crowd, surrounding me, exclaimed. Yes, I said, and I put you all in his power after tying you. Loud protests followed these words.[17]

It is evident that Cazotte was stepping into a land of make-believe to counterbalance the horrors of his "slow and cruel agony," as he described his unbearable pain in his last known writing, *Révélations*, directly inspired by the Bible.[18] In that text, the author's torment was significantly expressed in religious terms, as he examined current events precisely in the light of the Bible. He was deeply convinced that there were striking correspondences between the Revolution, which he regarded as the end of the world, and the Apocalypse. Because religion, politics and personal experience of the Revolution were all closely interlaced for Cazotte, everything in his last years became colored through the prism of biblical interpretation and equation.

The writer viewed the Apocalypse as a key to understanding the tragedy he was living and the only hope left, like a light at the end of the tunnel. His reading of the religious text became a sudden "revelation" to him, a "secret" directly imparted to him by God. Just as in his correspondence but in greater detail and in a more vivid and inspired manner, the Revolution assumed, in Cazotte's last, apocalyptic writing, the identity of the monster, the "beast" of the Apocalypse, the all-devouring hydra, announcing the end of the world before its spiritual rebirth and regeneration.

The multitudinous aspects of the colossal "dragon," which Cazotte depicted all pointed to an already well-known common identity: "The chief of those satanic genii; yes, that creature of deception and rebellion," Lucifer himself, the bearer of infernal light and the agent of evil (*DA* 267). Just as

Satan had been unsuccessful before, the Revolution/devil was bound to be
again defeated on the gigantic battlefield of Armageddon. Cazotte's powerful
prose thus evoked, for the reader, the terrifying visions that now haunted him
and the prophetic voices that spoke to him. He was no longer simply a
"writer." He was transformed into a seer, a prophet, the messenger of God,
as well as the interpreter of Nostradamus's prophetic almanacs (*Corr.* 164,
199).

In that process of mimesis and metamorphosis, "reality" was gradually
transformed into myth. And, inversely, myth became reality. For Cazotte,
the Revolution *was* both the devil and his work, in the chaotic world of the
new Apocalypse. The writer himself was part of that transformation. A new
seer, he resembled old king Phineus, the blind prophet, whom he mentioned
in one of his letters (*Corr.* 192).

As we saw earlier, the French king had gone through the same process
of transfiguration in Cazotte's mind. Although the writer occasionally referred
in his letters and other writings to the traditional association, in France, of the
"throne" and "altar"--that is, the close historical alliance between king and
church, dating back to Frankish King Clovis in 496--he would now mostly
worship his king as a representative of God on earth: "Good Lord, I must
love my king since I love you; your cult and his cannot be separated"
(*Révélations, DA* 266). The term *cult* here indicates that the king represented
much more to Cazotte than a mere political entity. He was, indeed, equated
with the "King of Kings," Christ himself. For Cazotte's deep grief was caused
not only by the ransacking and destruction of churches, the prosecution and
murder of priests, but also, and fundamentally, by the woes and indignities
suffered by the king and his family. The suffering, the Passion of Christ, and
those of the king were one in Cazotte's eyes. The author believed that he
himself participated in that general transfiguration through his own suffering:
"No . . . My suffering is dear to me; through it, I can share my king's
affliction" (*Révélations, DA* 266). The writer's pain became a necessity for
him, his reason for living and dying, as die he must, on the scaffold, even
though he would be offered an extaordinary chance to avoid death. But he
would refuse that opportunity because it denied him the martyrdom to which
he now aspired.

After his first arrest on August 18, 1792, and a speedy trial, Cazotte was
found guilty. But before he received a death sentence, his beautiful daughter,
Elizabeth, imprisoned with him, pleaded with their jailers to have her father
released. She managed to touch them as well as the crowds that had invaded
the prison for the September massacres. In a rare move, amid the terror and
the blood, Cazotte and his daughter were miraculously set free. Among all
the prisoners who fervently desired to leave jail and escape certain death,
Cazotte, who was ready to die for his faith and king, was paradoxically the
one selected not to meet that fate, at least, not yet.

After his astonishing liberation, the old man stubbornly refused to listen
to his friends and family who were urging him to run away, emigrate, or hide.
He knew that his situation was precarious and that his prosecutors would soon

rearrest and sentence him to death in view of the damaging documents they had in hand. The argument Cazotte made to remain home and accept his destiny is true to character. To the "enlightenment" of the *philosophes*, he always preferred "*les lumières de la religion*" (enlightenment from religion, *Corr.* 123). In other words, he sought *knowledge*, as he declared it, in "the Holy Scriptures, the only antidote for all the philosophical musings that have led us astray" (*Corr.* 211-212). Thus, the Bible held the key to his decision regarding his conduct after release from prison. A friend of the family, Mme d'Hautefeuille, reports in her book *La Famille Cazotte*, based on conversations with Cazotte's son, Scévole, and other witnesses, that the author, opening his Bible, would tell his friends and family the story of the prophet Eleazar in the Book of Maccabees.[19] Cazotte insisted that he wanted to follow the prophet's example in refusing his friends' entreaties to hide and escape from death:

Considering what he owed his venerable age, his white hair, an emblem of his natural generosity of heart, and his life of innocence, without blemish since his youth, he (the prophet Eleazar) answered: "In dying with courage, I will prove more deserving of my age, leaving to the young an example of courage and patience, instead of seeking to retain a few more days, which are not worth preserving." (Hautefeuille, 288)

Thus, Cazotte chose to identify not with the Greek philosopher Socrates in comparable circumstances--a choice that would have conformed better to the predominant neoclassical and republican taste of the day--but with a biblical prophet, thereby confirming for posterity both his opposition to the new political order, and the new religious role he assumed for himself in a blasphemous and ignominious dark world, dominated by Satan.

The old sage went through a second trial and was finally sentenced to death. Climbing the steps up to the guillotine with courage and a peaceful smile, he is reported to have said: "I am dying as I have lived all my life, faithful to God and my king"--*Deo et regis fidelis*, the very same terms French Illuminists used as their motto.[20] In his final words, Cazotte manifests a mystical stoicism that owes nothing to the world of antiquity, which had once been dear to him, and everything to "divine light"--an Illuminism all his own through his experience of suffering, death, and hope for regeneration.

NOTES

1. Marquis de Sade, *Contre l'Etre Suprême*, 1st ed. (Paris: Quai Voltaire, 1989), 22. All translations from the French in this chapter are mine.

2. Georges Décote, *Correspondance de Jacques Cazotte*, critical edition (Paris: Klincksieck, 1982), 215; letter of July 28, 1792, to his friend Pouteau (henceforth referred to as *Corr.*).

3. Jacques Cazotte, *Le Diable amoureux*, preface and notes by Georges Décote (Paris: Gallimard, 1981); 1st ed., 1772; important modifications in text

of 2nd ed. (1776). Décote's edition, consulted for this chapter, henceforth referred to as *DA* in text and notes.

4. Among the writers who were influenced in the last decade of the eighteenth century and in the nineteenth century by Cazotte's novel and its approach, the most often cited are: M. G. Lewis, himself the creator of the gothic and "black" novel; E.T.A. Hoffmann, the author who borrowed the most extensively from Cazotte; Schiller, Poe, Nodier, Mérimée, Maupassant, and so on. Some of the greatest nineteenth-century French poets, fascinated by Cazotte's exotic creation, Biondetta, the she-devil, were Nerval, Baudelaire, Gautier and Apollinaire, who mention her in their poetry and critical writings.

5. See Pierre-Georges Castex, *Le Conte fantastique en France de Nodier à Maupassant* (Paris: Corti, 1951); Louis Vax, *L'Art et la littérature fantastiques* (Paris: PUF, 1960) and *La Séduction de l'étrange; étude sur la litterature fantasique* (Paris: PUF, 1965); Roger Caillois, *Images, images, essais sur le rôle et les pouvoirs de l'imagination* (Paris: Corti, 1966); Max Milner, *Le Diable dans la littérature française, de Cazotte à Baudelaire, 1772—1861* (Paris: Corti, 1960) and *Jacques Cazotte. Le Diable amoureux* (Paris: Garnier-Flammarion, 1979); and most importantly Tzvetan Todorov, *Introduction à la littérature fantastique* (Paris: Seuil, 1970).

6. Jean-François de La Harpe, "Prédictions de Cazotte," in *Oeuvres choisies et posthumes* (Paris: Migneret, 1806). *See* "Prophétie de Cazotte rapportée par La Harpe," *DA* 203-211. The event, which was reported and published eighteen years after the facts, may have been fabricated by La Harpe *a posteriori*, as a reported "postcript" to his story, denying its veracity, might seem to indicate. However, that postscript, allegedly seen by his secretary and publisher, was left unpublished and has since "disappeared," thus leaving the question unresolved and essentially shrouded in mystery. Several other "witnesses" swear that the incident at the dinner party did indeed take place, but their assertions were published much later even than La Harpe's. Despite Georges Décote's interesting demonstration in his *Itinéraire de Jacques Cazotte* (Genéve: Droz, 1984, 339-352), the issue can be considered moot at this point, particularly in view of one of Cazotte's writings, which appears to anticipate some of the most gruesome aspects of the Revolution, notably the theme of heads cut off; see *Ollivier* (1763), in *DA* 189-195.

7. The Estates General were originally composed of the three major social classes in the *ancien régime*: the nobility, the clergy and the bourgeoisie; the bourgeosie was the *Tiers Etat* (Third Estate), which then did not include the *peuple* (the people), that is, peasants, manual workers, and generally speaking, the lower social classes. Only during the Revolution did the Third Estate and the "people" begin to merge into one entity, for a time, before the final victory of the bourgeoisie and gradual exclusion of the *peuple*.

Throughout this chapter, the term *people* is used with this political meaning, corresponding to the French word *peuple*; the words "bourgeois" and "bourgeoisie" specifically refer to the sociopolitical appellation it then had in France.

8. The *taille* was a French tax levied on the Third Estate and all commoners. The clergy and nobility were exempt from it. Of all the taxes, it was the most arbitrarily apportioned. Branded as the very symbol of inequity, it was universally hated. "Industrious part" here refers to the Third Estate and the people, in contrast to the idle aristocracy.

9. Nicolas Bergasse, *Considérations sur la liberté du commerce* (La Haye, 1780), 61.

10. Jacques Cazotte's son, Scévole, was also influenced lastingly by his father's mystic "illuminism," as well as by the ambient "mesmerism" or "magnetism" to which he was exposed in prerevolutionary France. This influence is evidenced not only in Scévole Cazotte's first book, *Témoignage d'un royaliste* (Paris: Le Clère, 1839), but also and essentially in his last writing, *Témoignage spiritualiste d'outre-tombe sur le magnétisme humain, fruit d'un long pélerinage, par J.-S.C. . . .*, published posthumously and anonymously by Abbé Loubert (Paris, 1860). Robert Darnton, in *Mesmerism and the End of the Enlightenment in France* (Cambridge, Mass.: Harvard University Press, 1968), erroneously attributes the son's last publication to his father, Jacques Cazotte, and gives an incorrect publication date for it (Darnton 1968: 71 n.15).

11. Well into the Revolution, Cazotte would still believe in the sanctity of the people, whom he considered simply misguided by political agitators when they misbehaved; see, for instance, *Corr.* 130 and *Révélations, DA* 268-269.

12. It was with a certain irony that Cazotte called the duke "duc de Pique," which I have translated as 'Duke of Pikes,' for lack of a better word in English that would express the dual meaning of *pique*. The term *pique* has several connotations in French, probably all of which Cazotte implied in this locution. Its first semantic value, "spade," refers to a playing card, notably the jack of spades here, with all its pejorative connotations. *Pique* also signifies "pike," suggestive of the weapon carried by the *sans-culottes*, a perceived infamy for a duke. Furthermore, in this sense, Cazotte's appellation was historically correct; the duke was reputed to have provided the revolutionaries with enormous quantities of pikes. Finally, Cazotte's choice of word was particularly apt as far as his own version of the Revolution was concerned. He was convinced that the French Revolution was the work of the devil, and, indeed, the pike is reminiscent of the devil's attribute. This appellation of the duke was definitely an all-around uncomplimentary pun.

13. Louis XVI, now a virtual prisoner of his people, was denied the right to practice his religion freely. This, together with his concern for the security of his family, was his primary motive for trying to escape from France. The determining factor that spurred him to do so on June 20, 1791, happened two months earlier when he was forbidden to attend Easter mass in St. Cloud.

14. See most of Cazotte's letters to Pouteau in which the writer constantly refers to Satan as the major agent of all revolutionary evils and to the revolutionaries themselves as the devil's fiendish partners.

15. See Décote's comments both on the identification of Christ and Louis XVI and on the close association between politics and religion in Cazotte's writings, *Corr.* 209 n.3, and *L'Itinéraire de Jacques Cazotte*, notably 395-397.

16. See E. P. Shaw, *Jacques Cazotte (1719—1792)* (Cambridge, Mass.: Harvard University Press, 1942), 113 n.384. Marat, the well-known radical revolutionary, was the opposite of Cazotte. He wrote violent articles against the king, the monarchy and moderate politicians in his newspaper *L'Ami du Peuple* (*Friend of the People*). Marat's assassination in his bath by young Girondist Charlotte Corday on July 13, 1793--ironically, less than a year after Cazotte's execution--is one of the major events recorded in the revolutionary chronicles. He was to be venerated by the people as their first great republican "martyr," just as Cazotte had felt himself to be a martyr of his own political and religious cause.

17. *Mon songe de la nuit du samedi au dimanche de devant la Saint-Jean* (*My Midsummer Night's Dream . . . 1791*), *DA* 257-258; first published posthumously in *Oeuvres badines et morales, historiques et philosophiques de Jacques Cazotte*, Vol. 1 (Paris: Bastien, 1817). The term *tie, lier* in the French text, has a mystical value for Cazotte. In his last years, awake or dreaming, Cazotte would "tie" evil people and spirits, that is, render them powerless through various signs and spiritual commands in the fashion of spiritualists and Illuminists such as Martines de Pasqually and Louis-Claude de Saint-Martin, whose influence on Cazotte before the Revolution had been considerable.

18. *Révélations, DA* 266;   text first published, posthumously, in *Oeuvres badines et morales, historiques et philosophiques de Jacques Cazotte*, Vol. 1 (1817), 18.

19. Hautefeuille, comtesse d' [pseud. Anna Marie], *La Famille Cazotte* (Paris: Waille, 1846).

20. Auguste Viatte, *Les Sources occultes du romantisme: illuminisme--théosophie, 1770—1820*, Vol. 1. (Paris: Champion, 1928), 196.

REFERENCES

Bergasse, Nicolas. *Considérations sur la liberté du commerce*. La Haye, 1780.

Caillois, Roger. *Images, images, essais sur le rôle et les pouvoirs de l'imagination*. Paris: Corti, 1966.

Castex, Pierre-Georges. *Le Conte fantastique en France de Nodier à Maupassant*. Paris: Corti, 1951.

Cazotte, Jacques. *Ollivier*, 1763. See under Georges Décote, *Jacques Cazotte. Le Diable amoureux*, 127-201.

————. *Le Diable amoureux, nouvelle espagnole*. Naples et Paris: Le Jay, 1772.

See also two other modern editions of *Le Diable amoureux* under the names of their respective editors below (Décote 1981; Milner 1979).

————. Consult *Le Diable amoureux* in *Romanciers du XVIIIe siècle*, edited by Etiemble et Marguerite du Cheyron. Vol. 2. Paris: Gallimard, Pléiade, 1965, 303-378.

————. Consult *Oeuvres badines et morales de M********, Vol. 2, for revised second edition of *Le Diable amoureux*. Amsterdam and Paris: Esprit, 1776.

————. *Mon Songe de la nuit du samedi au dimanche de devant la Saint-Jean 1791*. (*My Midsummer Night's Dream . . . 1791*). Published posthumously in *Oeuvres badines et morales, historiques et philosophiques*. Paris: Bastien, 1817. See in *Jacques Cazotte. Le Diable amoureux* (Décote 1981), 255-260.

————. *Révélations*. Published posthumously in *Oeuvres badines et morales. . .* 1817. Probably written in mid-1792. See *Jacques Cazotte. Le Diable amoureux* (Décote 1981), 261-279.

Cazotte, Jacques-Scévole. *Témoignage d'un royaliste*. Paris: Le Clère, 1839.

————. *Témoignage spiritualiste d'outre-tombe sur le magnétisme humain, fruit d'un long pélerinage par J.-S.C. . . . .*, published by Abbé Loubert. Paris, 1860.

Darnton, Robert. *Mesmerism and the End of the Enlightenment in France*. Cambridge, Mass.: Harvard University Press, 1968.

Décote, Georges. *Correspondance de Jacques Cazotte*. Critical edition. Paris: Klincksieck, 1982.

————. *L'Itinéraire de Jacques Cazotte (1719—1792). De la fiction littéraire au mysticisme politique*. Genève: Droz, 1984.

————. *Jacques Cazotte. Le Diable amoureux*. Preface and notes by Georges Décote. Paris: Gallimard, Folio, 1981. (Referred to as *DA* in this chapter).

Hautefeuille, Anne-Albe-Cornélie de Beaurepaire, comtesse Charles d' [pseud. Anna Marie]. *La Famille Cazotte*. Paris: Waille, 1846.

La Harpe, Jean-François·de. "Prédictions de Cazotte." In *Oeuvres choisies et posthumes*. Paris: Migneret, 1806. See "Prophétie de Cazotte rapportée par La Harpe," in *Jacques Cazotte. Le Diable amoureux* (Décote 1981), 203-211.

Milner, Max. *Le Diable dans la littérature française, de Cazotte à Baudelaire, 1772—1861*. Paris: Corti, 1960.

_____. *Jacques Cazotte. Le Diable amoureux*. Preface and notes by Max Milner. Paris: Garnier-Flammarion, 1979.

Rushdie, Salman. *The Satanic Verses*. London: Viking, 1988.

Sade, Donatien-Alphonse-François, marquis de. *Contre l'Etre suprême*. Paris: Quai Voltaire, 1989.

Shaw, Edward Pease. *Jacques Cazotte (1719-1792)*. Cambridge, Mass.: Harvard University Press, 1942.

Todorov, Tzvetan. *Introduction à la littérature fantastique*. Paris: Seuil, 1970.

Vax, Louis. *L'Art et la littérature fantastiques*. Paris: PUF, 1960.

_____. *La Séduction de l'étrange; étude sur la littérature fantastique*. Paris: PUF, 1965.

Viatte, Auguste. *Les Sources occultes du romantisme: Illuminisme--théosophie, 1770—1820*. Paris: Champion, 1928.

5

The Concept of Virtue in Literature and Politics During the French Revolution of 1789: Sade and Robespierre

Gislinde Seybert

Ideal and reality part company, as they usually do, in the French Revolution of 1789, known as the Great Revolution. The contradictory ideals of liberty, equality, fraternity, elaborated by the Age of Enlightenment, were to be transposed into practice in very different ways, and culminated in the period of Terror during which the Revolution devoured its offspring.

Two very different personalities representing literary and political life during the French Revolution were preoccupied with the concept of "virtue." Their divergent treatment of this concept is investigated here. The first personality is D.A.F. de Sade, descendant of a once-illustrious noble family and pursued by the *parlements* of the *ancien régime* which criminalized the young marquis for his sexual orgies. All his life he insisted on the professional title of *homme de lettres* (man of letters) and rightly so; the impact of his works was immense. The other is Maximilien Robespierre, an advocate and deputy elected by the inhabitants of Arras, who made his career as one of the most influential members of the *Comité de salut public* (Committee of Public Safety). Finally, shortly before his fall, he was elected president of the Convention.

With respect to the careers of these two figures, the concepts of social ascent and descent are highly questionable. Are the usual criteria of evaluation regarding social "descent" acceptable in the case of a member of the former aristocracy becoming a man of letters of historical importance? And what is social "ascent" worth if the powerful revolutionary leader ends up under the guillotine? Nevertheless, Sade and Robespierre present an interesting parallel in the political and cultural effects of their lives, both being implicated, by their deeds and work, in the problem of violence. So we could summarize the subject of this inquiry as follows: What connections between virtue and violence are to be found in the written testimonials of the two authors?

ROBESPIERRE AND THE REVOLUTIONARY RHETORIC OF VIRTUE

In the French Declaration of the Rights of Man, which was discussed in the *Assemblée constituante* from August 17 to 26, 1789, and became the preface to the Constitution of 1791, the concept of virtue plays only a minor role. It comes up just once in Article Six where it figures in a parallel construction with the talents of man.

Law . . . expression of the general will. All citizens, being equal before it, are all similarly eligible for all offices, positions and public posts, according to their capabilities and without any other distinction than that of their *virtues* and their *talents*. (All translations by Peter Hosford and Gislinde Seybert)

In the attempt to create a world of justice to supersede the impracticable customs of the corrupt ancien régime, the new equality is to be differentiated from it by reference to the "capabilities" of the citizens, their virtues and talents. The old system based on the privileges of nobility, clergy and social influence by means of capital is supposed to be destroyed and replaced by the measure of individual capabilities, the value on which bourgeois ideology is based. That individuals need some preconditions to develop their capabilities does not enter the constitutional frame.

In his addresses to the Convention and to the *club des Jacobins*, Robespierre insists on the concept of virtue as the foundation of his ideological system of revolutionary politics. He takes on a tone of moral indignation to confound the enemies of the Republic, the allied monarchies and their paid agents. The system of republican values corresponds to the theological doctrine of Christian religion, with its exclusion of the unbeliever. The friends of the republic are identified with the whole range of attributes of virtue and purity (*vérité pure; zèle pur*) (pure truth; pure zeal), while the republican values of *liberté, courage* and *civisme* are used synonymously with, and in the same phrase as, *vertu républicaine* and *vertu civique* (republican virtue and civic virtue). In the opposite position in this world of black and white, good and evil, is vice, the term attributed to the allied monarchies suffocating revolutionary France: "How edifying is the piety of tyrants! and how agreeable the shining *virtues* of the courts must be to heaven. . . . Of what god do they speak to us? Do they know other gods besides pride, debauchery and all the *vices*?"[1]

The high-risk political (and, it must be remembered, at that time military) antagonism is thus expressed in the religious and moral dualism of good and evil, virtue and vice. So the political ideology is a secularization of Christian mythology and, at the same time, a reawakening of the Roman tradition whereby republic and "father"-land (*patria*) were linked in a semi-religious way with the ideal of virtue and heroic manliness. The Latin *virtus* means both "virtue" and "courage." Robespierre, whose style is saturated with Roman history and mythology, explicitly terms the vices "the gods of pride and debauchery," thus personifying moral categories. Virtue is addressed as a person and worshiped as a powerful god: "O *virtue* of *great hearts*! what are all the agitations of pride and the pretentions of *small* souls against you! O *virtue*, are you any less necessary in the founding of a republic than in the governing of it in peacetime?"[2] Here Robespierre plays on the opposition of great (good) and small (evil) with respect to the heart and soul, invoking what were originally religious metaphors.

Another quotation from the speech *Sur les principes du gouvernement révolutionnaire*, addressed to the Convention in the name of the Committee of Public Safety and delivered on December 25, 1793, develops the opposition of virtue and vice into a political scheme:

> . . . for if the *Convention* does not govern, the tyrants will reign. . . . All the *vices* fight for them; the republic has nothing to protect her but the *virtues*. The *virtues* are simple, modest, poor, often ignorant, gross sometimes; they are the apanage of the unhappy and the patrimony of the common people. The *vices* are surrounded by riches, armed with all the charms of voluptuousness and the seductions of perfidy; they are accompanied by all the dangerous talents employed in crime.[3]

In these reflections, Robespierre defines a clear sociological principle derived from virtue and vice. In his opinion, virtue determines the behavior of the common people, virtue having been bestowed on them by poverty, which leads to modesty and ignorance. In contrast, vice coincides with wealth, voluptuousness, perfidy and crime. The rich need not obey moral laws, being able to buy themselves immunity. Thus, the lower classes, who are supposed to profit from the new republican government and whose support Robespierre wants to mobilize, are praised with the label of virtue, whereas the upper classes who accept the rule of tyrants (the monarchy) are blamed as vicious and denounced as enemies of the Republic.

Virtue and vice, as two opposite behaviors, synonymous with the good and evil of religious and moral tradition, are used as concepts through which political practice is defined. The increasing Terror needed a clear distinction between republican citizens and monarchist agents. Thus, a sharp dualism arises in political discourse which exploits a rhetoric of friends and enemies of the revolutionary government; the political practice will prove somewhat more difficult. In the same speech quoted above, Robespierre denounces the "perverted"--"stupid or perverted sophists who are trying to confound the opposites."[4] It is interesting to note the parallel construction that gives a certain equivalence to the terms *stupidity* and *perversion*, and acts as an indicator of the damning attributes that lead to the moral and physical annihilation of men.

This moralization of politics, which brings Robespierre's and the revolutionary political speeches so close to preaching, provoked in Sade a literary reaction to the republican ideology which did not create more justice in a better world, at least not in Sade's experience of life.

THE CARNIVALIZATION OF
REVOLUTIONARY VIRTUE IN *JUSTINE*

The emphatically moral rhetoric of the Revolution leads Sade, in his literary promulgation of a new morality, to a reversal of virtue and vice. Vice and crime thus become the prevailing values of the libertines, evoking the most extraordinary effect of "carnivalization," of a world turned upside down (*verkehrte Welt*).

Sade's theoretical and fictional texts deal with the contradictory positions of the Age of Enlightenment, the antagonism between individual and social interest, and the belief in the perfectibility of human behavior. The libertine's extreme, ruthless liberty radically rejects equality and fraternity, the other two revolutionary demands; Sade invents the literary protagonist of the Libertine with the aim of proving the incompatibility of individual liberty with the Enlightenment's two other prerequisites for ideal human behavior. From their indisputably Christian origins in the gospel of charity, the demands for equality and fraternity negate the liberty of the single individual. Yet liberty was not to be excluded, its importance being stressed by the first rank allotted to it.

Sade identifies with the sadomasochistic position of the libertine: his extreme need for liberty and power on one side and the victim's never-ending capacity for suffering on the other. This is the clear (but at first confusing) message of his literary texts. The victim's position, exemplified by Justine, represents the Christian and enlightened demand for virtue, its realization and execution for the sake of personal and public well-being. The libertine, on the contrary, propagates the reversal of virtue into vice, and indulges in the supposed peak of lust and self-gratification, with all the destructive consequences that this entails.

Justine, protagonist of the novel of the same title published in 1791, is the personification of virtue and the eternal victim. Her first attempt to obtain support and subsistence from a vicar after the death of her parents ends in an attack on her virtue:

Justine, in tears, goes to see her priest; she paints her situation with the energetic candor of her age. . . . She was dressed in a little white fur coat; her fine hair was casually bound under a white bonnet; her bosom, barely noticeable, was hidden under two or three yards of gossamer; her pretty face was somewhat pale because of the suffering that devoured her; tears swam in her eyes giving them an abundance of expression.[5]

Justine's decently veiled beauty moves the vicar to make her an indecent offer and to kiss her. The negation of the traditional picara who survives all the perils of adventurous fiction without being harmed, Justine is the person who suffers harm continually. She stumbles from one trap to the next, struggling to protect her virtue the whole time. In Rodin's public school, Justine-Thérèse barely avoids rape. Rodin, the headmaster, and his friend Rombeau, the doctor, discuss Justine's, their victim's, virginity: "Virgin, well she is almost a virgin, said Rodin. Just once, she was raped, against her will, and from then on, not the least thing."[6]

Justine, begging for her half-virginity, an ironic hint at the impossible paradox of this idea, falls down at their feet and offers her life for her honour:

I fell down at the feet of my torturers, I offered them my life and demanded honour from them. But as you are no longer a virgin, said Rombeau, what does it matter? You won't be guilty of anything, we're going to rape you the way you have been raped already and so there will be not the slightest sin on your conscience; violence will have robbed you of everything.[7]

This is the sophistic argumentation of Rombeau, who wants to obtain Justine's submission; being forced, she will not be responsible; there will be no danger to her salvation. Rombeau's argument stays within the clerical frame and takes no account of Justine as a moral person. After Justine has been raped and so definitely loses her virginity, she suffers an attack of desperation:

An attack of furious despair assailed my soul. I who placed *all my glory, all my happiness in my virtue*, I, who could console myself against all the misdeeds of fortune provided I had always behaved properly, could not bear to think of the horrible prospect of seeing myself so cruelly degraded by those from whom I should have expected the utmost in help and consolation: my tears roll abundantly, my cries make the vault resound; I roll on the floor, I beat my breast, I tear my hair, I plead with my torturers and beg them to put me to death.[8]

Justine, as the martyr of Kant's moral law (*Sittengesetz*), ranks her virtue as her most precious possession; her virtue is the source of her glory and happiness. Justine exhibits an attitude that internalizes the concept of virtue imprinted by patriarchal society. The identification with the aggressor's morality increases the psychic pain suffered by the victim, while the bodily pain and the humiliation inflicted by the violence would have been sufficiently overwhelming in themselves. One of society's most rigorous demands is for a woman's virtue, both in the era of the French Revolution and, implicitly, today. The virtue of chastity is a specific variety of sexual oppression, which is first of all directed against woman and insists on her complete submission to social rules, not only with regard to behavior, but also with regard to her way of thinking and feeling. This demand has been promulgated in response to the supposed necessity of limiting and channeling female sexuality, which has been conceived as insatiable. The demand to remain virtuous produces in the mind of the woman who internalizes the rule a kind of confusion that holds her back from fulfilling her own inclinations. When she tries to realize herself, she faces the task of combining the alienation of the enforced virtue with her own yearning for sexual completion.

During the Age of Enlightenment and the French Revolution, sexual behavior, especially for women, was so strictly regulated by social rules (except for the noble and the rich) that no self-determined sexual behavior was openly possible. Prostitution, the playground for the noble and the rich, was a kind of public institution according to the police reports read to Louis XV by his mistress Madame de Pompadour; it had nothing to do with a free sexual life for women.[9]

Sade's critique of the social situation of women in *Justine* implies the necessity of offering women the possibility of self-determination through a revision of a questionable social order. The exaggerated, parodistic and ironical representation of women's oppression in the violence to which they are subjected by every single male in the family system (the fathers, husbands, lovers and their own sons), as well as by the representatives of social institutions such as church, school and medical profession, pushes the situation to its extreme.

Most certainly, Sade sees violence against every individual, male and female, occurring whenever the individual is hindered in his growth by society and the representatives of its institutions. As a former privileged member of high nobility, he must have perceived the process of the increasing appropriation of the individual by the network of social power, especially during the Revolution. In the female protagonist, the helplessness of the individual is reinforced in a piquant and alluring way by the additional dimension of sadistic sexual oppression.

By the term *carnivalization*, Mikhail Bakhtin characterizes the transfer (into literature) of carnival structures (the world turned upside down), such as, for example, the fall of a person from the highest rank to the deepest degradation. Carnivalization can also be regarded as the free intermingling between man and his world, through the dissolving of hierarchies by uncontrolled human contact and combination, allowing sexual expression free from norms and taboos and leading to all kinds of eccentric behavior culminating in obscenity.[10] Justine's fall through insulting and degrading treatment, and finally through the loss of her virginity, is an example of carnivalization with its typically ambivalent effects of awe and laughter. Suffering torture, losing her virginity, and being struck by the lightning's mystical course through her body (at the end of the novel) become metaphors for the carnivalization of Justine's body and its familiarization with the world, and Sade's (and the reader's) symbolic fulfillment of the fantasy of profaning and martyring a saint.

In *Justine*, the carnivalization is not only moral but also linguistic, as the use of adjectives demonstrates. Adjectives of emotional color like *malheureux* (unfortunate) in the sympathetic mode, and *exécrable, impudent, scélérat* (wicked) in a context of condemnation, uttered from a perspective opposite to that of Christian morality, confuse the reader's moral and affective system and give Sade's texts their effect of emotional terror.

Sade's literary reaction to a world turned upside down (the pre-revolutionary period must have had this effect on the privileged classes already, not to mention the events *during* the Revolution which came close to a state of collective madness) consists in the conscious invention of a phantasmagorical world that gives the powerful free disposition over the weak without any inhibition by law. His long isolation in prison and the unprecedented change in the outer world must have had a powerful impact on Sade's unconscious, enabling him to produce fantasies of archaic regression tearing down the walls of the super-ego (*Uber-Ich*). On the other hand, his aggressiveness toward legal and religious limitations can be interpreted as an understandable consequence of rationally and emotionally motivated resistance to oppression and imprisonment.

VIOLENCE AND VIRTUE

In conclusion, it can be said that the concept of virtue as a secularized religious value plays an eminent role in literature and politics during the Revolution. It is used at that turning point of history which gave "modern times" their ambivalent kick. Increasing centralization in all realms, secularization of the state and the educational system, supposedly free access to positions of influence, the individual's liberty coupled with his dispensability, and bureaucracy and automatization--all came dressed in the costume of virtue as *vertu civique*. In the name of virtue, social integration by self-control was enforced for every individual who wanted to take part in the blessings of community, that is, civilization. The definition of virtue as a political term, discriminating between good and bad citizens, is transposed from clerical institutions to revolutionary institutions such as the Convention, the Committee of Public Safety, the *Comité de sûreté générale* (Committee of General Security), and the *Tribunal révolutionnaire de Paris*.

The *Comité de sûreté générale* issued passports, certificates of citizenship (*certificats de civisme*), and warrants of arrest.[11] Thus, it was the institution that approved the acceptance of people as citizens by publicly declaring their virtue. This became a matter of life and death during the period of Terror, when public institutions controlled the thoughts and feelings of the individual and endowed him with the label of "virtuous." Control and determination from outside as a fact of alienation made self-determination impossible and required self-imposed behavioral restrictions as a condition of survival.

Sade, as the eternal criminal, saw the precariousness of the concepts of virtue and vice and their inevitable iniquity in the denunciation of individuals and their exclusion from the community of citizens. He experienced this new political system based on the law of nature (*droits naturels*, *Naturrecht*) as just another regime of injustice. The revolutionary tribunal put him, the radical opponent of capital punishment, on the list of those sentenced to death in spite of his activity in support of the Revolution. In his literary texts, he expressed in never-ending tales of terror his contempt of any social organization based on law and legal punishment, by reversing its social values. The *desire* he describes in his texts is the *reverse side* of *law*.[12]

Desire only comes into being through the existence of prohibition. Because of prohibition, the individual desires liberty from suffocating norms. The desire for liberty is, according to Lacan, something that first appears during the French Revolution. Lacan presumes that the Revolution had its origins in the will to fight for the liberty of desire. Robespierre's demand for virtue defeats Danton's original call for a liberty of desire. In the end, it is the violence of power exercised by the group achieving the consensus of the collectivity that remains victorious.

In his book *Sade mon prochain*, Pierre Klossowski gives a profound interpretation of Sade's work. In the view of Klossowski, the pamphlet *Français, encore un effort si vous voulez être républicains*, inserted in *La Philosophie dans le boudoir*, calls into question the revolutionary values of 1789 by propagating them. Klossowski supposes that Sade embraces the philosophy of Enlightenment in order to reveal its dark foundations.[13] Horkheimer and Adorno come to a somewhat comparable conclusion in their *Dialektik der Aufklärung*.[14] Klossowski insists that Sade's political nihilism is a criticism of the period's violent collective process; his apology for crime satirizes the political instinct, which is always the instinct of preservation of the collective. Writes Klossowski:

With a profound satisfaction, a people exterminates those who counter them. The collectivity always sniffs out those who are harmful to it, whether they are right or wrong, and therefore, it can confound cruelty and justice without the slightest feeling of remorse. The rituals which the collectivity invents around the scaffold liberate it from the drama of pure cruelty, the face and effects of which are thus conveniently veiled.[15]

We thus owe a debt to Sade and we must acknowledge his [Sade's] function of denouncing the dark powers camouflaged as social values by the collective mechanisms of defence.[16]

So the ultimate significance of *Justine* lies in the idea that a "virtuous" life is seen to prove the integration of the individual into the collectivity, while the accusation of indulging in vice reflects nonintegration, like Sade's, which leads to criminalization and exclusion from the social body. Justine's constant need to protect her virtue must be interpreted as the inherent need (of the female outsider) for social acceptance. Justine's paradox is that she cannot integrate into a society that is a collectivity of vice by trying to fulfill its normative and ideological demands. Justine's paradox ultimately turns out to be the paradox of a society whose individual members do not live up to its moral claims. The antinomies between how the people live and how they should live are intensified, in the case of *Justine*, by the crucial adventures of a *woman* with mostly *male* representatives of society in the somehow lawless realm of privacy--that is to say in the absence of "objective," disinterested witnesses.

NOTES

1. Maximilien Robespierre, *Textes choisis*, Jean Poperen (ed.), Vol. 3 (Paris: Editions sociales, 1974), 83-93.

2. Ibid., 104.

3. Ibid.

4. Ibid., 100.

5. D.A.F. de Sade, *Justine ou les malheurs de la vertu* (Paris: 10/18, 1969), 17-18.

6. Ibid., 119.

7. Ibid., 119-120.

8. Ibid., 136-137.

9. Otto Flake, *Marquis de Sade* (Frankfurt am Main: Fischer Taschenbuch Verlag, 1981).

10. Mikhail Bakhtin, *Literatur und Karneval: Zur Romantheorie und Lachkultur* (München: Hanser Verlag, 1969), 49-50.

11. Marc Bouloiseau, *Nouvelle Histoire de la France contemporaine*, Vol. 2 (Paris: Seuil, 1972), 108.

12. Jacques Lacan, "Kant avec Sade: Postface de 'La Philosophie dans le boudoir,'" in *D.A F. de Sade: Oeuvres Complètes*, Vol. 3 (Paris: Cercle du livre précieux, 1966).

13. Pierre Klossowski, *Sade mon prochain* (Paris: Seuil, 1947).

14. Max Horkheimer and Theodor W. Adorno, *Dialektik der Aufklärung* (Frankfurt am Main: S. Fischer Verlag, 1969), 74.

15. Klossowski, *Sade mon prochain*, 86.

16. Ibid., 87.

6

Mme. De Staël: Comparative Politics as Revolutionary Practice

Susan Tenenbaum

Although Mme. de Staël has not been a neglected figure in intellectual history, her fame has largely attached to her work as a literary critic and novelist, as well as reflected an abiding fascination with her legendary persona. Recently, however, scholars have begun to rediscover Mme. de Staël as a political thinker.[1] I want to emphasize the term *rediscover*, for the impact of Mme. de Staël's political writing on her own day was considerable, and her legacy so vital that her biographer Albert Sorel dubbed her the "muse of Restoration liberalism."[2]

Yet Mme. de Staël does not receive even a footnote in contemporary surveys of political thought. She has long been dismissed as a polemicist whose political writings offer little of permanent value, and criticized for arguments that were, in the words of Jean Touchard, "essentially confused."[3] In this chapter, however, I shall be guided by the counsel of the poet and historian Lamartine who assessed most generously that quality of eclecticism that later critics have been less eager to applaud: "Her voice was like an antique chorus, in which all the great voices of the drama unite in one tumultuous concord."[4]

Following Lamartine, I suggest that Mme. de Staël's practical political involvements and divided intellectual allegiances establish a claim on our attention. The intellectual tensions in her work reflect her status as a thinker at the crossroads of eighteenth- and nineteenth-century cultures, and reveal an insatiably inquisitive mind eager to assimilate wide-ranging currents of ideas and apply them to the problems of her revolutionary era. If these problems were tied to the particular circumstances of her day, Mme. de Staël simultaneously perceived them as enduring political questions: What are the causes of revolution? the determinants of political stability? the prerequisites of a free society? These larger questions were, in turn, intimately bound to problems of practical politics: the building of consensus in an age of partisan extremism; the writing of new constitutions; the arresting of revolutionary change. The dynamic interaction between Mme. de Staël's theoretical concerns and her practical political objectives is evidenced throughout her major writings, and provides the frame for my present inquiry into her uses of comparative political analysis.

Mme. de Staël frequently turned to comparative analysis as a tool of instruction and persuasion. Nearly all of her major works--*On Literature*, *On Germany*, *Corinne*, *Considerations on the French Revolution*, *Ten Years of Exile*--are informed by a comparative perspective. This intellectual disposition, inherited from Montesquieu, was reinforced by her travels through Europe and her assiduous study of foreign cultures. Like Montesquieu, Mme. de Staël was intrigued by social diversity and dismayed by the narrow ethnocentrism of the French. Years earlier, Montesquieu had deployed incredulous Persians to indict French parochialism;[5] Mme. de Staël, his disciple, turned to comparative analysis to penetrate France's "Great Wall of China."[6] Her portraits of foreign cultures introduced new intellectual perspectives and contained detailed descriptions of unfamiliar societies. Nonetheless, these portraits were highly tendentious and linked to specific partisan purposes. Mme. de Staël presented the English Constitution as the model of good government, whose adoption by the French would consolidate the gains of the Revolution and serve as a foundation for the practical political reconciliation of the nation. Her portraits of Italy, Germany and Russia served strategic roles in her campaign against Napoleon.

Before turning to these explicitly partisan dimensions of Mme. de Staël's analysis, I should first like to bring to the surface a number of key intellectual tensions that characterize Mme. de Staël's work as a comparativist. These tensions owe as much to the divergent traditions of argument she sought to synthesize as to her shifting political alignments and polemical strategies. At least three distinct perspectives may be distilled from her writings:

1. *Comparison to illuminate sociocultural differences.* Mme. de Staël's celebration of the unique character of each national society had roots in her Montesquieuian inheritance and was later nourished by her contact with German nationalist thought. Montesquieu had ascribed to each society a distinctive "general spirit," arising from its unique combination of physical and moral causes (the latter comprising religion, laws, customs, and commerce).[7] In *On Literature*, Mme. de Staël extended Montesquieu's method to explore the sociology of culture, and she cautioned against the dangers of cultural arrogance, of recognizing no values besides one's own, as well as of taking profound differences in culture too lightly through imitation of alien literary styles. For example, she warned that "European states, particularly France, lose the advantages of national genius by imitating the writers of Italy."[8] Later, in *On Germany*, she continued to stress the importance of each nation's cultural self-expression, arguing that only authentic national cultures were worthy of admiration and that the "grafting on" of foreign cultures was a cause of social instability.

2. *Comparison to modify sociocultural differences.* Mme. de Staël's celebration of the multiplicity of national cultures was tempered by her cosmopolitanism. Thus, she was critical of exaggerated national differences and turned to comparison as a means of modifying these differences by a mutual "balancing" or "checking" of national characteristics. In *On Germany*, for example, she exposed the "excessively worldly" French to the "excessively

religious" Germans with a view to moderating the pronounced tendencies of each nation, reconciling both on a cosmopolitan middle ground.[9]

3. *Comparison to illustrate a theory of historical progress.* The theme that history is governed by general laws entailing advancement toward a universally valid form of society and a common human nature recurs throughout Mme. de Staël's major writings. In her writings prior to the *Considerations*, Mme. de Staël compares two broad historical types--ancient and modern societies. In the *Considerations*, she adopts a three-stage theory of history. Both frameworks identify modernity with a liberal constitutionalist state founded on the universal springs of human nature--"self-interest" and "sympathy." Unlike the first category of comparison, the present category appeals not to the richest expression of national differences, but to the historical emergence of a common humanity. Thus, we find Mme. de Staël awkwardly straddling positions as a cultural relativist and as an exponent of universal standards, deriving from a kind of secular natural law. Although, as I argue later in this chapter, this tension was powerfully reinforced by the strategic requirements of her politics, it was also nourished, on a deeper level, by the intellectual traditions of her day. Montesquieu, for example, drew no mutually exclusive distinctions between appeals to comparative and natural law.[10] And to the extent that Mme. de Staël sought to synthesize traditions as disparate as utilitarianism and pre-romanticism, her thought was simultaneously enriched and confused. My present concern is not, however, to delve more deeply into these intellectual sources, but rather to examine how Mme. de Staël drew on them to define her position as a "moderate" during an age of revolutionary upheaval.

If Mme. de Staël, by reason of her sex, was never a practitioner of political power, she nonetheless actively exercised the role of critic and polemicist. Her outlook was centrist, a posture that defined itself against the revolutionary extremes of radicalism and reaction. This middling approach, though compatible with strategic shifts in allegiance between monarchical and republican forms of government, was characterized by adherence to a core set of liberal principles: constitutionalism, representative institutions, the protection of civil liberties, and limited political equality. Before examining how these political convictions gave shape to Mme. de Staël's studies of Italy, Germany, Russia, and England, I should like to touch briefly on how they informed her theory of historical progress.

Mme. de Staël's concept of historical progress furnished a double-edged weapon with which to repudiate Jacobin reverence for classical antiquity, as well as to disavow the veneration of tradition by reactionary royalists. With Mme. de Staël, the idea of progress was enlisted in the service of political moderation. Her comparative models of ancient and modern society, formulated in collaboration with Benjamin Constant under the Thermidorian Republic, challenged Jacobin ideals of classical democracy. Mme. de Staël's strategy was to accuse the Jacobins of ahistoricism; of refusing to recognize the changes in social conditions that rendered their ideals of civic virtue, community and social democracy anachronistic and oppressive in the context

of modern social life. Unlike modern society, the ancient polity was characterized by smallness of scale, the absence of domestic life (given woman's
inferior social status, the gratifications of domesticity remained secondary to
active civic involvement with one's equals in the affairs of state), and a
rudimentary economy. Modern society, by contrast, was marked by a richly
rewarding domestic life and a highly developed commercial sector. The rise
of the "private" sphere as the locus of worthwhile endeavor, Mme. de Staël
argued, transformed the classical Jacobin ideal of civic self-sacrifice into an
instrument of political oppression.[11]

Mme. de Staël's adoption of a three-stage model of progress in the
Considerations reflected a shift in the balance of political forces under the
early Restoration: the reactionary aristocracy had replaced the Jacobins as the
principal threat to Mme. de Staël's vision of order. Their demands for a
return to the autocratic arrangements of the Old Regime countered her own
efforts to legitimate the "gains" of the Revolution. Omitting all reference to
classical antiquity, Mme. de Staël's model now comprised three successive
states: feudalism, despotism, and representative government. These stages
were distinguished by the degree of liberty secured by each: feudalism--
limited liberties; despotism--no liberty; representative government--liberty to
all citizens. By depicting feudalism as a system of limited monarchy in which
the power of the crown was curbed by the privileges of the nobility, Mme. de
Staël fashioned a political strategy that was simultaneously conciliatory and
critical. She conceded that the feudal constitution contained anticipations of
her cherished liberal form of government ("it is liberty that is ancient, and
despotism which is modern"),[12] acknowledging thereby the historical claims
of the nobility. Yet her model implicitly criticized the reactionary portrait of
the Revolution as an aberrant and criminal phenomenon; it affirmed the
Revolution's continuity with the historical struggle for liberty and celebrated
its universalization of liberal principles in 1789.[13]

Turning from Mme. de Staël's comparative historical typologies to her
treatment of contemporaneous societies, the model of England found in the
Considerations may be regarded as the most complete portrait of Mme. de
Staël's ideal of a modern free society. The models of Italy, Germany and
Russia set out, respectively, in *On Germany, Corinne* and *Ten Years of Exile*,
occupy a more ambivalent status in her work. They neither embody Mme. de
Staël's preferred forms of government nor receive her blanket censure.
Instead, they encapsulate various traits that during the course of the
Revolution, Mme. de Staël deemed essential to the triumph of her cherished
values. Thus she lauded the "enthusiasm" of the Germans and the "military
spirit" of the Russians during a period when the overthrow of Napoleon was
foremost in her thoughts. These models also served Mme. de Staël's political
purposes on another level: by focusing on the manifold variety of European
cultures, she implicitly repudiated Napoleonic designs for French hegemony.
Ultimately, however, such concessions to relativist standards are superseded
by her belief in the universal validity of a liberal social order. On this view,
Mme. de Staël's comparative investigations of Germany, Italy and Russia

function in a manner analogous to her concept of despotism: they counterpoint her model of a free society.

Mme. de Staël's homage to England in the *Considerations* had historical roots reaching back to the Huguenots, who celebrated English liberty in order to condemn French despotism following the revocation of the Edict of Nantes. Enlightenment *philosophes* like Montesquieu, Voltaire and Rousseau regarded themselves as either Anglophiles or Anglophobes. And, most immediately, the English model had played a strategic role in debates throughout the revolutionary era.[14] Members of the nobility promoted an aristocratic image of England as a means of defending their position first against the crown and, later, against the Third Estate. Against this aristocratic vision, Anglophile reformers like Jacques Necker depicted England as a model of an enlightened liberal and commercial order. It was this image of England that Necker transmitted to his daughter and that she enshrined in the *Considerations* as a model to be imitated by France: "We cannot believe that Providence has placed this fine monument of social order so near France, merely to give us the pain of never being able to emulate it."[15]

To claim England as a model, Mme. de Staël had to overcome not only her grim personal experience of English intolerance for "superior women," but also a relativism that disallowed the wholesale importation of alien social forms. Mme. de Staël's advocacy of English institutions, though nourished by her desire to compose the *Considerations* as a testament to Necker and a vindication of his policies, was nonetheless rooted in practical political judgments. Political conditions in France appeared to augur well for reception of the British model: England had established her credentials as the foremost opponent of Napoleon and liberator of France; the king and nobility had been restored to French political life; and, not insignificantly, all other constitutional solutions had been exhausted.

Mme. de Staël's portrait of England replicated the sweep of Montesquieuian analysis. She ascribed to England an animating passion--love of liberty--and explored how this passion informed English legal, political, social, and cultural institutions. Her investigation of England's constitutional structure focused on its "balanced government," founded on a tripartite sharing of power by king, lords and commons, and on its protection of individual rights. She explored how the English love of domesticity functioned as a barrier against state interference, and pioneered a concern for the "sociology of leisure" by describing the English penchant for solitary walks as suited to the dynamics of a free and privatized society.

Mme. de Staël's liberal criterion of good government had earlier served as a potent weapon against Napoleon, yet Napoleon's hegemonic designs on Europe simultaneously nurtured her wariness of any universalistic claims. Thus, she rallied resistance to the Emperor by championing the pluralistic expression of national cultures. French domination of Italy was a focus of her novel *Corinne* which depicted Italy as corrupt, fragmented and enervated under foreign rule, but as possessing the resources of a rich culture and an inspirational past. The novel is a sociological *tour de force*: plot lines dissolve into political argument and cultural exposition; protagonists are caricatures of their national traits rather than unique personalities.

In the novel, Mme. de Staël appealed to historical example to renew and rejuvenate the Italian people. Ancient ruins, often described in guidebook detail, serve as metaphors of lost dignity and as inspirations to national rebirth.[16] If Mme. de Staël had earlier alluded to the dangers of classical principles in modern society, she conceded their relevance to present-day Italian politics. To the ancients, freedom meant the absence of alien rule and the capacity to participate in public life--ideals with which to awaken Italy's dormant civic consciousness. The novel's heroine Corinne embodied the spontaneity, imagination and sensuality that Mme. de Staël deemed character-istic of Italian culture. If she condemned these qualities as inimical to a modern liberal society, she simultaneously applauded them as distinctive national traits, setting Italian creativity against the cold rationality of the French and the banal practicality of the English. This juxtaposition of national characters animates the love story between the novel's two protagonists--Corinne and the quintessentially English Oswald.

Like *Corinne*, *On Germany* was focused on an historically fragmented society which, under Napoleon, was being forged into a centralized state. Among the purposes of the treatise was to awaken a consciousness of national identity in order to incite rebellion against French hegemony. By joining these goals, Mme. de Staël opposed the views of German intellectuals like Hegel and Fichte who defended French rule precisely on the grounds that it was instrumental to the formation of a modern German state. Like Italy, Germany was depicted by Mme. de Staël as characterized by a divorce between politics and intelligence, albeit diverse national causes channeled Italian energies into the fine arts and German into philosophy. Mme. de Staël distinguished "enthusiasm," an elevation of the soul linked to apprehension of the sublime, as the animating passion of the German nation.[17] Enthusiasm lent an abstract contemplative quality to German philosophy, which led to a deprecation of worldly interests. Although this disposition militated against political activism, it nonetheless nourished a romantic aesthetic that, for Mme. de Staël, could be used to indict the prevailing French classicism. Whereas the romantic was "organic," "progressive," and "complex," the classical was "mechanical," "closed," and "simple." Because Mme. de Staël equated the tenets of classicism with the principles of despotic rule, her espousal of romantic aesthetics challenged the ideological foundations of the Napoleonic system, and thus brought into question its entire apparatus of control.[18]

Mme. de Staël's profile of Russia is found in her memoirs, *Ten Years of Exile*, which record her travels through that nation in 1812. Although the work was not intended as a political tract, the sections pertaining to Russia were drafted in the wake of the French invasion and directly reflect her Manichaean view of the 1812 war. Her largely sympathetic portrait of Russian life owed much to her perception of Russia as the instrument of Napoleon's defeat. She applauded Russia's primitive martial vigor, yet recognized it to be incompatible with the spirit of a free society; she admired Czar Alexander, yet acknowledged his power to be "despotic."

Mme. de Staël's designation of "martial vigor" as the animating passion of the Russians was informed by earlier Western accounts of Russian "primitivism," as well as by her own political sympathies. The image of Russia, massed as a nation and directing its unbridled barbaric energies against the Napoleonic menace, had captured her imagination. Mme. de Staël's politics merged once again with her sociological concerns as she offered a sustained investigation of the physical and moral causes that combined to form the distinctively Russian character type. She called attention to the harshness of the Russian terrain and the severity of its climate, the absence of a middle class that would support liberal institutions, education interrupted at an early age by military service, and an economy marked by extremes of luxury and privation.[19]

In the case of Russia, as in the cases of England, Italy and Germany, Mme. de Staël's practical political involvements served as a spur to her scholarship. Thus, she transmitted Montesquieuian sociological methods to the next century and enlarged his perspectives to accommodate a focus on the interrelationship between political and cultural life. With this focus she became celebrated as a herald and expositer of romanticism. Her comparative historical typologies nurtured the rebirth of historiographical research in the work of Restoration liberals like Guizot. While rooted in partisan purposes, Mme. de Staël's use of comparative analysis bequeathed an intellectual legacy that extended well into the postrevolutionary era.

NOTES

1. See, for example, E. Hofmann and A-L Delacrétaz (eds.), *Le Groupe de Coppet et la Révolution Française* (Paris, 1988).

2. Albert Sorel, *Mme. De Staël* (Paris, 1907), 197.

3. Jean Touchard (ed.), *Histoire des idées politiques*, Vol. 2 (Paris, 1959), 522.

4. Alphonse de Lamartine, *History of the Girondists*, Vol. 1 (New York, 1849), 198-199.

5. Charles-Louis de Secondat, baron de Montesquieu, *Lettres persanes*, in *Oeuvres complètes*, ed. R. Caillois (Paris, 1951).

6. Germaine de Staël, *De l'Allemagne*, Vol. 1 (Paris, 1968), 47.

7. Montesquieu, *De l'Esprit des lois*, in ibid., Vol. 2, Book XIX.

8. Germaine de Staël, *De la Littérature*, in *Oeuvres complètes*, Vol. 4 (Paris, 1820), 243-244. Translation mine.

9. Staël, *De l'Allemagne*, Part IV, Chap. 1.

10. On this point, see Melvin Richter, *The Political Theory of Montesquieu* (Cambridge, 1977), 20-30.

11. Germaine de Staël, *Des Circonstances actuelles qui peuvent terminer la Révolution et des principes qui doivent fonder la République en France* (Paris, 1906), Part I, Chap. 3.

12. Germaine de Staël, *Considérations sur la Révolution Française*, Vol. 1 (Paris, 1862), 7.

13. See Stanley Mellon, *The Political Uses of History* (Stanford, Calif., 1968), Chaps. 1-3.

14. On the role of the English model in French politics, see F. A. Ascomb, *Anglophobia in France 1763—1789* (Durham, N.C., 1950); G. Bonno, *La Constitution britannique devant l'opinion Française de Montesquieu à Bonaparte* (Paris, 1932); and P. Reboul, *Le Mythe anglais dans la littérature Française sous la Restoration* (Lille, 1962).

15. Staël, *Considérations*, Vol. 2, 210.

16. Germaine de Staël, *Corinne, Or Italy*, trans. A. Goldberger (New Brunswick, N.J., 1987), Book IV.

17. Staël, *De l'Allemange*, Vol. 2, Part IV, Chap. 10.

18. On this point, see Susan Tenenbaum, "The Coppet Circle: Literary Criticism as Political Discourse," in *History of Political Thought* 1, No. 3 (December 1980), 453-473.

19. Germaine de Staël, *Dix Années d'exil* (Paris, 1966), Chaps. 11-19.

7

Revolution in the Boudoir: Mme. Roland's Subversion of Rousseau's Feminine Ideals

Mary Trouille

The enthusiastic response of eighteenth-century women to Rousseau's sexual politics presents an intriguing paradox. How can one explain the puzzling fact that his views on women's nature, role, and education--views that seem re-actionary, paternalistic, even blatantly misogynic today--had such tremendous appeal and influence among women of the revolutionary era? More intriguing still is the passionate admiration for Rousseau and his writings expressed by talented and independent-minded women such as Mme. de Staël, Mme. Roland, Mary Wollstonecraft, and Olympe de Gouges, whose turbulent lives and political and literary activities seem incompatible with the feminine ideals of domesticity and self-effacement set forth in *Julie* and *Emile*.

To probe Rousseau's paradoxical appeal to women readers, I will examine how one woman of the revolutionary period--Marie-Jeanne Phlipon, who later became Mme. Roland--responded to his views on women and, speci-fically, how she interpreted his cult of domesticity as an empowering discourse. Her case is a particularly striking illustration of Rousseau's influence, since of the women mentioned earlier, Mme. Roland was the one who made the greatest effort to conform her outward behavior to the limited role he prescribed. Yet, while seeming to conform to these feminine ideals and norms, she in fact undermined them by blurring the gender dichotomies and the distinction between public and private spheres that lay at the very core of Rousseau's discourse on women. Her subtle transgression of traditional gender barriers did not go unperceived and was capitalized on by the Rolands' political enemies in the campaign of slander and persecution that eventually led her to the guillotine.

A PASSIONATE DISCIPLE OF ROUSSEAU

Born in 1754, Marie-Jeanne (or Manon as she was affectionately called) was the only child of a Parisian engraver. M. Phlipon's small but thriving trade permitted him to provide his gifted daughter with an education far above that customary for her sex and social rank, as well as excellent marriage prospects. However, M. Phlipon's reckless business speculations after the death of his wife considerably dimmed Manon's hopes for the future. It was at this critical juncture in her life, at the age of 21, that she first read *La Nouvelle Héloïse*. By then, Manon had perused the works of an impressive number of authors, in virtually every period, field, and genre, including all the major *philosophes*--except for Rousseau, conspicuous by his absence. Mme. Phlipon, who in general had given her daughter complete freedom in the choice of her readings, seems to have taken special care to prevent her contact with Rousseau, apparently fearing the negative influence he might have on Manon's passionate, sensitive nature.[1] It was only after her mother's death in 1776 that Manon read *Julie*, which a friend gave her to help calm her grief. The novel made a profound impact on her and was to have a determining influence on the course of her life. In her *Mémoires*, she recalls: "It seemed to me that I then found my true substance, that Rousseau became the interpreter of feelings and ideas I had had before him, but that he alone could explain to my satisfaction. . . . Rousseau showed me the domestic happiness to which I had a right to aspire and the ineffable delights I was capable of enjoying."[2] At a time of stress and crisis in her own life, when Manon had practically given up hope of finding a suitable husband because of her modest personal circumstances and idealistic expectations, Rousseau renewed her faith in the future through his appealing picture of the domestic felicity and motherhood to which a virtuous woman could aspire. Far from being considered a trap, this cult of motherhood and of enlightened domesticity seemed to offer a new power and dignity to women, regardless of their socio-economic status.

After reading *La Nouvelle Héloïse*, Manon devoured Rousseau's works one after the other. Her correspondence of the period expresses the enthusiasm he inspired in her. In a letter to a friend, she wrote:

I find it strange that you are surprised by my enthusiasm for Rousseau. . . . Who else portrays virtue in a more noble and touching manner? Who makes it more appealing? His works inspire love for truth, simplicity, and goodness. I truly believe that I owe him the best part of myself. His genius has inspired me; I feel myself elevated and ennobled by him. . . . His *Héloïse* is a masterpiece of sentiment.[3]

In the course of this same letter, each of Rousseau's works is praised in turn, including *Emile*. Nowhere in her writings does Mme. Roland explicitly criticize the ultraconservative, repressive view of women set forth in the fifth book of *Emile*. However, when raising her daughter Eudora, Mme. Roland would conscientiously apply the principles outlined for the education of Emile, while ignoring the far more limited education prescribed for Sophie. Like Rousseau, Mme. Roland felt that a woman's place was in the domestic sphere; however, contrary to Rousseau's view in *Emile*, she did not feel that a woman's activities should be limited to purely domestic tasks. In this respect, she was not unlike other Rousseau fans of the period, who did not hesitate to adapt and even distort his views according to their own needs and values.

Mme. Roland's response to *La Nouvelle Héloïse* has generally been described by her biographers as a revelation or even as a conversion experience.[4] However, as Mme. Roland herself observes in her *Mémoires*, she was predisposed both by her character and her upbringing to embrace Rousseau's cult of domesticity, as well as his pre-romantic, prerevolutionary spirit. Rousseau simply confirmed--and gave eloquent expression to--her deepest convictions and aspirations: "When I read Rousseau or Diderot, but especially the first, I felt transported by a tremendous enthusiasm; they seemed to have captured my deepest convictions, expressing them in ways I myself would no doubt have been incapable of matching, but that I could fully appreciate because they were feelings I shared."[5] That Manon Phlipon was a firm believer in the cult of domesticity long before she read Rousseau is borne out by the following passage of her memoirs where she recalls Sunday walks with her parents as an adolescent and her growing aversion for the crowded public promenades of the capital:

After these walks, I felt a terrible emptiness, anxiety and disgust. . . . Is it merely to attract attention and to receive vain compliments that the members of my sex acquire talents and are schooled in virtue? Do I exist only to waste my time with frivolous concerns and tumultuous feelings?--Oh, surely I have a higher destiny! . . . The sacred duties of wife and mother will one day be mine: my youth should be spent preparing me for these roles; I must study their importance and learn to control my inclinations, so that I can direct those of my children. Above all, I must become worthy of the man who will one day win my heart and be able to assure his happiness.[6]

Although Manon's domestic ideals may seem self-limiting to modern readers, her refusal to be reduced to a *femme-objet* and to engage in the frivolous games of vanity and ostentation so prevalent at that time constituted a conscious act of revolt on her part against what she considered an oppressive gender system. Above all, this passage reflects an independent mind and a strong desire for dignity and for a useful, meaningful life.

In her quest for happiness through companionate marriage and motherhood, Manon seemed to take Julie as her model by accepting as her husband an erudite and austere man twenty years her senior. During their six-year stay at Le Clos, Roland's modest country estate, Manon took great pleasure in emulating the sober domestic virtues embodied in Julie's life at Clarens. Like the Wolmars, Mme. Roland viewed the domestic sphere and rural life as the privileged locus of happiness and virtue. During her peaceful retreat at Le Clos, which she affectionately referred to as "mon Ermitage," Mme. Roland conscientiously fulfilled her role as wife and mother--educating her daughter (whom she had dutifully nursed in infancy), running her household, serving as doctor and benefactress to the local peasants, and overseeing the farmwork when her husband was away on his frequent tours as regional inspector of manufactures.

ROLAND'S EARLY WRITINGS: THE SPECTER OF *EMILE* AND THE PROPER LADY

In addition to these domestic and maternal tasks, Mme. Roland actively collaborated with her husband on numerous technical and scholarly works, including his three-volume *Dictionnaire des Manufactures, Arts et Métiers* for the revised edition of Diderot's *Encyclopedia*. Manon had a direct hand in the research, writing and proofreading of every article. Yet, far from satisfying any personal ambition on her part, this work was in her eyes merely an extension of her devotion to her husband:

It was almost as natural for me to write with him as it was to eat with him. Existing only for his happiness, I devoted myself to what brought him the greatest pleasure. If he wrote about industrial arts, I wrote about them too, although they bored me. Since he liked scholarship, I helped him in his research. If it amused him to send a literary piece to an academic society, we worked on it together.[7]

Although well aware of her intellectual and literay talents, Mme. Roland consistently refused to publish anything (even works entirely her own) under her name, preferring to remain anonymous or hide behind her husband's signature. She seems to have subscribed wholeheartedly to Rousseau's ideals of female modesty and self-effacement and to his views of the "natural" superiority and domination of the male sex. Her interiorization of female inferiority and of traditional prejudices against women writers and scholars is particularly apparent in a letter written to a male family friend in the early years of her marriage:

I believe in the superiority of your sex in every respect. . . . You have strength, and everything that goes with it: courage, perseverance, wide horizons, and superior talents. It is up to you to make the laws in politics and discoveries in the sciences. Govern the world, change the face of the globe, be proud, terrible, clever, and learned. You are all that without our help, and because of it you are destined to be our masters. But without us, you would not be virtuous, loving, loved, nor happy. So keep your glory and authority. For our part, we have and wish no other power than over your morals, no other throne than in your hearts. I will never claim anything beyond that. It often irks me to see women claiming privileges which suit them so poorly. Even the name of author . . . strikes me as ridiculous when applied to them. However gifted they may be, women should never show their learning or talents in public.

And she concluded her Rousseauistic credo by declaring: "I can imagine no destiny more rewarding than that of assuring the happiness of one man alone."[8]

Mme. Roland firmly believed that women who pursued ambitions and desires outside the domestic sphere jeopardized not only their happiness, but their reputation as well. She was, moreover, acutely aware of the double standard and prejudices affecting women writers:

I never had the slightest temptation to become an author; it became clear to me very early that a woman who earned this title for herself lost much more than she gained. She is disliked by men, and criticized by her own sex. If her writing is bad, people make fun of her, and rightly so; if her works are good, people deny that she wrote them . . . [or] they attack her character, morals, behavior, and talents to such an extent that they destroy her reputation as an author through the notoriety they give her.[9]

When a friend predicted that she would one day write a book, she retorted: "Then it will be under someone else's name; for I would eat my fingers before I ever became an author."[10]

Despite her passion for learning and the intense pleasure Mme. Roland experienced as a writer, she carefully avoided calling attention to her scholarly and literary activities, fearing the ridicule and censure generally encountered by *les femmes de lettres*: "I am not interested in becoming a scholar, nor is it my goal to earn a reputation for wit or talent or the pleasure of being published; I study because I need to just as much as I do to eat. . . . My work brings me happiness and much pleasure, or at least some consolation for my troubles."[11] Convinced that a woman's place was out of the public eye, Manon voluntarily relegated herself to the domestic sphere both before and after her marriage: "I like the shadows, and twilight is enough for my happiness. As Montaigne says, one is only at ease in the backshop."[12]

The six years spent at Le Clos unquestionably represent the most serene period in Mme. Roland's life. With peaceful resignation, she looked forward to finishing out her days in tranquil domesticity, enlivened by readings from her favorite authors: "Yes, I feel that I will spend my whole life in the country, in peace and contentment," she wrote her husband; "all I need are the works of Jean-Jacques; reading them will make us shed delicious tears and rekindle feelings that will bring us happiness whatever our fate may be."[13] Her formerly keen interest in political events waned under the influence of domestic preoccupations. To a Parisian friend who kept her informed of the latest news, she quipped: "I no longer dabble in politics."[14] However, Mme. Roland's political apathy was not destined to last, for the events of 1789 jolted her out of this comfortable and secure routine and, in their wake, brought to the surface unfulfilled aspirations and talents that had lain dormant during her nine-year retreat into domesticity.

THE REVOLUTION'S IMPACT:
BREAKING OUT OF THE DOMESTIC MOLD

Fervent disciples of Rousseau's political and social thought, the Rolands greeted the Revolution with immediate and unbounded enthusiasm: "The Revolution took hold of all our ideas and subjugated all our plans; we devoted ourselves entirely to our passionate desire to serve the public welfare."[15] All personal feelings and private activities were relegated to the background in favor of the national events that were making history. The *aurea medocritas* --the notion that happiness can be found only in obscurity--by which she had lived for so many years, now seemed totally forgotten in the flurry of excitement and exhilaration. Under the pressure of events, Mme. Roland's life and writings underwent a radical politicization. Her character and tone grew more energetic and direct, even brusque at times, as a result of her revolutionary zeal. In her letters from Le Clos to friends in Paris, her charming vignettes à la Sévigné gave way to urgent exhortations and warnings expressed in a trenchant, sometimes violent style: "It is true that I no longer write of our personal affairs: where is the traitor who today has other affairs than those of the nation?"[16] When some of her letters disappeared in the mail, censured perhaps because of their radical antimonarchism, she angrily warned the culprits: "If this letter does not reach you, let the cowards who read it blush with shame upon learning that these words were written by a woman, and let them tremble to think that she can inspire a hundred men who will in turn inspire a million others."[17]

Increasingly conscious of the power of words and of her own ability to use them to further the revolutionary cause, Mme. Roland became a regular, albeit anonymous, contributor to republican journals. In 1790 Roland was sent to represent Lyon in the Constitutional Convention in Paris, where he became an active member of the Jacobin Society. When he was appointed secretary of the club's correspondence committee, Mme. Roland eagerly shared his work. Convinced that shaping public opinion could play a vital role in the success of the Revolution, she put all her literary skill into answering the many letters from provincial correspondents. After Roland's unexpected appointment as minister of the interior, her collaboration became even more crucial to the success of his career. She was not only the moving force behind the propaganda bureau set up by her husband, the famous *Bureau d'Esprit Public*, but also served as Roland's secret political advisor and ghost writer.[18] She composed many of the key documents of his ministry, including his protest to the Pope concerning French prisoners in Rome, as well as his famous letter of protest to Louis XVI. Published by the Assembly (at Mme. Roland's urging), Roland's letter to the king led to the dissolution of the first cabinet and played a significant role in turning the tide of public opinion against the monarchy.

As in her earlier journalistic endeavors, Mme. Roland remained resolutely anonymous: "It was with intense pleasure that I wrote these pieces, because I felt they could be useful. I found greater satisfaction in doing it anonymously. . . . I have no need of glory."[19] As before, she claimed that her work was simply an extension of her devotion to her husband. In response to charges that she had secretly run her husband's ministry, she loyally defended Roland's probity and capabilities. She insisted that she merely served as his secretary and had always refrained from influencing his decisions: "I never meddled in administrative affairs. . . . Why should it detract from a man's professional reputation or merit if his wife serves as his secretary?"[20] However, from Mme. Roland's own testimony elsewhere in her *Mémoires*, it is abundantly clear that she was much more than a mere scribe and that charges that she was the hidden power behind her husband's ministry were not unfounded. Moreover, this subtle subversion of her husband's authority can be seen as an indirect challenge to Rousseau's male-centered view of power relations between the sexes.

It is also clear from her *Mémoires* that Mme. Roland derived a secret pleasure and amusement from the important role she played behind the scenes:

A letter to the Pope, written in the name of the Executive Council of France, secretly composed by a woman in the austere office that Marat liked to call a boudoir--the situation struck me as so amusing that I laughed about it quite a while afterward. It was the secrecy of my participation that made these contrasts so amusing.[21]

At one point in her memoirs, she could not resist discreetly poking fun at Roland's tendency to take her talents and efforts for granted and to appropriate them as his own: "If one of his pieces was singled out and praised for its graceful style, . . . I took pleasure in his satisfaction without remarking that I had written it, and he often ended up convinced that he had truly been inspired when he had written a passage that I myself had composed."[22] Although on the surface, this passage suggests that Mme. Roland was being exploited by an ungrateful and egotistic husband, her ironic tone conveys quite a different impression--that if Roland became the powerful political figure that he was, it was due less to his exploitation of her than to her clever manipulation of him. He became in a sense her mouthpiece, just as she was his hidden voice.

In the early years of their marriage, Mme. Roland had been somewhat intimidated by her husband's greater age, knowledge and experience. Eventually, however, she gained enough confidence in her abilities and judgment to voice her own opinions.[23] She began to resent Roland's autocratic, self-centered manner and the fact that she had always sacrificed her happiness for his, but she carefully repressed any resentment behind a mask of submission and devotion to him and his work:

After considering only my partner's happiness for so long, I finally realized that there was something missing in my own. . . . I often felt that our relationship was unequal, due to Roland's dominating character and the twenty-year age gap between us. If we lived alone together, I sometimes had a difficult time with him; if we went out into society, I was admired by people, some of whom I sensed might attract me. I plunged myself into my husband's work--another excess which had its disadvantage, for he became too dependent upon my help, . . . and I wore myself out.[24]

This passage suggests that Mme. Roland plunged herself into her husband's work not simply to prove her devotion and worth to him, but also to fill emotional and intellectual needs that her marriage had not satisfied, as well as to protect herself from the attractions of younger men. Her collaboration on her husband's work may also have helped compensate for the disappointments of motherhood. For despite all Mme. Roland's efforts, Eudora remained a rebellious and indolent child of mediocre intelligence, utterly lacking in intellectual curiosity and artistic gifts.[25]

The Revolution gave Mme. Roland a unique opportunity for self-ful-fillment outside the domestic sphere--the chance she had secretly longed for to play an active role in shaping the ideal republic she had dreamed of ever since she first read Plutarch at the age of eight. As a young woman, she had lamented the powerlessness and obscurity to which she seemed condemned by both her sex and her inferior social status:

I am truly vexed to be a woman: I should have been born with a different soul or a different sex or in another century. I should have been born a woman in Rome or Sparta, or else a man in France. At least then I could have chosen the republic of letters as my country, or another of those republics where as a man, one only needs to obey the law. . . . I feel imprisoned in a class and an existence that is not at all mine. . . . Everywhere I turn, my mind and heart run up against the con-straints of opinion and prejudice, and all my strength is consumed in vainly struggling against my chains. . . . My enthusiasm for the welfare of society seems utterly wasted, since I am unable to contribute anything to it![26]

Conscious of her rich inner gifts, Manon felt stifled and out of place in the petit bourgeois world of her father. For lack of proper training and a stimulating environment, she felt that her intelligence and imagination were being wasted.[27] Ardently, she aspired to a higher level of existence, to a place in the "republic of letters" where her intellectual and literary endeavors would be appreciated and encouraged. She bitterly resented the socioeconomic and gender barriers that prevented her from traveling abroad and from partici-pating actively in the cultural life of her period. In several letters to Sophie Cannet, she fantasized about dressing like a man in order to gain greater freedom to study, to travel and to develop her talents.[28]

Parallel to Manon's frustrated intellectual and artistic ambitions as a young woman of the petite bourgeoisie were her frustrated political aspirations--her desire to participate in the political life of her country, to contribute actively to the public good in accordance with her republican convictions. At the age of twenty, she had written to Sophie:

It seems to me that man's vocation is to be useful to his fellow creatures, that the first and most admirable virtue lies in working for the public good. . . . You can imagine how frustrated I feel to be confined to the narrow circle of my private life, living only for myself and totally useless to others.[29]

MME. ROLAND'S REVOLUTIONARY SALON: FUSION OF PUBLIC AND PRIVATE SPHERES

Mme. Roland's important contribution to her husband's work during his two terms as minister of the interior enabled her to participate covertly in the public sphere and to help shape the future of the new French Republic without having to sacrifice her outward conformity to Rousseau's ideals of female modesty and domesticity. When her husband first became active in the Jacobin Club in early 1792, Mme. Roland's home served as an informal gathering place for Brissot, Robespierre and other deputies who at the time constituted the radical left. After Roland became minister, she had dinner gatherings twice a week for his political associates.

As a hostess, Mme. Roland maintained a simple, almost Spartan style of entertaining. There were generally no more than fifteen guests at a time. Moreover, women were strictly excluded from the gatherings in her home--in accordance with Rousseau's dictum concerning the segregation of the sexes and his notion of separate spheres.[30] During the discussions that followed dinner, Manon officiated with simplicity and tact and--what was even more appreciated--in silence. In her *Mémoires*, she insists that she never allowed herself to utter a word until the meetings were over, although occasionally she had to bite her lip to keep from disagreeing with what was being said. Deliberately seating herself outside the circle of men, she quietly did needlework or wrote letters while the debates went on. Yet despite her voluntary self-effacement, Mme. Roland does not deny that she listened attentively to all that was said; nor did she hesitate to offer her opinion when it was asked for. Moreover, since Roland's associates tended to call on him at home rather than at his office, political matters were frequently discussed in his wife's presence. Under the pretext of leaving messages for the absent Roland, they got in the habit of calling on Manon and presenting their case to her, for they were well aware that she would be consulted anyway. In her *Mémoires*, Mme. Roland tries to repudiate accusations that she was running her husband's ministry, insisting that because she was nearly always at home and enjoyed her husband's fullest confidence, she found herself quite naturally "in the midst of things without intrigue or vain curiosity."[31] But she hardly needed to resort to intrigue or subterfuge to impose her views, for in the intimacy of the Girondin circle her opinions carried increasing weight.

THE VIRTUOUS MARTYR: RELIVING JULIE'S PASSION

Mme. Roland's "secret" collaboration in the political affairs of the Girondists seemed to offer the ideal opportunity to satisfy her unfulfilled political ambitions. However, by putting her in contact with dynamic young men, her role as Egeria of the Girondist party exacerbated the equally painful dilemma of her unfulfilled desire for romantic love and sensual pleasure--desires that Mme. Roland recognizes quite openly in her *Mémoires*.[32]

In the fall of 1792, when the Girondists were under constant attack from the Montagnards, Manon fell passionately in love with the Girondist deputy François Buzot. Young, handsome, eloquent, and dynamic, he was everything Roland was not: a worthy Saint-Preux-like foil to the aging and "sexless" Roland. Despite her disenchantment with marriage and motherhood, as well as her growing disillusionment with the Revolution, Mme. Roland stoically resisted yielding to her passion, which was shared by Buzot with equal ardor. Like Julie's death, Mme. Roland's imprisonment and execution resolved her

moral impasse. By allowing herself to be imprisoned in place of her husband,
Mme. Roland was able to free herself from conjugal duties and to give full
expression to her love for Buzot, without restraint or remorse. In a letter to
Buzot from prison, she expressed her secret joy:

I was not greatly distressed to be arrested. They will be less angry and vindictive
toward Roland. . . . If they put him on trial, I will be able to defend him in a
manner that will enhance his reputation. And in this way I can pay the debt I owe
him for his sorrows. Don't you see that by being alone, it is with you that I remain?
Through imprisonment I can sacrifice myself for my husband and keep myself for
my friend, and it is to my persecutors that I owe this reconciliation of love and duty.
Don't pity me! Others may admire my courage, but they don't know my joys.[33]

Mme. Roland firmly rejected all plans for her escape, for she was convinced
that freedom would not bring her happiness, "but only replace [her] chains
with others that no one can see."[34]

    In a final message to Buzot (embedded in her "Dernières Pensées"), she
wrote:

And you whom I dare not name! . . . who respected the barriers of virtue in spite
of the most overwhelming passion, will you grieve to see me go before you to a
place where we will be free to love each other without crime, where nothing will
prevent us from being united? . . . There I will await you. . . . Adieu. No, in
leaving the earth, I am not leaving you, but bringing us closer together.[35]

The parallels with the dénouement of *La Nouvelle Héloïse* are of course
striking, for on her deathbed, Julie had expressed herself in almost identical
terms in a letter to Saint-Preux.[36]

ROLAND'S SUBVERSION OF ROUSSEAU'S FEMININE IDEALS

    In her final farewell to the man she loved, as throughout her adult life,
Mme. Roland had followed the inspiring example of Rousseau's heroine. Like
Julie, Mme. Roland had conscientiously devoted herself to an idealized view
of marriage and motherhood, and, like her--rather than accept moral defeat
or disenchantment--had heroically sacrificed her life in order to preserve the
precarious balance between duty and passion, virtue and sensibility. However,
while seeming to conform to the feminine ideals and norms advocated by
Rousseau in his novels, Mme. Roland in fact subverted those models by
undermining the gender dichotomies (public/private, self-assertion/self-
effacement, reason/sensibility) that lay at the very core of his discourse on
women. While appearing to relegate herself to a role of silence and self-
effacement in the domestic sphere, she in fact transformed her home into a
public forum, her tiny office into the unofficial center of Roland's ministry,
and her devotion to her husband into a dynamic political partnership--there-
by giving herself the power to influence public affairs in a very direct
and dramatic manner. Furthermore, through her ability to combine qualities

traditionally reserved for men (reason, authority, energy, superior intelligence, and strength of character) with traits traditionally ascribed to women (sensitivity, charm, intuition, and persuasiveness), Mme. Roland was able to command the respect of her husband and colleagues and to make herself valuable, indeed indispensable, to their political cause. As Mme. Roland herself remarks in her *Mémoires*:

Roland would have been no less a fine administrator without me; his capabilities, diligence, probity are entirely his own. With my help, he caused more of a sensation because I infused his writings with that special mixture of strength and gentle persuasiveness, that blend of reason and authority with the charms of sentiment, which perhaps only a sensitive woman with a sound mind is capable of achieving.[37]

Mme. Roland's elevated opinion of her husband's capabilities is disputed somewhat by biographers and historians. They generally agree that Roland was a dedicated, hard-working administrator, but that without his wife's conviction, boldness, literary talents, and shrewd judgment of character "he could be rated barely higher than a superior clerk."[38]

That Mme. Roland was a woman of exceptional talents--with a distinctly androgynous character and style--is confirmed by numerous contemporary accounts, including a review of her *Mémoires* in the *Analytical Review* of 1795: "She possessed a mind uncommonly vigorous and masculine, and her situation as wife of the minister Roland in a moment of great peril called forth all her energy [to display] talents which will not fail to rank her among the distinguished ornaments of her sex."[39] As for the "virile" quality of her writing, even Rousseau had been fooled by it. After an unsuccessful effort to meet her idol during his last stay in Paris, Manon's disappointment had been somewhat allayed by the fact that Rousseau had mistaken her letter of introduction for that of a man: "Surely it was not you who wrote a letter like that," reported Thérèse, as she blocked the door. "Even the handwriting looks like that of a man."[40] Contrary to traditional eighteenth-century views of women as victims of their imagination, emotions and sexual desires (views clearly reflected in Rousseau's portrayal of Sophie), Mme. Roland underlines her belief in the primacy of reason and consistently portrays herself as in control: "I kept my imagination in check and followed lines of reasoning. . . . I channeled my imagination through studying."[41] Her "masculine" firmness, self-possession, and strength of character inspired even her strongest critics with a grudging sort of admiration, mixed with deep ambivalence and distrust.

Gita May maintains that Mme. Roland's transgression of traditional gender restrictions was involuntary and largely due to the unusual circumstances in which she found herself. If Mme. Roland contradicted her own convictions regarding the proper role of women, argues May, it was not through any personal ambition or will to power on her part, but through a disinterested, self-sacrificing devotion to the revolutionary cause.[42] She goes on to defend Mme. Roland against the criticism of pro-Jacobin historians who,

in May's view, unjustly question her intentions and motives. Although there
is little doubt that these historians were unduly harsh and often misogynic in
their judgment of the Girondists' Egeria,[43] May seems to give too much
credence to the mask of modesty and self-effacement that Mme. Roland
assumed in an effort to defend herself against similiar attacks by her
contemporaries. She tends to take Mme. Roland's self-justification at face
value and to ignore or minimize the importance of passages in her memoirs
and correspondence where she momentarily lets her mask fall, revealing a
woman of intense personal and political ambitions. The passages expressing
her desire to develop her talents to the fullest, her secret pleasure at
manipulating power relations behind the scenes, and above all, her deep
satisfaction at fulfilling her adolescent dream to escape the confines of her sex
and class in order to help shape the future of the new French Republic--all
these passages reveal the woman behind the mask who consciously subverted
the limited gender role imposed on her by society.[44]

ON TRIAL: MISOGYNIC ATTACKS BY
THE PRESS AND REVOLUTIONARY LEADERS

Mme. Roland's subtle transgression of traditional gender barriers did
not go unperceived and was capitalized on by the Rolands' political enemies
in the campaign of slander and persecution that eventually led her to the
guillotine. As the Girondists' popularity declined, Jacobin politicians and
journalists multiplied their attacks against the Rolands. As a woman, Mme.
Roland was particularly vulnerable to denunciations and satire. No insult or
innuendo, no matter how far-fetched or obscene, was spared to destroy her
influence and to belittle her party by picturing the Girondists as wholly
dominated by a scheming female--a form of ridicule particularly withering to
the Gallic ego. For example, in an issue of his highly popular *Ami du peuple*,
Marat inserted "Un mot à la femme Roland" (A word to the Roland woman)
which read: "Roland is only a ninny whose wife leads him by the nose; it's
she who is Minister of the Interior."[45]

Ten days later (in late September 1792) Roland went before the
Assembly to resign as minister in order to become a simple deputy; however,
upon the urging of a majority of the deputies, he agreed to retain his post.
Hearing this, Danton rose from his seat and launched his famous sarcasm:
"No one does justice to Roland more than I, but if you invite him to be
minister, you should also extend the invitation to Mme. Roland; for everyone
knows that he was not alone in his department! As for me, I was alone in
mine." He then added: "We need ministers who see through other eyes than
those of their wives."[46] The following spring, Danton would again make Mme.
Roland the butt of his sarcasm in an effort to save the Girondists from an
assassination plot hatched by Varlet: "Those glib talkers [*beaux parleurs*]
are not worth such a fuss," quipped Danton; "They are as enthusiastic and
flighty as the woman who inspires them. Why don't they choose a *man* as

their leader? That woman will lead them to their destruction. She's the Circe of the Republic!"[47]

Following Danton's lead, the Jacobin press tirelessly harped on the theme that it was not M. Roland but Mme. Roland who actually ran the Ministry of the Interior. Day after day, the popular press echoed with outrageous reports of the "orgies" over which Mme. Roland had presided and of the sexual and political favors she had distributed in order to maintain her influence. In his popular *Père Duchesne*, Hébert artfully exploited both the antifeminist and antiaristocratic sentiments of Mme. Roland's enemies by comparing her to Marie-Antoinette and to various royal mistresses--minus their beauty, for he later describes her as a toothless, balding old hag:

The tender wife of virtuous Roland is ruling France just like the Pompadours and the du Barrys, Brissot is the grand squire of this new queen, Louvet is her chamberlain, Buzot her chancellor. . . . [Barbaroux, Vergniaud, Guadet, Lanthenas, are then each assigned a role.] This is the new court that is running things today. Like our former queen, madame Coco, stretched out on a sofa, surrounded by all those *beaux esprits*, talks on endlessly about war, politics, supplies. It is from this den of corruption that daily proclamations issue forth to the public.[48]

In the midst of Hébert's grotesque slander, one recognizes a man who is perceptive and well informed and who does not strike at random. All the politicians who were among Mme. Roland's circle of close friends are named. Moreover, Hébert rightly guesses that several of them (and Buzot in particular) might be enamored of her and that she might not be insensitive to their admiration. In the following issue of *Pére Duchesne*, Brissot is "overheard" saying to Buzot:

Admit that you are fortunate to serve as the righthand man of someone like me. I got you in with the *beaux esprits* that are governing France. If it weren't for me, you wouldn't be the favorite among the admirers of the virtuous wife of the virtuous Roland. What a pleasure it must be to rehearse at her feet the role you will play at the Convention the following day, to hear her applaud you when you recite a fiery tirade against Robespierre, to see her swoon in your arms when you have passed some fine decree banishing loyal revolutionaries or encouraging civil war.[49]

In general, Mme. Roland chose to maintain a dignified silence in response to such slander. Referring to Marat's repeated attacks, she told her husband: "He is foolish enough to imagine that I would be sensitive to such nonsense, that I would answer him in writing, and that he would have the pleasure of dragging a woman into the public forum in order to ridicule her husband." And defiantly, she declared: "Let them slander me as much as they like; I won't complain or even concern myself with them."[50] In prison, however, she felt physically threatened by the danger of mob violence that might result from the increasingly inflammatory articles published by Hébert. When an angry group began to shout insults and threats outside the window of her cell, she dashed off a fierce letter of protest to Garat, who was then minister of justice.[51]

The viciousness and frequency of the attacks against Mme. Roland reflect the degree of power and influence that were attributed to her. Like her subsequent imprisonment, trial and execution, they constitute a paradoxical tribute to her importance as a political figure. The misogynic nature of the charges made against Mme. Roland by both the periodical press and the revolutionary government--the fact that she was condemned more for alleged moral transgressions and for overstepping traditional gender barriers than for any specific political act--illustrates how women's political and intellectual activities were associated with moral and social deviance. It is interesting, moreover, to note how in their allusions to Roland's writing her enemies make use of double entendres to equate literary self-revelation with sexual promiscuity. For example, in one of his articles in *Père Duchesne*, Hébert recounts how Mme. Roland "unbuttoned herself/spoke frankly to" Père Duchesne, and "lui a découvert le pot aux roses"--that is, revealed her secret plots/private parts.[52] Similarly, in the formal act of accusation against the Girondists, Amar refers to the "prodigieuse facilité" with which Mme. Roland provided the Bureau d'Esprit Public with propaganda pamphlets in order to corrupt the public. Once again, ease of writing in a woman is associated with easy virtue, and both are directly linked to corruption of the public mind and morals. The connection between women's writing and female sexuality (and sexual promiscuity) is illustrated most graphically--and grotesquely--in another issue of *Pére Duchesne* in which Hébert reports an alleged visit to the Rolands on New Year's Eve:

It was around midnight and, in the arms of her lackey Lanthenas, the virtuous Mme. Roland was diverting herself from the moral pleasures provided by her feeble old husband. Pregnant with a discourse that the billboarders would deliver in the morning, she was right in the midst of her labor when little Louvet rushed in and interrupted their love-making.[53]

In this passage, Hébert evokes the hackneyed comparison of writing to child-birth in order to mock Mme. Roland's literary and political activities more effectively. By appealing to misogynic prejudices and stereotypes (women writers and politicians as witches, whores and monsters), he and his colleagues added highly effective ammunition to their campaign of verbal terrorism against the Girondists and their ill-fated Egeria.

Well aware of the misogynic tenor of the charges against her, Mme. Roland strove to counterbalance them by underlining her strict conformity to traditional gender roles. In the speech prepared for her trial she maintained:

I took a keen interest in the public welfare and in the progress of the Revolution, but I never went beyond the limits prescribed for my sex. It was no doubt my talents, knowledge, and courage that turned people against me. . . . Only odious tyrants would sacrifice a woman whose sole crime was to possess a few merits about which she never boasted.[54]

Much to her chagrin, Mme. Roland was never permitted to deliver her speech or indeed to utter more than a few words at her trial. However, during the two interrogations that preceded it, she cleverly turned the antifeminism of her examiners against them. When questioned about her husband's political activities, she replied that as a woman it was not her role to meddle in public affairs and that her only knowledge of events had been through the newspapers. This, of course, was hardly the case; but when her examiners insisted that she must have had more information than the average citizen, she coolly observed that a woman was not expected to make special inquiries into matters that did not concern her sex.[55] When asked about various pamphlets distributed by Roland's propaganda bureau, she maintained that they were available for anyone to read and that it was up to the public and not to her, a mere woman, to pass judgment on them. She also firmly denied accusations that she had directed the propaganda bureau or any other of her husband's political operations.[56] Finally, when her interrogators demanded to know Roland's whereabouts, she responded that no human law could force her to betray her loyalty to her husband--another dictum of the Rousseauistic code. She then attempted to defend her husband's probity as an administrator and his loyalty to the Revolution, but was rudely interrupted, accused of being a chatterbox, and ordered to respond to all further questions with a simple yes or no. Resisting the prosecutor's efforts to intimidate and silence her, and rejecting the self-incriminating script he tried to impose on her, Mme. Roland appealed to higher principles of justice and reason to affirm her innocence.[57] She even tried to seize control of the proceedings by ordering the court clerk to write under her dictation. But this open defiance of the prosecutor's authority only served to infuriate him so much that he abruptly ended the interrogation, thereby silencing her definitively.

That Mme. Roland was imprisoned and condemned to death more for overstepping traditional gender barriers than for any specific political act is clearly underlined by newspaper accounts of her execution. For example, *Le Moniteur Universel* wrote: "In a short period of time, the revolutionary tribunal has given women several valuable examples that will not be lost for them." After unflattering epitaphs to Marie-Antoinette and to the feminist Olympe de Gouges (both executed the same month as Mme. Roland, along with Mme. du Barry), the memory of Mme. Roland was then evoked in blatantly misogynic terms:

That woman Roland, who fancied herself a great mind with great plans, a philosopher, was in every way a monster. Her disdainful attitude, her proudly opinionated replies, her ironic gaiety, and the firmness she displayed on the way to her execution prove that she was devoid of any grief. She was a mother, but she sacrificed nature. . . . The desire to be learned led her to forget the virtues of her sex. Such negligence is always dangerous and caused her to perish on the scaffold.[58]

In other accounts of her execution, Mme. Roland's courage was invariably construed as proof of her insensitivity and baseness: a truly virtuous woman, a truly loving wife and mother, would have shown regrets, weakness, tears.[59]

It is clear from all these commentaries that Mme. Roland's execution, like that of Olympe de Gouges and other "public" women, was being used as a warning to women activists: if they did not give up their political activities and conform to the passive domestic role prescribed for them by the revolutionary government, they, too, would risk imprisonment and death. After pointing to Mme. Roland's example, the article in *Le Moniteur Universel* ended with the following exhortation:

Women, do you wish to be true republicans? Then love, follow and teach the laws that guide your husbands and sons in the exercise of their rights. . . . Be diligent in your housework; never attend political meetings with the intention of speaking there; but let your presence serve as an example for your children. The fatherland will then bless you, for you will truly have given what it expects from you.[60]

Similarly, in the ruling banning women's participation in political clubs and meetings, Chaumette, head counsel of the Paris Commune, pointed to the cases of Mme. Roland and Olympe de Gouges as irrefutable justification for the ban:

Remember *la Roland*, that haughty wife of a stupid, perfidious husband, who thought herself fit to govern the republic and who rushed to her downfall. Remember the impudent Olympe de Gouges, who was the first to set up women's societies, who abandoned the duties of her household to meddle in politics, and whose head fell beneath the avenging knife of the law.[61]

It is indeed ironic that Mme. Roland--who had so painstakingly conformed her outward behavior to Rousseau's cult of domesticity--should be frequently cited along with the militant feminist de Gouges as a pernicious example for others of their sex by revolutionary leaders and journalists.[62] The charges against the two women were surprisingly similar, despite the striking differences in their lives and characters. Both were accused of neglecting their duties as wives and mothers in order to meddle in politics, of attempting to usurp male powers and prerogatives and, graver still, of forgetting their proper place as women. Both were victims of the revolutionary government's increasingly repressive policies toward women--policies strongly influenced by Rousseau's writings.[63]

ROUSSEAU'S PARADOXICAL INFLUENCE ON ROLAND'S LIFE AND WRITINGS

Above all, Mme. Roland was a victim of long-standing tensions within herself between the Rousseauistic ideals of domestic happiness and female self-effacement and an irrepressible urge to develop her talents to the fullest--an urge that impelled her, almost in spite of herself, to take an active part in the intellectual and political life of her period. As the attacks against her in the press became increasingly frequent and violent, Mme. Roland bitterly lamented the loss of her anonymity:

Those who have lifted the veil under which I wished to remain have done me an ill turn indeed! . . . If they had judged the facts as they really were, they would have spared me the kind of celebrity for which I had no desire. Instead of having to defend myself against their slander by writing my confession, I could brighten the solitude of my imprisonment by reading the essays of Montaigne.[64]

Despite all her protestations of modesty, Mme. Roland was secretly grateful to her persecutors for giving her the ideal pretext to write her autobiography. For it was an opportunity not only to justify herself in the eyes of posterity, but also to fulfill her talents and ambitions as a writer. Recounting her life's story and the political personages and events she had witnessed proved to be a richly rewarding experience. Despite the gloom of prison and the spectre of impending death, Mme. Roland ended her *Mémoires* with a proud affirmation of her powers as a writer, mixed with the regret of being unable to develop her talents more fully: "If I had been allowed to live," she declares, "I would have had only one ambition: to record the annals of my century and to be the Macaulay of my country; I was going to say the Tacitus of France, but that would be immodest, and . . . some might say that I am not quite up to his level."[65] Overtly mocking the conventions of modesty and inferiority imposed on women--conventions to which she had always previously deferred--she then expressed her confidence that with time and practice, and on a subject of equal richness, she might well have rivaled the writings of Tacitus. By composing her memoirs and correspondence, Mme. Roland was in fact able to fulfill her ambitions at least partially, for together they provide a vivid chronicle of her period and a rich sampling of what she might have accomplished as a writer had she lived longer and pursued a literary career.[66]

Despite her special fondness for Tacitus and Plutarch, it is Rousseau whom Mme. Roland most often evoked as her literary and spiritual father. From her prison cell, she wrote to a friend: "These memoirs will be my *Confessions*, for I will not conceal anything. . . . I've thought about it carefully and made up my mind. I will tell all, absolutely everything. This is the only way to be useful."[67] Following Rousseau's example in his *Confessions*, Mme. Roland gave free rein to her thoughts and feelings in her memoirs and, like Rousseau, attempted to justify herself in the eyes of posterity by presenting an authentic self-portrait and self-analysis to counter what she perceived as misrepresentations of her character and motives by her contemporaries. In the course of her autobiographical venture, Mme. Roland emerged from anonymity as her husband's secret political advisor and ghost writer to become a writer and public figure in her own right, as well as a woman with passions and ambitions outside the domestic sphere to which she had voluntarily--on the surface at least--confined herself until then. However, without the Revolution and the Terror, without the creative impulse provided by the constant threat of death and the desire to justify herself in the eyes of future generations, would Mme. Roland have felt impelled to write her memoirs? Given her earlier reluctance to pursue a literary career and to publish under her own name, this appears rather doubtful.

Rousseau's influence on Mme. Roland's life and writing is therefore crucial, yet paradoxical. For although on the surface she appeared to conform to his cult of domesticity and sensibility, her superior intelligence and education, coupled with her political and literary activities, made her a very different woman indeed from the feminine ideal advocated in *Julie* and *Emile*. In fact, because of her involvement in politics, she was the very kind of woman Rousseau would have been inclined to criticize. Perhaps the most paradoxical aspect of Rousseau's influence on Mme. Roland is that, following his bold example in the *Confessions*, she dared to transgress social and literary conventions of female modesty and silence to reveal her most intimate thoughts, feelings and experiences in ways that both shocked and thrilled her readers.

NOTES

1. "Probablement mon excellente mère, qui voyait bien qu'il fallait laisser exercer ma tête, ne trouvait pas grand inconvénient que j'étudiasse sérieusement la philosophie, au risque même d'un peu d'incrédulité," Mme. Roland later surmised. "Mais elle jugeait sans doute qu'il ne fallait pas entraîner mon coeur sensible, trop prêt à se passionner. Ah! mon Dieu! que de soins inutiles pour échapper à sa destinée!" *Mémoires de Madame Roland*, ed. Paul de Roux (Paris: Mercure de France, 1966), 277. [All subsequent references to Mme. Roland's memoirs are to this edition unless otherwise indicated.]

2. Ibid., 302. [All translations are mine unless otherwise indicated.]

3. Letter to Sophie Cannet, March 21, 1776, in *Lettres de Madame Roland*, ed. Claude Perroud, 4 vols. (Paris: Imprimerie Nationale, 1900–1915), I, 393.

4. See in particular Gita May, "The Revelation of Jean-Jacques Rousseau," in *Madame Roland and the Age of Revolution* (New York: Columbia University Press, 1970), 55-72; and "Voltaire détrôné par Rousseau," in *De Jean-Jacques Rousseau à Madame Roland* (Génève: Droz, 1964), 76-93. Also see May's article "Rousseau's Antifeminism Reconsidered," in Samia Spencer, *French Women and the Age of Enlightenment* (Bloomington: Indiana University Press, 1984), 309-317.

Gita May's work on Roland has been a source of great inspiration to me, but my approach differs from hers in several important respects. May views Roland's response to Rousseau as a conversion experience that inspired a life-long effort to live up to his idealistic views on women. I, on the other hand, see Roland's initial enthusiasms for Rousseau as a confirmation of the deepest convictions and longings of her youth. This enthusiasm gradually gave way to a questioning and subversion of his narrow ideals under the pressure of external events and in response to her own evolving aspirations

--political, literary, and romantic--as a mature woman. It is this gradual evolution in Roland's response to Rousseau, from young militant to married conformist to subverter of his ideals, that I have sought to trace in this chapter.

5. Fragment of journal, 1777, in *Mémoires de Madame Roland*, ed. Claude Perroud, Vol. 2 (Paris: Plon, 1905), 422. In this passage, Mme. Roland negates gender differences at the experiential level, but not at the creative level. She recognizes woman's (and specifically her own) ability to experience the same thoughts and aspirations as men, but underlines the superior ability of male writers (and specifically of Rousseau) to express them.

6. *Mémoires*, 264. Similarly, recalling the Sunday dances at Soucy (the estate of a farmer general where her great aunt and uncle Besnard had worked as housekeeper and intendant), she writes: "je ne rassasiais personne de ma présence, et, après une heure de délassement, j'échappais aux curieux, en me retirant avec mes parents pour la promenade, dont je n'aurais pas sacrifié les doux instants au plaisir bruyant et toujours vide pour mon coeur d'une sorte de représentation" (276).

7. *Mémoires*, 154.

8. Letter to Bosc, July 29, 1783, in *Lettres*, III, 257.

9. *Mémoires*, 304.

10. Ibid., 321.

11. Letter to Sophie, March 27, 1776, in *Lettres*, I, 396. Similarly, when Manon wrote to Rousseau to try to arrange a meeting with him, she carefully kept her plans secret: "Je n'avais pas envie de me donner aux yeux d'une infinité de gens une teinte de philosophie que mes goûts me donnent déjà assez: l'enthousiasme pour les grands hommes est un ridicule au jugement de ceux qui ne le sentent pas" (Ibid., 383).

12. Letter to Sophie Cannet, October 2, 1776, in *Lettres*, I, 492.

13. Letters to Roland, November 22 and 18, 1787, in *Lettres*, III, 709 and 695.

14. Letter to Bosc, June 10, 1783, in *Lettres*, III, 254.

15. *Mémoires*, 337. Similarly, in another passage of her memoirs, she writes: "Séduite par la Révolution, . . . pénétrée du désir de voir prospérer mon pays, la tourmente des affaires publiques me donnait une fièvre morale qui ne me laissait pas de relâche" (154). It is interesting to note Mme. Ro-

land's repeated use of amorous terms and images to describe her revolutionary zeal. More than once in the course of her memoirs, the Revolution is personified as a seductive but ultimately faithless lover.

16. Letter to Bosc, July 26, 1789, in *Lettres*, IV, 53. The shift in her character and tone brought about by the Revolution is particularly well reflected in the following passage of her *Mémoires*: "Tant que je suis demeurée dans un état paisible et concentré, ma sensibilité naturelle enveloppait tellement mes autres qualités, qu'elle se montrait seule ou les dominait toutes. Mon premier besoin était de plaire et de faire du bien. . . . Depuis que les circonstances, les orages politiques et autres ont développé mon caractère, je suis franche avant tout, sans regarder d'aussi près aux petites égratignures qui peuvent se faire en passant. . . . [J]' aime à faire justice à force de vérités, et j'enonce les plus terribles en face des intéressés, sans m'étonner, m'émouvoir, ni me fâcher, quel qu'en soit l'effet sur eux" (202).

17. Letter to Bosc, July 26, 1789, in *Lettres*, IV, 53.

18. Cf. de Roux, 93 n.1: "Champagneux, arrêté le 4 août 1793, eut à se défendre d'avoir dirigé ce service dont le véritable chef fut probablement Mme. Roland."

19. *Mémoires*, 155.

20. Ibid., 305.

21. Ibid.

22. Ibid., 304.

23. Recalling her work on her husband's articles as a young bride, she writes: "J'en remplissais la tâche avec une humilité dont je ne puis m'empêcher de rire lorsque je me la rappelle, et qui paraît presque inconciliable avec un esprit aussi exercé que je l'avais; mais elle coulait de mon coeur; je respectais si franchement mon mari que je supposais aisément qu'il voyait mieux que moi, et j'avais tant de crainte d'une ombre sur son visage, il tenait si bien à ses opinions, que je n'ai acquis qu'après assez longtemps la confiance de le contredire" (*Mémoires*, 333).

24. *Mémoires*, 332-333.

25. In 1788, when Eudora was seven, Mme. Roland expressed her discouragement and frustration in a letter to Lavater: "Enseignez-moi à vaincre, à diriger un caractère indocile, une trempe insouciante, sur qui les douces caresses, de même que les privations et la fermeté, n'ont presque aucun empire. Voilà mon tourment de tous les jours. L'éducation, cette tâche si

chère pour une mère à l'égard d'un enfant qu'elle aime, semble être la plus rude des épreuves qui m' aient été réservées" (July 7, 1788, in *Lettres*, IV, 22). Four years later in prison, Mme. Roland expressed her disenchantment with motherhood with surprising frankness: "J'ai une jeune fille aimable, mais que la nature a faite froide et indolente; je l'ai nourrie, je l'ai élevée avec l'enthousiasme et les sollicitudes de la maternité; . . . mais jamais son âme stagnante et son esprit sans ressort ne donneront à mon coeur les douces jouissances qu'il s'était promises" (*Mémoires*, 42).

26. Letter to Sophie Cannet, February 5, 1776, in *Lettres*, I, 374-375.

27. "Je suis désolée que mon imagination reste inutile, faute de talent pour l'exercer . . . je reste pauvre parce que je ne peux pas employer mes richesses. Il faudrait à mes désirs une étude constante, et des secours de toute espèce pour l'étendre au possible; je manque de tout; je ne ferai jamais rien de bon, et je serai à jamais un petit être tronqué, déplaisant à ceux de mon espèce parce que je ne leur ressemble pas, et n'ayant point assez d'acquis pour m'élever jusqu'aux autres. Je suis déplacée autant qu'on peut l'être" (Letter to Sophie Cannet, December 10, 1776, in *Lettres*, I, 527-528).

28. "Quelquefois je suis tentée de prendre une culotte et un chapeau, pour avoir la liberté de chercher et de voir le beau de tous les talents. On raconte que l'amour et le dévouement ont fait porter ce déguisement à quelques femmes. Ah! si je raisonnais un peu moins, et si les circonstances m'étaient un peu plus favorables, tête bleue! j'aurais assez d'ardeur pour en faire autant." A few months later, in another letter to Sophie, Manon expressed her enthusiasm for d'Holbach's *Système de la nature* and confided: "Je ne saurais te dire quelle envie il me donne d'étudier la physique, l'astronomie, choses que probablement je ne pourrais jamais apprendre; je suis bien ennuyée d'être fille; je crois qu'un petit grain de folie de plus et une santé plus forte, je me déguiserais pour me débarrasser de mes entraves, et je me plongerais dans l'étude sans distraction." However, the conclusion of her letter clearly suggests that Manon did not really feel the need to be a man in order to engage in serious intellectual pursuits: "Le sort en est jeté, j'ai commencé à raisonner, à chercher, je raisonnerai et je chercherai toujours. J'ai motivé ma conduite, je me suis fait des règles pour agir, et j'éprouve que le bonheur dépend moins des opinions que du caractère" (Letters to Sophie Cannet, August 25 and November 13, 1776, in *Lettres*, I, 465, 519).

29. Letter to Sophie Cannet, May 9, 1774, in *Lettres*, I, 195.

30. "Lorsque mon mari fut au ministère, je m'imposai la loi de ne faire ni recevoir de visites et de n'inviter à manger aucune femme; je n'avais pas de grands sacrifices à faire à cet égard; d'ailleurs je ne m'étais livrée nulle part à la grande société, parce que j'aime l'étude autant que je hais le jeu et que je m'ennuie des sots. Habituée à passer mes jours dans l'intérieur de mon

domestique, je partageais les travaux de Roland et je cultivais mes goûts particuliers. C'était donc à la fois conserver ma manière d'être, et prévenir les inconvénients dont une foule intéressée environne les personnes qui tiennent aux grandes places, que d'établir cette sévérité dans mon hôtel" (*Mémoires*, 72).

Mme. Roland attempts to justify her exclusion of women from her home as a means of maintaining an atmosphere suitable for serious political discussion, free from frivolity and intrigue (both amorous and political). She also viewed it as a means of preserving her independence and privacy, in keeping with her cult of domesticity. For the same reason, she refrained from participating in the social life of the capital. In maintaining this austere lifestyle, she claims to have merely been following the positive example set by Mme. Pétion, wife of the mayor of Paris. However, her exclusion of women from her home and her refusal of their invitations suggests that Mme. Roland had interiorized her male contemporaries' distrust and scorn for women. Throughout the passage cited above one senses a thinly veiled misogyny.

31. Ibid.

32. "Je ne vois le plaisir, comme le bonheur que dans la réunion de ce qui peut charmer le coeur comme les sens et ne point coûter de regrets. Avec une telle manière d'être, il est difficile de s'oublier et impossible de s'avilir; mais cela ne met point à l'abri de ce qu'on peut appeler une passion, et peut-être même reste-t-il plus d'étoffe pour l'entretenir" (*Mémoires*, 253). And, in her self-portrait, she underlines her natural sensuousness: "Quant au menton, il a précisément les caractères que les physionomistes indiquent pour ceux de la volupté. . . . Je doute que jamais personne fût plus faite pour elle et l'ait moins goûtée" (ibid).

33. Letter to Buzot, June 22, 1793, in *Lettres*, IV, 484.

34. Letter to Buzot, July 6, 1793, in *Lettres*, IV, 498.

35. "Mes Dernières Pensées," [Last Will and Testament written by Mme. Roland, October 8, 1793], reprinted in de Roux's edition of her *Mémoires*, 342, 346.

36. "No, I am not leaving you; I shall wait for you. The same virtue that separated us on earth will unite us in heaven. . . . I am only too happy to sacrifice my life for the right to love you forever without crime, and to be able to say it to you freely once again" (Jean-Jacques Rousseau, *Julie ou La Nouvelle Héloïse*, in *Oeuvres Complètes*, Vol. 2 [Paris: Pléiade, 1969] 743.)

37. *Mémoires*, 155.

38. May, *Mme. Roland and the Age of Revolution*, 206.

39. *Analytical Review* 22 (July-December 1795), 145. The reviewer's compliments were double-edged, however, since he or she then added: "While her husband continued in office, she assisted him in his political labours, and by her uncommon exertions, rendered herself the centre of a numerous group of enthusiastic admirers." The lengthy four-part review was signed "E.D."--initials sometimes used by Mary Wollstonecraft, who was a frequent contributor to the *Analytical Review* at the time Mme. Roland's *Mémoires* were published, as well as a passionate observer of the French Revolution. If indeed Wollstonecraft wrote the review, her ambivalence toward Roland's political role--reflected in the repetition of the term *uncommon* and in the sexist phrase "distinguished ornament of her sex"--would strikingly illustrate the power of traditional gender stereotypes over even the most progressive minds of the period.

40. Anecdote recounted in a letter to Sophie Cannet, February 29, 1776, in *Lettres*, I, 384.

41. *Mémoires*, 303; 34.

42. "C'est par un sincère dévouement à la cause révolutionnaire plus que pour assouvir son ambition personnelle qu'elle en vint à contredire ses principes restrictifs sur la femme et sur son rôle dans la vie politique et sociale," writes May. "Des événements extraordinaires lui forcèrent en quelque sorte la main. Témoin des éternelles hésitations et vacillations des Girondins, de l'inefficacité de leur programme politique, elle ne pourra s'empêcher de prendre une part grandissante dans leurs délibérations en petit comité, de les seconder et de les conseiller" (Gita May, *De J-J Rousseau à Mme Roland*, 187).

43. See, for example, Gerard Walter's note on Mme. Roland in his critical edition of Michelet's *Histoire de la Révolution française*, Vol. 2 (Bibliothèque de la Pléiade, 1952), 1521; Albert Mathiez, *La Révolution française*, Vol. 2 (Paris, 1958), 46-47; and Vol. 3, 85; and Louis Madelin, *La Révolution française*, Vol. 2 (Paris: Hachette, 1910). Cited by May, *De J-J Rousseau à Mme. Roland*, 186-187.

44. These passages are all cited and discussed in the course of this chapter. See, in particular, Mme. Roland's *Lettres*, I, 195; 374-75 and her *Mémoires*, 155; 305; 338-339.

45. "Vous êtes priée de ne plus dilapider les trésors de la nation à soudoyer deux cents mouchards pour arracher les affiches de l'Ami du Peuple. . . . Roland n'est qu'un frère coupe-choux, que sa femme mène par l'oreille; c'est elle qui est le ministre de l'intérieur" (Jean-Paul Marat, *Ami du Peuple* 684 (September 19, 1792), in *Oeuvres de J.-P. Marat*, A. Vermorel (ed.), (Paris: Décembre-Alonnier, 1869), 230.

46. Cited by Chaussinand-Nogaret, *Madame Roland, Une femme en Révolution* (Paris: Eds. du Seuil, 1985), 263.

47. Ibid.

48. Jacques-René Hébert, *Le Père Duchesne* 202 (December 20, 1792).

49. *Père Duchesne* 204 (December 25, 1792).

50. *Mémoires*, 90.

51. "Je lui faisais honte de l'administration qui expose l'innocence déjà opprimée aux derniers excès d'un peuple aveuglé. Je ne prétendais pas le convertir; je lui envoyais mes adieux comme un vautour pour ronger son coeur" (Ibid., 175).

52. *Père Duchesne* 243 (June 20, 1793).

53. *Père Duchesne* 205 (January 1, 1793).

54. "Projet de défense," in *Mémoires*, ed. de Roux, 371-373.

55. "Interrogatoire de Mme. Roland," in *Mémoires*, ed. de Roux, 95.

56. "Notes sur mon procès et l'interrogatoire qui l'a commencé," in *Mémoires*, 367.

57. "L'accusateur public, qui posait cette question, eut soin de la charger, comme toutes celles qu'il se mêlait de faire, d'épithètes outrageantes . . . il requit de m'interdire les détails; et lui et le juge . . . employèrent tous les moyens pour me réduire au silence ou me faire parler à leur gré. Je m'indignai, je dis que je me plaindrais en plein tribunal de cette manière vexatoire et inouïe d'interroger; que je ne m'en laissais point imposer par l'autorité; que je reconnaissais, avant tout . . . la raison et la nature" (ibid).

58. *Le Moniteur universel* (November 19, 1793), cited in Dauban, 537-538. The charges against Mme. Roland, Marie-Antoinette, and Olympe de Gouges were remarkably similar, despite the striking differences in their lives and characters. All three were criticized for being unfaithful wives and bad mothers and for meddling in politics, thereby forgetting their proper place as women: "Marie-Antoinette, élevée dans une cour perfide et ambitieuse, apporta en France les vices de sa famille; elle sacrifiait son époux, ses enfans et le pays qui l'avait adoptée, aux vues ambitieuses de la maison d'Autriche. . . . Elle fut mauvaise mère, épouse débauchée." As for Olympe de Gouges, "née avec une imagination exaltée, [elle] prit son délire pour une inspiration de la nature . . . elle voulut être homme d'Etat, et il semble que

la loi ait puni cette conspiratrice d'avoir oublié les vertus qui conviennent à son sexe" (ibid., 537).

59. "Une femme qui aurait eu la conscience de sa vertu, ou qui aurait sacrifié sa vie à la République n'aurait pas eu ce maintien," insists Sylvain Maréchal in le *Calendrier républicain*. "Le vrai courage ne rit pas," maintains Audouin in *le Journal Universel*. Not surprisingly, the most insulting commentary on her execution is found in Hébert's *Père Duchesne*: "Mieux vaut tuer le diable que la diable ne nous tue. . . . Les sans-culottes ont donc bien fait, dame Coco, de te faire jouer à la main chaude; car si ton vieux cocu de mari ne s'était pas cassé le nez, tu aurais été une seconde Autrichienne" November 9, 1793).

60. *Le Moniteur universel* (November 19, 1793), cited in Dauban, 538.

61. Cited in *Women in Revolutionary Paris, 1789—1795*, Darline Gay Levy, Harriet Branson Applewhite, and Mary Durham Johnson (eds.), (Urbana: University of Illinois Press, 1979), 220.

62. The negative portrayals of Mme. Roland by hostile journalists and politicians form a curious contrast with the glowing description of her shortly before her death by Count Beugnot, a fellow prisoner at the Conciergerie. Despite his political differences with her and his natural aversion to intellectual, agressive women, he was rapidly won over by her dignity and charm. He was especially moved when she spoke of her family: "No one defined better than she the duties of a wife and mother and proved more eloquently that a woman knows happiness only in the accomplishment of these sacred duties. The picture of domestic life took on ravishing colors when she painted it; tears fell from her eyes whenever she spoke of her daughter and husband." See *Mémoires du Comte Beugnot*, ed. Robert Lacour-Gayet (Paris: Hachette, 1959), 139.

63. Rousseau's home-and-hearth ethic was enthusiastically advocated by the revolutionary government as a vehicle for its program of social reform. The public discourse of the period is filled with references to the bourgeois ideals of simplicity, efficiency and frugality extolled in *Julie* and *Emile*. The Rousseauian cults of motherhood and domesticity and the principle of separate spheres underlying them were frequently invoked by revolutionary leaders (notably Mirabeau, Robespierre and Chaumette) to justify the continued subordination of women, as well as the persecution of feminist militants and the suppression of women's revolutionary clubs.
For further discussion of the influence that Rousseau's views on women had on the leaders of the revolutionary government, see Marie Cerati, *Le Club des citoyennes républicaines révolutionnaires* (Paris: Editions sociales, 1966), and Ruth Blum, *Rousseau and the Republic of Virtue: The Language of Politics in the French Revolution* (Ithaca, N.Y.: Cornell University Press, 1986).

See especially Blum's chapter titled "The Sex Made to Obey," 204-215.

64. *Mémoires de Mme. Roland*, 304-305.

65. Ibid., 338-339.

66. "Par le feu qui les anime, ses souvenirs de la Révolution constituent à coup sûr l'un des textes les plus énergiques et les plus suggestifs de l'époque," maintains Gita May. "Plus précieux encore sont sans doute ses *Mémoires* particuliers. Chronique de la vie privée de la moyenne bourgeoisie parisienne entre 1760 et 1780, ils nous offrent un document admirable sur la sensibilité, les moeurs, les idées et le goût à la fin de l'Ancien Régime. Nous y découvrons en outre un écrivain alerte, parfois délicieux" (*De J.-J. Rousseau à Mme. Roland*, p. 30). Mme. Roland's writing was, of course, greatly admired by important writers and critics of the romantic period, including Sainte-Beuve, Lamartine, Brunetière, Stendhal, and the Goncourts.

67. Letter to Jany, October 1793, in *Lettres*, IV, 527-528.

8

French Women Writers and the Revolution: Preliminary Thoughts

Catherine R. Montfort

Les femmes furent à l'avant-garde de notre révolution.
    Michelet, *Les Femmes de la Révolution*, 1854

When one considers the fate of French women writers throughout the ages, one notices that, until recently, most of them have been "outsiders" in some sense of the word. For example, in the Middle Ages, Christine de Pisan, though well adjusted to her times, a happy wife, and the mother of three children, was subjected to repeated attacks and innuendos when, after the death of her husband, she decided to write in order to become economically independent. Her life became a series of struggles when she not only defended women against medieval misogyny, in particular the misogynist attacks of Jean de Meung in *Le Roman de la Rose*, but also affirmed the intellectual capacity of the "feminin sexe." In spite of such writings as *L'Epître au Dieu d'Amours, Le Trésor de la Cité des Dames*, and *Le Chemin de longue étude*, the "querelle des femmes," as it was then called, went on unchanged after her death.

In the sixteenth century, Louise Labé only seemingly partook of the so-called Renaissance.[1] Although she was lucky enough to be educated, her relative independence after marriage gave birth to calumny: she was accused of publishing Maurice de Scève's works under her own name; she was also accused of being a courtesan. As for Mlle. de Gournay (1565–1645), she received only criticism, although Montaigne thought highly of her and called her his "fille d'alliance." Since she was an old maid and somewhat ugly, Mlle. de Gournay's virtue was not questioned like Louise Labé's, but her writings were never taken seriously. Her *Equality of Men and Women*, written in 1622, had no impact on the *Grand Siècle* (the seventeenth century).

In the seventeenth century, Mme. de Sévigné and Mme. de la Fayette were ladies of the salons and were well regarded in their lifetime, but neither was a professional writer. Mme. de Sévigné wrote only personal letters; Mme. de la Fayette's *Zaïde* was published under a friend's name, and her best novel, *La Princesse de Clèves*, appeared without the name of an author. The previous examples are far from being exhaustive but are enough for our purpose: in the centuries-old patriarchal system that regulated sexual roles and rights, there was no room or only very little room for women writers.

It is only with the French Revolution that the fate of women in general and of women writers in particular slowly began to take a new turn.[2] The willingness of Enlightenment philosophers to question the basic immutability of apparently natural characteristics had had revolutionary implications for the status of women. However, the promises of the Revolution were slow to materialize. Women hoped for much, and in particular they hoped for improved education. They received little. The main point of this chapter is to investigate how a woman of genius, Mme. de Staël, born in 1766 and educated before the Revolution, fared after this upheaval--particularly when France, after an attempt at being a Republic, became the prey of a new absolute ruler, Napoleon. Her fate at that time will be compared with the fate of another aristocrat, Mme. de Sévigné. The two women, both of whom are now viewed as important, were judged very differently at the turn of the century.

Let us see what they have in common. They both belonged to the aristocracy through birth or marriage, although both were brought up in bourgeois families. They were both well educated and at ease in salons where they shone because of their conversational skills. Paris was the city they liked best. They were both married according to the mores of the time; love was not considered, only the name or the wealth of the spouse. They both had children--Mme. de Sévigné developing a strong attachment to her daughter and Mme. de Staël remaining strongly attached to her father. Both of them were religious. Both of them were writers.

The similarity, however, stops there. Mme. de Sévigné was married and soon a widow. She never married again and refused lovers. Mme. de Staël, soon after her marriage, began taking lovers, and she had many throughout her life: Louis de Narbonne, Benjamin Constant, Prosper de Barante, and John Rocca, to name a few. Mme. de Sévigné was Catholic, leaning toward Jansenism. Mme. de Staël was a strong Protestant; she thought that Protestantism was the only religion compatible with a republic because it promoted morality and reduced dogma to a minimum. Mme. de Sévigné traveled within France, mainly to go to her estate in Brittany or to visit her daughter in Provence. Mme. de Staël was exiled from France by Napoleon and was somehow forced into traveling. Besides England where she had gone early in life, she eventually went to Italy, Germany and Russia, which gave her a cosmopolitan outlook in spite of herself. Finally, and more importantly, Mme. de Sévigné wrote mainly to her daughter whom she loved. She did not think of publication. Mme. de Staël wrote to be published--from her *Lettres sur J.J. Rousseau* in 1788 to the posthumously published *Considérations sur la Révolution Française*. She wanted to make an impact on the public.

How both of these women were judged at the end of the eighteenth century and the beginning of the nineteenth century is illuminating. To understand what happened at that time, we need to be aware of the way the aristocracy was judged after the Revolution. Recent events had been shocking: the king had been beheaded; the upper classes had been exiled, and the poor were dancing in the street. A moral judgment followed: the upper classes had been living a sinful life with too much freedom outside the family, not enough religious practice, too much sexual freedom, and too much leisure. The bourgeois ideal was extolled, in particular the ideal of enlightened domesticity. This ideal was not brand new; from 1750 on it had been discussed by philosophers, doctors and statesmen. For example, Rousseau, the most well-known theoretician of maternal love, had proposed an ideal picture of motherhood in *La Nouvelle Héloïse*. Julie, his heroine, in spite of having married without love according to her father's wishes, becomes an exemplary mother. Rousseau above all praised her as an educator--education being the cornerstone of any debate about how society can be changed. Although in the past education was based on authority, Rousseau believed that it should be based on tenderness and devotion. However, the limitations Rousseau imposed on mothers are important. First, men control the education. Second, because of their maternal duties, women are excluded not only from civil, political and economic activities, but also from intellectual activities.

In addition to philosophers like Rousseau, doctors also emphasized that women were made for maternity. Unfortunately, they were limited to maternity only and, to make things worse, were acknowledged to be subject to inherent weaknesses and to have a sensibility to be feared. Starting with Pierre Roussel, whose *Système physique et moral de la femme* in 1775 was very successful, this view marks the whole of the nineteenth century.[3] In *Histoire des mères du moyen age à nos jours* Yvonne Knibielher and Catherine Fouquet cite the *Dictionnaire des sciences médicales* (1812—1822): "The existence of woman is only a fraction of the existence of man. She does not have an existence of her own, but lives for the multiplication of the species, together with man. This is the only goal that Nature, Society and Morals acknowledge."[4] Before Freud, doctors said that anatomy was a destiny.

Finally, statesmen joined the ranks of philosophers and doctors. A noteworthy, albeit temporary, change takes place at the time of the Revolution. Although at the beginning of the Revolution women played an active role in newspapers and clubs, they were soon pushed away from political life. The first important blow was dealt by Robespierre when he closed the clubs in 1793. Then the *Convention* forbade all gatherings of women and finally entrance to political assemblies. Eventually, statesmen found themselves praising women for their private role and condemning them whenever they wanted to be included in political life. As one member of the Convention, Amar, put it rhetorically: "Should women have political rights and meddle in matters of government? . . . No, because they would be forced to sacrifice more important duties to which nature calls them."[5] Women, then, were excluded from political life because of the importance of their maternal role--in particular procreation.

Altogether, the new ideal at the turn of the century was for women to be mothers first. This view holds true whether we question the Republicans inspired by Rousseau or the Royalists who had come to accept his judgment. Women were seen principally as educators, particularly of very

young children, and were always under the guidance of men. This role
implies that staying in the home was imperative: mothers did not have a
public role. Besides, they had to stay at home to remain faithful to their
husbands. The *Journal des Débats* of March 1800 stresses all these points:

Is it proper for a woman whose most sacred duty is to be a faithful wife and a tender
mother, whose first virtue must be modesty, is it proper for her to leave this sweet
obscurity imposed upon her by her sex to hand her whole life over to a public, who
after having judged her writings, has the right to judge her actions?[6]

That Napoleon backed this ideal is important because of the many
measures he took or instigated from 1800 to 1815. His own misogyny is well
known, and it can be explained partly by his personal history. He was raised
in a patriarchal society. His mother, married when she was fourteen years old
and a widow at thirty-five, had thirteen children. Her austerity, lack of
ambition and discretion made her a model for him--the perfect role model at
the imperial court, in direct contrast to the coquettish Joséphine de
Beauharnais, an extravagant spendthrift and, above all, sterile. First as
consul, and then as emperor, Napoleon sought to restore order and organize
society. For example, he founded the *lycées* (high schools) in 1802 and
organized the university in 1806, but both institutions were forbidden to
women; consequently, he prevented young girls of the aristocracy or the rich
bougeoisie from being educated. He also promoted science and founded the
first chair of gynecology in 1806, but his ulterior motive was to produce more
soldiers for the *Grande Armée*. Finally, in 1804, when he instituted the *Code
Civil*, the purpose of which was to reorganize French society, Napoleon made
the married woman an eternal minor. The Code contains a double standard
of morality for men and women; adulterous women were punished by prison,
but adulterous men paid only a fine.

As far as literature was concerned, Napoleon wanted to promote or
sponsor writers as long as they did not criticize the new order he was
establishing. Some writers tried to please him; others were censured or
exiled, as we will see shortly with Mme. de Staël.

Louis XIV was Napoleon's chosen model; Enlightenment philosophy was
rejected. In 1800 the stated intent of the newly established *Mercure de France*,
in its Prospectus of messidor VIII, was to "contribute to the destruction,
in today's ideas and style, of those barbarous texts that the influence of the
18th of brumaire steadily effaces from revolutionary laws."[7] And in 1801,
fructidor IX, the journal pointed to the seventeenth century as a model to be
emulated: "Imagination and good taste like to reflect and dwell on the good
old days of Louis XIV's century."[8]

In this respect, Mme. de Sévigné looked particularly attractive. She was
a representative of the seventeenth century which, in comparison with the
recent upheaval, seemed a model of order: one king, one religion and an
ordered society. She never rebelled against the government or tried to have
a political role. She was religious. She wrote delightful and unpretentious
letters. Above all she loved her daughter. Consequently, she was praised for

her role as "mother." Her letters were published many times in their entirety: for example, by Vauxcelles in 1801 and by Grouvelle in 1806; and also in *Sevigniana* and *Lettres Choisies*, the latter to be read by the young with the idea of educating them. In 1803, Levizac, in a second edition of his *Lettres Choisies de Mesdames de Sévigné et de Maintenon*, mentions the dual goal of his publication: to save time for "young persons" who have so much to learn, and to expurgate from the letters details that could be "poison for youth."[9]

Besides the journal articles and editions, plays were written in which Mme. de Sévigné held the major role. In 1805 Bouilly wrote a play entitled *Madame de Sévigné* in which Mme. de Sévigné appeared as the perfect mother. As Bouilly said in his advertisement: "Where is the tenderhearted mother who does not know that patience and gentleness are the surest ways to elicit love from one's children, to win their trust and to save them from the fire of the passions."[10] The play emphasized Mme. de Sévigné's devotion to her children. For example, Mme. de Villars mentions that Mme. de Sévigné, a widow at the age of twenty-five, devoted her life to the education of her children, in spite of her youth and beauty.[11] Also to M. Darmenpierre, who asks her about her daughter, Mme. de Sévigné is shown replying, in reference to her son who is in trouble with gambling debts: "The heart of a mother is an altar meant for many sacrifices."[12] In another play written by Dupaty in 1808, *Ninon chez Madame de Sévigné*, the author shows Ninon, the famous courtesan, giving up the marquis's love for the sake of his mother, Mme. de Sévigné, and his chosen bride:

Instead of a fickle love which lasts only a few days/ Learn to deserve the two immortal loves/ That of a spouse, and that of a mother/ Far from blinding you the latter enlightens you.[13]

Napoleon must have been very pleased.

Though highly praised, Mme. de Sévigné is distorted according to the needs of the time. The woman as mother gets too much emphasis, and the genius of the writer is treated as secondary. The proliferation of *Lettres Choisies* carefully selected for the education of the young therefore betrayed who she was as a whole. It was a major force in developing an antiseptic Mme de. Sévigné.[14]

Mme. de Staël did not fit the new ideal. On the one hand, she held that education was fundamental. "If women, rising above their fate, dared to aspire to the education of men; if they knew what to tell men to do; if they had the conviction of their actions, what noble destiny would be theirs."[15] On the other hand, she aspired to more than marriage and motherhood. Not only did she choose to be a writer in spite of her father's disapproval and that of society at large, but she also believed that a writer should be political, for politics was the key to everything. She could never remove herself as a writer from social life, or literature and philosophy from the domain of political action.[16] Consequently, she wrote on many topics, from literary criticism, to political issues, to philosophy. And because she was the daughter of a high government official and the wife of an ambassador, she was in the spotlight.

For this reason, her opinions, her writing and her public and private behavior came under intense scrutiny. In 1794, when she published her *Réflexions sur la Paix adressées à M. Pitt et aux Français*, followed in 1795 by her *Rélexions sur la Paix Intérieure*, the Committee of Public Safety was outraged and exiled her to Switzerland.

A few years later, Napoleon came to the same conclusion. He thought she was a threat to the new order he was in the process of establishing. Napoleon and Mme. de Staël's conflict can best be summarized in the famous confrontation: when Mme. de Staël asked him which woman was most worthy of praise, Napoleon answered the one with the most children. As we saw, Napoleon believed that women belonged in the home, being faithful and raising children. Consequently, everything about Mme. de Staël was antipathetical to him: her above-average education, her desire to play a role in politics, her sexual freedom, her critical mind, her belief in the philosophy of the Enlightenment, most of her writings. *Delphine* (1802), with its apology for divorce, *Corinne* (1807), with its apology for the independence of nations and its praise of England, and *De l'Allemagne* (1810), with its praise of German writers and philosophy--all angered him immensely. "Never will M. Necker's daughter come back to Paris," he exclaimed, after the triumph of the first novel.[17] In 1806 when Mme. de Staël came close to Paris to correct the galleys of *Corinne* and see her friends, Napoleon wrote to Fouchet from Prussia: "Do not let that rogue of a woman, Mme. de Staël, come close to Paris."[18]

As a result, Mme. de Staël was exiled most of her life, becoming along the way, with Chateaubriand, the most famous of the French writers of this period. We will mention here only what she describes in *Corinne*: the portrayal of a woman of genius. This novel shows that Mme. de Staël had a difficult time accepting the fact that being a woman of genius entailed loneliness and misunderstanding. Corinne, the heroine, is a loser at the end in spite of her genius. The mother figure in the novel is either absent or very harsh. Men are depicted as weak and powerless. Mme. de Staël could neither abide by the new rules of obedience, submissiveness and lack of power, nor accept fully her status as woman of letters. The new ideal of domesticity was absolutely unacceptable to her, but at the same time it was strong enough to imbue her with a sense of culpability.

The fate of these two women shows us that fitting into the mold of society is as bad as not fitting; Mme. de Sévigné's world was distorted in the sense that her maternal love was held up as the ideal norm, whereas anyone who reads all her letters realizes that her "passion" for her daughter was exceptional, and indeed, somewhat "abnormal." Besides, her genius as a writer was overlooked while her "motherly" role was extolled. The letters being printed as extracts gave a poor idea of the richness and variety of her genius. Paradoxically, Mme. de Staël was betrayed in a similar manner. Because she did not fit the current mold, she was attacked as a foreigner, and as a loose and overbearing woman. Although her role in French romanticism is a major one, she was quickly forgotten by the nineteenth century, and until recently appeared as a secondary author in anthologies of French literature. Being judged according to wrong criteria seems to be the fate of women writers. Let us hope that all the "outsiders" of the past centuries are recalled to life--from Louise Labé to Olympe de Gouges, from Mme. Roland to Mme. de Genlis, from George Sand to Colette.

NOTES

1. See the article by Joan Kelly "Did Women have a Renaissance?," in *Becoming Visible: Women in European History* (Boston: Houghton Mifflin, 1977), 137-164.

2. See Olympe de Gouges's statement in her Déclaration des Droits de la Femme et de la Citoyenne, in 1791: "La loi . . . doit être la même pour tous: toutes les citoyennes et tous les citoyens, étant égaux à ses yeux, doivent être également admissibles à toutes dignités, places et emplois publics, selon leurs capacités, et sans autres distinctions que celles de leurs vertus et de leurs talents." "Law . . . must be the same for everyone: all citizens, male or female, being equal before the law, must be eligible for all positions and public jobs, according to their abilities, and with no other distinction than that of their virtues and their talents." Quoted in Paule-Marie Duhet, *Les Femmes et la Révolution, 1789—1794* (Paris: Julliard, 1971), 69-70. All translations are by the author.

3. See Yvonne Knibielher and Catherine Fouquet, *Histoire des mères du Moyen Age à nos jours* (Paris: Edition Montalba, 1977), 147-148.

4. "L'existence de la femme n'est qu'une fraction de celle de l'homme. Elle ne vit pas pour elle-même, mais pour la multiplication de l'espèce, conjointement avec l'homme. Voilà le seul but que la Nature, la Société et la Morale avouent." Ibid., 149.

5. "Les femmes doivent-elles exercer les droits politiques et s'immiscer dans les affaires du gouvernement? . . . Non, parce qu'elles seraient obligées d'y sacrifier des soins plus importants auxquels la nature les appelle." Duhet, *Les Femmes*, 154-155.

6. "Convient-il bien à une femme dont le devoir le plus sacré est d'être épouse fidelle et mère tendre, dont la première vertu doit être la modestie, lui convient-il bien de sortir de cette douce obscurité dont son état lui impose la loi, pour livrer son existence toute entière à un public qui après s'être établi juge de ses écrits, a le droit de devenir juge de ses actions?"

7. "Contribuer à dètruire, dans les idées et le style modernes, ces textes de barbarie que l'influence du 18 brumaire efface de jour en jour dans les lois révolutionnaires."

8. "L'imagination et le goût aiment à revenir sans cesse vers les beaux jours du siècle de Louis XIV."

9. "Poison pour la jeunesse." M. de Levizac, *Lettres Choisies de Mesdames de Sévigné et de Maintenon* (Paris: Gabriel Dufour, 1803), viii.

10. "Quelle est la mére sensible qui ne remarque pas que la patience et la douceur sont les moyens les plus sûrs de se faire aimer de ses enfants, d'avoir leur confiance, et de les sauver de la fougue des passions?" Jean-Nicolas Bouilly, "Madame de Sévigné, in *Suite du Répertoire du Théâtre français*, tome 8 (Paris: Mme. Veuve Dabo, 1822), 245.

11. "Education de ses enfants." Ibid., 257.

12. "Le coeur d'une mère de famille est un autel destiné à bien des sacrifices." Ibid., 332.

13. "Pour un amour léger qui passe en peu de jours; /Sachez donc mériter deux immortels amours: /Et celui d'une épouse, et celui d'une mère./ Loin de vous aveugler celui-là vous élaire!" Emmanuel Dupaty, "Ninon chez Mme. de Sévigné," in *Collection des Théâtres Français: Fin du Répertoire*, tome 31 (Senlis: Tremblay, 1829), 57.

14. See my monograph, Catherine Montfort-Howard, *Les Fortunes de Madame de Sévigné au XVIIème et au XVIIIème siècles* (Paris: Jean-Michel Place, 1982).

15. "Si les femmes, s'élevant au-dessus de leur sort, osaient prétendre à l'éducation des hommes; si elles savaient dire ce qu'ils doivent faire; si elles avaient le sentiment de leurs actions, quelle noble destinée leur serait réservée!" Mme. de Staël, *Oeuvres Complètes de Madame la baronne de Staël-Holstein* (Slatkine Reprints), Vol. 1, 111.

16. Simone Balayé, *Madame de Stael: Lumières et Liberté* (Paris: Klinchsieck, 1979), 13.

17. "Jamais la fille de M. Necker ne rentrera à Paris." P. Gautier, *Madame de Staël et Napoléon* (Plon: Paris, 1921), 97.

18. "Ne laissez pas approcher de Paris cette coquine de Mme. de Stael." Ibid., 185.

REFERENCES

Abensour, Léon. *La Femme et le Féminisme avant la Révolution.* Paris: Leroux, 1923.

Balayé, Simone. *Madame de Staël: Lumières et Liberté.* Paris: Klincksieck, 1979.

Bouilly, Jean-Nicholas. "Madame de Sévigné." Comédie en trois actes représentée pour la première fois au Théâtre Français, le 6 juin 1805. In *Suite du Répertoire du Théâtre français.* Tome 8. Paris: Mme. Veuve Dabo, 1822, 241-364.

Diesbach, Ghislain de. *Madame de Staël.* Paris: Perrin, 1983.

Duhet, Paule-Marie. *Les Femmes et la Révolution,* 1789—1794. Paris: Julliard, 1971.

Dupaty, Emmanuel. "Ninon chez Mme de Sévigné." Comédie en un acte et en vers, mêlée de chants. Musique de H. Berton. Représentée pour la première fois sur le théâtre de l' Opéra-Comique, le 26 septembre 1808. In *Collection des Théatres Français: Fin du Répertoire.* Tome 31. Senlis: Tremblay, 1829, 1-60.

Gautier, P. *Madame de Staël et Napoléon.* Paris, 1921.

Journal des Débats, March 1800.

Kelly-Gadol, Joan. "Did Women have a Renaissance?" in *Becoming Visible: Women in European History.* Renate Bridenthal and Claudia Koonz (eds.), Boston: Houghton Mifflin, 1977, 137-164.

Knibielher, Yvonne, and Catherine Fouquet. *Histoire des mères du Moyen Age à nos jours.* Paris: Editions Montalba, 1977.

Levizac, M. de. *Lettres Choisies de Mesdames de Sévigné et de Maintenon.* 2ème ed. Paris: Gabriel Dufour, 1803.

Mercure de France, Messidor an VIII 1800, Fructidor an IX 1801.

Montfort-Howard, Catherine. *Les Fortunes de Madame de Sévigné au XVIIème et au XVIIIème siècles.* Paris: Jean-Michel Place, 1982.

Staël, Anne-Louise Germaine Necker de. *Oeuvres Complètes de Madame la baronne de Staël-Holstein.* Slatkine Reprints, 1836.

9

The Sublimity of Speech as Action: The Myth of Mirabeau, 1791–1848

Patricia A. Ward

In coming to grips with the Revolution of 1789, historians, memorialists, and literary figures of the nineteenth century early recognized the power of revolutionary discourse. Charles Nodier, writing of the Convention, suggests that the life of great men is exhibited in their speech (*parole*), implying that speech was action for orators like Vergniaud.[1] More explicitly, Barante comments that "the history of an assembly takes place in large measure at the tribune; speeches are always actions."[2] For the romantics, revolutionary oratory, viewed in retrospect, brought into focus their own ambivalence about the changing social order in France and their role in the political arena. Speech as action (*verbe* as *événement*) posed in an indirect fashion the question of the relationship of literature to the political world: Does writing make a difference in the social order? Does it reflect that order or does it seek to change it? The fact that Chateaubriand, Lamartine, Hugo, and others carved out for themselves public careers to supplement their roles as men of letters illustrates the depth of this political-literary connection.

The figure of Honoré-Gabriel Riqueti, comte de Mirabeau, struck a responsive chord among writers, publishers, and readers during the Restoration and July Monarchy, for his support of a constitutional monarchy, and his role as a leader of the masses seemed to correspond with the spirit of the Charter of 1814 and the early years of the July Monarchy. Mirabeau came to symbolize the ambiguous currents at the heart of French political life. A myth of Mirabeau gradually emerged, a myth that constituted a projection onto his life and character of the desires and fears of post-Napoleonic France and of its writers. In a passage dated November 1821, in the *Mémoires d'outre-tombe*, Chateaubriand recounts his own encounters with Mirabeau, noting the mythic grandeur that the orator had already achieved, particularly owing to the empty political stage of post-Napoleonic France.

Mirabeau has already undergone the metamorphosis which takes place among individuals of whom the memory must last; dragged from the Pantheon to the gutter and then restored to the Pantheon, he has been elevated the all-time height which serves today as his pedestal. We no longer see the real Mirabeau but the Mirabeau as the painters render him in order to make him the symbol or the myth of the era which he represents; he is thus becoming more false and yet truer. Out of so many reputations, so many actors, so many events, so many ruins, only three men remain, each of whom is linked to one of the three great revolutionary epochs: Mirabeau stands for the aristocracy, Robespierre for democracy, and Bonaparte for despotism. The restored monarchy has nothing: France has paid dearly for three figures of renown whom virtue cannot acknowledge as its own.[3]

In a more technical sense than Chateaubriand's reference to Mirabeau's symbolic stature in the nineteenth century, the term *myth* can be applied to the particular narrative with which he became associated in the public and literary imagination. This narrative is composed of "mythemes," or constituent units, that can stand alone or be substituted for one another, for each unit, as well as the narrative as a whole, has a fixed association with Mirabeau. The myth or its mythemes function like clichés (frozen lexical expressions) as part of the coinage of post-Napoleonic culture. Some of these mythemes come to represent the sublimity of speech as action, encapsulating the complex motivations of nineteenth-century writers to speak (write) and to act (elicit change), but to remain somehow within the established order.

At the time of Mirabeau's death in April 1791, the narrative of his life was already apparent. *L'Orateur du peuple* commented:

Let us distinguish between the two men in Monsieur Mirabeau; the second part of his political career tarnished the brilliance of the first part. Why was it that he never associated the talents of Cicero with the honesty of the consul of Rome? Why did the vile love of money suck dry the pure springs of patriotism within him? Oh! In that case his tomb would be watered by the tears of all the centuries to come! People praise his eloquence but forget the treacherous use he made of the veto, of martial law, etc. People praise his eloquence, but the devil, according to Milton, is also eloquent![4]

Thus, even as all of Paris was following Mirabeau's funeral cortège to the Pantheon, the controversy that had surrounded him in life was continuing. Attempts to idealize him as an orator were as strong as the criticisms.

Monsieur de Mirabeau is dead. We who knew him intimately and sincerely cherish his affectionate and sensitive character, admiring greatly his superior gifts, owe him tears--and we have shed them. . . . I swear that from the ashes of the great Mirabeau will rise thousands of athletes and orators who will double as fearless defenders of the people. Released from its mortal shell, his shade will be present in all the purity of true principles in our midst.[5]

The scandal of Mirabeau's earlier life and his career as a writer of sorts, eclipsed by the brilliant but brief blaze of his oratory between 1789 and 1791--these are the two early mythemes of the narrative. His rapid fall owing to the exposure of his own secret contacts with the court constitutes a third. In a way, Mirabeau was bound to be overshadowed by subsequent events of the Revolution, but the Jacobins destroyed his bust and the Convention covered the one that stood in the hall where it met, as if to obliterate him from the historical record. By late 1792, within little more than a year of his death,

Mirabeau had sunk into relative oblivion owing to his own scheming and the increasingly radical nature of the Revolution.

Within the Restoration, Mirabeau's fortunes were to undergo a tremendous change. The Revolution was the event that the nineteenth century could no longer repress. As the historiography of the Revolution began to emerge, Thiers' preface to his *Histoire de la révolution française* (1823—1827) is representative of this sense of psychic necessity.

I have no illusions about the difficulties of the undertaking, because passions once extinguished under the influence of military despotism have just been reawakened. Suddenly, men bent with years and toil have experienced the rebirth of feelings which had seemed dormant, and have communicated them to us, their sons and inheritors.[6]

As the historiography and autobiography of the Revolution evolve, further, more detailed, mythemes are added to the narrative of Mirabeau's life: his physical appearance, the transformation of Mirabeau when at the *tribune*, the sublimity of his speech, the identification of Mirabeau with Roman orators and tribunes. A single moment, when speech constituted an exemplary act, setting in motion a chain of defiant acts, became for the nineteenth century the central event of this narrative. This was Mirabeau's protest to the marquis de Dreux-Brézé on June 23, 1789, when the *tiers-état* refused the order of the king to terminate its session. According to the *Moniteur* at the time, Mirabeau declared that "if you were ordered to make us leave this place, you will have to ask for permission to use force, for we will not leave our places except by the force of bayonettes."[7] But the popular version was even more defiant: "Go and tell your master that we are here through the will of the people and that we will leave only through the force of bayonettes."

Madamme de Staël's portrait of Mirabeau in her *Considérations sur les principaux événemens de la révolution française* (published posthumously in 1818) is remarkable for the immediacy of its style. Many of the elements of the myth are present: immorality, physical traits, and a striking power, transforming the decadent aristocrat into the represenative of the people.

The opinion one had of his wit was augmented in a peculiar way by the fear caused by his immorality; yet it was this very immorality which reduced the influence his amazing abilities should have brought him. It was difficult not to keep on looking at him once you caught sight of him: his large head of hair marked him as did Samson's; his face took on expression from his very ugliness. Everything about him gave the impression of an irregular power, but of just the sort of power one would imagine in a tribune of the people.[8]

The dramatist Népomucène Lemercier was probably even more influential than Mme. de Staël for details of the narrative surrounding Mirabeau the orator-tribune. In 1818 he also published a little treatise on declamation and the national theater. In *Du Second Théâtre Français*, Lemercier advised young actors to study the great scenes of history. Then Lemercier evokes the scene of the constituent assembly where "the most astonishing political actor" was found who can serve as a model for young actors on the stage. This actor was, of course, Mirabeau, and in a long Ciceronian passage Lemercier paints his physical appearance, delaying his name until a fitting climax is reached.

He was ugly; his shape conveyed simply an ensemble of massive contours; when you focused your eyes on his face, it was with repugnance that you endured his sallow, pitted complexion, his furrowed cheeks, his sunken eyes set beneath high eyebrows in their hollow sockets, his crooked mouth, and finally, his disproportionate head borne by his large chest.[9]

Lemercier has fleshed out in striking detail the ugliness to which Mme. de Staël referred in generic terms. He then continues his description to show, in a remarkable passage, the sublime transformation wrought in Mirabeau by the power of his speech--a particular form of the speech event, reminiscent in its imagery of Longinus's treatise *On the Sublime*. For Longinus, the influence of sublime speech is that of a spell, a reign of power and irresistible might. "Sublimity flashing forth at the right moment scatters everything before it like a thunderbolt, and at once displays the power of the orator in all its plenitude." With this evocation of the oratorical tradition of the sublime, well known in France through Boileau's translation of Longinus, Lemercier originates in the figure of Mirabeau a unique personification of sublime energy.

He spoke first in a drawling voice with a catch, sustained gradually by the inflections of his knowledge and intelligence, and suddenly soaring with a supple mobility to the full, varied, majestic tone of the ideas which his ardour produced. In this he was like those large birds who lumber forth out of the depths as though weighted down, but whose flight becomes light when they spring forth into the high clouds; from there the eagle soared; it trifled with storms; it launched a thousand bolts of lightening; it struck everything. Strong in his male eloquence, tall through his declamation, Mirabeau's ugliness would disappear; he would be revealed as truly handsome; his vigour would be touched with grace, such was the extent to which his inspiration (âme) completely transformed him. How well that inspiration made use of his robust stature in the energy of his expressions! How it controlled his rare, but distinctive gestures! How it strengthened his proud carriage, his lion-like bearing! How nobly his genius brought into total harmony his fiery glances, the shuddering muscles of his forehead, his excited, quivering face, and the movement of his lips with intonations of truth, of vehemence, of menace, and of irony.[10]

Lemercier concludes the passage on Mirabeau with an allusion to the famous confrontation with Dreux-Bréé:

I would have been curious to see what the ambitious captain, who congratulated himself for subjugating everything to the sovereignty of gold and iron, could have done in defiance of the freedom of this moral colossus who so proudly scorned what he called the power of the bayonnettes.[11]

Lemercier's discourse is remarkable, for the subtext created by his imagery is that of primal, male, sexual, immoral energy that is transformed and directed through speech into moral action.

The literary descriptions of 1818 were followed by the publication of a number of editions of Mirabeau's works in the 1820s and 1830s: for example, the *Oeuvres oratoires* (3 vols., 1819), with a historical note on Mirabeau's life which makes use of the passage in Lemercier; *Les Discours et opinions de Mirabeau* (3 vols., 1820); the *Oeuvres choisies* (5 vols., 1820—1821, 2nd ed., 1821), and the *Oeuvres* (9 vols., 2 editions, 1826—1827, with a third edition in 1834—1835). All these editions contained prefaces with a historical note on the life of Mirabeau. At the same time, personal accounts of either the Revolution or of Mirabeau began to appear, along with histories of the Revolution: Jacques Peuchat's *Mémoires sur Mirabeau et son époque* (4 vols., 1824), Dumont's *Souvenirs sur Mirabeau et sur les deux premières Assemblées legislatives* (1832), and Montigny's *Mémoires biographiques, littéraires et politiques de Mirabeau* (8 vols., 1834—1835, 2nd ed., 1841). Both Hugo and Chateaubriand were acquainted with the volumes by Montigny, as they were with the article on Mirabeau by Beaulieu et Foisset l'aîné in Volume 29 of the Michaud *Biographie universelle*, published in 1821. Lemercier's description was reproduced in part in this biographical article.[12]

Two outstanding histories of the Revolution by the liberals Thiers and Mignet refuse to place Mirabeau in a legendary context, although they recognize the force of his presence in the period 1789 to 1791. Mignet, more than Thiers, portrays Mirabeau in a broader historical context. Mirabeau was a man whose moment in history had come, and he took advantage of it to gain preeminence at the tribune. The middle class triumphed in the first phase of the Revolution, ushered in by the events of July 14; the Constituent Assembly, the National Guard and the Town Hall were its domain, with Mirabeau, La Fayette, and Bailly, respectively, dominating each institution.[13]

Mirabeau gained the same ascendancy at the tribune as Sièyes in the committees. Here was a man who was only awaiting the opportunity to become great. During the height of the Republic in Rome, there would have been one of the Gracchi, during its decline, a Cataline; during the Fronde, a cardinal de Retz; and during the decrepitude of a monarchy when someone such as Mirabeau could only use his enormous abilities in agitation, he gained attention by the vehemence of his passions, by the blows he suffered at the hands of authority, and by the life he devoted to causing confusion and to suffering for it. . . . Without the revolution Mirabeau would have missed his destiny, for it is not enough to be a great man; one has to reach greatness at just the right moment.[14]

After the July Revolution, the new government took advantage of the revolutionary climate of 1830 and of the emerging historiography of 1789.[15] For instance, it used painting for political purposes, and in September 1830, Guizot, minister of the interior, proposed a series of competitions for artists in order to decorate the Palais Bourbon with historical paintings. The first competition, held in December of that year, was devoted to Louis-Philippe taking his oath, August 9, 1830. In 1831 three subjects were proposed: Mirabeau and Dreux-Brézé, Boissy d'Anglas at the Convention, and the Convention after the vote for the execution of Louis XVI. These particular paintings were to decorate the wall opposite the hemicycle of the Chamber of Deputies. (The Mirabeau painting remained there until 1839 when it was replaced by the Minerva in the Salle des Pas Perdus.) The subject of Mirabeau drew more than thirty entries, including proposed paintings by Delacroix and Désiré Court, but Alexandre Hesse was declared the winner. The first issue of *L'Artiste* (February 1, 1831) contained an article, "Mirabeau à l'Ecole des Beaux-Arts," on the relative merits of the two paintings by Delacroix and Court.[16]

In 1834, when Victor Hugo wrote his essay, "Sur Mirabeau," first as a booklet and then as part of *Littérature et philosophie mêlées*, he was consciously making a statement in the context of both the Revolution and the cultural tradition I have been outlining. Hugo had just begun his liaison with Juliette Druot in 1833, and the case can be made that Hugo's underlying psychological and physical drives, as well as his conscious literary and political ambitions, underlie his identification with the figure of Mirabeau. With his awareness of the failure of the July Revolution and his awakening social consciousness, Hugo declared himself to be, like Mirabeau, "an event which speaks."[17] The figure of Mirabeau and the lexical choices present in his evocation of the orator at the tribune were to remain part of Hugo's imaginative storehouse, to be reworked in new contexts, throughout the rest of his career, until the writing of *Ouatre-vingt-treize*.[18]

Hugo depicts Mirabeau as the symbol of the people in his 1834 essay, and this is his particular contribution to the myth, a theme taken up later by Michelet in his lectures on the Revolution at the College de France. But Hugo's identification with Mirabeau represents an ambiguous liberalism; it is the aristocrat who speaks, who creates, and whose energies are transformed into a moral force on behalf of the people with whom he links himself. The sublimity of this transformation is not lost on Hugo; he writes in the tradition of Lemercier:

The true Mirabeau is the speaking Mirabeau. The Mirabeau who speaks--he is flowing water, a foaming wave, a sparkling fire, a soaring bird, a thing which produces a noise peculiar to itself, a nature fulfilling its own law. A spectacle forever sublime and harmonious![19]

Hugo takes up the imagery of energy and force, the theme of the ugliness of Mirabeau, and the defiance of Dreux-Brézé. One example will illustrate Hugo's own powerful style--his portrait of Mirabeau at the tribune.

Everything about him was powerful. His abrupt and violent gesture was replete with authority. At the tribune he made a colossal movement of his shoulders like an elephant carrying its armed tower into battle. But Mirabeau, he was bearing his thought. His voice . . . had a formidable revolutionary accent which one discerned in the assembly as the roaring of a lion in its den. His head of hair, when he shook it, had the appearance of a mane. . . . His head had an awe-inspiring ugliness of which the effect, like lightning, was electric and terrifying.[20]

Hugo concludes that the Revolution opened up the great testament of history. Mirabeau, Robespierre, and Napoleon have inscribed their particular word on the pages of history, but who will sign the book in 1834? Not a revolutionary, but a man of progress, like Hugo himself, who will carry out the long laborious harvest of the seed sown by revolutionaries. "Mirabeaus are no longer necessary; therefore, they are no longer possible."[21]

As the political climate changed further in the 1840s, the power of the myth of Mirabeau to speak to the time, to regulate the popular perception of the Revolution, and to reflect the hesitancies of the July Monarchy began to disappear. Robespierre was to supersede Mirabeau as the dominant personality of the Revolution. By 1847, Borély, the *procureur général*, opened himself to dismissal by Guizot merely for suggesting that a statue to the memory of Mirabeau be erected in Aix-en-Provence.

In his first two lectures of his course on the Revolution at the College de France, Michelet portrayed Mirabeau as the symbol of the people, using Montigny and Hugo among his sources. For this he was roundly denounced. In his published work he defends Mirabeau but in a moderate, less enthusiastic way.[22]

Lamartine takes into account some of the mythemes surrounding Mirabeau in his *Histoire des Girondins*, also published in 1847, but his final judgment is severe. When viewed as a whole, the Revolution was much more than speech, and speech could never be mistaken for action.   As Mirabeau's ascendancy waned, "his genius had paled before that of the revolution itself; dragged inevitably to a precipice by the very chariot which he had launched on its course, he clung in vain to the tribune."[23] A new agenda for political action had now displaced the aristocratic Mirabeau. Vergniaud, the Mirabeau of the Girondins, now becomes the sublime orator, but the myth that symbolized the Revolution as a speech act has begun to crumble.[24]

NOTES

1. Charles Nodier, "Convention Nationale, Eloquence à la tribune" in *Souvenirs, Episodes et Portraits pour servir à l' histoire de la révolution et de l'empire*, Vol. 1 (Paris: Alphonse Levavasseur, 1831), 135.

2. M. de Barante, *Histoire de la Convention Nationale*, Vol. 1 (Paris: Furne, Langlois, Leclercq, 1851—1853), xi. The translation into English of this and all subsequent citations is my own.

3. Chateaubriand, *Mémoires d'outre-tombe*, 2nd ed., reviewed and amended by Maurice Levaillant, Vol. 1 (Paris: Flammarion, 1949), 229.

4. Philippe-Joseph-Benjamin Buchez et Prosper-Charles Roux, *Histoire parlementaire de la révolution française*, Vol. 9 (Paris: Paulin, 1834—1838),

393 (hereafter cited as Buchez et Roux).

5. *Annales politiques*, cited in Buchez et Roux, Vol. 9, 392.

6. Adolphe Thiers, *Histoire de la révolution française*, Vol. 1 (Paris: Lecointe et Durey, 1823), 1-2. Volumes 1 and 2, coauthored with Félix Bodin, appeared in 1823. Thiers revised these opening remarks somewhat in later editions.

7. Buchez et Roux, Vol. 1, 22.

8. Mme. de Staël, *Considérations sur les principaux événements de la révolution française*, 2nd ed., Vol. 1 (Paris: Delaunay, 1818), 186.

9. Népomucène L. Lemercier, *Du Second Théâtre Français, ou Instruction relative à la déclamation dramatique* (Paris: Nepveu, 1818), 36 (hereafter cited as Lemercier).

10. Lemercier, 37.

11. Ibid., 38.

12. A.W.R. James reproduces Hugo's notes for his essay on Mirabeau, alluding to sources, in Vol. 2, 450-452, of his edition of *Littérature et philosophie mêlées* (Paris: Klincksieck, 1976); this edition is hereafter cited as Hugo.

13. François-Auguste-Alexis Mignet, *Histoire de la Révolution française depuis 1789 jusqu'en 1814*, 6th ed., Vol. 1 (Paris: Didot, 1836), 108 (hereafter cited as Mignet). This work first appeared in 1824.

14. Mignet, Vol. 1, 112-113.

15. For a complete treatment of the political use of art by Louis-Philippe, see Michael Marrinan, *Painting Politics for Louis-Philippe: Art and Ideology in Orléanist France, 1830—1848* (New Haven, Conn. and London: Yale University Press, 1988).

16. See Albert Boime, *The Academy and French Painting in the Nineteenth Century* (New York: Phaidon, 1971), 115-121, Frank Anderson Trapp, *The Attainment of Delacroix* (Baltimore and London: Johns Hopkins University Press, 1971), 104-110, and Marrinan, *Painting Politics*, 82-86.

17. Hugo, Vol. 2, 317.

18. Patricia A. Ward, "Hugo et le mythe de Mirabeau au dix-neuvième siècle" in *Hugo le fabuleux*, introduction by Jacques Seebacher (Paris: Seghers, 1985), 335-346 (hereafter cited as Ward).   Raymond Tousson, without citing this previous work, gives a summary of major romantic accounts of Mirabeau in his essay, "Mirabeau vu par les écrivains romantiques," *Dixhuitième siècle*, 20 (1988), 415-430. Tousson notes the mythic nature of Hugo's major writings on Mirabeau but does not explore the function of the figure of Mirabeau in Hugo's imagination over his entire career.

19. Hugo, Vol. 2, 299.

20. Ibid., Vol. 2, 301-303.

21. Ibid., Vol. 2, 323.

22. Ward, 342.

23. Alphonse de Lamartine, *Histoire des Girondins*, Introduction et notes de Jean-Pierre Jacques, Vol. 1 (Paris: Plon, 1984), 30 (hereafter cited as Lamartine).

24. See Lamartine, Vol. 1, 241, 529.

10

French Theater and Revolution: The Eve and the Aftermath

Mario Hamlet-Metz

Upon his return from England, one century before the battle of *Hernani*, an enthusiastic Voltaire publicly proclaimed his sincere admiration for most British institutions, including theater, and including, yes, Shakespeare. Voltaire was indeed one of the first writers of his century to realize the urgent need for reform in French tragedy, a genre that was falling into a sad state of stagnation in the post-Racine years; thus, he began to create plays in which the rigorous structure of French classicism was skillfully combined with the onstage action and violence characteristic of the plays of the Bard. In the dedication of his *Zaïre* (1730), inspired directly by *Othello*, Voltaire openly admitted his debt to Shakespeare and said that by adopting certain aspects of the Shakespearean play he hoped to contribute to the birth of a type of tragedy unknown to the French. He was clearly posing as innovator. But in 1776, when the French appointed Letourneur as official translator of the first edition of the complete works of Shakespeare, the jealous Voltaire vociferously denied his initial enthusiasm for the British poet, denouncing him within the august walls of the French Academy as being nothing but a monster and a clown: "And to think that it was I who, years ago, was the first to speak of Shakespeare; it is I who showed the French a few jewels that could be found in the midst of all his rubbish."[1] The fate of Shakespearean theater in France and of French theater itself during the years that preceded 1789 could have been quite different indeed had Voltaire given the British poet an accolade rather than a deadly blow in the assembly of the forty Immortals.

But the revolutionary trumpets were not being heralded by Voltaire alone. As early as 1747, in the preface to his François II, Président Jean-François Hénault introduced a modern French theme and defended his choice by saying that the cardinal of Lorraine and the duc of Guise plotting the murder of the prince of Condé were just as interesting dramatically as the confidants of Ptolemaeus deliberating about the death of Pompeus, and that Catherine de Medici was just as valid a character as Cleopatra and Agrippina. In addition, Hénault vehemently defended, in the name of logic, his breaking the rule of unity of time, because it was practically impossible to observe it when depicting events that took place over a period of seventeen years. "I have not written a tragedy . . . just a new way to present the facts that could prove advantageous."[2]

In addition to the well-known but relatively pacific efforts to modernize the French theater by Diderot and Sedaine, and the popular translations of Shakespeare by Ducis, there were the much more fiery attempts by Sébastien Mercier, the most outspoken advocate of theatrical reform in France on the eve of 1789. In his essay *On Literature and Writers* (1778), Mercier accuses the French classical authors of having created nothing but elegant copies and a theater totally foreign to the civic and political interests of the French. He goes on to foretell the definitive advent of Shakespeare and of naturalness in French theater and does not hesitate to redefine in his own terms the mission of the modern playwright--to identify the (dramatic) issues that affect his society and his times and to present them to his contemporaries in the most meaningful manner. According to Mercier, true masterpieces would be produced once again in France only when a new and unknown genre came forth, a genre daring in its structure and picturesque in its content--both qualities that were usually sacrificed at the time in the name of theatrical conventions, useful to poor authors and harmful to art.[3] Mercier, who in the eyes of the Academicians was nothing but a fool (let us notice, however that he announced from afar Stendhal, whose articles for *Le Globe* and whose *Racine and Shakespeare* in the 1820s were written in the same vein), had an immediate success abroad, especially in Germany, where his essays were translated and where his ideas were in perfect agreement with the literary doctrine that Goethe was beginning to adopt in his *Goetz von Berlichingen* and that Schiller would follow in his *Raeuber*. Because both German authors had a considerable influence on French literature of the early nineteenth century, it is safe to state that Mercier's revolutionary message was indeed heard in his own country but that it arrived there indirectly, with some delay, via Germany.

The social and political chaos that followed the outbreak of the Revolution became evident in the theatrical world as well. In November 1789 forty consecutive performances welcomed Marie-Joseph Chénier's tragedy *Charles IX* at the Théâtre de la Nation. In spite of its moderate tone, the disrespect shown in this play to monarchy and religion, two sacred institutions that had remained untouched until then, initiated the pandemonium that reigned on the Parisian stage for several years. In fact, from that moment on, an avid populace filled the boulevard theaters night after night, hungrily demanding to see on stage viciously scornful and violent antimonarchic and antireligious plays, in which royalty, nobility and clergy would be punished for their crimes, while the people would finally be avenged for their sufferings. Fanaticism took the place of moderation; a strict and tyrannical censorship outlawed and destroyed plays and promptly sent their authors to the popular courts. Citizen Barrère, speaking in the name of the Public Health Committee, gave theater a didactic role of the utmost importance, saying that theaters were the elementary schools of the unenlightened and that, in general terms, they provided an excellent supplement to public education.[4] In 1793, for example, François de Neufchâteau was nearly sent to the guillotine because in his *Paméla* equality did not triumph in the end. Olympe de Gouges (the author of *L'esclavage des nègres [The Enslavement of the Negroes]*, the 1790 play for which actors refused to put black makeup on their faces) had her *Le général Dumouriez à Bruxelles ou les Vivandiers* performed at the beginning of the 1793 season. Full of action, marches and battles, this play offered some interesting innovations in staging but it brought to mind the uselessness of the execution of Louis XVI; the play was booed, people starting singing the carmagnole, and the author was accused of being a royalist and sent to the guillotine.

On 6 nivôse of the year II, *Lovelace français ou la jeunesse du duc de Richelieu (French Lovelace, or the Youth of the Duke of Richelieu)* by Duval and Monvel premiered at the Théâtre de la République. In this work, the duke, disguised as a butler, seduces the wife of his tapestry-maker. The play pleased the crowds for its indecent scenes, but its few true literary merits (knowledge of the stage, purity and correctness of style) passed unnoticed. Aware of the frenzy for theater, some authors looked for new settings, and Spain, exotic and adventurous Spain, became a popular source of inspiration, especially after Beaumarchais. Ten days after the premiere of the above-mentioned *Lovelace*, citizen Dorveau had his *Contre-révolutionnaires jugés par eux-mêmes (Counter-Revolutionaries Judged by Themselves)* received with popular acclaim. In it, a waiter disguised as a Spanish ambassador enters a café where he learns the secret plottings of a nobleman, a parliamentarian, a priest, and a powerful merchant. Much to the audience's delight, they are promptly arrested, sent to court, and sentenced to death.

Two of the numerous plays produced during the Convention in 1793 caused a real uproar. The first one, Jean-Louis Laya's *L'ami des lois (The Friend of the Law)*, opened during the trial of Louis XVI. In it, the author foresees the abuses of the Jacobins and denounces false patriotism. Nine days before the execution of the king, the authorities ordered the theater to cancel any further performances of this play. This interdiction could not, however, prevent Laya's eloquent and pointed message from going straight to the hearts of those who had seen and later on read the play, which in the end caused a profound impact. The second one was Marie-Joseph Chénier's *Fénelon*; in the preface, the author wanted to pass for a revolutionary, innovator and precursor. Just like Mercier, he was misunderstood and seemed to be writing for the generation to come, for his words were those of a true romanticist, especially when he declared himself the enemy of all prejudices in the theater and said that he intended to use the theater as a tribune from which he hoped to contribute to the improvement of his society's morals and to form new men for the new laws.[5] In the play itself, his protagonist complains bitterly about the present state of morals and hopes that, under the wise mentor Telemaque's influence, his people and humanity in general will rediscover the value of truth and virtue:

We have forgotten nature and its laws.
The cries of prejudice have silenced its voice.
Searching for truth beneath falsehood,

Taking the generous route to virtue
May our successors, more enlightened than ourselves,
Dissipate the errors which led us astray . . .
Telemaque will instruct docile youth . . .
Hence I will plead humanity's cause. (III, 2)[6]

However revolutionary this may sound, in 1793 Chénier's play was qualified as weak. The *Journal des spectacles* criticized this weakness by comparing the author to the more courageous Corneille who in the seventeenth century came out eloquently in defense of republicanism, and to Molière who dared denounce hypocrisy under a tyrannical regime. Interestingly, the same article stated that the Revolution would be authenticated in art only after a radical change had taken place in theaters, in the plays themselves, and in literature in general. Republicanism, which had become synonymous with Revolution, would have to be found in all spheres of French society, including literature. In point of fact, it would be this republicanism that would help the French to maintain their predominance in the world of letters. "Everything around us must take on the severe and male character of republicanism. . . . The French have lifted themselves above all modern nations through their literature, and especially through their dramatic plays. Let us maintain this superiority. The Revolution is a new source of energy."[7] Hence, the success of *Scipion l'Africain* in the year VI of the Republic, in which the young general Bonaparte was artfully praised. All this tells us that the Revolution was being presented as a source of ideological and literary inspiration.

Toward the end of the eighteenth century, the most popular plays belonged to a totally new genre, melodrama, which hardly contributed to the improvement of the quality of French theater. This genre, meant to appeal to the illiterate spectators of the boulevards, was placed outside of literature from the very beginning, even by its most important representative, Guilbert de Pixerécourt, who admitted that neither linguistic subtleties nor stylistic purity could be understood by the masses. Whatever the literary value of melodrama, this genre, which had begun by identifying itself with the principles of the Revolution (punishment of evil, triumph of justice and virtue), and had cleverly adapted itself to the aspirations and to the taste of the subsequent political regimes, managed to survive in its initial form not only the revolutionary period, but also the Empire and even the Restoration, until the advent of romantic drama of the 1830s, which it greatly influenced. Years later, Charles Nodier came out in defense of melodrama, qualifying it as an "indispensable genre for its times," because it satisfied completely the taste and demands of the people.[8]

The end of the Terror was followed by a relatively peaceful period, politically, socially, and also artistically. The exaggerated violence and disrespect seen on the streets and on the stage declined and made room for a period of transition, during which politicians and writers, without forgetting the principles of 1789, searched relentlessly for new and durable laws and institutions for the seemingly aimless French society. Among the literary figures who followed this direction at the very end of the eighteenth century and in the early nineteenth century, one must mention Népomucène Lemercier. In his 1797 *Agamemnon*, despite the classical subject, he succeeded in introducing new dramatic elements, such as the unprecedented "thee-ing" and "thou-ing" of the characters, and precise indications as to the costumes. From that moment on, Lemercier proudly thought he was the great innovator of the French theatrical system. *Agamemnon* is followed by *Pinto*, the first of a series of historical comedies, a new but short-lived genre. However, Lemercier, being more interested in tragedy, adroitly continued to exploit classical subjects at a time when the Emperor, after prohibiting the performances of all plays that could be interpreted as anti-Napoleonic, encouraged the revival of Greek and Roman tragedies.

It was not only in the subsidized theaters that a rebirth of interest in traditional classicism could be perceived. As a matter of fact, judging by the records (titles and box offices), it seems that most Parisian theatergoers were not ready yet for any drastic change or innovation in the theater. The best proof for this was given by the success of plays of the type of *Chapelain ou la ligue des auteurs contre Boileau* (1804), at the end of which the mediocre Cottin triumphantly exclaimed that the Boileaus of this world would disappear and authors of his own caliber would claim eternal victory.[9] The failure of Constant's *Wallstein* proved that, for the time being at least, the French did not want direct influence coming from the other side of the Rhine either. All in all, one must admit that during the early years of the Empire, French theater hardly made any progress at all, except maybe at the Opera, where just about everything was allowed, and where the enthusiastic support of the Emperor contributed a great deal to the modernization of the venues, as well as of the lyric genre itself.

On the other stages, the predominant atmosphere was one of fear, both of the implacable censorship and of losing the little ground that had been conquered since the revolutionary days. As early as 1804, a daring article published in the *Mercure* encouraged young writers to create plays inspired by national history. This article explains the enormous success of the *Templiers* (*The Templars*), by Raynouard, performed in 1805. The author used French history directly and moved spectators to tears with his pathetic and eloquent description of the fate of the brave and woeful knights. And Sébastien Mercier took up the challenge once again, this time with a series of anti-classical and pro-German satires.[10] The most innovative play of those years was undoubtedly Lemercier's *Christophe Colomb*, which premiered in 1809. The appearance onstage of a ship, a complete violation of the rule of unity of place, and the modernity of the subject, at a time when neoclassicism and David were the only accepted authorities in art, caused such a scandal that at the end of the first performance the theater had to be evacuated by the national guards. In the midst of this controversy, Lemercier obviously lost public favor and, of course, the favor of the Emperor himself who had supported him until then. The same controversy followed by a prohibition happened once again again one year later (1810) with Raynouard's *Les Etats de Blois* (*The Estates at Blois*), in which the author proved himself a good historian and poet but dared praise the Bourbons a trifle too much, while denouncing the revolutionaries.

Let us conclude this chapter (1789—1814) of the history of French theater by saying that the modernization of structure and themes which had started full speed at the beginning of the Revolution did not go very far, and that by the end of the Napoleonic era a status quo was still apparent in things theatrical. Maurice Albert defines this period correctly when he says that it produced plays that were historically interesting, in that they were a perfect mirror of public opinion and of the people's state of mind.[11]

The sad state of affairs in French theater was one of the first things noticed by all those, visitors or *émigrés*, who returned to France with the Bourbons. The visitors limited themselves to criticizing French plays, especially the still much respected classical repertory. Thus, the sarcastic Lady Morgan wrote that French tragedies were nothing but copies of the medieval mystery plays and of Greek and Roman history and theater, whose uninteresting facts and poetic restrictions they shared in full.[12] The émigrés, all French, began working at once on modernization; Madame de Stäel, timidly, and Sismondi, forcefully, recommended that young playwrights follow the example of foreigners, namely the Germans. The debate between conservatives/classicists and innovators/romanticists (the word *romanticism* was being used for the first time) grew in passion on a daily basis.

Analyzing Racine and Calderon, for example, the viscount de Saint Chamand wanted to prove at all costs the superiority of the French, whose discreet, introverted depiction of suffering could not be compared with the "undignified," extroverted Spanish style. The viscount concluded that the price to pay for the few beauties found in Calderon was too dear.[13] On the other hand, Chénier, the same author of the above-mentioned *Charles IX* (1789), who had started the literary revolt, declared eloquently that France was in dire need of authors with a profound knowledge and sense of history, politics and morals, and who were strongly against prejudices of any kind and willing to serve uncompromisingly the cause of liberty.

The results of this kind of strong harangue was felt almost immediately, with the general acceptance of the so-called historic tragedy or drama, a genre that had been in the making since the early days of the Revolution and took its definitive shape during the Restoration. It was this genre that would contribute most to the renovation of themes in French theater and greatly influence the masses in favor of romanticism, in its final battle against classicism. The year 1819 was particularly productive and interesting because of the innovations--moderate rather than revolutionary innovations--introduced by at least four remarkable plays peformed in succession: Lebrun's *Marie Stuart* (adapted from Schiller), Delavigne's *Les Vêpres siciliennes*, D'Avrigny's *Jeanne d'Arc*, and Ancelot's *Louis IX*. All four of them have in common the treatment of (new) romantic subjects in a style that still maintained many classical characteristics. (Lamartine would do the same a year later in his *Premières Méditations poétiques*). For all their moderation, these plays did indeed contribute to the cause of romanticism because their success meant that a first breach had finally been made in the formidable bastions of the Comédie-Française and the Odéon.

Yet another early blow to the classicists came in 1821, with the publication of the Guizot edition of the complete works of Shakespeare. In the preface, Guizot, who is just as opposed to the stagnant classical plays as to the chaotic melodrama still reigning on the boulevards, proclaims that only Shakespearean plays provided the right models for contemporary authors, and that the new theatrical system, though freed from traditional rules, would have its own strict laws, perhaps even stricter than those that supposedly prevented chaos and licentiousness.[14] The Guizot edition, the most serious one published to that date, gave the young playwrights better knowledge of the author who was to be their model and literary idol. It is true that it was still a bit early for the masses to accept Shakespeare, either because of their literary pride which still attached them strongly to classical plays, or because of their historical pride which was still bleeding from the Waterloo wounds. Thus, the scandalized reaction to Desdemona's handkerchief during the historical performance of *Othello* in 1822 that brought to an abrupt end the first appearances in Paris of a British touring company; at the drop of the curtain, the crowd screamed mercilessly: "Down with Shakespeare! He's a lieutenant of Wellington! . . . Down with the English! No foreigners in France!"[15]

The Shakespearean cause, synonymous with freedom, was not at all defeated by this failure. On the contrary, it encouraged the two factions of romanticists (liberals and royalists) to forget their differences momentarily and to unite their efforts in their common battle. At all levels, the blows against classicism were multiplied. Journals and magazines such as the *Mercure*, *Pandore*, and especially *Le Globe* published strong articles. On the Parisian stages, weak plays still inspired by the seventeenth century, such as Guiraud's *Macchabées* and Soumet's *Saül* and *Clytemnestre*, alternated with a series of new plays well worth mentioning: Ancelot's *Fiesque*, Pichat's *Léonidas*, and most importantly Lebrun's *Le Cid d'Andalousie* (1825). *Le Cid*, imitated from Lope de Vega, had the rare merit of being the first not to shock the audiences in its frequent transitions from tragic to less serious passages. One should not forget to mention those plays that were not meant to be produced on the stage, but that followed closely the romantic principles as recommended by Stendhal in the *Globe* and in his *Racine and Shakespeare* (1823 — 1825). To this category of new plays belong Prosper Mérimée's *Théâtre de Clara Gazul*, Rémusat's *Les Rénégats de Sainte-Domingue*, and Dittmer and Carre's *Soirées*.

Last but not least, there was a young poet at the beginning of his long and prolific career. The avant-garde skirmishes preceding the definitive battle are well known: the success of the second British touring company and Hugo's preface to *Cromwell* in 1827, the translations of Goethe's *Faust* by Nerval and of *Othello* by Vigny, and Delavigne's *Marino Faliero* and Dumas's *Henri III et sa cour*. On the eve of the battle of *Hernani*, the classicists used satire as a last resort to defend themselves against the inevitable final defeat, denouncing the vulgarity of the upcoming romantic plays. "The touching sufferings of Andromaque and the Cid / No longer inspire tears in the spectator; / He needs the scaffold, the executioner, torture; / That's what is called nature today."[16] By that time it was too late; at the sound of Hernani's horn the French proclaimed in February 1830 the advent of freedom--that is, the advent of a new genre proudly baptized as *drame romantique*.

All those who were seeking reforms in the name of reason during most of the eighteenth century did indeed enjoy some days of glory immediately after 1789. The throne and the altar were upset, and pushed by a forceful initial enthusiasm, the revolutionaries could hardly wait to begin building the new social and political edifice that would have for its foundation the principles of liberty, equality and fraternity. Alas, the ensuing nineteenth century proved that reform was easier to formulate in theory than to accomplish in practice. Despite the actual value of the principles themselves, despite the courage of the revolutionaries, and despite the full commitment of the followers of '89, the construction of a more just, more tolerant and more democratic new society turned out to be a long, arduous, and often frustrating task. Interestingly, the same can be said when referring to the history of French theater of the time. The efforts to reform it started timidly in the first part of the eighteenth century, became violent during the Revolution, and did not come to fruition until well into the nineteenth century. In a word, the theatrical revolution in France had its own precursors, martyrs and disciples, all of whom were conscious or unconscious contributors to the triumph of modernity and liberty in 1830.

It would be unfair to attribute the victory of the Revolution in French theater (and in French literature in general, for that matter) exclusively to the writers of the 1820s. Whatever the weaknesses of the French plays produced on the eve, during, and immediately after the Revolution, it must be said that the awareness of the need for reform was indeed there, and that the authors who were trying to introduce reform did so at the risk of being booed, persecuted, and even tried and sentenced in courts of justice. The delay in the acceptance of the ideas originally introduced by Voltaire, Mercier and others proves once again that in the field of aesthetics, just as in politics, the application of revolutionary principles, whatever their urgency, is achieved only after a long and persevering struggle, at the end of which a large majority is sincerely persuaded of the theoretical and operational value of these principles.

NOTES

All translations into English by author of this article.

1. Voltaire, *Oeuvres complètes*, Vol. 18 (Paris: Garnier, 1882), 58.

2. Charles Jean-François Hénault, *François II* (Paris: N/N, 1747).

3. Sébastien Mercier, *De la littérature et des littérateurs* (Paris: Yverdon, 1778), 22-24.

4. Maurice Albert, *La littérature française sous la Révolution, l'Empire et la Restauration* (1789—1830) (Paris: Lecène and Oudin, 1891), 334.

5. Marie-Joseph Chénier, *Fénelon ou les religieuses de Cambrai* (Paris: Moutard, 1793), XI.

6. Ibid. (Editor's translation)
   Nous avons oublié la nature et ses loix
   Les cris des préjugés ont fait taire sa voix.
   Cherchant la vérité sous le voile des fables,
   Conduits à la vertu par des routes aimables,
   Puissent nos successeurs un jour plus éclairés,
   Dissiper les erreurs qui nous ont égarés,
   . . . .
   Télémaque instruira leur jeunesse docile
   . . . .
   Là de l'humanité je plaiderai la cause. (III, 2)

7. *Le Journal des Spectacles*, year II of the Republic, Wednesday, November 11, 1793, (editor's translation). ("Il faut que tout ce qui nous environne prenne le caractère mâle et sévère du républicanisme. . . . Les Français se sont élevés au-dessus de toutes les nations modernes par leur littérature, et surtout par leurs pièces dramatiques. Conservons cette supériorité. La Révolution est un nouveau ressort.")

8. Charles Nodier, *Mélanges de littérature et de critique*, 2 vols., Vol. 2 (Paris: Raymond, 1820), 330.

9. Barre, Radet et Desfontaines, *Chapelain ou la ligue des auteurs contre Boileau* (Paris: Masson, 1804), 22.

10. Sébastien Mercier, *Satires contre Racine et Boileau* (Paris: Hénée, 1808), 20.

11. Albert, 59, (editor's translation). ("pièces historiquement très curieuses parce qu'elles reflètent avec fidelité l'opinion publique et l'état des esprits.")

12. Lady Morgan, *La France*, 2 vols., Vol. 2 (Paris: Treuttel, 1817), 139.

13. Vicomte de Saint Chamand, *L'anti-romantique ou examen de quelques ouvrages nouveaux* (Paris: Le Normant, 1816), 215 (editor's translation).

("les beautés sont trop chèrement payées par les sottises où elles sont
enchâssées.")

14.   *Oeuvres complètes de Shakespeare précédées d'une notice
biographique et littéraire sur Shakespeare par F. Guizot*, 13 vols., Vol 1
(Paris: Ladvocat, 1821), cli-clii (editor's translation). (le nouveau système
dramatique s'établira "comme la liberté, non sur le désordre et l'oubli de tout
frein, mais sur des règles plus sévères et d'une observation plus difficile peut-
être que celles qu'on réclame encore pour maintenir ce qu'on appelle l'ordre
contre ce qu'on appelle la licence.")

15.   J. L. Borgerhoff, *Le théâtre anglais à Paris sous la Restauration*
(Paris: Hachette, 1912), 14 (editor's translation).   ("A bas Shakespeare!
C'est un lieutenant de Wellington! . . . A bas les Anglais!   Pas d'étrangers
en France!")

16.   Baron d'Ordre, *Les classiques et les romantiques* (Paris: Chez les
marchands de nouveautés, 1829), 6 (editor's translation).   ("D'Andromaque
et du Cid les touchantes douleurs /Au parterre blasé n'arrachent plus de
pleurs;/Il lui faut le gibet, le bourreau, la torture;/Voilà ce qu'on appelle
aujourd'hui la nature.")

11

Rewriting the Revolutionary Past in *Les Prussiens en Lorraine*

Barbara T. Cooper

Moments of civil strife seem to have held a particular fascination for nineteenth-century French dramatists eager to portray their nation's past. In the early decades of the century, at a time when direct reference to the Revolution of 1789 was frequently cause for censorship, dramatists chose the "safer"--because more distant--Hundred Years War and the religious wars of the sixteenth century as the setting for their representations of the internal dissensions that were inevitably linked to questions of national identity. Gradually, however, within the ideological limits defined by successive nineteenth-century political regimes, the Revolution made its appearance on Parisian stages.[1]

When it premiered at the Théâtre de la Gaîté in Paris in March 1840, Gustave Lemoine's and Prosper-Parfait Goubaux's *Les Prussiens en Lorraine, ou l'Honneur d'une mère* was by no means the first work whose historical and geographical backdrop unequivocally recalled the French Revolution.[2] On the contrary, if the representation of "la patrie en danger" (the fatherland in danger) was not already a *topos* almost as familiar as the Vendean Wars, it would soon become so.

The act-long prologue to the play is set in an isolated castle at the edge of the Ardennes forest. It is early September 1792 and the city of Verdun has just fallen into the hands of Prussian soldiers allied with royalist forces seeking to put an end to the Revolution. The remaining three acts of the piece take place in 1813, in Prussia, where a regiment of French troops, advancing ahead of the Grande Armée, has temporarily set up headquarters in an isolated castle. The deliberate opposition of these temporally and physically defined landscapes suggests that they constitute what Pierre Nora has called "des lieux de mémoire," that is, the sites around which collective memories crystallize or at which they are stored (xvii). Memories, however, like dramas, are notorious for their distortion of the past, and thus we need to examine *Les Prussiens en Lorraine* to discover how it represents the Revolution and its meaning to the audience.

We can perhaps be helped in this endeavor if we consider Claude-Joseph Rouget de Lisle's "La Marseillaise" as an intertext.[3] Composed in April 1792 as a "War Song for the Army of the Rhine," the "Marseillaise" was written in response to the same military invasion we find dramatized in the prologue of *Les Prussiens*. Indeed, with its Manichaean characters and its didactic purpose, Rouget de Lisle's hymn is in many ways already a melodramatic text. The juxtaposition of this revolutionary anthem and Lemoine's and Goubaux's play ought to, therefore, help us determine how, if at all, the representation and the significance of an historical event change over time. Enhanced by a myriad of pathos-inspiring details, the prologue of *Les Prussiens* closely parallels the situation described in the first stanza of the "Marseillaise." In the opening bars of Rouget de Lisle's song, the citizens of the French Republic are called to arms to defend their country against the bloodthirsty forces of tyranny massing on France's eastern border. The "ferocious soldiers" whose voices echo across the countryside are said to be coming "into your midst,/To slit the throats of your sons, your wives." Similar characters and events are depicted in the prologue of Lemoine's and Goubaux's play. Upon learning that Prussian troops are advancing through his district, Georges de Malsanne, a liberal nobleman who is a representative to the Legislative Assembly, seeks to organize area peasants into a militia that will fight to safeguard their homes and families. Meanwhile, a detachment of Prussian soldiers known as "the hussars of death" is being led into the nearby village of les Islettes by a red-headed officer referred to only as "Le Tueur" (the Killer). After one soldier drowns a six-year-old boy in a well for trying to retrieve the blanket ripped from his sick, elderly grandmother's shoulders, a group of Prussians seeks sanctuary in the village church. Local peasants, eager to avenge the boy's death, quickly surround the church. Rejecting even this most legitimate act of popular violence, Malsanne will not hear of the Prussian prisoners being massacred by Frenchmen.[4] "That would be imitating the barbarity of the foreigners" (prologue, 5, 5), he claims. He leaves his wife Constance, his six-year-old son Ernest, Constance's wet-nurse la mère Séraphin, and her son Antoine alone in his isolated castle while he goes off to les Islettes to prevent his fellow countrymen from committing an atrocity. In his absence, "Le Tueur" and those of his henchmen responsible for the most heinous crimes perpetrated in les Islettes enter the castle where they drink themselves into a brutal fury. They beat and later kill la mère Séraphin as Antoine, who has been tied to a hitching post, watches with helpless rage. Constance is raped (out of sight of the audience) by "Le Tueur" who, upon learning that she is the wife of a representative, decides to carry her off and burn the castle. As she is dragged away, Constance cries to the shackled Antoine to save Ernest whom she had hidden away in a secret room in a castle wall now menaced by fire.

    The play, with its attribution of the horrors of rape, pillage and murder to counterrevolutionary forces, perpetuates, in slightly varied form, a theme already present in Rouget de Lisle's celebrated song. What both the "Marseillaise" and the prologue of *Les Prussiens* share is an ideologically inflected version of the myth of the barbarian. As Pierre Michel observed in his book *Les Barbares, 1789—1848: un mythe romantique*, the French Revolution marked an important turning point in the evolution and meaning of the myth of the barbarian. For partisans of the Revolution, the Frankish invasion of Gaul was cast in a new light (28ff). The Franks came to represent the aristocracy and its foreign allies who, by dint of might rather than right, subjugated the Gauls (the people, the Third Estate) and deprived them of their native liberty.[5] The second stanza of the "Marseillaise" reflects this politicized version of French history when it proclaims: "Frenchmen for us, ah!, what an outrage;/What transports it ought to stir up./It is we whom they dare contemplate/Returning to our *ancient state of slavery*" (emphasis added). *Les Prussiens* similarly portrays the opponents of the Revolution as barbarian invaders. Unlike the song, however, the play presents the image of a national community united under the paternal direction of liberal aristocrats in the fight against those alien forces menacing family, property and liberty.[6] Such a scenario brings to mind a vision of the Revolution once held by men like La Fayette and Philippe d'Orléans, and no doubt served to sustain the fiction that the July Monarchy was in some way the legitimate heir to the Revolution. What is more, the erasure of any French presence on the side of tyranny meant that the barbarian was completely "other." He might, therefore, be portrayed as cruel, vicious and destructive without enflaming political divisions and class hatred in Louis-Philippe's France.

Nonetheless, the image of the barbarian is, as Pierre Michel (23) reminds us, but one part of a dialectic. It has as its counterpart the representation of a civilized individual. This antithesis is evident in the third stanza of the "Marseillaise" where proud French warriors are set in opposition to those foreign cohorts and mercenary phalanxes who serve the cause of despotism, and again in the fifth stanza where the French are enjoined to behave more humanely than their enemies: "Frenchmen, as magnanimous warriors,/Strike or withhold your blows;/Spare those poor victims,/Who reluctantly arm themselves against us." Similarly, in the prologue of Lemoine's and Goubaux's play, when Georges de Malsanne learns of the villager's intention to massacre the Prussians who have taken refuge in the church in les Islettes, he is determined to prevent his fellow countrymen from imitating the barbaric, lawless actions of the invaders. "No, no," he exclaims; "let the horrors of war be his [the foreigner's]! let the shame of massacres and calculated cruelties be his!" Despite the potential dangers and the lateness of the hour, Malsanne will not postpone his departure. To his way of thinking, "It is never too late to spare the unfortunate and to save Frenchmen from committing a crime" (both quotes, prologue, 5, 5). His words, like those of the "Marseillaise," suggest that partisans of the Revolution must adhere to a higher standard of behavior than that practiced by their opponents, a standard marked by justice and compassion.[7]

Civic virtue does not preclude family sentiment, however. On the contrary, as both the "Marseillaise" and *Les Prussiens* make clear, for civilized individuals, devotion to one's family and service to one's country are inextricably intertwined. In stanza one of the "Marseillaise," for example, it is as "*children* of the Fatherland" (emphasis added) that Frenchmen are called upon to defend their loved ones and their liberty. In the prologue to *Les*

Prussiens, the connection between family and country is affirmed in a slightly different manner, but nonetheless maintained. Thus, before leaving for les Islettes, Georges de Malsanne comforts his wife by telling her:

Are you not both in my thoughts every day, every instant? (He picks up his son). Dear child! . . . (He embraces him). If I am proud to represent my fellow citizens, it is for him . . . it is so that one day our peasants may say when they see him: look, there is the son of the man who once defended our fields and our liberty, the man who fought back the invasion with us, in our ranks! . . . It is so that one day the memory of his father may protect the head of my child (prologue, 6, 6).

His words suggest that public service guarantees security both for one's community and for one's family, that defense of the nation's general interests (land, liberty) safeguards one's personal interests (reputation, safety) as well. What is especially important about Malsanne's remarks is that they appear to locate the source of individual prestige in a new quarter. As Malsanne sees it, in the future, status will derive from recent actions rather than from ancient rights.

To this point, Lemoine's and Goubaux's play has presented the public with a vision of the French Revolution articulated around the well-defined, well-worn antithesis of the barbarian versus the civilized individual. In contrast to the "Marseillaise" where that dialectic was exploited in terms of pro-Revolutionary versus counterrevolutionary sentiments, the prologue to *Les Prussiens* has defined the conflict as a Franco-Prussian confrontation and thus has transformed partisan virtues into national ones. The twenty years separating the action depicted in the prologue from that described in the remaining acts of the play further underscore that transformation by insisting on the permanence of certain characteristics across time and space.[8]

Act one of *Les Prussiens* again rehearses the barbarian-civilized dialectic enunciated in the prologue, but this time the audience's attention is focused on the count de Rutner, a Prussian nobleman previously introduced as "Le Tueur."[9] More than a mere restatement of Prussian barbarity, the depiction of Rutner's uncivilized behavior in Act One emphasizes the enduring nature of his shameful conduct and extends it from a foreign to a domestic space and from the public to the private sphere. Though never explicitly evoked, the example of the now-deceased Georges de Malsanne inevitably presents itself as a positive antithesis to Rutner's barbaric behavior. Thus, whereas Malsanne served the national interest in Lorraine in 1792 (Cf. prologue, 3, 3: ". . . have I not been sent by the Assembly to organize all the means of defense in this region?"), Rutner serves his own self-interest in the hostilities that pit France against Prussia in 1813 (Cf. 1, 2, 13: "Ah! you refuse my services, ungrateful government! Well then! I will wage war on my own account, and you'll still hear tell of the old lion.") He promotes rather than prevents popular violence by organizing disgruntled ex-soldiers into a guerrilla movement ready to combat the invading French army. What is more, in contrast to the magnanimous attitude Malsanne adopted vis-à-vis the Prussian prisoners in les Islettes some twenty years before, Rutner firmly believes that "the bravest man is one who does the greatest harm to his enemy" (1, 3, 13). Finally, Rutner is repeatedly portrayed as an unfeeling, uncaring husband and father. Ready to leave his castle to fight the French, Rutner refuses to waste any time saying good-bye to his wife and daughters (1, 4, 13). Malsanne, on the other hand, did not hesitate to comfort his wife and embrace his child before leaving his castle to save Prussian lives (see quote from prologue, 6, 6 cited above).

If Act One makes the point that Rutner's barbarity has persisted across time and space, it also affirms the permanence of French virtues. Thus, although Malsanne is long dead, his generosity and compassion are presented as national characteristics that are now embodied in the next generation. (Cf. "the children's stanza," a stanza added to the "Marseillaise" in October 1792: "We will enter the ranks,/When our elders are no longer there./We will find their path/And the traces of their virtues").[10] Twenty-seven-year-old Colonel Ernest Sirmet, a graduate of the military academy who has served his country for the past eleven years, is a perfect example of those who carry on in the place of men like Malsanne. Described by one of his subordinates as "a good-hearted man with one of the most noble personalities in the army; but an orphan since childhood" (1, 12, 18), he is, I believe, meant to be perceived by the audience as a "child of the Fatherland" whose status derives from his actions and whose qualities are those of all Frenchmen.[11]

Leader of a detachment of French hussars advancing through Prussia ahead of the Grande Armée, Sirmet insists that his troops behave in an exemplary manner. He announces that he will punish any acts of vandalism in the nearby village or in the count de Rutner's castle which he has taken over for his headquarters (1, 11, 18). In contrast to the Prussian solder who, twenty years before, had stolen an ailing grandmother's blanket in les Islettes, Sirmet surrounds with kindness and attention the blind and impoverished Madame Marguerite whom he encounters in Rutner's castle. (The screen Sirmet places behind the chair he has set in front of the fireplace for her may be read as a functional equivalent of the blanket since it both envelops and helps to warm Marguerite [1, 16, 19].) Instead of brutalizing the women and servants left alone in the castle, the French treat them with courtesy and respect. Thus, after having attended to some urgent business, the colonel's first words to Madame de Rutner and her daughters are: "Please forgive me, ladies, if my duty has made me delay for even an instant paying you my respects" (1, 12, 18). The true extent of Sirmet's virtues has not been measured, however, because his concern for national honor has yet to come into conflict with his personal sentiments. It will be the purpose of Acts Two and Three to test Sirmet's character and to show how he responds to the apparent contest between his filial and his patriotic duty.

Initially, it is the behavior of Séraphin (Antoine), Sirmet's sergeant and surrogate father, that brings matters to a head. Although he has always behaved in a generous, civilized manner in other countries where the Grande Armée has triumphed, in Prussia Séraphin plunders and commits acts of brutality. Even when Sirmet threatens to withhold a recommendation for a

medal and a promotion the sergeant otherwise deserves, Séraphin is unrepen-
tant. He explains that his actions are intended to exact vengeance for his
mother's death at the hands of Prussian soldiers and that he is indifferent to
their personal cost. Torn between his affection for his surrogate father and his
sense of national honor, Sirmet concludes that he must transfer Séraphin to a
unit in Germany so that he will not have to witness or punish the sergeant's
barbaric behavior.

Later that day, as he passes through the Rutner family portrait gallery,
Séraphin identifies the count, whom he has not seen in person in the castle,
as "Le Tueur." This discovery allows the sergeant to deliver the letter
Sirmet's father, Georges de Malsanne, had written to the young man on his
deathbed twenty years earlier. From the letter, the colonel learns of his
mother's rape and kidnapping and of his father's wish that he avenge her
honor. This knowledge, coupled with Rutner's continued misdeeds, temporarily transforms Sirmet into a hard-hearted, vengeful individual, insensitive
to appeals for clemency on the villain's behalf. In the end, however, even
though the colonel has the power and Napoleon's permission to exact
vengeance, he is touched by the appeals from both Rutner's family and
Madame Marguerite, and he rescinds the count's death sentence. Sirmet's
wish that his mother forgive him for failing to punish her persecutor is
immediately granted as Madame Marguerite, recognizing herself in the
colonel's story about his mother, embraces her child. Moments later,
providence (and melodramatic convention) intervene and Rutner dies in an
explosion he sets off in the castle to kill its French occupants. Thus,
national honor is preserved and familial honor restored without French hands
having been sullied by blood.

Indeed, the message of the play seems to be that personal vengeance is
contemptible and barbaric. The villagers surrounding the church in les
Islettes, Rutner, and Séraphin are all motivated by a desire for familial
vengeance to commit acts of violence, and all are chastised or condemned by
those characters in the play who represent the nation (Georges de Malsanne
and Sirmet) for their actual or intended misdeeds. Even Sirmet's reunion with
his mother, that is, with the one person who alone can give meaning to the
acts he performs on behalf of his country (cf. 1, 15, 19), depends for its
occurrence on his renunciation of violence.[12]

But if *Les Prussiens* communicates the message that compassion and
justice are rewarded, it also suggests--in contrast to the "Marseillaise"--that
these virtues are specifically and permanently French. Thus, the opposition
the play establishes between the barbaric foreigner and the civilized
Frenchman not only defines the national character, but also creates an image
ripe for political exploitation in an age of nationalism. Written at a time when
the Belgian question and the crisis in the Orient brought back into focus not
only the matter of France's natural border (the Rhine), but also the importance
of its place among European power brokers, *Les Prussiens* would be revived
again in 1870, in the context of the Franco-Prussian War.[13] The portrait it
paints of the Prussian as a barbarian who rapes, pillages and murders would

be repeated in a myriad of caricatures published in the newspapers of that time and would, as Ouriel·Reshef has shown in *Guerre, mythes et caricature*, shape the mentality of the generation that fought in World War I.

Transformed from a divisive civil war into a unifying moment in the nation's history, the Revolution as presented in *Les Prussiens* did not inspire fear in the hearts of the government's theater censors who reviewed the manuscript of the play in December 1839 (AN F 21 977). This is not surprising when we consider that Lemoine's and Goubaux's piece (1) shows the various classes united to repulse a barbaric, foreign enemy rather than fighting among themselves, (2) accords a leadership role in the battle to the most enlightened elements of society (i.e., liberal aristocrats and bourgeois), and (3) espouses moderation and compassion as virtues and adopts them as national characteristics. Such a tableau is surely a falsification of history, but it is a falsification that tells us much about the political climate in France in 1840. As an example of the way history was used for propogandistic purposes during the July Monarchy, *Les Prussiens en Lorraine* deserves to be set beside Louis Festeau's conciliatory "Marseillaise de 1840" (see Robert 1981: 73-74), Nicolas-Toussaint Charlet's controversial prints (see Driskel), and the paintings depicting the events of the period from 1789 to 1815 which Louis-Philippe had commissioned and hung at Versailles (see Marrinan 1988, especially Parts III and IV). When sandwiched between those contemporary works and Rouget de Lisle's "Marseillaise," its ideological inflections become especially clear.

NOTES

1. For background on the censorship of works representing the Revolution, see Krakovitch (1989). I wish to thank Mme. Krakovitch for sending me the manuscript of this talk which she presented at a conference in Paris in October 1989. All translations in this study are my own.

2. The play, variously described as a melodrama in four acts or with a prologue and three acts, had a total of thirty-one performances over a period of two months. It was also printed and performed in Lisbon and Madrid in the mid-1840s. For biographical background concerning Lemoine, see Larousse, Vol. 10, 354. Regarding Goubaux, see Larousse, Vol. 8, 1386 and Legouvé, "Notice biographique." For the tendency, common during the July Monarchy and reflected in the chronology of this play, to view the Revolution as extending through the period of the First Empire, see the headdress of the figure of the Revolution in François Rude's "The Departure of the Volunteers," a.k.a. "La Marseillaise" (1835—1836), on the Arc de Triomphe (Agulhon, 44-48). Debate as to whether the Empire continues or marks the end of the Revolution persists even today. Cf. the recent special issue of *L'Histoire*, "Napoléon: Révolution ou Dictature?"

3. I wish to note here that Goubaux's short story "Souvenirs des invasions"

(dated August 1839) is the actual source of the plot and that neither the drama critics nor the government's official theater censors mention any similarity at all between play and song. The "Marseillaise" was officially banned at the time of the play's composition and production. It resurfaced briefly, with government authorization, in July 1840 as part of the protest against the treaty signed by the Allied powers regarding the Orient. Two of the best recent histories of the "Marseillaise" are those written by Vovelle and Luxardo.

4. This rejection of popular violence and bloodshed, even in the name of legitimate vengeance, is typical of the way in which the representation of the Revolution is frequently distorted in nineteenth-century dramas.   It constitutes a departure from the fervent call heard in the refrain of the "Marseillaise": "Let [their] impure blood water our furrows."

5. The introduction of the gallic cock as a symbol of the nation also dates from this period, as do the images painted on pieces of earthenware (*faïence*) of a cock astride a canon with the slogan "I stand watch for the nation/for liberty." For the antirevolutionary forces, the barbarians were the people, a bloodthirsty group of lower class individuals and their allies, who were destroying the centuries-old civilization of France in their attempt to achieve a new world order. While disagreeing over the precise identity of the barbarian, both the prorevolutionary and the counterrevolutionary groups appear to have settled on a common set of "barbarian" characteristics, one of which is red hair.

6.   The anonymous voice that issues the orders found in the "Marseillaise"--"allons," "formez," "marchez"--becomes that of the liberal aristocrat Georges de Malsanne in the play.

7.   Once de Malsanne has left for les Islettes, Antoine judges his master's actions as follows (prologue, 9, 6): "By God, you have to admit that the master is a brave man; deliberately going out of his way, at night, for a bunch of Prussians; not to mention the fact that there's a fierce storm brewing; you talk about your citizens, well there's a daring one for you!"

8. Ernest Legouvé attributes the following statement to Goubaux in the "Biographical Note" he wrote to his friend's *Nouvelles*: "A child in the first act, an old man in the last! That's where the interest lies, in the changes the march of time brings to all things human, to fortune, to character, to appearance, even to the soul . . . in the gradual and almost inevitable development of good or bad sentiments" (unnumbered page vi).

9. McCormick notes the basic melodrama formula Bouchardy used in the plays he wrote for the Gaîté (40-42). Many of the same conventions, including use of a prologue and character name changes, are at work in *Les*

Prussiens. Name changes here create suspense and postpone the dénouement. Rutner's identity as Le Tueur is revealed to the audience in Act One, but Antoine/Séraphin, Ernest/Colonel Sirmet, and Constance de Malsanne/ Madame Marguerite do not discover it until late in Act Two. Similarly, Ernest and Antoine are kept from discovering their relationship to Constance/Marguerite until the final moments of the play.

10. For information on and reaction to Louis-Philippe's declamation of this stanza at ceremonies at Saint-Cyr in 1837, cf. *La Gazette de France*.

11. Sirmet is in fact the child of Georges and Constance de Malsanne. He has only vague memories of his mother whom he believes to be dead. Sirmet clearly does know who his father was. The young man's change of name from the aristocratic de Malsanne to the bourgeois Sirmet is, in my view, a way of showing the democratization of his father's "noble" qualities.

12. Contrast this with the "Marseillaise" where those Frenchmen who serve the cause of despotism are described as "Those tigers who, without pity/Tear open their mother's [i.e., their country's] breast."

13. See Krakovitch, *Hugo censuré* (242), for information on the revival of *Les Prussiens*. Its reprise coincides with the publication of such novelistic representations of the 1792 invasion of eastern France as Erckmann and Chatrian's *Histoire d'un paysan (1789—1815)*, first published in 1868—1870 and Alexandre Dumas père's *La Terreur prussienne* (1868).

REFERENCES

Agulhon, Maurice. *Marianne into Battle. Republican Imagery and Symbolism in France, 1789—1880*. Trans. Janet Lloyd. Cambridge: Cambridge University Press; Paris: Eds. de la Maison des Sciences de l'Homme, 1981.

Archives Nationales, Paris. F 21 977. [Théâtre de la Gaîté, December 1839: Ms. of Censor's Report on *Les Prussiens en Lorraine*.]

Driskel, Michael Paul. "Singing 'The Marseillaise' in 1840: The Case of Charlet's Censored Prints." *Arts Bulletin* 69, No. 4 (1987): 603-624.

Dumas, Alexandre. *La Terreur prussienne*. Paris: Michel Lévy, 1868.

Erckmann, Emile, and Alexandre Chatrian. *Histoire d'un paysan (1789—1815)*. 2 vols. Paris: J. J. Pauvert-Serpenoise-Tallandier, 1987.

Goubaux, Prosper-Parfait. *Nouvelles*. Paris: impr. de Napoléon Chaix, 1861.

Krakovitch, Odile. *Hugo censuré: La Liberté au théâtre au XIXe siècle*. Paris: Calmann-Lévy, 1985.

-----. "La Révolution vue par le théâtre parisien de 1815 à 1870 et sa répression." Paper presented in October 1989, Paris, France, at the conference on "La Révolution française et le XIXe siècle" sponsored by the Société d'histoire de la révolution de 1848 et des révolutions du XIXe siècle.

Larousse, Pierre. *Grand Dictionnaire universel du XIXe siècle.* 17 vols. Paris: Larousse & Boyer; Admn. du Grand Dictionnaire, 1866—1878.

Legouvé, Ernest. "Notice biographique." P. P. Goubaux, *Nouvelles.* Paris: impr. de Napoléon Chaix, 1861. N pag.

Lemoine, Gustave [and Prosper-Parfait Goubaux]. *Les Prussiens en Lorraine, ou l'Honneur d'une mère.* "Le Magasin théâtral." [Paris: Marchant, 1840.]

Luxardo, Hervé. *Histoire de la "Marseillaise."* Paris: Plon, 1989.

Marrinan, Michael. *Painting Politics for Louis-Philippe: Art and Ideology in Orléanist France, 1830—1848.* New Haven, Conn. and London: Yale University Press, 1988.

McCormick, John. "Joseph Bouchardy: A Melodramatist and His Public," *Performance and Politics in Popular Drama: Aspects of Popular Entertainment in Theatre, Film and Television, 1800—1976.* Eds. David Bradby, Louis James, and Bernard Sharrat. Cambridge: Cambridge University Press, 1980, 33-48.

Michel, Pierre. *Les Barbares: 1789—1848, un mythe romantique.* Lyon: Presses universitaires de Lyon, 1981.

"Napoléon: Révolution ou dictature?" Special issue, *L'Histoire* 124 (1989).

Nora, Pierre. "Entre mémoire et histoire. La Problématique des lieux." *Les Lieux de mémoire: La République,* Vol. 1. Ed. Pierre Nora. Paris: Gallimard, 1984, xvii-xlii.

Reshef, Ouriel. *Guerre, mythes et caricature.* Paris: Presses de la Fondation Nationale des Sciences Politiques, 1984.

Robert, Frédéric. "Genèse et destin de 'la Marseillaise'." *La Pensée* 221-222 (1981), 72-85.

"Souvenir de 92--La Marseillaise." *La Gazette de France* 14 (June 1837), 1.

Vovelle, Michel. "La Marseillaise: La Guerre ou la paix." *Les Lieux de mémoire: La République,* Vol. 1 Ed. Pierre Nora. Paris: Gallimard, 1984, 85-186.

12

Prosper Mérimée Is Thinking the Revolution

Evlyn Gould

During the first half of the nineteenth century in France, thinking about the Revolution of 1789 produced a new kind of historical consciousness. Historians responded to the demands of a new discipline called "history" by endeavoring to recount the facts and events of the Revolution. Writers of realist fiction responded to the discovery that social reality is essentially historical by attempting to represent the lingering effects of the Revolution on modern life.[1] Both relied on the supposition that history is essentially genetic or evolutionary--that is, that the study of the past may explain the contradictions of the present--and both had recourse to narrative discourse to sketch out this new program for historical consciousness (Jameson 1988, 2: 154-156). One direct impact of the Revolution on both nineteenth-century historiography and realist literature can thus be seen in their common desire to think the Revolution.

In his *Metahistory*, Hayden White explains that the new historiography defined itself in opposition to the literary or, more specifically, to the rhetorical, by purporting to follow a factual and literal "historical method" (White 1973: 41-42, n.7). Although writers of realist fiction would, in some sense, develop their own kinds of historical methods, they also appeared to be troubled by this new discipline that both echoed their goals and excluded their participation. As a result, many writers came to mount what might be called a tacit attack on historical narrative by turning their attentions to the deficiencies of a historical method and by elucidating the problematic status of historical consciousness itself.[2] In other words, a certain trend in nineteenth-century realist fiction can be read as possessing the theoretical stance that Fredric Jameson (1988) refers to as "existential history," the experience by which historicity itself may be conceived as a relativized contact between a historian's mind and the cultural objects that mind chooses to study. In taking up this stance, much realist fiction not only dramatizes the difficulties inherent in writing a history of the effects of the Revolution, but it also suggests that thinking about revolutions now past may actually program new modes of revolutionary thought and, in this way, produce new revolutionary futures.[3]

Prosper Mérimée's *Carmen* is one of these realist fictions insofar as it renders the relationship of history and literature problematic by questioning the "objective truth" of the historical method and by deconstructing the ways in which the manipulation of narrative may surreptitiously produce mixed ideological messages. Mérimée accomplishes this critical perspective by openly distinguishing between the story of *Carmen* and the narrative of *Carmen*. The "Carmen story" itself recounts a tale of desire and of human degradation concerned primarily with the nefarious effects of Bohemian life on the moral fabric of modern society. Insofar as Bohemia is synonymous, during the nineteenth century, with revolutionary spirit, this message emphasizes the persistently destructive influence of the revolutionary ideals of 1789 on the increasingly unstable contours of a contradictory present. It also promulgates a return to order.

The formal contours of Mérimée's narrative, however, propose a very different message. When studied in relation to the historian-subject who narrates, the formal play of the narrative may be more accurately conceived of as a treatise on historical consciousness that dramatizes the ways in which the integrity of that very consciousness may be unconsciously revolutionized by the destructive forces it seeks to control. That is, the formal disposition of Carmen's narrative offers an existential history that maps out the difficulties inherent both to circumscribing an object of historical research and to restraining the speaking subject of historical discourse. From this perspective, *Carmen* echoes Jerrold Seigle's definition of Bohemia as an ambiguous cultural phenomenon associated both with revolutionary spirit and with a reinforcement of bourgeois values (Seigle 1986: 7-11). On one hand, *Carmen's* formal contours work to maintain the status quo by following certain rhetorical rules designed to ensure the veracity and objectivity of historical discourse (a kind of formal return to order). At the same time, however, these same contours also disrupt the status quo by unmasking the ideological presuppositions that sustain that discourse (a kind of formal revolution or, what I call, an "aesthetic anarchy").

To understand fully the ambivalent revolutionary force of the formal contours of Mérimée's novella, it must be read as an exploration of the aesthetic problems confronted by the writer of history, that writer who sets out to relate objective, impersonal facts about the past but whose objectivity is undermined by personal fascinations and choices about chronology, value, point of view, and identity. The narrative voice that introduces *Carmen* is that of a historian whose study conforms to what White (1973: 5-42) identifies as the rhetorical rules or transformative discursive operations that govern nineteenth-century historiography. Following a research phase, these rules include (1) the representation of events as having the order of a chronicle; (2) the "emplotment" of the events into a story with identifiable beginning, middle, and end phases; and finally, (3) the evaluation or interpretation of these emplotted events (White 1988: 12). Although White's work uncovers the pervasive and unconscious insistence of these rules in nineteenth-century historiography, I propose that Mérimée's *Carmen* consciously cultivates and calculates these same transformative operations. In this way, it works within the conventions of nineteenth-century historiography to reveal the limits of those very conventions, primarily the convention that presumes that historical narrative can be objective and devoid of political force if it adopts a particular rhetorical stance.

THE RESEARCH PHASE

At the opening of *Carmen*, the historian sets out to correct the geographical details of Caeser's last battle. As a historian depicted in the "research phase of his work," he is, to use White's words, "concerned to discover the truth about the past and to recover information either forgotten, suppressed, or obscured" (White 1988: 11). He begins *Carmen* with the following description of his intent:

I have always suspected geographers of not knowing what they are talking about when they place the battle field of Munda in the country of the Bastuli-Poeni, close to the modern Monda, approximately two leagues north of Marbella. . . . I thought it necesary to search the neighborhood of Montilla for that memorable spot where, for the last time, Ceasar played for double or nothing against the champions of the republic. Finding myself in Andalusia at the beginning of the autumn of 1830, I made a rather long excursion in order to shed light on the doubts that still remained.[4]

In this passage, doubts about the "official" history of the geographical location of Caesar's last battle center, somewhat ironically, on a simple language problem--the difference between an "o" and a "u" (Monda and Munda). The supposition is that the events of official history may well have been altered because of a mistranscription or mere typographical error. In this way, the unconscious slips of language in any writing or reading of history are already slated to play a determining role in this one.

Although the obscure historical detail may not be as provocative as the historian supposes, it becomes more interesting when considered in light of its association with the "autumn of 1830." Because of this date, marking a second French Revolution, Caesar's "double or nothing" triumph over the champions of one republic necessarily comments on the unwieldy establishment and subsequent demise of other, more recent republics. With the image of Caesar, our historian calls to mind Napoleon's rise to power in the waning days of the first troubled French Republic. And with the notion of a double or nothing gamble, he also evokes the duplicity of the conciliatory government of Louis-Phillipe's July Monarchy that also triumphed, double or nothing, over the modern champions of revolutionary change. Like Caesar's and Napoleon's reign, Louis-Phillipe's reign triumphed in a "double" or politically ambiguous manner by offering the republicans certain new privileges while, at the same time, squashing their revolutionary ideals.

Given this subtle suggestion that history repeats itself rather than progressing logically in a linear manner from cause to effect, this writer of

1845 may also be hoping to encourage new republican champions by subtly playing with the sense of an "autumn." To use the expression the "autumn of those years" ("the autumn of 1830") is to suggest a waning or dying out of revolutionary politics. In relation to a summer, however, this "autumn" also supposes a new beginning, a movement forward in time, and in relation to a summer monarchy, a new revolutionary call to arms. The double or nothing gamble thus confuses and enriches the historical object of research by pitting the present of the historian/writer in 1845 against a historical narrative that begins in the ambiguously suggestive "autumn" of 1830 by recalling the waning of the ideals of 1789 while, at the same time, looking forward to the Revolution of 1848. It thereby clues us into the writer's unspoken sense that any attempt to think about a revolution now past may both revise that past and produce repetitive futures.

This double or nothing gamble also epitomizes the duplicity of the narrative historian himself who quickly draws our attention to the fact that he is both a historian and a storyteller. On one hand, his research into the location of Caesar's last battle continues to fuel both his travels and his discourse, causing a productive series of chance encounters designed to assure both the objectivity of his "historical" point of view and the scholarly honesty of his chronicle. On the other hand, the object of the historian's research also takes a literary detour. He writes: "While waiting for my dissertation to resolve, once and for all, the geographical problem that holds all of scholarly Europe in suspense, I want to tell you a little story" (609). The irony of the historian's tone regarding the significance of his geographical problem displaces our attention away from official historical questions by asking us to concentrate, rather, on a "little story" or an unofficial history. Because this historian never does get back to the interesting question of Munda, we could say that the object of his research shifts away from the historical past toward a more literary present, suggesting that the desire to solve historical dilemmas may itself produce historical fictions. Moreover, this shifting away from the initial research does introduce the first transformative operation characteristic of historical discourse: the representation of events as having the order of a chronicle.

WRITING A CHRONICLE

The chronicle begins by describing an encounter with a noble stranger whom the historian refers to as "a traveler like myself, though a bit less of an archaeologist" (611). The fact that this historian sees the stranger as being a traveler like himself is an initial clue that the objectivity of his point of view is already in peril. Nonetheless, the historian proceeds to outline a new object of study. Because of his knowledge of Spanish culture, he quickly establishes a cultural fraternity with the stranger that allows a detailed study of the physiognomy and linguistic habits of his specimen. His cultivated distance from this new object of study is underscored through the use of explanatory footnotes: "The Andalusians breathe in their esses" (611), for example.

This scholarly objectivity is soon undermined, however, as the historian decides that, in this traveler, he recognizes the face of the infamous bandit, José-Maria.

With charmed delight, the historian dons the cloak of a bad detective, bad because this is not José-Maria. (Indeed, it is not until the opening of the third chapter that the bandit is identified as Don José de Navarre). Nonetheless, the interesting result of his misreading of the signs is a slip in assumptions and, therefore, in the factuality of his chronicle that recalls the suspected slip in vowels that got him started in the first place. An effort to rectify one error leads to the production of new ones. More importantly, the historian's search for forgotten facts is transformed into a game of potential truths as his concern for the past becomes a study of the present, and the values of his stuffy bourgeois sensibilities give way to a fascination with the more exciting values represented by this supposed Bohemian.

As he draws us into the "little story," ("But let *us* respect his incognito") (613, emphasis mine), the historian is seduced by his own idealized version of the stranger's identity. In fact, when the historian's guide decides to denounce the bandit in the hopes of securing a financial reward, the historian protectively alerts him to the forthcoming denunciation. This act in turn provokes a rationalization of his own motives, a kind of crisis of consciousness. He writes:

Had I not betrayed my guide who was upholding a lawful cause; had I not exposed him to the vengeance of a scoundrel? But the responsibilities of hospitality! . . . Prejudice of a savage, I said to myself; I will have to answer for all the crimes the bandit is going to commit. . . . On the other hand, is it a prejudice, this instinct of conscience that resists all reasoning? (Author's ellipses)

The as yet unidentified subcultural values of Bohemian life--hospitality, instinct, liberty, justifiable crime, and a savage prejudice that resists the logic of reason--dismiss fear of the bandit's future crimes, soften the anguish of culpability, and justify the breaking of the law. By emphasizing his own sensitivity rather than obedience to the law, the historian proves his unconscious allegiance to the laws of Bohemia, an allegiance that allows both the dissolution of the moral values of the man and the disintegration of the subjectivity of the narrator. Just as morality slides, the subject and object of history seem to slide. From Caesar to Spanish culture to Bohemia and its bandits, the historian becomes an archaeologist, an ethnographer, a bad detective, and then a moral criminal who cannot help but identify with a Bohemian he himself has constructed. His initial duplicity, whether historian or storyteller, thus gives way to a multiplicity of possible roles to play, as if between the two theoretically opposed poles, all sorts of fantasy self-representations were possible. The borders that separate the speaking subject from the object of his gaze thus become just as elusive as those that distinguish the savage Bohemian from the moral Bourgeois.

The historian's unconscious identification with this supposed Bohemian calls to mind a phenomenon that psychoanalysis refers to as *Verleugnung*--

denial, disavowal, or denegation. In his *Clefs pour l'Imaginaire ou l'Autre Scène*, Octave Mannoni (1969: 166) relies on this phenomenon to explain that belief in dream scenes or in fantasms, that is, in unconscious fantasy scenarios, is possible only because the subject in question is able to deny any real participation in the events of the scenario. Mannoni uses the formula "I *know very well* but *even so*" to illustrate the way patients begin to tell of their dream scenes or fantasy scenarios as if they were already denying them. In this case, it is because the historian believes that the cultures of the Bohemian and the bourgeois are distinguished that he is able to participate in his game of fantasy role-playing. And it is because he can deny any association with Bohemia that he is able to identify, on an unconscious level, with the fascinating bandit. In the last scene, for example, he resolves his own crisis of consciousness by offering his guide some money and by signing a false declaration certifying that he has not been the bandit's accomplice (619). These acts reassure the security of his bourgeois identity.

Once acquitted, the historian returns to his research at the Dominican library in Cordoba on manuscripts relating to the "interesting problem" of Munda. He opens his second chapter by relating a new encounter: "There, one takes pleasure in a spectacle that is well worth one's attention" (619). This "spectacle" is a daily ritual comprised of a group of female workers who leave their tannery to gather at the end of day by the banks of the Guadalquivir. There they disrobe and bathe. As he describes this ritual, the historian recultivates his distant look, but he also comments on the ways in which a literary (and fantasy-oriented) imagination may contaminate what attempts to be an objective relation of facts. His choice of the pronoun *on* (one) is already suggestive of both his distance from and his involvement in the spectacle, and his use of the verb *jouir* (to partake in an erotic pleasure) predicts something more than an indifferent attitude toward the scene. Indeed, his description of the bathers reeks of unconscious desire:

At the last stroke of the clock, all of these women undress and go into the water. Then there are cries and laughter, an infernal noise-making. From the top of the quay, the men contemplate the bathers, squint their eyes, and don't see much. Yet the white, uncertain forms drawn upon the somber azure of the river put poetic minds to work and, with a little imagination, it is not difficult to see before oneself (literally, to represent before oneself) Diana and her nymphs bathing, without having to fear the destiny of Acteon (619-620).

In this description, the infernal noise-making of what can only be prostitutes bathing becomes a poetic vision of the goddess Diana and her nymphs. Both the erotic and the political force of these female workers is tamed by a poetic reading of mythic proportions.

Although this poetic reading tends to reassure the objective distance of the historian's discourse, it also works to hide the energetic, if disavowed, work of desire. The historian once again denies reality--here the eroticism of the scene--in order to replace it with a personal poetic fantasy. And, once again, the formula for fantasy based on denial or denegation is set in operation: he *knows* he need not face the destiny of Acteon--to be devoured by the dogs of the huntress--and this safety allows him to justify and to deny his own personal voyeuristic pleasure. He is not like those other men who strain their eyes to see and see little. By concentrating on the painterly aspect of these chiaroscuro drawings in space, he sees much more than what is actually there. Evidently, the contrast between the Dominican fathers and this spectacle of "infernal" prostitution which their teachings would both forbid and promote is obviously too much for this ethnographer to reconcile. He poeticizes the scene and, quite literally, represents it for himself, sublimating an erotic experience into an artistic vision.[5] An analogy can be drawn between this instance of subtle denial and the historian's earlier examination of motives that also justified and denied a loss of personal integrity. It is once again an effort to constitute Bohemia as "other," and thus, to distinguish himself from it, that summons the energy of desire. This denied desire unleashes the historian's own Bohemian tendencies and causes the un(self)conscious historian to misread or slip up. As a result, the objectivity of a scholarly account of Guadalquivir is undermined by a literary and fantasmatic productivity.

The historian's misapprehension of the bathing scene and denial of his own capacity to play the role of Acteon serves as a prelude to a magical and charming encounter with Carmen, one of the engaging bathers our researcher wants to misrepresent. Curiously, although this third encounter with Bohemia appears to move the chronicle forward, it also twists itself into a repetition of the encounter with José. First, it is the strange, animal beauty of this gypsy that charms and finally seduces him. "It was a strange and savage beauty, a face that was astonishing at first, but a face one could never forget" (622). The historian makes excuses and again calculates his distance by punctuating his thoughts with footnotes. Unfortunately, the footnotes give way to "savage prejudices," to an overemphasis on his own poetic sensibilities, and thus, to a denial of Bohemia's seductive powers (ibid). Then, an unexpected interruption of his tête-à-tête with Carmen forces the narrator into a renewal of criminal thoughts: "Already I had my hand on the foot of one of the bar stools, and I was syllogizing to myself to determine the precise moment at which it would be appropriate to throw it at the head of the intruder" (623). The potential murder is only staved off by the fact that this jealous intruder is none other than the bandit, don José, whom "I regretted a bit not having let hang" (623). What was once only a fantasy fascination with crime now becomes a reality, and the identification with an imaginary version of the "bandit" José is thoroughly complete.

EMPLOTMENT

At the opening of the third chapter, the historian learns that the bandit is named Don José de Navarre (a name that identifies him, ironically, as a bourgeois gentlemen "much like himself") and that he has been imprisoned and sentenced to death for the murder of Carmen. In this third chapter, don

José takes over the discursive function of storyteller as the historian listens to a tale of moral dissolution disquietingly similar to the one he himself has just experienced. Although José tells his own story, he also rectifies the details of identity and chronology contained in the historian's chronicle of events. Therefore, José's narrative can be called, in White's words, a transformation by way of "emplotment," a chronicle recast as a "story with identifiable beginning, middle, and end phases" (White 1988: 12). In fact, by the end of this third chapter, it is clear that José has recounted the story that our historian has just lived and that the exchanging of narrators signals a more interesting exchange of identities. Like the historian, José is a bad reader of signs, the result being that he, too, idealizes and is seduced by his own personal version of Bohemia. Like the historian, José liberates a Bohemian prisoner, the infamous Carmen, with whom he also identifies: "She spoke a broken basque, and I believed she was Navarrese" (632-633). And like the historian, José's life is summed up by a series of degradations from officer to brigadier, to bad detective, to soldier, to jealous lover, to murderer, so that he, too, takes on a multiplicity of different roles to play. At the conclusion of his story, José condemns Bohemia, making it clear that neither he nor Carmen is at fault, but, rather, the nefarious Bohemia that always corrupts (660). In his final evaluation, this reading is reiterated by our supposedly objective historian, thus, rounding out the series of associations that make him like his protagonist.

EVALUATION

In the final chapter of *Carmen*, a formal argument is being adduced in order to establish, as White (1973, 1988) suggests, the ethical, cognitive, and aesthetic meaning of the now "emplotted" chronicle. Both José's story and the historian's original object of research are temporarily and emotionally distanced as the cool voice of the historian returns, but in an even more dissertative tone, to give an impersonal but erudite evaluation of Bohemian life.[6] This evaluation essentially repeats José's indictment of Bohemia by recasting elements of the story we have just read into the shape of a scholarly interpretation. In so doing, this historian does not correct the geography of Caesar's last battle but, rather, the official history of Bohemia itself. Whereas previous research in the field extolled the positive virtues of Bohemian life--liberty, fraternity, equality--the historian has made it his business to guard us against its evils.

On a formal or textual level, however, the "moral of the story" is quite different. The mirror effect that plays across a narrative frame both to distinguish and to ally the historian and José works against the historian's reactionary evaluation. Although the historian conquers the revolutionary forces that the nefarious Bohemia has come to represent, he also shows us that a program of cultural classification such as the one in which he is engaged may force an identification of a historian and the object of his research. For in his setting up of Bohemia as a dangerously seductive "other," the historian proves, by way of his own actions, that it is impossible to escape its alluring appeal. Looking outward, the historian merely finds himself projected into a world inevitably reorganized or, finally, revolutionized, by his very attempt to organize and study it. Despite his ethical evaluation of Bohemia, therefore, the historian's cognitive contact with it nurtures the very destructive forces his discourse would guard against. He, like Caesar, has also gambled "double or nothing."

This anarchical reorganization of the world sends an opposing political message to the reader of *Carmen* by suggesting that it may be precisely the constraints of an ordered vision of society (and of historiography) that actually causes revolutions or, at least, productive disruptions. The idealizations, misreadings and unanalyzed desires provoked by Bohemia actually push *Carmen* foward and program new identities, releasing the intense utopian energy of an aesthetic violence. To secure the borders of the story by following the rules of nineteenth-century historiography is to believe one secures those of society as well, but as the story is reordered by the transformative operation of discourse, so are its life-styles and its identities.

Finally, the confused chronology of the tale at the level of its narrative structure permits an unresolved sense of the present and tacit speculations about the future of France. Insofar as José, the nobleman, can be read as belonging to the *ancien régime*, corrupted and seduced by the champions of a republican life-style, it is clear that, by 1830, this life-style has been both imprisoned and compromised. The traveling historian then condemns those revolutionary forces that destroyed don José. But in his critique of those forces, our historian also borrows them, promulgating liberty, fraternity and an unconscious equality, an invitation to identify with the Bohemian values of a countercultural life-style. This leaves us with the writer of 1845 whose nostagia for those waning ideals of 1830 and of 1789 releases a utopian energy that looks forward to 1848 by showing us his poetic capacity to rewrite the world he sees. Indeed, he may be said to represent a world violently reordered by a disavowed, and thus, inevitable identification with Bohemian style. Like the Bohemians, his style wanders as it breaks the rules (of historical narrative), cultivating visions of Bohemia that confuse art and life. Bohemia does become an artistic call to freedom and a social force for change as the participation of poets and artists in the insurrection of 1848 demonstrates (Seigle 1986: 404).[7] And beyond 1848, *Carmen* continues to program innovative revolutionary art forms in the work of Georges Bizet, Enrst Lubitsch, Roland Petit, Otto Preminger, and more recently, Peter Brook, Carlos Saura, and Jean-Luc Godard.

NOTES

1. Hayden White makes this point both in his *Metahistory* (1973, 1-5) and in his "'Figuring the Nature of Times Deceased': Literary Theory and Historical Writing" (May 1988, 3, 41-42 n.7), a paper distributed during a faculty seminar at the University of Oregon.

2. In the preface to his *Comédie Humaine*, for example, Balzac talks about filling in the gaps of an "official" history by writing novels about the history of social mores. See his well-known "Avant Propos de la *Comédie Humaine*" written after many of his novels in 1842 (Balzac 1976, 1: 7-20).

3. See White 1973, 45-48. Although it is outside the scope of this limited discussion to pursue this point, two examples effectively illustrate this concern. Balzac's *Le Père Goriot* presents a monarchist view of life during the Restoration in Paris that highlights the negative effects of postrevolutionary bourgeois equality. At the same time, however, it also stages the compelling force of revolutionary ideals (and, thus, of bourgeois equality) through its portrayal of Vautrin's seductive influence on the unsuspecting young hero, Rastignac. It thereby questions the very possibility of using historical narrative to promulgate any one single view of how the Revolution has affected modern life. Likewise but differently, Flaubert's *La Tentation de Saint Antoine* reduces all of history to a subjective drama in which it is necessarily reorganized into personal versions of truth. Any linear or evolutionary conception of history as a series of causes and effects is transformed into a circular structure of repetitions or revolutions. On this ironic view of history in *La Tentation*, see my *Virtual Theater from Diderot to Mallarmé* (1989, 103-140).

4. Mérimée 1951, 609. All further citations from *Carmen* will refer to this Pléiade edition. This and all further translations of passages from *Carmen* are my own.

5. This transformation recalls Michel Foucault's argument about the repressed and, therefore, celebrated sexuality of the Victorians in *The History of Sexuality* (1980).

6. The fourth chapter was, in fact, added later by Mérimée, in 1847.

7. Seigle (1986, 403) also writes: "Those who built the image of Bohemia self-consciously recalled the Romantics of the 1830s, but in terms that transformed the real Romantic estrangement into an idealization of bourgeois youth." On this new poetic Bohemia, see also Henry Murger, *Scènes de la Vie de Bohème* (1851, 5-10).

REFERENCES

Balzac, Honoré de. *Oeuvres Complètes*. 9 vols. Paris: Gallimard, 1976.
Flaubert, Gustave. *La Tentation de Saint Antoine*. Paris: Louis Concard, 1924.
Foucault, Michel. *The History of Sexuality*: Volume I: *An Introduction*, trans. Robert Hurley. New York: Vintage Books, 1980.

Gould, Evelyn. *Virtual Theater from Diderot to Mallarmé*. Baltimore: Johns Hopkins University Press, 1989.

Jameson, Fredric. *The Ideologies of Theory* 2 vols. Minneapolis: University of Minnesota Press, 1988.

Mannoni, Octave. *Clefs pour l'Imaginaire ou l'Autre Scène*. Paris: Seuil, 1969.

Mérimée, Prosper. "Carmen" In *Oeuvres Complètes*. Paris: Gallimard, 1951.

Murger, Henry. *Scènes de la Vie de Bohème*. Paris: Calmann-Lévy, 1851.

Seigle, Jerrold. *Bohemian Paris: Culture, Politics, and the Boundaries of Bourgeois Life, 1830—1930*. New York: Penguin Books, 1986.

White, Hayden. *Metahistory*. Baltimore: Johns Hopkins University Press, 1973.

_____. "'Figuring the Nature of Times Deceased': Literary Theory and Historical Writing." Paper delivered at the University of Oregon, May 1988.

13

Georges Sorel and the "Dreyfusard Revolution"

Jeffrey Mehlman

The nearly simultaneous initiatives by the embassies of fascist Italy and the Soviet Union to erect monuments to Georges Sorel after his death in 1922 has in part obscured a very different and equally striking chapter in the history of the reception of his thought: the reaction of the literary leaders of Anglo-American modernism.[1] *Réflexions sur la violence* was translated in 1916 by the philosopher of art T. E. Hulme, who, in his preface, referred to Sorel as "one of the most remarkable writers of the time, certainly the most remarkable socialist since Marx."[2] That translation was reviewed in *The Monist* of 1917 by T. S. Eliot, who claimed that the book gave, "more than any other book [he was] acquainted with, an insight into . . . 'our directions.'"[3] The skepticism of Renan and Sainte-Beuve, he wrote, was "almost an aesthetic pose. . . . But the skepticism of the present, the skepticism of Sorel, is a torturing vacuity which has developed the craving for belief,"[4] as though the breviary of anarchosyndicalism were, in fact, a dry run for "The Waste Land." Finally, there is the case of the great painter-writer Wyndham Lewis--"wrong," wrote Ezra Pound, "about everything except the superiority of live mind to dead mind; for which basic verity God bless his holy name."[5] *The Art of Being Ruled* (1926) was an ongoing commentary on and debate with Sorel, whom Lewis regarded as "the key to all contemporary political thought."[6]

Lest the Sorelianism of Hulme, Eliot, and Lewis, in their reactionary modernism, seem too quaintly remote and easily circumscribable, there is the case of the role our thinker--directly or indirectly--may have played at the wellspring of what has been called postmodernism. The reference to Sorel is explicit in Walter Benjamin's "Critique of Violence" and all but there in the pessimistic and apocalyptic leftism of the "Theses on the Philosophy of History."[7] There is a second case: now that cirumstance has led many to speculate on the influence Hendrik de Man may have had on his nephew Paul, Zeev Sternell's observation that Hendrik de Man's thought may be read essentially as a prolongation of Sorel's may prove a source of fruitful provocation to historians of critical theory.[8] Finally, there is the case of Jules Monnerot, one of the last survivors of the fabled Collège de Sociologie. In 1974, when he opted to gather a number of his essays, written over some thirty years, under the title *Inquisitions*, the last was entitled "La Fièvre de Georges Bataille." The first (and best) was "Georges Sorel ou L'Introduction aux mythes modernes."[9] Clearly, from the explicit acknowlegment of Sorel's importance in the work of the modernist trio of Eliot, Hulme, and Lewis, to the more subterranean and indirect impact in that of the postmodernists Benjamin, de Man, and the Collège de Sociologie, Sorel's work invites reconsideration in terms of the concerns of our current textualist consensus.[10] Such will be the horizon of the inquiry broached in these comments.

The motifs in Sorel's thought that anticipated the central concerns of critical "theory" are manifold. His polemic against parliamentary socialism in the name of a myth of violence may be read, for instance, as an attack against a realm of representation--Parliament--construable above all in terms of specularity: "Nothing so resembles a representative of the bourgeoisie as a representative of the proletariat."[11] Indeed, one feels that the distinction left-right remained ultimately a specular trap for him. During the Dreyfus Affair, he referred to Anatole France as the Jules Lemaître of the left, but to Jules Lemaître as the Anatole France of the right.[12] Then there was the performative or "irrefutable" status of the "myth" intended to shatter that realm, its "catastrophic" opposition to every "organic" take on history[13]--not to mention the insistence on irreducible polemical difference in the face of every dream of ascendant or idealizing union.[14] Surely, these are obsessions that a generation of postmodernists shares with the lonely thinker Péguy used to call "notre maître."[15]

But what is most gripping in Sorel, I believe, may be intuited by isolating two central motifs in his thought and observing the sparks generated between them. On the one hand, Sorel as a historian was fascinated by the phenomenon he referred to as "revolutions occurring in periods of decadence" or what he elsewhere called a "double movement of degeneration causing both bourgeois and proletarians to stray far from the paths assigned to them by theory."[16] Indeed, it has been suggested that "entropy" is perhaps the dominant intuition of Sorel's thought,[17] so that a certain degenerative violence suffered by dialectic-*qua*-revolution is the sorry spectacle Sorel finds himself endlessly railing against. On the other hand, were one to isolate the motif best characterizing Sorel's contribution to Marxist thought, it would be his freeing of that thought (by way, first, of Bergsonian myth, then of Jamesian pragmatism) from the teleology intrinsic to dialectic itself. So we have both a positively marked agression against dialectic (irrefutable "myth") and a negatively marked one ("entropy"), and the question that remains undecidable is how to distinguish between the two.

The case is somewhat reminiscent of Benjamin, for whom the liberatory image, in his *Passagen-Werk*, was conceived as that violent yoking together of past and present in a "constellation" bringing "dialectic" to a "standstill" ["Bild ist die Dialektik im Stillstand"].[18] Yet the conclusion of his second "Arcades Exposé" is devoted to a crucial image or constellation of "standstill" that strikes Benjamin as "infernal," but no less exemplary for that.[19] It is the model of eternal return sketched by Louis-Auguste Blanqui in his late and

almost mystical text, *L'Eternité par les astres*.[20]   Here the "hell" of
dialectic--or revolution--squandered in a phantasmagoria of endless
recurrence is indistinguishable from the liberatory gesture of the image
bringing dialectic to a standstill.   The undecidability is profound and
profoundly Sorelian as well.

But perhaps the undecidability was scripted by Marx himself. I refer
to that freezing of the dialectic in *The Eighteenth Brumaire of Louis
Bonaparte*, whereby bourgeoisie and proletariat remain undialectically in
place, as the unseemly dropouts from the class struggle, the *lumpen-
proletariat* of the Bonapartist Society of December 10, rise to the pinnacle of
society.[21] If ever there were a revolution, in Sorel's words, "possessing an
ideal of retrocession," it was this:[22] "An entire people," wrote Marx, "which
had imagined that by means of a revolution it had imparted to itself an
accelerated power of motion, suddenly finds itself cast back into a defunct
epoch."[23] Yet the question that remains, in all its crudity, is why this most
undialectical (or un-Marxian) of texts remains Marx's finest achievement as
a historian. It is as though between Benjamin's liberatory "dialectic at a
standstill" and the maleficent "freezing" of the dialectic lamented by Marx a
contamination had taken place, but it is a contamination essentially
continuous with the twin violences wreaked on dialectic (in Sorel) by entropy
and myth.

Now the configuration is further complicated--or enriched--by the fact
that one of Sorel's important texts, *La Révolution dreyfusienne* (1909) is, at
crucial junctures, studded with allusions to *The Eighteenth Brumaire*.[24] It is
to that work that I would like to turn now. Before doing so, however, let us
pause to consider the relations between the Bonapartist coup of 1851 and the
Dreyfus Affair. Daniel Halévy was, no doubt, among the most eloquent to
have pointed out an affinity between the two episodes, referring, in 1910, to
"le coup Dreyfus" as a "more overt, more gratuitous, and more stupid crime
than the coup d'état of 1851."[25] The threat to the Republic posed by such
would-be demagogues as Paul Déroulède and Jules Guérin, leader of the *Ligue
Antisémite*, was as ominous, if not as effective, as the menace posed years
earlier by Louis Bonaparte.

Perhaps the most brilliant individual who prolonged that interpretative
tradition was Hannah Arendt in *The Origins of Totalitarianism*. Her manifest
intent was to view the Dreyfus Affair, with its widespread rioting against the
Jews in 1898, as a dress rehearsal for the Nazi regime, a "foregleam," as she
puts it, of the twentieth century.[26] Yet her rhetoric manifestly harks back to
Marx's analysis of the second 18 Brumaire. Whereas Marx refers to Bonaparte's success in gathering to his cause the "scum (*Auswurf*), offal (*Abfall*),
and refuse (*Abhub*) of all classes," that parody of a class, the lumpen-
proletariat, Arendt on the Dreyfus Affair speaks at length about the "mob,"
in which "the residue of all classes are represented."[27] If Marx's lumpen-
proletariat was the parody of a class, Arendt's mob is a "caricature of the
people."[28]   "While the people in all great revolutions fight for true
representation, the mob will always shout for the 'strong man,' the 'great

leader.'"[29]   And in the case of the Dreyfus Affair the "caricatural" great leader whom the mob--and Arendt--alight upon is Jules Guérin, in whom "high society found its first criminal hero."[30]   First?   For Marx, the criminal Bonaparte's world was that of what he called in English the "swell mob," thus combining the two components Arendt divides into "high society" (swell) and "mob."[31] In brief, in Arendt's reading, but for the success of the Dreyfusards, the Affair could very easily have turned into the 18 Brumaire of Jules Guérin.

Consider now Sorel's *Révolution dreyfusienne*, or rather consider it in its relation to the central motif of Marx's *Eighteenth Brumaire*, revolution as "farce."   The stage is set at the very beginning of the text by a lengthy discussion of the speech delivered by Renan, in 1889, the year of the centenary of the Revolution, upon welcoming Jules Claretie, director, Sorel writes, of the Maison de Molière, to the Académie Française. The principal theme is the somewhat comic notion that in a revolution, it is frequently acts and individuals deserving of the greatest contempt outside the revolutionary context that emerge, through their very contemptibility, as heroes or highpoints of the revolution: "Those artisans who have performed a labor of giants seen in themselves are pygmies."[32]   Their alleged genius is an illusion engendered by the gravity of the turmoil amid which they lived.

That point of view eventually leads Sorel to quote the celebrated opening of *The Eighteenth Brumaire*--the second time as farce--and to offer something of a corrective to Marx. Given what he takes to be the accuracy of Renan's position, Sorel opines that the great Revolution itself was no doubt always already something of a farce: "it was as ridiculous as its imitation in 1848."[33] Meanwhile, the bulk of Sorel's essay consists of efforts to show how grotesque--or farcical--many of the heroic figures of the Dreyfus Affair, in fact, were: Zola's more Hugo-esque statements are quoted to devastating effect; Anatole France's about-faces on the issue of Zola's literary and human merits are exploited cruelly; Jaurès's propensity to hamming and Picquart's subservience to Clemenceau are similarly cast in a somewhat nasty light. It is all a rather ungenerous performance, to say the least.

Now at the book's end the reference to *The Eighteenth Brumaire* resurfaces in an odd light. Marx's riotously "Bohemian" Society of December 10, Bonaparte's motley crew of followers, is evoked as a parallel to the political element surrounding the radical government triumphant in the wake of the Dreyfus Affair: "The Dreyfusard revolution . . . brings us back to a social regime, rather close to the one that existed under the Second Empire. . . . The parliamentary regime is becoming more and more of a farce."[34] A text beginning with the Maison de Molière thus ends with Marx's farce. But note how the intertext has changed from its very plausible application by Arendt. Whereas for her the Affair, in retrospect, came perilously close to being the 18 Brumaire of Jules Guérin, leader of the *Ligue Antisémite*, for Sorel it was in fact the successful 18 Brumaire of Prime Minister Waldeck-Rousseau (and his followers).

Now this, on the face of it, was a very odd activation of the Marxian intertext. What Sorel offers in its support is the elaborate and indecorous manipulation of the judiciary by the Dreyfusards once in power: the rather singular "contempt of the Dreyfusards for the courts."[35] The central element is the final rehabilitation of Dreyfus, long after the pardon of 1899, in July 1906. For that rehabilitation, consisting in the Cour de Cassation's annulment of the verdict of the Rennes court-martial without ordering up a new trial, was on the face of it unconstitutional. Any annulment of a prior verdict that did not, in fact, dispel the existence of the crime itself (and no one claimed that treason had not been committed) required a new trial. The fact that the Dreyfusard government managed to spare Dreyfus that ordeal was viewed as the juridical centerpiece of a Dreyfusard 18 Brumaire.

Sorel's explicit argument does not tell the whole story, of course. Unmentioned is the fact of just how unpopular the Dreyfusard cause was in France.[36] It should not be forgotten, as well, that after a string of resignations, the only minister of war prepared to make the Army swallow a pardon for Dreyfus was Galliffet, the infamous "massacreur" of the Commune. Finally, there was the overarching fact that the Affair had served to lure a good portion of the left firmly into the republican or democratic camp. As Sorel put it explicitly in *La Décomposition du marxisme*: "The Dreyfus Affair can well be compared to a political revolution. For it would have resulted in a complete deformation of society if the entrance of many anarchists into the syndicates during that period had not oriented workers toward the path of revolutionary syndicalism and strengthened the idea of class struggle."[37] The Dreyfus Affair, in the larger perspective, the perspective that makes of *La Révolution dreyfusienne*, a text integrally linked to *Réflexions sur la violence*, was thus a "revolution," but a counterrevolutionary one--as such, a reactivation of what was at stake in *The Eighteenth Brumaire of Louis Bonaparte*.

What remains is the strange chiasmus that has Sorel invoking the same Marxian subtext as Hannah Arendt but to opposite effect: the Affair not as the would-be coup of the protofascists, but as the successful coup of the unprincipled democrats. If, however, the Dreyfus Revolution can be construed as a counterrevolutionary revolution, a revolution played out in the decadent mode (and the orgy of social legislation through which the Dreyfusard bourgeoisie manifested its ethos was, for Sorel, proof of this), there remains the question of the extent to which it constitutes as well a Sorelian "myth," or, to resort to Benjamin's locution, a--liberatory--instance of "dialectic at a standstill."

Now that "standstill," I believe, can best be produced by following Sorel in what Benjamin might have called a "tiger's leap into the past," and demonstrating that the author's Dreyfusard Revolution was in a strong sense a *repetition* of an earlier configuration he had, in fact, elaborated in 1889 before the famous *bordereau* attributed to Dreyfus was even written. I refer to one of Sorel's earliest books, *Le Procès de Socrate*.[38]

Like *La Révolution dreyfusienne*, *Le Procès de Socrate* was an effort at sympathy with those who condemned an innocent man--sympathy provoked by a sense of just how ultimately corrupt the advocates of his innocence, in the course of time, would prove themselves to be. What was Socrates's crime? Sorel answers (in terms that already anticipate the argument of his book on Dreyfus): "Socrates did much to break the bonds that tied the citizen of antiquity to the *polis*. The bonds were those of military discipline. The citizen was a soldier, kept under strict surveillance. . . . In the ideal city of the Socratics, the mind would have been supervised (*surveilleé*), directed, and oppressed. Plato outdid his master, but he followed the same principles."[39] Old Athenian democracy, Sorel argues, was essentially military in its ethos. The new values associated with Socrates were sophistical, oriented toward elaborate verbal performance and the notion of government by those in the know. Those later values were conducive to the plans of the oligarchs (known as the "Thirty"), who suborned the old military values. That oligarchy, moreover, was in fact a form of demagogy, proud of its openness to all classes.[40] In addition, Socrates was a religious and erotic mystic of sorts, given to much resented cults of Eastern provenance. Those who contested the decline of the old military values at the hand of the oligarchy--fast-talking, effete, alien in its religiosity--and who intuited just what kind of utopian tyranny post-Socratic Socratics such as Plato had in store for them cannot but be forgiven for the verdict they delivered.

Moreover, the best guide to the truth of Sorel's argument, it is suggested, is a reading of Aristophanes, in his send-ups of Socrates. Socrates's trial, that is, is best read as comedy--or farce. Like Sorel's Dreyfusard Revolution. But Sorel's Dreyfusard and Socratic farces are at a fundamental level identical: the innocent victim embodying the challenge to a waning military society; the resentment toward foreign religiosity; the resistance to a new society rooted in skills of verbal and monetary exchange (Socrates is said to admire in Sparta a city in which money reigned: "its magistrates were corrupt");[41] the subversive role of philosophical clubs called "loges" in the French (the allusion to Freemason lodges seems patent); and above all, the fear of the utopian pretensions of the Socratic party. In 1889 Sorel compared the Socratics to the Calvinists, who were fond of free expression only when they felt their adversaries had been effectively silenced. Those enemies were, of course, the Catholics. If one replaces "Socratic" with "Dreyfusard," one perceives just how fine an anticipation of (his own version of) French history Sorel was offering in his early work on Greece. Or to resort to another metaphorico-metonymical chain in Sorel's phantasmagoria of French history: the "sophists" of *Le Procès de Socrate* become the "intellectuals" of *La Révolution dreyfusienne*--with the "philosophes" of *Illusions du progrès* supplying a transitional term.[42]

The idiosyncrasy of Sorel's reading of Socrates's fate is perhaps best revealed by playing it off against another work with the identical title, *The Trial of Socrates*, published a hundred years after Sorel (without mentioning him), in the teeth of academic resistance, by the independent journalist I. F. Stone. Stone, too, attempts to absolve the Greeks for what he admits was an unjust verdict, but the differences are as striking as in the case of Arendt's divergences with Sorel in the Dreyfus case, even as they parallel them.

Stone's story centers on Socrates's affinities with the three "political earthquakes" of the years surrounding Socrates's trial: in 411 and 404, "disaffected elements in connivance with the Spartan enemy, overthrew the democracy, set up dictatorships, and initiated a reign of terror. In 401, two years before the trial, they were about to try again. The type of rich young men prominent in the entourage of Socrates played a leading role in all three civic convulsions."[43] The differences with Sorel could not be clearer. For the Frenchman, the oligarchy of the Thirty, as it was called, is remarkably like the Third Republic: antimilitarist, verbose, money-oriented. For the American, the model is perhaps that of a Nazi or Nazi-collaborationist government. For Sorel, the trial of Socrates became the trial of Alfred Dreyfus (and the Dreyfusards).[44] For Stone, it becomes an unduly harsh purge trial for collaboration with a violently fascist regime.[45] In sum, on the question of Socrates, I. F. Stone's relation to Sorel is the same as Hannah Arendt's on the question of the Dreyfus Affair. Each shares with Sorel a fundamental presupposition (*The Eighteenth Brumaire* as subtext in one case, imaginative sympathy with Socrates's jury in the other) but proceeds to read the data in a manner fundamentally opposed to Sorel's.

We emerge, then, with a double chiasmus, the repetition of whose difference offers a particularly bracing image of dialectics at a standstill. Beyond that, what is striking is the extent to which the very idiosyncratic terms (or myths) used, in our post World War II democracies, to stigmatize fascism--or otherness--itself have served historically to characterize (and stigmatize) democracy. The existence of such a configuration, and such a forgetting, is but testimony to the immense act of historical repression that World War II brought in its wake. But that is a subject that would take us far afield from the subject at hand.[46]

NOTES

1. The twin initiatives of Italy and the Soviet Union are evoked by Isaiah Berlin in *Against the Current: Essays in the History of Ideas* (London: Penguin Press, 1982), 331.

2. *Reflections on Violence*, translated with an introduction by T. E. Hulme (London: George Allen and Unwin, 1916).

3. *The Monist* (London), Vol. 27 (1917), 478.

4. Ibid., 478.

5. Quoted in Hugh Kenner, *Wyndham Lewis* (New York: New Directions, 1954), xiii.

6. *The Art of Being Ruled* (Santa Rosa, Calif.: Black Sparrow, 1989), 132.

7. For an incisive discussion of Benjamin's use of Sorel in his "Critique of Violence," see Wolfgang Fietkau, "A la recherche de la révolution perdue: Walter Benjamin entre la théologie de l'histoire et le diagnostic social," in *Walter Benjamin et Paris*, ed. Heinz Wismann (Paris: Editions du cerf, 1986), 285-332.

8. Zeev Sternhell, *Ni droite ni gauche: L'idéologie fasciste en France* (Paris: Seuil, 1983), 136.

9. Jules Monnerot, *Inquisitions* (Paris: José Corti, 1974), 7-47. For Monnerot, Sorel's synthesis of myth (or "phantasm") and shock (or "trauma") has important resonances with Freud's thinking during the same period.

10. A final contemporary marked, however unwittingly, by the Sorelian tradition was Michel Foucault. His announced project (in conversation with the author, 1978) of offering a leftist critique of the Enlightenment for the first time in France constituted an odd forgetting, if not repression, of the author of *Les Illusions du progrès*. Another Sorelian motif in Foucault's thought was his affirmation of a "political spirituality," which manifested itself in his culminating enthusiasm for the early stages of Khomeini's antiprogressivist revolution--"perhaps the first great insurrection against the planetary system, the most modern form of revolt--and the most insane." The original French texts of articles on Iran published by Foucault in 1978 in *Corriere della sera* are quoted at length in Didier Eribon, *Michel Foucault (1926—1984)* (Paris: Flammarion, 1989), 298-313.

11. Georges Sorel, *Réflexions sur la violence* (Paris: Marcel Rivière and Cie, 1972), 46.

12. *Propos de Georges Sorel*, ed Jean Variot (Paris: Gallimard, 1935), 176.

13. In *The Illusions of Progress*, trans. J. & C Stanley (Berkeley: University of California Press, 1972), 139, illusory progress is condemned for "being like an organic movement."

14. See, for instance, Wyndham Lewis's exemplary evocation of Sorel's stance in *The Art of Being Ruled*, 21: "For this *up* and *down*, this *higher* and *lower*, this *betterment* of 'progress' and democratic snobbery, with its necessary unification into a whole, suppressing of *differences* and substituting for them an arbitrary scale of values, with the *salon* at the top, the syndicalist would substitute an equally dogmatic egalitarian *this* and *that*, a horizontal diversity."

15. Georges Goriély, *Le Pluralisme dramatique de Georges Sorel* (Paris: Marcel Rivière and Cie, 1962), 173.

16. *Réflexions sur la violence*, 103, 98.

17. Claude Polin, Preface to *Réflexions sur la violence*, xx.

18. Walter Benjamin, *Das Passagen-Werk*, ed. Rolf Tiedemann (Frankfurt: Suhrkamp, 1983), 578.

19. Ibid., 77.

20. Ibid., 75. This text presents the idea of an eternal return ten years before *Zarathustra* in a manner that is only slightly less moving and with an extreme aptitude for hallucination.

21. I have presented such a reading of *The Eighteenth Brumaire* in *Revolution and Repetition* (Berkeley: University of California Press, 1977), 5-41.

22. *Réflexions sur la violence*, 102.

23. *Der achtzehnte Brumaire des Louis Bonaparte* in Marx, *Werke*, Vol. 8 (Berlin: Dietz Verlag, 1960), 117.

24. Georges Sorel, *La Révolution dreyfusienne* (Paris: Marcel Rivière and Cie, 1911).

25. Daniel Halévy, *Apologie pour notre passé* (Paris: *Cahiers de la quinzaine*, 1910), 112.

26. Hannah Arendt, *The Origins of Totalitarianism* (New York: Harcourt Brace Jovanovich, 1951), 93.

27. Marx, *The Eighteenth Brumaire*, 161; Arendt, *Origins of Totalitarianism*, 107.

28. Arendt, 107.

29. Ibid., 107.

30. Ibid., 111.

31. Ibid., 11.

32. *La Révolution dreyfusienne*, 9.

33. Ibid., 32.

34. Ibid., 72.

35. Ibid., 50.

36.   See, for instance, Minister of War Galliffet's note to Waldeck-Rousseau in September 1899: "Let us not forget that the great majority of people in France are anti-Semitic. Our position would be, therefore, that on the one side we would have the entire army and the majority of Frenchmen, not to speak of the civil service and the senators." Quoted in Arendt, 115.

37.   "The Decomposition of Marxism," trans. I. L. Horowitz in I. L. Horowitz, *Radicalism and the Revolt Against Reason: The Social Theories of Georges Sorel* (Carbondale, Ill., Southern Illinois University Press, 1961), 253.

38.   Georges Sorel, *Le Procès de Socrate* (Paris: Alcan, 1889).

39.   Ibid., 7.

40.   Ibid., 34, 179.

41.   Ibid., 246.

42.   *Le Procès de Socrate* is in many ways Sorel's *Birth of Tragedy*; it praises Aeschylus for his extravagance, and it derides the lack of vitality of Euripides, whose work is associated with Socratic "optimism." It establishes a quite remarkable parallel between Greek and French history whereby the trio Aeschylus-Euripides-Socrates is superimposed on that of Corneille-Racine-Voltaire. At the time he wrote the book, Sorel had not yet read Nietzsche.

43.   I. F. Stone, *The Trial of Socrates* (New York: Doubleday, 1988), 140.

44.   Indeed, even in their divergences, the two cases are curiously aligned. If Zola comes in for mockery for going into exile, is it not because of the argument supplied by Socrates in the *Crito*? And if Dreyfus is regarded as contemptible for agreeing to withdraw his request for a retrial, and thus accept a pardon with its complement of attendant guilt, is it not because of the reason Socrates gives in *The Apology* for refusing to propose a counter-punishment lest he admit his own guilt?

45.   See Stone, 141: "The 'Socratified' youth of *The Birds*, with their Spartan-like clubs, . . . had become the storm troopers with which the Four Hundred in 411 and the Thirty in 404 terrorized the city."

46.   The subject is broached in my *Legacies: of Anti-Semitism in France* (Minneapolis: University of Minnesota Press, 1983).

14

Revolution in the *Education sentimentale*: Structure, Theory and History

Gail M. Schwab

STRUCTURE AND REVOLUTION

Flaubert actually wrote two books called *L'Education sentimentale*, but he published only one of them. Surprisingly few critics have dealt with the 1843 novel, the notable exception being, of course, Jean Bruneau. Bruneau considers the *Première Education* the first "real" flaubertien novel, but explains that Flaubert did not publish it, and, indeed, could not have published it, because

> it does not really conform to the aesthetic of its author. Firstly, the psychological analysis of the main characters is insufficient; secondly the style is uneven, the novel was written too quickly. . . . Finally, and mainly, as Flaubert himself saw perfectly, the novel lacks unity.[1]

It might be said to show that "défaut de ligne droite" (lack of a straight line) which Frédéric Moreau will blame for his failure. Flaubert himself says the book lacks the link of cause and effect, and he writes in 1852 to Louise Colet, who was clearly pressuring him at that time to publish it:

> it would be necessary . . . , which seems to me the most difficult of all, to write a missing chapter, which would show how the same trunk inevitably had to bifurcate. . . . The causes are shown, the results also; but the link of cause and effect is not. That is the flaw of the book, and the way it belies its title.[2]

Flaubert was referring here to the bifurcation of the destinies of his two heroes, Jules and Henry, who start out together on a parallel course dreaming of art and love, only to end up moving apart drastically at right angles to each other. Henry will become a successful bourgeois, eventually a deputy, Flaubert hints, sort of a Martinon, at the end of the book, and Jules will turn out to be a great writer who, of course, has no counterpart in the 1869 *Education*, and could well be the young Gustave himself coming to terms with his vocation. Bruneau claims that the missing chapter Flaubert talks about "would doubtless have been placed after the return of Henry to France, because nothing is yet lost for him at that point, nothing prevents him, after the failure of his love, a failure parallel to that of Jules, from becoming a great artist as well."[3]

I agree with Bruneau's assessment to the extent that it is quite true that that which should have effected the split between the heroes' destinies and linked cause to result, that is, Henry's and Mme. Renaud's expatriation to New York, does not succeed in doing so. Trips, as we all know (and this could be an entry in the *Dictionnaire des idées reçues*) "forment la jeunesse" ("are educational for young people"), and they are one of the classic conventions of the *bildungsroman* genre. The hero will leave his home and family to go out and discover the world, to learn and change and grow. Emilie and Henry undertake precisely that. At great peril to life and limb, with very little money and no discernible means of earning any more, they go off to make their way together in the New World. It is not that Henry and Emilie do not learn and change in New York. They do, and Flaubert analyzes with great subtlety the evolution of their passion, its ups and downs, and eventual waning, exactly as he will do later for Emma in *Madame Bovary*. But when the two lovers return to France, Henry and Emilie are welcomed back into the bosom of their respective families, and far from remaining the déclassé Bohemians they had been in New York, they again become the same respectable bourgeois that they had been before they ran off. Time went by, and great events came to pass, but no sentimental (that is emotional) growth occurred--a summary with which readers of Flaubert are all familiar.

Bruneau was quite right in assuming that Flaubert would have needed another chapter after the return from New York. Something else would have had to have happened in order for the differentiation between Henry and Jules to be clearly psychologically motivated. The trip, as Flaubert conceives it novelistically, is insufficient as a structuring element.

In an article entitled "La Seine, le Nil et le voyage de rien", Philippe Berthier shows how Flaubert undercuts the voyage topos in the 1869 *Education*. While at the opening of the *Première Education* Henry leaves for Paris to study law, and then later goes off to Le Havre to set sail for New York, like the quasi-romantic hero that he is, a kind of Rastignac, Frédéric in the opening scene of his story is actually leaving Le Havre by way of Paris and is on his way home to his mother and small provincial town. Berthier writes: "Since he is coming back to his family instead of leaving it in order to launch himself into the future, our first sight of Frédéric catches him in a contradictory movement: a return to the nest which ironically takes on the trappings of a great departure."[4]

Flaubert mercilessly deconstructs his earlier theme because by this time he has found another, monumental enough to structure his whole novel--the political theme of revolution. There is a very convincing 1987 article by Françoise Gaillard in which she discusses Flaubert's long trip to the Orient with Maxime du Camp, and she shows how it was, at least in part, motivated by the pain caused by the disappointments of 1848, and the desire to escape from all that was happening politically in France at that time.[5] The voyage, far from being a profound motivating factor, is actually motivated by historical events. And, of course, what finally happens to the voyage theme at the end of the 1869 *Education* is that it disappears into the famous *blanc*. The revolution theme comes to replace the interlude/intermezzo that was Henry's and Emilie's trip to New York, and travel constitutes just part of the more or less gratuitous activity that fills in the vacuum separating the assassination of Dussardier--which actually signifies the end of all meaningful action, political, sentimental or otherwise in France for twenty years to come--from the final "action" of the novel, the visit of the by now well into middle-age Mme. Arnoux.

It is also noteworthy that Flaubert's young adult life--his own sentimental education--lies between 1843 when he first conceived the story of a sentimental education and 1864 when he finally did begin to write his definitive version of it. Although the Revolution of 1848 actually took place only five years after the *Première Education* was begun, it constitutes, along with its subsequent political repercussions and eventual *coup d'état*, the virtual end of the novel. I am not trying to make the case here for some sort of "autobiographical" reading of *L'Education sentimentale*, but am simply underlining the fact that the Revolution is conceived as having brought the education process to its completion. It "makes the hero's education" ("faire son éducation"). In fact, although the 1869 *Education sentimentale* seems to proceed randomly and "à défaut de ligne droite" ("lacking a straight line"), it builds systematically to the climax/anticlimax of the revolutionary years. The intertwining themes of love, friendship, and ambition are woven together and finally tightly interlocked in the extremely dense and concentrated Part III, during the relatively short period of time between early 1848 and late 1851. And it is possible to follow any one of these threads up to some sort of climax relating to the revolutionary period. The love plot culminates in the liaisons with Rosanette and Mme. Dambreuse, both of which are brought to an abrupt end by the auction of Mme. Arnoux's furniture, where Frédéric sacrifices all-- the courtesan, the *grande dame*, and a brilliant future, for Mme. Arnoux's sake. She herself disappears in Part III, finally reappearing at the end to play out the love scene that we had all been awaiting since the beginning of the novel.

Bruneau, in an article entitled "Sur la Genèse de *l'Education sentimentale*," analyzes the vicissitudes of the composition of the 1869 *Education*. In the beginning, it was supposed to be "Quite simple . . . the husband, the wife, the lover,"[6] and "*Madame Moreau* [the original title] was the counterpart of *Madame Bovary*; Parisian mores of provincial mores, an obvious reference to the *Comédie humaine*."[7] The 1869 *Education* was originally conceived to resemble the *Première Education* and, by extension, *Madame Bovary*. Flaubert was for quite a long time at great pains to conceive the plan of this book, which was not at all unusual for him, but Bruneau shows that the novel actually begins to take shape as the political theme takes on more and more importance, and as Flaubert comes to realize that what he wants to do, as the Goncourt claim he told them, is to "put everything into it, the movement of 1830, the physiognomy of 1840, and 1848, and the Empire . . . fit the ocean into a carafe."[8]

Antoine Compagnon, in *La Troisième République des lettres*, underlines the close relationship of the 1869 *Education* to *Bouvard et Pécuchet*. "The two projects were in competition in 1863. Flaubert was hesitating between them in Notebook 19. He decides on the *Education*: on the reprise of a project from prior to 1848. The addition of the revolution theme permits him to bring it to fruition."[9] Compagnon analyzes the structure of *Bouvard et Pécuchet* and, far from reading it ahistorically, treats it as Flaubert's *Education politique*,[10] pointing out that Sartre claimed "la Révolution de 1848 a cassé la vie de Flaubert en deux" (the Revolution of 1848 snapped Flaubert's life in two).[11]

I would claim that revolution structures the entire *Education* of 1869, as Compagnon claims it structures *Bouvard et Pécuchet*. The novel fractures and re-fractures, over and over, through the lives of its multiple heroes-- Dussardier, Deslauriers, Sénécal, Arnoux, Dambreuse, Martinon, Le Père Roque, Rosanette, la Vatnaz, and Frédéric--the image of revolution and its determining role in focusing dreams, ambitions, goals, and fears. Each of the characters represents one possible orientation in the face of different political events. The same characters orient themselves differently as events change, but the central pivot they circle around is revolution.

Compagnon claims that Flaubert was an "antidemocratic liberal," of the ilk of a Taine or a Renan (it certainly seems a convincing label), and that he wrote *Bouvard et Pécuchet* as "une charge contre la Révolution française et ses retours" ("an attack against the French Revolution and its returns").[12] Flaubert may have been antidemocratic enough to write to George Sand, "Il faut que la Révolution française cesse d'être un dogme" ("The French Revolution *must* stop being a dogma"),[13] but he was too lucid a writer not to recognize that it was a dogma and not to place it at the center of his panorama of mid-nineteenth-century France.

THEORY AND HISTORY

It is evident that to affirm the essential importance of revolution as a structuring element for the *Education sentimentale*, and to have, hopefully, made a case for said affirmation, is not precisely to have dealt with the historicity of the novel. The question that must now be raised centers on the relationship between the novel and history, and between theory and history, which means that a brief history of the theory dealing with this very sticky problem of representation in the *Education* is indicated. Volume 12 (Spring 1984) of *Nineteenth Century French Studies* was devoted to this problem, resurrected now as an issue in this bicentennial year of the opening gambits of the French Revolution. Back in 1984, Graham Falconer placed himself "on the watershed,"[14] "an uncomfortable place for the critic to perch,"[15] with respect to historical readings of *L'Education sentimentale*, and he claimed, quite rightfully, that "in almost a century of Flaubert studies, most have backed away from the edge and settled for a more secure base of operations on one slope or the other."[16]   That is either on the slope of history, of referentiality and realistic representation, of mimesis--or on the slope of Flaubert's irony, his deconstructionism, his language games and mimicry.

Leading the campaigns in the enemy camps, we have on the side of historical realism Victor Brombert, a fellow-contributor along with Professor Falconer to the *NCFS*, number 12.   On the deconstructionist side, I think we must fill-in, imagine, a noncontributor to the issue whose absence was actually more of a felt presence, Jonathan Culler.   Culler's own "uncertainty"[17] would seem to have been echoed by Falconer three years later in a 1987 article in *Comparative Literature* entitled "Flaubert, James and the Problem of Unde-cidability," but "undecidability" actually designates once again the watershed position between the two opposing camps.   Falconer does a close analysis of the different techniques of irony and deconstruction used by Flaubert in *l'Education*, and then he concludes:

For reasons that include a coherent story line, a certain consistency in the behavior of the protagonists, and a description of the February Revolution sufficiently grounded in detailed observation to be taken as a serious source by professional historians--the playfulness I have been illustrating does not justify our treating *L'Education sentimentale* as a kind of Rousselian parody, even less as "*du Beckett avant la lettre*" ["Beckett before Beckett"]. . . . What Flaubert does in this particular novel is rather to oblige the reader (in quick succession, if not simultaneously) to read in two quite different, not to say mutually exclusive ways.[18]

Finally, at the 1987 Nineteenth-Century French Studies Colloqium at Northwestern University, Falconer asks (the following quotation is from the NCFS collection of abstracts of the conference papers):

Since history comes into *l'Education* through the medium of a spray of ready-made phrases, of devalorised clichés, does it still make any sense to use such a dubious text as if it were indeed the moral story of a generation?   Can the absurd con-versations not only in the *club de l'intelligence* but at the Dambreuse dinner-table really tell us anything of substance, anything authentic about values, or immorality, when the *énoncés* strung together are merely bits of found language?[19]

Obviously, this binary orientation in Flaubert studies is, or was, a problem for Falconer who tries to find reading strategies to overcome the opposition, but continues to pose the same, almost anxious, questions of the text.   This binarism also bothers a critic as different from Falconer as Dominick LaCapra, who writes: "I would like to make it clear that the interpretative method I recommend is hybrid [like the watershed], that it calls upon the talents of the historian and those of the literary critic.[20]

If I have included these quotations from Falconer and LaCapra, it is because I find in their rejection of the binary opposition and in their respective attempts at a dialectical synthesis the right approach to the *Educa-tion*.   The binarism cannot, however, be overcome by any critical method that is dependent on a structural linguistics that posits the divorce of language from historical and sociological phenomena. It is certainly true that much of the language of *L'Education sentimentale* is "found language" (a more flaubertien term might be "parroted language"), and indeed Flaubert's language from *Bovary* to the *Dictionnaire* is full of parroted language. But this should only constitute a methodological conundrum for us if we assume that language is somehow not history--that it floats above time and space in some sort of ideal, heavenly, nontime and nonspace--as in structural linguistics.

The watershed that we actually find ourselves perched on is the one separating structuralist and poststructuralist literary theory of the 1960s, 1970s and early 1980s, and contemporary "return to history" currents in criticism. It might be useful to use the linguistic theory of Mikhail Bakhtin to eliminate the watershed division altogether and to integrate literary theory into a continuum less bristling with barriers and boundary disputes. The Bakhtinian linguistic model postulates the ultimate importance of the historical and the sociological. For Bakhtin language is relational--an interlocking network of relationships among speakers, the spoken, and listeners; among writers, the written, and readers. Intersubjectivity and intertextuality are found at the level of the word, and there is no such thing as a "decontextualized" word. "Decontextualized" language is nothing, and every utterance carries with it the full weight of its historical and sociological context.[21]

Bakhtin had many idiosyncrasies, and one of them was his taste for obscure, long-lost literary genres that supposedly no one had practiced and hardly even studied for hundreds of years. One of his very favorites among these was the menippean satire, and I should like to show how the menippean satire form applies with remarkable clarity to the *Education sentimentale*. Menippean satire is characterized first of all by carnival scenes, which abound in *l'Education*. The February Revolution scene itself, of course, need hardly be mentioned, but there are many other less obvious ones--the many balls, parties and orgies attended by the hero over the course of his education are all examples. Particularly noteworthy are the oft-analyzed in the context of discussions of Flaubert's depiction of the Revolution of 1848: the dinner *chez* Dambreuse and the ridiculous meeting of the *Club de l'Intelligence*. Both scenes can also be clearly read as typically menippean *coena*/symposium sequences, banquets where the "serious" problems of existence are discussed and "encyclopedic" erudition and/or ironic magpie mimicry of erudition are displayed.[22]

Carnival always involves role reversal, topsy-turviness and the *monde à l'envers*,[23] and this turnabout brings about an inevitable profanation of the sacred. Each of the above-mentioned examples from the novel is associated with the profanation theme, which as we know from Brombert permeates the whole novel.[24] To deal briefly with the revolution scene--there is the profanation of ideal love as Frédéric makes love to Rosanette in the boudoir prepared for Mme. Arnoux; there is a "prolétaire-magot" (grotesque prole-tarian) sitting on the throne of the monarchs of France, and a prostitute posed as the Statue of Liberty; there are convicts rolling about on the beds of princesses. Hussonnet, in whose company Frédéric witnesses the mob taking the Tuileries, is perhaps the characterological representation of profanation, and he sneers something about "the sovereign people" smelling bad. There are many other examples. The races at the *Champ de Mars* constitute another carnival sequence, and here Rosanette outrageously insults Mme. Arnoux as she stands up in her carriage to attract the attention of all the surrounding gentlemen to herself by calling out "Yoohoo, over there, you honest women, my protector's wife, yoohoo!"

These reversals, highs and lows, contradictions, idiot/kings, prostitute/ideals characterize the entire book and are one of the principal elements of the menippean tradition.

The menippean satire is a genre of language, of, in fact, reported language, or of found, parroted language. Julia Kristeva, who was one of the first to recognize Bakhtin's overwhelming importance, wrote an article dealing with the *ménippé* back in 1969 entitled "The Word, Dialogue and the Novel." Kristeva calls the ménippé a "pavage de citations" (a mosaic of citations), a sort of catalog of the journalism of its times. Its discourse, according to Kristeva who here is following Bakhtin, externalizes the political and ideological conflicts of the moment and articulates contemporary social and political thought.[25]

A 1981 collection on *L'Education* entitled *Histoire et language dans l'Education sentimentale de Flaubert* deals precisely with the problem of language and/in/as history in the *Education*. Bakhtinian theory is not part of the avowed methodology of the collection, but some of the work included illuminates Bakhtin's "historical word" with illustrations from Flaubert.[26] Michel Crouzet, who discusses in detail the dinner *chez* Dambreuse and the meeting of the *Club de l'Intelligence*, claims that *l'Education* is a

calendar-novel; the political facts noted as news items of the day, taken up as subjects of conversation, are the best way of dating the episodes, and our contact with history; if public opinion is king in democracy, history is what is thought, repeated, in any case what is said. Time is scanned, or better yet, constituted by the news items the dialogues carry along, as if this verbal milieu, derived from another, unevoked environment, the newspaper, defined an oral tradition, which the characters create by talking about it, which makes them the actors of history as soon as they are its speakers.[27]

History, in *l'Education* according to Crouzet, becomes this reported language, picked up in casual discussions, or in casual reading, and circulated. It becomes a mosaic of citations--a sort of menippean satire.

Maria Cajueiro-Roggero, in an article entitled "Dîner chez Dambreuse: La Réaction commençante" ("Dinner *chez* Dambreuse: The Reaction Beginning"), gives a very specific and telling illustration of the way Flaubert constructs his mosaic. In the "pre-text" of *l'Education*, that pre-text which is generally so vast for Flaubert's novels, and which is now in the process of being carefully studied by de Biasi, Duchet, and others, Flaubert writes in a note under the rubric "language": "Language: social problem, problem of

poverty--solidarity--workers--laborers--exploitation of man by man--organize--
unnatural rage--the word workshop everywhere."[28] This is precisely a list of
"reported language," a mosaic of citations that Flaubert notes down in order
to be sure to work them into the text. It is the discourse of the period that
Flaubert wants to record. Cajueiro-Roggero adds, "Flaubert is referring to a
pre-existing text, and integrating it into his novelistic discourse."[29]

The historical discourse does not always have a precise [speaking] subject. In the
manuscript Flaubert hesitates on the choice of the speaker. . . . The indifference to
the choice of the speaker indicates that the historical discourse takes precedence; the
intentions of Flaubert being to reproduce a reactionary speech, it can be attributed
to any of the guests at the party, with the exception of Arnoux.[30]

She then goes on to show how Flaubert puts the locution, "to govern France,
we need an iron hand," first into the mouth of M. Dambreuse and then finally
ends up attributing it to *le Père* Roque.[31] It doesn't matter who says it; what
matters to Flaubert is pinning down this bit of language, the historical
discourse of the beginning of the reactionary period. It is important to note
the precision here. Flaubert is capturing a specific moment. As long as the
language is recorded, any one of the numerous reactionary *imbéciles* chez
Dambreuse will do nicely as speaker.

It is now time to parrot Falconer's questions. Can we then read
l'Education sentimentale as the "moral story" of a generation? I propose that
we must. "Can it tell us anything of substance, anything authentic about
values or immorality when the *énoncés* strung together are merely bits of
found language?" Language is always social, it always originates in relation
to an Other, to the Other's language, and to an historical/sociological context.
It is always found language. What Flaubert's infamous parroting technique
actually does is articulate both the origin and the functioning of language in
society.

So can Flaubert's parroted language "tell us anything about values,
morality or immorality"? Yes--values, morality and immorality are found
language and are articulated by found language. They are recuperable in
language as all social phenomena are recuperable in language for it is in
language that all social phenomena are played out. I quote the great
Bakhtinian scholars Michael Holquist and Katerina Clark:

Language is a unitizing noun developed for the action of what is a scattered and
powerful array of social forces. Whether or not social interaction is conceived as
class struggle, social forces are never conceived otherwise than as being in conflict.
. . . Bakhtin argues that language is where those struggles are engaged most
comprehensively and at the same time most intimately and personally. It is in
language, not in the nation-state (which is also language by the way) that social force
finds its most realized expression.[32]

This is precisely what Flaubert was showing in those fetishized texts--
the dinner *chez* Dambreuse and the meeting at the *Club de l'Intelligence*. After

the guns are thrown down and the barricades torn down, the struggle goes on in words. So reported discourse *is* reported history, and it is at the level of found language that we can read the Revolution of 1848 through the *Education sentimentale*.

NOTES

1. Jean Bruneau, *Les Débuts littéraires de Gustave Flaubert* (Paris, 1962), 460. This translation and all those that follow are my own.

2. Gustave Flaubert, *Correspondence*, January 16, 1852. Cited in ibid., 412-413.

3. Bruneau, *Les Débuts*, 413.

4. Philippe Berthier," La Seine, le Nil et le voyage de rien," *Histoire et langage dans l'Education sentimentale de Flaubert* (Paris, 1981), 5.

5. Françoise Gaillard, "La Révolte contre la Révolution," *Gustave Flaubert: Procédés narratifs et fondements épistémologiques* (Tubingen, 1987), 43 and *passim*.

6. Jean Bruneau, "Sur la Genèse de *l'Education sentimentale*," *Flaubert e il pensiero del suo secolo: Atti les convegno internazionale, Messina, 1984* (Messina, 1985), 237.

7. Ibid., 247.

8. Ibid., 240. Here Bruneau is quoting the Goncourts.

9. Antoine Compagnon, *La Troisième République des lettres*, (Paris, 1983), 259.

10. Ibid., 260.

11. Ibid., 255.

12. Ibid., 281.

13. Ibid.

14. Graham Falconer, "Reading *l'Education sentimentale*: Belief and Disbelief," *Nineteenth Century French Studies* 12 (Spring 1984), 331.

15. Ibid.

16. Ibid.

17. Jonathan Culler, *Flaubert: The Uses of Uncertainty* (Ithaca, N.Y., 1974).

18. Graham Falconer, "Flaubert, James and the Problem of Unde-cidability," *Comparative Literature* 39, no. 1 (1987), 12.

19. The Nineteenth Century French Studies Colloquium traditionally provides a collection of abstracts of all conference papers for colloquium participants.

20. Dominick LaCapra, "L'Effondrement des sphères dans *L'Education sentimentale*," *Annales: Economies, sociétés, civilisations* 42, nos. 1-3, (1987), 628-629.

21. See my "*La Tentation de saint Antoine*: Flaubert and the Menippean Satire," *Cincinnati Romance Review* 5 (1986): 121-131. *La Tentation* is "even more" menippean than the *Education* and constitutes an extraordinary modern example of the genre, as does *Bouvard et Pécuchet*. However, extensive menippean elements can be found in all of Flaubert's narratives, including *Madame Bovary*, *Salammbô*, and the *Trois contes*. An extensive study of the problem would be interesting.

22. Another critic who is interested in the menippean tradition is Northrup Frye. So Bakhtin was not unique. Frye analyzes the symposium aspect of menippean satire in the *Anatomy of Criticism* (Princeton, N.J., 1957), 308-312.

23. Julia Kristeva, "Le Mot, le dialogue et le roman," *Séméiotiké* (Paris, 1969), 165-166.

24. Victor Brombert, *The Novels of Flaubert: A Study of Themes and Techniques* (Princeton, N.J., 1966): cf. chapter on the *Education sentimentale*.

25. Kristeva, 165-166. The above sentence is my own transposition into English of Kristeva's sentence.

26. Perhaps one of the drawbacks of Bakhtin's predilection for obscure *genres* and writers is that he very rarely mentions Flaubert, whom he probably considered the epitome of the monologic novelist, on a par aesthetically with a Tolstoy, only somehow worse because he was not even Russian. It was Bakhtin's loss, considering Flaubert was an accomplished practitioner of the menippean satire.

27. Michel Crouzet, "*l'Education sentimentale* et le 'genre historique'," *Histoire et language dans l'Education sentimentale de Flaubert* (Paris, 1981), 98.

28. Maria Cajueiro-Roggero, "Dîner chez Dambreuse: La Réaction commençante," *Histoire et langage dans l'Education sentimentale de Flaubert* (Paris, 1981), 98.

29. Ibid.

30. Ibid.

31. Ibid.

32. Katerina Clark and Michael Holquist, *Mikhail Bakhtin* (Cambridge, Mass., 1984), 220.

REFERENCES

Berthier, Philippe. "La Seine, le Nil et le voyage de rien." *Histoire et language dans l'Education sentimentale de Flaubert*. Paris: Editions CDU/SEDES réunis, 1981, 3-16.
Brombert, Victor. *The Novels of Flaubert: A Study of Themes and Techniques*. Princeton, N.J.: Princeton University Press, 1966.
Bruneau, Jean. *Les Débuts littéraires de Gustave Flaubert*. Paris: Colin, 1962.
————. "Sur la Genèse de *L'Education sentimentale*" *Flaubert e il pensiero   del suo secolo: Atti les convegno Internazionale, Messina, 1984*. Messina: Facoltà di lettere e filosofia, 1985, 235-248.
Cajueiro-Roggero, Maria. "Dîner chez Dambreuse: La Réaction commençante." *Histoire et langage dans l'Education sentimentale de Flaubert*. Paris: Editions CDU/SEDES réunis, 1981.
Clark, Katerina and Michael Holquist. *Mikhail Bakhtin*. Cambridge, Mass.: Harvard University Press, 1984.
Compagnon, Antoine. *La Troisième République des lettres*. Paris: Seuil, 1983.
Crouzet, Michel. "*L'Education sentimentale* et le 'genre historique'." *Histoire et langage dans l'Education sentimentale de Flaubert*. Paris: Editions CDU/SEDES réunis, 1981, 77-110.
Culler, Jonathan. *Flaubert: The Uses of Uncertainty*. Ithaca, N.Y.: Cornell University Press, 1974.
Falconer, Graham. "Flaubert, James and the Problem of Undecidability." *Comparative Literature* 39, no. 1 (1987), 1-18.
————. "Reading *L'Education sentimentale*: Belief and Disbelief." *Nineteenth Century French Studies* 12 (Spring 1984), 329-341.

Frye, Northrup. *The Anatomy of Criticism*. Princeton, N.J.: Princeton University Press, 1957.

Gaillard, Françoise. "La Révolte contre la Révolution." *Gustave Flaubert: Procédés narratifs et fondements épistémologiques*. Alfonso de Toro (ed.) Tubingen: Narr, 1987, 43-55.

Kristeva, Julia. *Séméiotiké*. Paris: Seuil, 1969.

LaCapra, Dominick. "L'Effondrement des sphères dans *l'Education* sentimentale de Flaubert," *Annales: Economies, Sociétes, Civilisations* 42, no. 1-3 (1987), 611-629.

Schwab, Gail. "*La Tentation de saint Antoine*: Flaubert and the Menippean Satire." *Cincinnati Romace Review* 5 (1986), 121-131.

15

Cities, Bourgeois, and the French Revolution

Charles Tilly

In a delightful dialectic, the decay of one social interpretation is giving rise to another. The pamphleteering Marxist account of the French Revolution, with its transfer of power grounded in a straightforward succession of ruling classes and modes of production, lies in tatters after a generation of critical flailing. Judging from the titles of papers presented during the bicentennial conference, The French Revolution of 1789, few specialists get any joy from beating that nearly dead horse. But is it dead or just sleeping? The critique of the social interpretation has often led away from any serious consideration of the actual processes by which France changed in the critical years after 1787. In its better moments, however, the critique has called attention to the importance of changes in state power Marxist historians long neglected, which in turn has made it possible to see that a "social interpretation" actually has a good deal of explanatory power. Although recent rhetoric has gone in quite a different direction, historians are on the way to rediscovering the bourgeois revolution in a more precise and sophisticated form.

If we insert the French state's history in the general transformations of European states as we have long inserted the transformation of France's social classes in the general history of European capitalism, we will understand both better. Let me sketch a line of explanation stressing the interaction of cities and states, the shift from indirect to direct rule, and the place of capitalists in both momentous processes. It will give some reasons for thinking of revolution and counterrevolution as complementary elements of the same processes of state formation, and for considering the French Revolution to have been a bourgeois revolution after all.

In its simplest form, my argument runs as follows: In France, as elsewhere in Europe, towns and cities formed two analytically distinct hierarchies: an imposed top-down hierarchy defined by coercion, conquest, and state power, and a bottom-up hierarchy defined by capital, trade, and manufacturing. The two hierarchies linked the same places in different ways, with some centers such as Versailles occupying very high positions in the coercive hierarchy and relatively low positions in the hierarchy of capital. War, preparation for war, and extraction of the means for war created the top-down hierarchy and crystallized it into a connected administrative structure.

Soldiers and state administrators held power in the top-down hierarchy; trade and manufacturing created the bottom-up hierarchy. Capitalists--those who made their living from the deployment of capital--held power in the bottom-up hierarchy. Transformations of the state inevitably affected the coercive hierarchy directly, but had lesser and more indirect effects on the hierarchy of capital.

Like other European states, the French state of the eighteenth century only extended its direct top-down rule to the level of the region, the level of the *subdélégation*, the *élection*, the *sénéchaussée*, the *grenier à sel*, and similar administrative units. At and below that level, the *ancien régime* state ruled indirectly, especially through the mediation of priests, nobles, and urban oligarchies. During the eighteenth century, in search of funds for past, present, and future military activity, state agents began pressing for various forms of direct rule that would bypass the privileges and resistance of the entrenched intermediaries. In the Revolution, the state's new managers, battling the old intermediaries for control of revenues, loyalty, and military power at the local and regional levels, improvised successive systems of direct rule in which capitalists, broadly defined, played the critical part. The creation of a new top-down administrative hierarchy drastically altered the relations between coercion and capital, and incited a new series of struggles for power within regions. Revolutionary attempts to institute direct rule and to displace old intermediaries incited wide spread resistance, which took the form of open counterrevolution where the intermediaries had large followings and the national network of capitalists had only thin support. The argument requires many explications, qualifications, and nuances. Yet it captures many implications of recent work on urban hierarchies, political processes, and struggle in France.

Europe experienced in its own more segmented way the interplay of the two processes that G. William Skinner detects in China: the bottom-up building of regional urban hierarchies based on trade and manufacturing, the top-down imposition of political control via a hierarchy of capital cities.[1] In his recent remarkable but easily misunderstood book on French urbanization in the eighteenth and nineteenth centuries, Bernard Lepetit identifies what he calls two "models" of urban systems.[2] They actually constitute two different sets of relations among cities. Europe's urban networks represented the hierarchy of capital; they comprised the higher levels of commercial connections that reached into towns and villages, linked by *colporteurs*, peddlers, and other more substantial merchants who made their business capital accumulation through local and regional trade. As an English king or a Burgundian duke reached into the countryside for taxes and soldiers, he found well-established commercial connections that he had played little part in creating and could not completely control. Indeed, Europe's bottom-up hierarchies long remained more complete, connected, and extensive than its top-down structures of political control. That was a major reason for the failure of the many post-Roman attempts to build empires spanning the continent.

The patterns of political covariation Skinner describes for China have European counterparts: administrative capitals in regions of scanty commerce in which a viceroy held power through direct military control but could produce little revenue for the king, or lower ranking royal officials surrounded by prosperous landlords and merchants with whom they had no choice but to negotiate. Consider the contrast between eastern Prussia, where the state's administrative apparatus overwhelmed merchants in favor of great landlords, and western Prussia, where a similar apparatus almost dissolved in the region's commercial activity. Gabriel Ardant pointed out thirty years ago that the "fit" between fiscal system and regional economy determines the cost and effectiveness of attempts to tax. In an area with little market activity, a land tax based on estimated value and levied in cash is likely to cost a great deal to collect, strike the population very inequitably, miss a good deal of potential revenue, and incite widespread resistance. In contrast, in a highly commercialized area a flat head tax generates less revenue at higher cost than a comparable tax designed to fit the loci of capital and the paths of commerce.

On the other hand (as Ardant did not observe), with high levels of commercial activity, merchants often hold considerable political power and therefore are in a position to prevent the creation of a state that will seize their assets and cramp their transactions. In Europe, the extent of commercial activity strongly affected the viability of the various tactics used to build state strength. Outside of Gdansk, which prospered with the quickening of Baltic trade, Polish merchants were unable to break the grip of great landlords. But the merchants of Amsterdam, Dubrovnik, Venice, and Genoa, high points in the commercial hierarchy, could dictate the terms on which any state would operate in their territories. Thus, Skinner's model of China sheds light on the geography of state formation in Europe.

Among other things, it helps explain the transition from indirect to direct rule. Before the seventeenth century, every large European state ruled its subjects through powerful intermediaries who enjoyed significant autonomy, hindered state demands that were not to their own interest, and profited on their own accounts from the delegated exercise of state power. The intermediaries were often privileged members of subordinate populations and made their way by assuring rulers of tribute and acquiescence from those populations. In southeastern Europe especially, the presence of multiple populations mixed by centuries of conquest and Mediterranean trade combined with the characteristic forms of Muslim rule through semiautonomous subordinates to produce a vast zone of indirect rule whose traces remain today in the region's cultural heterogeneity and its continuing struggles over the rights of minorities. Crucial intermediaries included clergy, landlords, urban oligarchies, and independent professional warriors, in proportions that varied along the continuum from capital-intensive to coercion-intensive regions. The centrality of these various intermediaries identified alternative systems of indirect rule.

Any system of indirect rule set serious limits on the quantity of resources that rulers could extract from the ambient economy. Beyond that limit, intermediaries acquired an interest in impeding extraction, even in allying themselves with ordinary people's resistance to state demands. In the same circumstances, however, rulers developed an interest both in undermining the autonomous powers of intermediaries and in making coalitions with major segments of the subject population. As war demanded greater resources, emphatically including manpower, and as the threat of conquest by the largest states grew more serious, ever more rulers bypassed, suppressed, or coopted old intermediaries and reached directly into communities and households to seize the wherewithal of war. Thus, national standing armies, national states, and direct rule caused each other.

The growth of domestically recruited standing armies offered a strong stimulus to direct rule. Although rented troops persisted in some armies through the eighteenth cenury, rulers in regions of capitalized coercion--especially in France, Prussia, and England--began to move away from wholesale engagement of mercenary armies during the seventeenth century. Mercenaries had the severe drawbacks of being unreliable when poorly paid, seeking booty and rapine when not closely supervised, causing widespread trouble when demobilized, and costing a great deal of cash. The effort to maintain substantial armies in peacetime, pioneered by such rulers as Prussia's Friedrich Wilhelm in the seventeenth century, exceeded the ability of most states to tax the essential revenues, especially in the face of competition from regional powerholders. These circumstances encouraged rulers to establish durable domestic military administrations, and then to conscript, coopt, and penetrate. These steps bypassed intermediaries and led the way from indirect to direct rule.

The domestic recruitment of large standing armies entailed serious costs. While discharged mercenaries had few enforceable claims on any states, veterans of a national force did, especially if they had incurred disabilities in the nation's service. Families of dead or wounded warriors also acquired benefits such as preference in the state-run sale of tobacco and matches. The garrisoning of troops within the country involved military officials and their civilian counterparts in food supply, housing, and public order. Eventually, the health and education of all young males, which affected their military effectiveness, became governmental concerns. Thus, military reorganization entered a wedge for expansion of state activity into what had previously been local and private spheres.

European states began forcing the choice between local and national loyalties during the eighteenth century. Although Enlightenment "reforms" often had the effect of reinforcing direct rule, the most sensational move in that direction was no doubt the work of the French Revolution and Empire. French actions from 1789 to 1815 forwarded the general European transition from indirect to direct rule in two ways: by providing a model of centralized government that other states emulated, and by imposing variants of that model wherever France conquered. Even though many of the period's innovations in French government emerged from desperate improvisations in response to threats of rebellion and bankruptcy, their battle-tested forms endured beyond the Revolution and Empire.

What happened to France's system of rule during the revolutionary years? Before 1789 the French state, like almost all other states, ruled indirectly at the local level, relying especially on priests and nobles for mediation. From the end of the American war, the government's efforts to collect money to cover its war debts crystallized an antigovernmental coalition that initially included the *Parlements* and other powerholders, but changed toward a more popular composition as the confrontation between the regime and its opponents sharpened. The state's visible vulnerability in 1788 — 1789 encouraged any group that had a stifled claim or grievance against the state, its agents, or its allies to articulate its demands and join others in calling for change. The rural revolts--Great Fear, grain seizures, tax rebellions, attacks on landlords, and so on--of spring and summer 1789 occurred disproportionately in regions with large towns, commercialized agriculture, navigable waterways, and many roads. Their geography reflected a composite but largely bourgeois-led settling of scores.

At the same time, those whose social survival depended most directly on the Old Regime state--nobles, officeholders, and higher clergy are the obvious examples--generally aligned themselves with the king. Thus, a revolutionary situation began to form: Two distinct blocs both claimed power and both received support from some significant part of the population. With significant defections of military men from the crown and the formation of militias devoted to the popular cause, the opposition acquired force of its own. The popular bloc, connected and often led by members of the bourgeoisie, started to gain control over parts of the state apparatus.

The lawyers, officials, and other bourgeois who seized the state apparatus in 1789 — 1790 rapidly displaced the old intermediaries: landlords, seigneurial officials, venal officeholders, clergy, and sometimes municipal oligarchies as well. At a local level, the so-called Municipal Revolution widely transferred power to enemies of the old rulers; patriot coalitions based in militias, clubs, and revolutionary committees and linked to Parisian activists ousted the old municipalities. Even where the old powerholders managed to survive the Revolution's early turmoil, relations between each locality and the national capital altered abruptly. Village "republics" of the Alps, for example, found their ancient liberties--including ostensibly free consent to taxes--crumbling as outsiders clamped them into the new administrative machine. Then Parisian revolutionaries faced the problem of governing without intermediaries; they experimented with the committees and militias that had appeared in the mobilization of 1789, but found them hard to control from the center. More or less simultaneously they recast the French map into a nested system of departments, districts, cantons, and communes, while sending out *représentants en mission* to forward revolutionary reorganization. They installed direct rule.

Furthermore, given the unequal spatial distribution of cities, merchants, and capital, the imposition of a uniform geographic grid altered the relations between cities' economic and political power, placing insignificant Mende and Niort at the same administrative level as mighty Lyon and Bordeaux. Within

Old Regime France, cities whose commercial rank exceeded their administrative stature included, for example, Nîmes, Saint-Etienne, Roubaix, and Castres; those occupying higher administrative than commercial rank included Tulle, Saint-Amand-en-Berry, Saint-Flour, and Soissons.

The Revolution reordered that relationship. Among capitals of the eighty-six original départements, fifty-four were indisputably the dominant cities within the new jurisdictions, three won out through size over others that had higher administrative and fiscal ranks under the Old Regime, six maintained their administrative priority despite smaller size, twelve became capitals despite being neither the largest nor the highest ranking of their regions, and ten were too close to call. Larger cities that failed to win departmental capitals clustered disproportionately in northern France, with Atlantic and Mediterranean ports also having more than their share. The great discrepancies, however, did not appear on the local level, but as inequalities among the eighty-six capitals, now all nominally occupying identical administrative relations to the national capital.

As a result, the balance of forces in regional capitals shifted significantly: In the great commercial centers, where merchants, lawyers, and professionals already clustered, departmental officials (who frequently came, in any case, from the same milieus) had no choice but to bargain with the locals. Where the National Assembly carved departments out of relatively uncommercialized rural regions, the Revolution's administrators overshadowed other residents of the new capitals and could plausibly threaten to use force if they were recalcitrant. But in those regions they lacked the bourgeois allies who helped their confrères do the Revolution's work elsewhere, and confronted old intermediaries who still commanded significant followings.

In great mercantile centers such as Marseilles and Lyon, the political situation was very different. By and large, the Federalist movement, with its protests against Jacobin centralism and its demands for regional autonomy, took root in departmental capitals whose commercial positions greatly outpaced their administrative rank. In dealing with these alternative obstacles to direct rule, Parisian revolutionaries improvised three parallel, and sometimes conflicting, systems of rule: (1) the committees and militias; (2) a geographically defined hierarchy of elected officials and representatives; and (3) roving commissioners from the central government. To collect information and gain support, all three relied extensively on the existing personal networks of lawyers, professionals, and merchants.

As the system began to work, revolutionary leaders strove to routinize their control and contain independent action by local enthusiasts, who often resisted. Using both cooptation and repression, they gradually squeezed out the committees and militias. Mobilization for war put great pressure on the system, incited new resistance, and increased the national leaders' incentives for a tight system of control. Starting in 1792, the central administration (which until then had continued in a form greatly resembling that of the Old Regime) underwent its own revolution: The staff expanded enormously, and a genuine hierarchical bureaucracy took shape. In the process, revolutionaries installed one of the first systems of direct rule ever to take shape in a large state.

That shift entailed changes in systems of taxation, justice, public works, and much more. Consider policing. Outside of the Paris region, France's Old Regime state had almost no specialized police of its own; it dispatched the Maréchaussée to pursue tax evaders, vagabonds, and other violators of royal will and occasionally authorized the army to quell rebellious subjects, but otherwise relied on local and regional authorities to deploy armed force against civilians. The revolutionaries changed things. With respect to ordinary people, they moved from reactive to proactive policing and information-gathering: Instead of simply waiting until a rebellion or collective violation of the law occurred, and then retaliating ferociously but selectively, they began to station agents whose job was to anticipate and prevent threatening popular collective action. During the Revolution's early years, Old Regime police forces generally dissolved as popular committees, National Guards, and revolutionary tribunals took over their day-to-day activities. But with the Directory the state concentrated surveillance and apprehension in a single centralized organization. Fouché of Nantes became minister of police in the Year VII/1799, and thenceforth ran a ministry whose powers extended throughout France and its conquered territories. By the time of Fouché, France had become one of the world's most closely policed countries.

Going to war accelerated the move from indirect to direct rule. Almost any state that makes war finds that it cannot pay for the effort from its accumulated reserves and current revenues. Almost all war-making states borrow extensively, raise taxes, and seize the means of combat--including men--from reluctant citizens who have other uses for their resources. Prerevolutionary France followed these rules faithfully, to the point of accumulating debts that eventually forced the calling of the Estates General. Nor did the Revolution repeal the rules: Once France declared war on Austria in 1792, the state's demands for revenues and manpower excited resistance just as fierce as that that had broken out under the Old Regime. In over-coming that resistance, the revolutionaries built yet another set of centralized controls.

Resistance and counterrevolutionary action followed directly from the process by which the new state established direct rule. Remember how much change revolutionaries introduced in a very short time. They eliminated all previous territorial jurisdictions, consolidated many old parishes into larger communes, abolished the tithe and feudal dues, dissolved corporations and their privileges, constructed a top-to-bottom administrative and electoral system, imposed expanded and standardized taxes through that system, seized the properties of emigrant nobles and of the Church, disbanded monastic orders, subjected the clergy to the state and imposed on them an oath to defend the new state church, conscripted young men at an unprecedented rate, and displaced both nobles and priests from the automatic exercise of local leadership. All this occurred between 1789 and 1793.

Subsequent regimes added more ephemeral changes such as the revolutionary calendar and the cult of the Supreme Being, but the early Revolution's overhaul of the state endured into the nineteenth century and set the pattern for many other European states. The greatest reversals concerned the throttling of local militias and revolutionary committees, the restoration or compensation of some confiscated properties, and Napoleon's Concordat with the Catholic Church. All in all, these changes constituted a dramatic, rapid substitution of uniform, centralized, direct rule for a system of government mediated by local and regional notables. What is more, the new state hierarchy consisted largely of lawyers, physicians, notaries, merchants, and other bourgeois.

Like their prerevolutionary counterparts, these fundamental changes attacked many existing interests and opened opportunities to groups that had previously had little access to state-sanctioned power--especially the village and small-town bourgeoisie. As a result, they precipitated both resistance and struggles for power. Artois (the Department of Pas-de-Calais) underwent a moderate version of the transition. In that region, large leaseholders dominated local politics, but only within limits set by their noble and ecclesiastical landlords. The Revolution, by sweeping away the privileges of those patrons, threatened the leaseholders' power. They survived the challenge, however, as a class, if not as a particular set of individuals. Many officeholders lost their posts during the struggles of the early Revolution, especially when the community was already at odds with its lord. Yet their replacements came disproportionately from the same class of comfortable leaseholders. The struggle of wage-laborers and smallholders against the *coqs de village* that Georges Lefebvre discovered in the adjacent Nord was less intense, or less effective, in the Pas-de-Calais. Although the larger farmers, viewed with suspicion by national authorities, lost some of their grip on public office during the Terror and again under the Directory, they regained it later and continued to rule their roosts through the middle of the nineteenth century. By that time, nobles and ecclesiastics had lost much of their capacity to contain local powerholders, but manufacturers, merchants, and other capitalists had taken their places. The displacement of the old intermediaries opened the way to a new alliance between large farmers and bourgeoisie.

Under the lead of Paris, the transition to direct rule went relatively smooothly in Artois. Elsewhere, intense struggle accompanied the change. The career of Claude Javogues, agent of the Revolution in his native Department of the Loire, reveals that struggle and the political process that incited it. Javogues was a huge, violent, hard-drinking roustabout whose close kin were lawyers, notaries, and merchants in Forez, a region not far to the west of Lyon. The family was on the ascendant in the eighteenth century, and in 1789 Claude himself was a well-connected thirty-year-old *avocat* at Montbrison. The Convention dispatched this raging bourgeois bull to the Loire in July 1793 and recalled him in February 1794. During those six months, Javogues relied heavily on his existing connections, concentrated on repression of the Revolution's enemies, acted to a large degree on the theory that priests, nobles, and rich landlords were the enemies, neglected and bungled administrative matters such as the organization of food supply, and left behind him a reputation for arbitrariness and cruelty.

Yet Javogues and his co-workers did, in fact, reorganize local life. In following his action in the Loire, we encounter clubs, surveillance committees, revolutionary armed forces, commissars, courts, and *représentants en mission*. We see an almost unbelievable attempt to extend the direct administrative purview of the central government to everyday individual life. We recognize the importance of popular mobilization against the Revolution's enemies--real or imagined--as a force that displaced the old intermediaries. We therefore gain insight into the conflict between two objectives of the Terror: extirpation of the Revolution's opponents and forging of instruments to do the work of the Revolution. We discover again the great importance of control over food as an administrative challenge, as a point of political contention, and as an incentive to popular action.

Contrary to the old image of a unitary people welcoming the arrival of long-awaited reform, local histories of the Revolution make clear that France's revolutionaries established their power struggle and frequently over stubborn popular resistance. Most of the resistance, it is true, took the form of evasion, cheating, and sabotage rather than outright rebellion. But people through most of France resisted one feature or another of revolutionary direct rule. In the bustling port of Collioure, on the Mediterranean close to the Spanish border, popular collective action during the Revolution, consciously or not, pursued the goal of preserving a certain cultural, economic, and institutional independence. In other words, popular action sought to challenge the French state's claims to intervene in local life in order to raise troops for international wars, to change religious organization, or to control trade across the Pyrenees. The issues differed from region to region as a function of previous history, including the previous relations of capital and coercion. Where the fault lines ran deep, resistance consolidated into counterrevolution: the formation of effective alternative authorities to those put in place by the Revolution. Counterrevolution occurred not where everyone opposed the Revolution, but where irreconcilable differences divided well-defined blocs of supporters and opponents on a large geographic scale.

France's South and West, through similar processes, produced the largest zones of sustained counterrevolution. The geography of executions under the Terror provides a reasonable picture of counterrevolutionary activity. The departments with more than two hundred executions included, in descending order: Loire Inférieure, Seine, Maine-et-Loire, Rhône, Vendée, Ille-et-Vilaine, Mayenne, Vaucluse, Bouches-du-Rhône, Pas-de-Calais, Var, Gironde, and Sarthe. These departments accounted for 89 percent of all executions under the Terror. Except for the Seine and the Pas-de-Calais, they concentrated in the South, the Southwest, and especially, the West. In the South and Southwest, Languedoc, Provence, Gascony, and the Lyonnais hosted military insurrections against the Revolution, insurrections whose geography corresponded closely to support for Federalism. Federalist movements began in the spring of 1793, when the Jacobin expansion of the foreign war--including the declaration of war on Spain--incited resistance to taxation and conscription, which in turn led to a tightening of revolutionary surveillance and discipline. The autonomist movement peaked in commercial cities that had enjoyed extensive liberties under the Old Regime, notably Marseilles, Bordeaux, Lyon, and Caen. Sustained rural counterrevolution, on the other hand, broke out chiefly in regions whose revolutionary capitals had occupied relatively low ranks in the Old Regime's administrative, fiscal, and demographic hierarchies, and whose bourgeois therefore had relatively weak influence in the surrounding regions. In those two kinds of cities and their hinterlands, France fell into bloody civil war.

In the West, guerrilla raids against republican strongholds and personnel unsettled Brittany, Maine, and Normandy from 1791 to 1799, while open armed rebellion flared south of the Loire in parts of Brittany, Anjou, and Poitou beginning in the fall of 1792 and likewise continuing intermittently until Napolean pacified the region in 1799. The western counterrevolution reached its high point in the spring of 1793, when the Republic's call for troops precipitated armed resistance through much of the west. That phase saw massacres of "patriots" and "aristocrats" (as the proponents and opponents of the Revolution came to be called), invasion and temporary occupation of such major cities as Angers, and pitched battles between armies of Blues and Whites (as the armed elements of the two parties were known).

The West's counterrevolution grew directly from the efforts of revolutionary officials to install a particular kind of direct rule in the region: a rule that practically eliminated nobles and priests from their positions as partly autonomous intermediaries, that brought the state's demands for taxes, manpower, and deference to the level of individual communities, neighborhoods, and households, that gave the regions bourgeois political power they had never before wielded. They consolidated their power through struggle. On October 12, 1790, at la Chapelle de Belle-Croix, Vendée, a number of people from neighboring parishes arrived for mass and vespers armed with clubs. "Seeing the local National Guard with their regular uniforms and arms, the strangers came up to them and said they had no right to wear the national uniform, that they were going to strip it from them, that they supported the cause of clergy and nobility and wanted to crush the bourgeois who, they said, were taking bread from priests and nobles." They then attacked the Guards and the Maréchaussée of Palluau, who only fought them off with difficulty. In the mouths of Vendeans, to be sure, the word *bourgeois* conflated class and urban residence; nevertheless, the people of that counterrevolutionary region saw clearly enough that the two connected intimately. In seeking to extend the state's rule to every locality and to dislodge all enemies of that rule, French revolutionaries started a process that did not cease for twenty-five years. In some ways, it has not yet ceased today.

In these regards, for all its counterrevolutionary ferocity, the west conformed to France's general experience. Everywhere in France, bourgeois-- not owners of large industrial establishments, for the most part, but merchants, lawyers, notaries, and others who made their living from the possession and manipulation of capital--were gaining strength during the eighteenth century. Throughout France, the mobilization of 1789 brought disproportionate numbers of bourgeois into political action. As the revolutionaries of Paris and their provincial allies displaced nobles and priests from their critical positions as agents of indirect rule, the existing networks of bourgeois served as alternative connections between the state and thousands of communties across the land. For a while, those connections rested on a vast popular mobilization through clubs, militias, and committees. Gradually, however, revolutionary leaders contained or even suppressed their turbulent partners. With trial, error, and struggle, the ruling bourgeoisie worked out a system of rule that reached directly into local communities and passed chiefly through administrators who served under the scrutiny and budgetary control of their superiors.

     This process of state expansion encountered three huge obstacles. First, many people saw opportunities to forward their own interests and settle old scores opened up in the crisis of 1789. They either managed to capitalize on the opportunity or found their hopes blocked by competition from other actors; both categories lacked incentives to support further revolutionary changes. Second, the immense effort of warring with most other European powers strained the state's capacity at least as gravely as had the wars of Old Regime kings. Third, in some regions the political bases of the newly empowered bourgeois were too fragile to support the work of cajoling, containing, inspiring, threatening, extracting, and mobilizing that revolutionary agents carried on everywhere. Resistance to demands for taxes, conscripts, and compliance with moralizing legislation occurred widely in France, but where preexisting rivalries placed a well-connected bloc in opposition to the revolutionary bourgeoisie, civil war frequently developed. In these senses, the revolutionary transition from indirect to direct rule embodied a bourgeois revolution and engendered a series of antibourgeois counterrevolutions.

     Many outstanding specialists will surely disagree with my analysis, in part or as a whole. Some will challenge the very agenda it broadcasts: investigation of class politics during the Revolution, of the implantation of revolutionary control, of organizational change in the state--old-fashioned topics that return us to issues long since raised by Jules Michelet, Jean Jaurès, and Georges Lefebvre. Vive la vivacité du combat! Let diversity reign. Yet it would be satisfying if, at the bicentennial of 1793, 1795, or 1799, people remembered the Hofstra conference of 1989 as the one at which scholars again began thinking seriously about the actual mechanisms of the sweeping political process by which the French Revolution became a world-historical event.

NOTES

     1. G. William Skinner, "Cities and the Hierarchy of Local Systems" and "Introduction: Urban Social Structure in Ch'ing China" in G. William Skinner (ed.), *The City in Late Imperial China* (Stanford, Calif.: Stanford University Press, 1977), 275-351, 521-553.

2. Bernard Lepetit, *The Pre-Industrial Urban System*, translated by Godfrey Rogers, New York, N.Y.: Cambridge University Press, 1994.

16

The Nobility's New Clothes: Revisionism and the Survival of the Nobility During the French Revolution

John Dunne

> Whoever won the Revolution the noble landlord lost.
>> R. Forster, "The Survival of the Nobility
>> During the French Revolution" (1967)[1]

> . . . the old landed families survive[d] the decade of
> Revolution with their estates intact.
>> R. Forster, "The French Revolution and the New
>> Elite, 1800-50," (1980)[2]

Forster's change of heart is a dramatic illustration of the remarkable shift that has taken place in historical opinion over the last twenty years concerning the "problem of the nobility and the French Revolution." Up until the 1960s, the notion that a decaying aristocracy paid for its resistance to the Revolution with its elimination as an effective social force was the one fixed point in a changing and uncertain historiography. Virtually all recent publications--both monographs and general histories of the Revolution--tell a very different story. The story goes roughly as follows. Far from the parasitic caste depicted in Sieyès' *What Is the Third Estate?*, the late eighteenth-century nobility was a remarkably open, diverse and--in its leading elements--dynamic group. It goes without saying that such a sociological nonentity was incapable of presenting a united front against the liberal revolution; indeed, many of the wealthiest and best educated nobles were in the vanguard of reform. Of course, as the Revolution careened onwards, many of them had second thoughts. But the idea of solid and implacable noble resistance to the Republic is now seen as a figment of radical rhetoric. In the end, however, not too much damage was done. Forster's contention that noble fortunes did not suffer unduly from the slings and arrows of revolutionary legislation seems to command general acceptance among the specialists. Indeed, for some the real issue is when in the course of the nineteenth century, and for what reasons, did the decline of the nobility actually begin.[3]

This historiographical u-turn, of course, forms part of the wider paradigm shift that has occurred within the field of French revolutionary studies since Cobban's initial onslaught on the classic "bourgeois revolution" interpretation.[4] With the waning acceptance of this particular Marxist model, it became possible for historians to think about the nobility in terms other than simply the losing side in a fight to the finish between old and new ruling classes. Conversely, the new writing on the nobility has been instrumental in establishing the current "revisionist" paradigm of the Revolution.[5] Most of the harder evidence that revisionist historians point to as demonstrating the superiority of their own version of events over the rival one relates directly to the nobility. The view that the Revolution in its constructive phase was the work not of a rising bourgeois class but of a mixed elite of property owners--noble as well as commoner--relies largely on evidence of the liberal or at least conciliatory inclinations of the second order prior to the meeting of the Estates General.[6] The argument that the Revolution was in its outcome, as well as its origins, a "revolution of the notables"--and its corollary that the period of the Terror was without material consequence--is similarly dependent on evidence of the order's long-term economic survival.[7]

Given their enormous strategic importance in the battle for the Revolution, the various revisionist theses on the problem of the nobility and the Revolution have been subjected to surprisingly little close critical scrutiny.[8] Even Marxist academics have accepted the empirical basis of much of this revisionist work, merely asserting that it is not necessarily resistant to a Marxian analysis of sorts.[9] In my view, this acceptance is premature. Undoubtedly, the evidence put forward by the revisionists succeeds in demonstrating the elements of distortion and caricature in the old view, but it does not seem to me sufficient to establish their own counterclaims. Although the point could be substantiated in relation to the nobles' role in the making of the Revolution, in the remainder of this chapter I will confine myself to the question of the impact of the Revolution on their economic position in French society.[10]

It might be objected that the kind of exercise I am about to engage in is rather trivial. Even if successful, does it not simply exemplify what to philosophers, if not always practitioners, of history is a truism? Namely, that no historical interpretation can accommodate all the bewildering mass of available evidence about the past. My justification is not merely that the matter of degree is important here. Revisionism, at least in Britain, has generally been held to represent the triumph of fact over theory, of Anglo-Saxon empiricism over Marxist a priorism.[11] If it succeeds in drawing attention to the naivete of this epistemological stance, this chapter will have performed some service.

What is the evidential basis for the shift in received opinion on the question of the survival of the nobility during the French Revolution? The most substantial body of material concerns noble landownership in postrevolutionary society. When in 1964 Cobban cautiously mused: "it would be interesting to know to what extent . . . the *noblesse* kept its lands during the Revolution, or regained them after temporary loss," French historians outside the field of Revolutionary history were already mining two sources that were to provide an indirect and partial answer: the cadastral surveys and electoral lists of the censitary political systems of the first half of the nineteenth century.[12] Conspicuous among the mass of resultant publications was Tudesq's pioneering study of the national political-cum-wealth elite of the July Monarchy which revealed for the first time the great preponderance of nobles among France's major landowners.[13] The cumulative effect of this laborious research at both national and departmental levels has been to show, as one recent synthesis concludes, "that the French nobility comes out of the revolution still in a position of strength . . . insofar as its economic base in land was concerned."[14] That this position was not simply the artificial product of an "aristocratic reaction" of the Bourbon Restoration is evident from subsequent work on the composition of provincial elites under Napolean.[15]

While sufficient to demolish the catastrophic view of the Revolution's impact on the nobility, this material is not quite up to the load placed on it by proponents of the alternative continuity position. The composite picture of the landownership of the old nobility in postrevolutionary France is deficient in two respects. In the first place, virtually all the studies from which it is made up contain a serious methodological flaw. To identify nobles on cadastral and electoral lists, historians have taken the presence of the *particule* in a name to indicate its bearer's noble status. If, as Gibson points out, it is understandable that, in view of the sheer practical difficulty of more correct procedures, historians have taken this shortcut, the consequences are nonetheless unfortunate.[16] Not only are men who, like Giscard's ancestor, usurped noble status by means of a simple name change confused with the real thing, but these more recent bearers of noble title also include a leavening of new creations of the Napoleonic and Restoration period alongside the *nobles d'ancien régime*. Just how great is the magnitude of error which might result has been demonstrated by Gibson in relation to the *conseil-général* of the Dordogne. In 1840, although 36.7 percent of members' names contained the *particule*, only one-fifth were actually descended (through the male line) from the former Second Estate.[17]

Second and more seriously, the electoral lists, which have attracted far more attention than the unwieldy cadastral surveys, have by their very censitary nature another defect. While identifying the many nobles who satisfied the admittedly modest tax qualifications for exercise of the vote, they cannot disprove the existence of a substantial impoverished nobility outside the propertied political nation. And since there is no way of carrying out a retrospective census of the noble population of postrevolutionary France, we cannot know what proportion "the many" represent. In an important article, which ultimately comes down on the side of the revisionists, Beck has attempted to circumvent this problem by setting the known number of noble electors in the 1840s against estimates of the noble population in 1789. The results are hardly supportive of his case. The former--despite including new and "self-made" nobles along with descendants of the old families--represent such a modest proportion of even the lowest estimated figure for 1789 that he is forced to conclude: "There appears to have been either a substantial decline in the number of nobles or the creation of a *noblesse pauvre* of sizable proportions." His reasons for preferring the first possibility are obscure and unconvincing.[18]

Even if Beck's intuition is correct (and most heads of *ancien régime* noble families under the July Monarchy were indeed alive and well and living in the propertied political nation), we should still be unable to conclude that their material health had not been seriously undermined by the ordeal of the revolutionary decade. The existence of an important landed base in the second quarter of the nineteenth century is no guarantee that it had not shrunk considerably as the result of revolutionary expropriations. Clearly, only comparative study of noble landholding before and after the Revolution can establish whether or not this was the case. Few such comparisons have been attempted--and their findings point in different directions. From a sample of twenty-eight communes Bois has concluded that no perceptible decline in noble landownership occurred in the Sarthe between 1777 and 1830.[19] Beck's comparison of his own data drawn from the electoral lists of the July Monarchy with Lefebvre's analysis of the prerevolutionary situation in six "representative" departments tells a different story, or rather a number of different stories: the drop in noble landownership ranges from 80 percent in the Côte d'Or to just 6 percent in the Haute-Vienne.[20] The average decrease, however, (which is not supplied), seems to have been close on two-thirds.

Since the "before and after" approach has so far produced only meagre and inconclusive results, the question of the impact of revolutionary legislation has to be addressed directly. It is because of their failure to properly pursue this line of inquiry that the revisionists' case fails to convince. The whole question of the financial losses sustained as a result of the Revolution's liquidation of the corporate society and seigneurialism is virtually absent in the recent literature. Consequently, the few pages devoted to this subject in Forster's article written in his prerevisionist phase remain the last word on the subject.[21] The more crucial issue of noble land losses resulting from the confiscation of émigré property has not been quite so neglected. Nevertheless, revisionist historiography has been less than wholehearted in its efforts to get to grips with the available evidence.

In 1967 Forster observed that for a proper assessment of the impact of revolutionary confiscations "we must first know what proportion of the Second Estate emigrated."[22] This apparently unobjectionable piece of advice has since gone unheeded. The revisionist argument that the effect on noble fortunes of anti-émigré legislation had been seriously overestimated has not been accompanied by any parallel attempt to similarly revise previous estimates of the incidence of noble emigration. None of the current generation of revisionist historians, including Forster himself, has bothered to refute the calculation made in his early "pessimistic" essay that "one noble family in four" was affected by emigration.[23] In the course of the most trenchant statement of the revisionist case to date, Blanning is unusual in feeling the necessity to minimize the significance of the émigré current: "for every Comte d'Artois who demonstratively emigrated, there were a dozen who stayed at home and quietly got on with making the best of it."[24] Yet he does so by a slight of the pen rather than statistical argument. This proportion is, in fact, virtually the same as the one taken as the basis for Forster's calculation. Since there is no doubt that emigration was an option taken essentially by adult male nobles, it follows that most of Blanning's dozen, stay-at-home conformists were women and children.[25]   In view of this consideration, the formulation "one noble family in four" surely conveys the order's experience more meaningfully.

In fact, there are good reasons for thinking that Forster's figure needs revising--but in an upward direction. Higonnet, at least, believes that Greer's estimate of the number of noble émigrés, which has been taken as standard, falls considerably short of the mark.[26]   More crucially, there is the vexed question of the overall extent of the noble population at the onset of the Revolution. All widely cited estimates of the incidence of emigration have taken a base figure of between five hundred thousand, used by Greer, and the two hundred thousand preferred by Forster.[27]   However, in the most recent study of the eighteenth-century nobility the arch-revisionist Chaussinand-Nogaret puts the number of nobles in 1789 at no more than 120,000.[28]   The specialists are as yet undecided on the merits of his case. Either way, however, revisionism in one form or another is the loser. If his figure is incorrect, then so is his depiction of the order on the eve of the Revolution as lean, fit, and thoroughly rejuvenated by frequent transfusions of new blood. On the other hand, if he is right, we must conclude with Beck that more than half of all noble families were affected by emigration during the Revolution.[29]

Of course, not all families affected by emigration suffered permanent land losses as a result. Some managed to prevent their estates going under the auctioneer's hammer; others sooner or later repurchased what they had lost. It is in these areas that revisionists have concentrated their fire, cataloguing the dodges employed by émigré relatives and lawyers to circumvent the revolutionary legislation, and accumulating instances of successful reconstitution.[30]   However, their efforts are some way from achieving the desired effect. First, this is because the evidence presented is so largely anecdotal in character; the fascinating family histories they relate could be countered by other very different ones.   Only Denis, for the Department of the Mayenne, has done the appropriate sums--calculating the proportion of sequestrated property actually sold off, which in one district amounted to just over a quarter (26 percent); and, by a most ingenious procedure, estimating that two-fifths of alienated propery was later repurchased by its former owners.[31]   However, as Denis, but not everyone who cites him, is well aware, the Mayenne is not France. Both its afforested character and, even more, the strength of counterrevolutionary feeling in this western department go a long way toward explaining the feeble impact of the sales. Second, proponents of continuity tend to conflate cases of avoidance of sales and repurchase, treating both as instances of economic survival.   In reality, repurchase repaired a family's influence and standing at great financial cost. In such cases, anti-émigré legislation effectively imposed anything up to a 100 percent tax on the offender's real estate. No doubt, indebtedness resulting from earlier efforts to reconstitute their patrimony was a major cause of what Denis calls "l'effacement des grands seigneurs," which occurred in the Mayenne during the Restoration, as the great court families sold up and left the department for good.[32]

The publicity given to Denis's important but localized findings contrasts with the current neglect of the only work to use quantitative national data on the impact of revolutionary confiscations and sales: Gain's monumental study-- published in the 1920s--of the Indemnity Law of 1825, which provided com- pensation for losses incurred through emigration.[33] The recent disappearance of this work from the historiography has been most convenient for the re- visionist case, since it offers strong support for the traditional view. Of the 25,000 émigrés from all classes of society who received some compensation for lands sold during the Revolution, it is Gain's conviction that the "majority . . . were nobles."[34] If this is so, we must conclude that however successful émigrés were subsequently in reconstituting their domains, comparatively few had avoided expropriation and sale in the first instance. Maybe--that is taking the worst possible case scenario based on the lowest estimate of their overall number--every other noble family suffered some significant loss.

It would be wrong to end this chapter on a definitive note. Firm conclusions are out of order in a field of study where answers to the basic quantitative questions--how many nobles were there in 1789, how many emigrated, and how many were expropriated?--rely on such a large dose of impressionism. (Indeed, this chapter is also intended as a plea for further research into such questions at a time when the vogue is for work to be pursued across rather than along the lines of *ancien régime* order).[35] All that can be said with any degree of confidence is that the balance of available evidence is on the side of Forster's first rather second thoughts. How has so much professional opinion reached the opposite conclusion? Surely it is because the revisionist paradigm has operated in the same way as Marxist theory before it. Rather than an assembly of empirical conclusions, revisionism is better seen as a cluster of a priori propositions that have governed the historians' selection of evidence. Unlike what is found in Marxism, these propositions are not derived from a positive theory or philosophy of history. Instead, they result from a negation or inversion of Marxist theses. After theory comes not empiricism but antitheory.

NOTES

1. R. Forster, "The Survival of the Nobility During the French Revolution" *Past and Present*, 37 (1967), 86.

2. R. Forster, "The French Revolution and the New Elite, 1800— 1850," in J. Pelenski (ed.), *The American and European Revolutions 1776—1848* (Iowa, 1980), 188.

3. Among the most influential works in English which articulate the

traditional view are G. Lefebvre, *The Coming of the French Revolution* (Princeton, N.J., 1947) and A. Soboul, *A Short History of the French Revolution* (Berkeley, 1965). The most forceful statements of the new view are to be found in: G. Chaussinand-Nogaret, *La noblesse au XVIII-siècle: de la féodalité aux lumières* (Paris, 1976), W. Doyle, *Origins of the French Revolution* (Oxford, 1980), and T. Blanning, *The French Revolution: Aristocrats versus Bourgeois?* (London, 1987). The debate on the timing and causes of the nobility's ultimate decline is carried on in D. Higgs, "Politics and Landownership among the French Nobility after the Revolution," *European Studies Review*, 1 (April 1971) and R. Gibson, "The French nobility in the Nineteenth century--particularly in the Dordogne," in J. Howorth and P. Cerny, *Elites in France: Origins, Reproduction and Power* (London, 1981).

4. A. Cobban, *The Social Interpretation of the French Revolution* (Cambridge, 1964).

5. Doyle makes a point of the importance of new writing on the nobility to the whole revisionist enterprise: *Origins*, 15.

6. Most notably in Chaussinand-Nogaret, *La Noblesse*.

7. Blanning, *The French Revolution*, 6 and 45.

8. This is almost as true of the entire revisionist approach to the Revolution and its outcome. However, Bill Edmonds "Successes and Excesses of Revisionist Writing about the French Revolution," *European History Quarterly* 17, no. 2 (April 1987) makes some telling criticisms of revisionist arguments against a revolutionary bourgeoisie but does not look at the other side of the coin.

9. The most striking case is G. Comninel, *Rethinking the French Revolution* (London, 1987).

10. I have done so in my MA dissertation (Hull University, 1986): *Counting Noble Heads: Nobility and Revolution in the Rouen Region. An Initial Report.*

11. See, for example, Doyle's historiographical survey which constitutes Part I of his *Origins*. By contrast, French revisionism with its association with *Annales* has no such antipathy to theory as such.

12. Cobban, *The Social Interpretation*, 87.

13. A. Tudesq, *Les grands notables en France (1840—1849): étude historique d'une psychologie sociale*, 2 vols. (Paris, 1964).

14. Gibson, "The French Nobility," 13.

15. L. Bergeron, *L'Episode napoléonien: Aspects intérieurs 1799-1815* (Paris, 1972), summarizes research up to the date of publication; my unpublished Ph.D. thesis, "Notables and Society during the Napoleonic Period: the Seine-Inférieure 1799–1815 (University of London, 1988), documents the importance of the noble presence in this area.

16. For this point--and much else in this chapter--I am indebted to Gibson, "The French Nobility," 6.

17. Gibson, "The French Nobility," 7.

18. T. Beck, "The French Revolution and the Nobility: A Reconsideration," *Journal of Social History* (1981), 226.

19. P. Bois, *Paysans de l'Ouest: des structures économiques et sociales aux options politiques depuis l'époque révolutionnaire dans la Sarthe* (Le Mans, 1960), 319-321.

20. Beck, "The French Revolution," 223.

21. Forster, "The Survival," 72-74.

22. Ibid.

23. Ibid., 75.

24. Blanning, *The French Revolution*, 44.

25. D. Greer, *The Incidence of the Emigration During the Revolution* (Cambridge, Mass., 1951), 84-85.

26. P. Higonnet, *Class, Ideology and the Rights of Nobles During the French Revolution* (1981), 285; Greer, *The Incidence of the Emigration*, 84.

27. Greer, *The Incidence of the Emigration*, 69; Forster, "The Survival," 75.

28. Chaussinand-Nogaret, *La Noblesse*, 48.

29. Beck, "The French Revolution," 227-228.

30. See, for example, the cited works by Higgs and Gibson.

31. M. Denis, *Les royalistes de la Mayenne et le monde moderne*

XIX-XX siècles) (Paris, 1977), 157-163.

32. Ibid., 15.

33. A. Gain, *La Restauration et les biens des émigrés*, Vol. II (Nancy, 1928).

34. Ibid., 470.

35. C. Lucas, "Notable against Notable," *Times Literary Supplement*, May 8, 1981, 525.

17

The Rights of Man and the Right to Vote: The Franchise Question During the French Revolution

Malcolm Crook

The study of elections is a poor relation of revolutionary historiography.[1] Many aspects of the subject remain unclear or little investigated, and the very nature of the franchise is frequently misunderstood, although the prolonged debate over how citizens should exercise their electoral rights was an extremely important one. This chapter seeks to clarify the situation, not only by reexamining suffrage legislation during the 1790s, but also by exploring its application at the local level. Limitations on the revolutionary franchise have often been exaggerated and sometimes blamed for inhibiting participation in electoral politics. I will argue that, on the contrary, it was the system of indirect elections, through the agency of electoral colleges, that constituted the real barrier to democracy, while the antiquated procedures inherited from the *ancien régime* constituted a major cause of widespread abstentionism.

By rendering the nation, or the people, the source of sovereignty in France, the revolutionaries placed the question of who should vote and how they should do so at the center of the political agenda. It was generally agreed, however, that the issue of "direct democracy" was already being raised in the districts of Paris and that the size of the country necessitated a representative system of some sort. The sovereignty of the people was, therefore, transformed into a *droit d'élire*, and a definition of the franchise became essential.[2] In a report presented to the *Comité de Constitution*, toward the end of July 1789, the influential abbé Sieyès had already floated the notion of a distinction between "active citizens" who voted and "passive citizens" who did not.[3]

Most deputies in the National Constituent Assembly agreed with Sieyès's ideas, which also reflected the accumulated wisdom of the *philosophes*.[4] When the *Comité de Constitution's* proposals on the franchise were presented to the National Assembly by its spokesman Jacques-Guillaume Thouret, on September 29, they duly reflected the prevailing consensus on the need for restrictions. Not just two categories of citizens, active and passive, were recommended, but four. Active citizens, who qualified by the payment of the equivalent of three days' local wages in direct taxation, had to cross a further hurdle of ten *journées de travail* in impositions before they became eligible for local office. Finally, in order to serve as a national deputy, a tax payment worth the weight of a silver mark was also required.[5] Access to active status thus became more selective the closer one came to the most important public offices.

What must be emphasized, however (for it is so often overlooked or misconstrued), is that the basic distinction between voters and nonvoters provoked little criticism in 1789. There was overwhelming acceptance from the Assembly, with the major exception of Robespierre who, when discussion commenced on October 22, subjected the *Comité's* proposals to a characteristically withering attack.   He maintained that the legislation was unconstitutional because it ran counter to no less than three articles of the Declaration of the Rights of Man and the Citizen, but few other deputies associated themselves with his protest.[6]

Muted opposition in the Assembly may not occasion too much astonishment, but the silence of the press is rather more surprising. As Aulard and Jaurès noted long ago, it was only when eligibility for office was discussed, as opposed to the basic right to vote, that protests of any magnitude began to be mounted within or outside of the Assembly.[7] What really aroused the ire of the deputies was not the *dix journées de travail* in taxation required for local office, but the *marc d'argent* (or tax payment to the value of roughly 50 *livres*) that was demanded of national deputies. It was this stipulation in particular that prompted warnings about the emergence of an "aristocratie de l'argent," while the lawyer Target observed that nineteen-twentieths of the electorate would be rendered ineligible for national office as a result.[8]

In the end it was decided that "in order to be eligible for the National Assembly, (the candidate) must pay a direct tax equivalent to the value of a *marc d'argent* and, in addition must have landed property of some sort."[9] There is no indication as to how many deputies voted against this decree, but opposition must have been considerable since this aspect of the franchise legislation, unlike the others, was to be reconsidered. In fact, on December 7, the *Comité de Constitution* was already prepared to soften its stance by the suggestion that, where a national deputy received 75 percent of the votes cast, the *marc d'argent* could be waived. Some lively debate occurred but the amendment was rejected, albeit by no more than a handful of votes.[10]

This time, however, the press did take up the gauntlet. The distinction between voters and nonvoters, like the modest fiscal requirement for local office, was still not called into question, but the *marc d'argent* for national deputies certainly was. Camille Desmoulins in *Les Révolutions de France et de Brabant*, declared, "It is enough to say that Jean-Jacques Rousseau, Corneille, Mably, would not have been eligible."[11] Marat's *L'Ami du Peuple* also inveighed against the pretensions of the emergent aristocracy of wealth, and Loustalot, in *Les Révolutions de Paris* exclaimed, "The aristocracy of wealth is established without shame," (before adding) "What! Our most worthy deputies at present will no longer be eligible." To be sure, the *marc d'argent* affected members of the National Assembly directly, in a way that the other franchise qualifications did not. As Jaurès comments somewhat sardonically, "It's the intellectual bourgeoisie that desires its place along side the bourgoisie of property."[12]

But what precisely did this complex franchise legislation mean in practice? When he presented the original proposals, Thouret had suggested that active citizenship would concern roughly one-sixth of the French population; he was to be proved right. A report drawn up by the *Comité des Contributions publiques* in May 1791 listed the number of *citoyens actifs* for each *département*, together with demographic and fiscal statistics.[13] Its total of 4,298,360 active citizens can be compared with a recent estimate for the number of French males who had reached the 25 years of age required to vote (though already some deputies had argued in favor of 21).[14] The resulting discrepancy suggests that over 2.5 million adult Frenchmen were excluded from the franchise, or roughly 40 percent of the age group. Dubois-Crancé was therefore wrong to suggest, during a debate on the admission of passive citizens to the National Guard in 1791, that "The only passive citizens who exist are beggars and vagabonds."[15]

In France as a whole there was considerable variation in the proportion of the population able to vote, ranging from 12.7 percent in the Haute-Vienne to 20.2 percent in the case of the Var. Generally speaking, however, the number of potential voters was relatively lower in the cities than in rural areas.[16] Dijon, for instance, had an active population of 12 percent, while the average for the Department of the Côte-d'Or was 18 percent. There are several reasons for the contrast, and first, there is the fact that taxes under the *ancien régime* tended to fall more heavily on the countryside. Second, towns tended to be penalized because they acted as a refuge for poorer people, especially at the end of the *ancien régime*. Third, it should not be forgotten that servants were not permitted to vote under the legislation passed in 1789. This might take quite a toll in the cities; Daniel Ligou has calculated that no less than 4 percent of the population of Dijon in 1790 comprised male servants! Finally, urban areas usually contained a more mobile population, and this could mean that even wealthy inhabitants might fall foul of the one-year residence qualification.[17]

It can, then, be concluded that no more than a quarter of French adult males were disenfranchised at the beginning of the Revolution on account of poverty. For the fixed, rural population, the suffrage was a very extensive one, especially in comparison with contemporary Britain or even with the fledgling United States.[18] On the other hand, voting regulations for the Estates General of 1789 had been more permissive since, in the countryside at least, *all* taxpayers had been allowed to vote.[19] Moreover, in 1789 no further qualification had been attached to eligibility, whereas further restrictions were imposed by the National Assembly in its franchise legislation later in the year. These additional requirements were by no means as draconian as many historians have implied. All too often the actual number of individuals who could serve on the departmental colleges, or fill local offices, in any given year has been confused with the huge pool from which they were chosen.[20] For whole departments where statistics are available, there is a range from 57 percent eligibility among active citizens in the Landes to 61 percent in the Calvados and 67 percent in the Doubs.[21] It can be concluded that roughly two-thirds of all *citoyens actifs* were also eligible for local offices in 1790--in other words a total in excess of 3 million Frenchmen, or almost half of all adult males.

The *marc d'argent*, however, demanded of such deputies was clearly a hurdle that few could cross; Target's contention, that no more than 5 percent of active citizens would qualify, was only a slight exaggeration. For the moment no rural statistics are at hand to compare with the urban situation at Dijon or Toulouse. Statistics available there would suggest that only half a million Frenchmen, or less than 10 percent of adult males, passed the national eligibility threshold at the outset of the Revolution.[22] Yet even this number was superior to the overall total of voters under the restored monarchy of the early nineteenth century. Given the breadth of the ordinary franchise and the generous degree of eligibility to local office, the focus of opposition in 1789 on the extremely exclusive *marc d'argent* becomes more comprehensible.

In any event, the *marc d'argent* was never applied because repeated campaigns to repeal it finally bore fruit in the summer of 1791. On August 5, Thouret, acting as *porte-parole* for the *Comité de Constitution et de révision*, proposed its withdrawal, though only at the cost of raising the contribution required for eligibility to the departmental electoral colleges.[23] After some stormy and prolonged debate, it was decided to institute a complex mechanism, which set particular eligibility conditions for different types of communities. Basically, the smaller the *commune*, the lower the annual property income that was needed (once again in terms of local wage levels) in order to become a member of the departmental electoral college.

These proposals were not put into effect in 1791, but they were employed in the later revolutionary Constitution of 1795. Registers compiled for eligibility to the departmental colleges after 1795 can provide a good indication of what would have happened under the proposed revisions of 1791, as well as illuminating levels of access during the final years of the Revolution. No statistics were published at the time, and none have been since, because they are by no means easy to unearth. In the Meuse, the urban canton of Bar (le Duc) listed 23 percent of its active citizens as *éligibles* for the elections of the year V (1797), and they included a minority of better-off artisans and shopkeepers.[24] By contrast, in rural areas of the department the proportions were generally lower, ranging downward to only 7 percent at Chardogne. Meanwhile, at Belle-Ile, a canton located off Quiberon point in the Morbihan, almost 9 percent of the electorate of the year VII (1799) were eligible for office.[25] Clearly, the legislation passed in 1795--like the intent of the revision of 1791--produced a severe reduction in the level of eligibility which in 1790 had been running above 60 percent.

The Constitution of 1795 had, in fact, reintroduced a qualification for the basic franchise, namely, the payment of "a tax which is direct, assessed upon land or paid individually."[26] But from 1792 to 1795, in between the so-called censitary periods of restricted suffrage, at the opening and closing of the revolutionary decade, a quasi-democratic franchise had been applied. Yet, all those adult males "en état de domesticité" remained excluded from voting, and the August decrees of 1792 stopped short of granting full universal manhood suffrage because the requirement that voters be self-supporting ruled out the large numbers dependent on welfare resources.[27] It was only the Constitution of 1793, which was accepted in a plebiscite but never implemented, that proclaimed a fully democratic franchise when it stated that: "Any man, born and residing in France who has reached his twenty-first birthday," could not only vote but also be elected to any office.[28]

It was the same ill-fated Constitution of 1793 that alone prescribed direct elections for national deputies. In the event after 1795, as before, all national elections were conducted according to a two-tier procedure, with primary elections in the cantons leading to the formation of departmental colleges. It is difficult to determine just how representative college delegates were of those who elected them in the primary assemblies. It would certainly be rash to associate the choice of national deputies with opinion in the departments as a whole.[29] Indeed, it was this indirect electoral procedure, inherited from the *ancien régime* and the elections to the Estates General in 1789, which constituted a much greater barrier to democratic participation than any restrictions on the franchise itself.

Deputies in the Constituent Assembly had adopted this traditional, two-step, electoral procedure in 1789 without demur, almost without discussion. A series of assemblies had, after all, served its purpose in elections to the Estates General by filtering out an enlightened elite of Third Estate representatives who were dedicated to reform.[30] For the same reasons and without considering any alternatives, the Assembly had also retained the tradition of voting in assemblies rather than individually.

When these details were debated in the National Assembly, in November 1789, they did prompt one complaint concerning the "excessive slowness" that such electoral assemblies might entail.[31] It was indeed extremely rare to complete an election of any sort in a single day. This was to impose an especially onerous burden on voters in rural cantonal elections because traveling was usually required to reach assemblies at the *chef-lieu*.

Such quaint procedures undoubtedly discouraged the development of new modes of electoral behavior after 1789, and further exploration of the whole issue would undoubtedly help to illuminate patterns of political culture of the Revolution. This particular treatment of the franchise question would not, however, be complete without a brief allusion to the levels of electoral participation that were actually recorded during the period. These, too, remain to be studied in a comprehensive fashion, but it is already apparent that, regardless of the regulations governing access to the franchise, many voters failed to attend the electoral assemblies.[32]

Indeed, the poorer the voter, the less likely he was to play any part. This conclusion can be drawn from a study of Toulon, where the franchise was universal from 1790 onward (in the absence of tax records from the *ancien régime*), but it was evident everywhere in 1792, when most restrictions were abolished. There were many reasons for low turnout, but it would not seem that limitation on the franchise was a major cause.

Universal manhood suffrage would not then, in itself, have automatically produced greater participation, whereas changes in the electoral mechanism might have done so. Needless to say, political stability and civic education would also have been required for a more effective apprenticeship in democracy in France during the 1790s.[33] Nevertheless, the Revolution did make a start by establishing a broad basic franchise throughout the decade and by accustoming the French people to the concept, if not always to the reality, of national sovereignty. Much remained to be done and setbacks were experienced during the early years of the nineteenth century, but the process was at least under way. When the Second Republic was created in 1848, universal manhood suffrage was immediately reinstated and this time it was to endure.

NOTES

1. J.-R. Suratteau, "Heurs et malheurs de la sociologie électorale pour l'époque de la Révolution française," *Annales: Economies, Sociétés, Civilisations* (1968), 560-580 and M. Edelstein, "Vers une sociologie électorale de la Révolution française: la participation des citadins et campagnards (1789−1793," *Revue d'histoire moderne et contemporaine* (1975), 508-529, are the ony two general surveys available, and both are, of course, no more than article length.

2. E. Thompson, *Popular Sovereignty and the French Constituent Assembly, 1789-1791* (Manchester, 1952), Chap. 3 passim.

3. E.-J. Sieyès, *Préliminaire de la constitution: reconnaissance et exposition raisonnée des Droits de l'Homme et du Citoyen* (Versailles, 1789), 13-14. See also M. Forsyth, *Reason and Revolution. The Political Thought of the abbé Sieyès* (Leicester, 1987), 162-165, for a sympathetic view of Sieyès's notions of citizenship; and W. H. Sewell, Jr., "Le citoyen/la citoyenne; Activity, Passivity and the Revolutionary Concept of Citizenship," in C. Lucas, (ed.), *The French Revolution and the Creation of Modern Political Culture.* Volume 2, The Political Culture of the French Revolution (Oxford, 1988), 107-108, which presents a less flattering interpretation of Sieyès's ideas on this subject.

4. D. Diderot, and J. L. d'Alembert, (eds.), Encyclopédie ou dictionnaire raisonné des sciences, des arts et des métiers, Vol. XIV, 243-246, cited in J. Lough, *The Philosophes and Post-revolutionary France* (Oxford, 1982), 46.

5. *Archives parlementaires de 1787 à 1860. Première série, 1789−1799* (1877), Vol. IX, 204-205, September 29, 1789, and see O. Le Cour

Grandmaison, "La citoyenneté à l'époque de la Constituante," *Annales historiques de la Révolution française* (1987), 250.

6. *Arch. parl.*, Vol. IX, 479, October 22, 1789.

7. A. Aulard, *Histoire politique de la Révolution française*, 4th ed. (1909), 70 and J. Jaurès, *Histoire socialiste de la Révolution française* (Editions sociales, 1968), Vol. 1 587-588.

8. *Arch. parl.*, Vol. IX, 598-599, October 29, 1789.

9. Ibid., Vol. IX, 600, October 29, 1789.

10. Ibid., Vol. X, 414-415, December 7, 1789.

11. *Les Révolutions de France et de Brabant*, No. 3, November 1789, and *Les Révolutions de Paris*, No. 17, October 31 - November 7, 1789.

12. Jaurès, *Histoire socialiste*, Vol. 1, 613.

13. *Arch. parl.*, Vol. XXVI, 532-533, Tableau 4, May 15, 1791.

14. L. Henry and Y. Blayo, "La population de la France de 1740 à 1829," *Population* (Numéro spécial, November 1975), 102.

15. *Arch. parl.*, Vol. XXV, 385, April 28, 1791.

16. Archives départementales de la Côte-d'Or (A.D.C.O.), L497, Tableaux des citoyens actifs, April-May 1790. Likewise in the Aude: M. Peronnet, and G. Fournier, *La Révolution française dans l'Aude* (Saint-Etienne, 1989), 101.

17. D. Ligou, "Population, citoyens actifs et électeurs à Dijon aux débuts de la Révolution française, 1790—1791," *Actes du Congrès national des Sociétés savantes* (Clermont Ferrand, 1963), 253.

18. R. R. Palmer, *The Age of the Democratic Revolution. A Political History of Europe and America, 1760—1800. Vol. 1, The challenge* (Princeton, N.J. 1959), 525-527.

19. F. Furet, "La monarchie et le règlement électoral de 1789," in K. M. Baker, (ed.), *The French Revolution and the Creation of Modern Political Culture, Vol. 1, The Political Culture of the Old Regime* (Oxford, 1987), 380-381. See also M. Crook, "Les élections aux Etats généraux et les origines de la pratique électorale de la Révolution," to be published shortly as part of conference proceedings at Grenoble, 1988 on "Les origines provinci-

ales de la Révolution française."

20. A. Cole, and P. Campbell, *French Electoral Systems and Elections*, 3rd ed. (Aldershot, 1989), 37, for a recent example of this misconception, and W. Doyle, *The Oxford History of the French Revolution* (Oxford, 1989), 124.

21. A.N. DIV bis 37 and 38, Listes de citoyens actifs, 1790−1791.

22. A.D.C.O., L232, Procès-verbaux des assemblées primaires de Dijon, June 1791, Sentou, J., "Impôts et citoyens actifs à Toulouse au début de la Révolution," *Annales du Midi* (1948), 177-178.

23. *Arch. parl.*, Vol. XXIX, 210, August 5, 1791.

24. Archives départementales de la Meuse, L347-348, Listes des citoyens des cantons, an V (1797).

25. Archives départementales du Morbihan, L246, Procès-verbal d'élection, canton de Belle-Ille, an VII (1799).

26. *Procès-verbal de la Convention*, Vol. 68, 68-69.

27. *Arch. parl.*, Vol. XLVII, 691, August 10, 1792 and Ibid., Vol. XLVIII, 29, August 11, 1792.

28. J. Godechot, (ed.), *Les constitutions de la France depuis 1789* (Flammarion, 1970), 83.

29. L. Hunt, *Politics, Culture and Class in the French Revolution* (Berkeley, 1984), 130 et seq., does try to establish a political geography of revolutionary France on the basis of deputies' political allegiances, but she is (p. 135) aware of the limitations of this approach. Her map shows the Vendée as a left-wing area!

30. Crook, "Les élections aux Etats-généraux."

31. *Moniteur*, 391, November 14, 1789.

32. M. Crook, "Les français devant le vote: participation et pratique électorale à l'époque de la Révolution," in *Les pratiques politiques en province à l'époque de la Révolution française* (Colloque de Montpellier, pub. Montpellier 1988), 27-37.

33. M. Genty, *Paris, 1789-1795. L'apprentissage de la citoyenneté* (1987).

18

Aux Urnes, Citoyens! The Transformation of French Electoral Participation (1789-1870)

Melvin Edelstein

The bicentennial of the French Revolution provides an opportunity to explore the Revolution's impact on electoral participation. Our subject is the emergence of democracy. The decade of the 1790s marked the origin of mass electoral politics in France. According to Franklin Ford, the revolutionary-Napoleonic era was a "watershed" in European history because of major changes, including "the increased public involvement in politics."[1] Charles Tilly has discerned a shift from local to national politics during the Revolution, a process that had gone far by the middle of the nineteenth century. He calls this shift the "nationalization of politics."[2]

Recently, however, the Revolution's pivotal role in integrating France's citizenry into national politics has been called into question, largely by historians of nineteenth-century France. Peter McPhee commented that the image of the French Revolution as a time of massive political mobilization sits awkwardly with the fact of low participation rates in national elections after 1789.[3] Comparing the first democratic national elections of August 1792 to the elections to the Constituent Assembly in April 1848, he asked a very important question that has been overlooked by historians: How does one explain the transformation from low electoral participation in national elections during the French Revolution to the high participation in national elections during the Second Republic? The participation rate of under 20 percent of adult males in August 1792 compares to 84 percent in April 1848. McPhee noted that participation in elections during the Revolution had not been high before 1792. The 1792 elections only continued a previous pattern of low participation, especially in national elections. He insists that the shift from low turnout during the Revolution to high electoral participation during the Second Republic represents a fundamental change in political behavior in France.

Rejecting modernization theory, McPhee disputed the explanation offered by Tilly and this author that increased political participation during the Revolution was the result of changes in the institutional framework, greater administrative centralization, and the development of communication networks and the mass media. Instead, he argued that the transformation of French electoral participation from the 1790s to 1848 was the result of greater involvement in a developing market economy. He discounted growing literacy because he doubted that the mass of the population was any more literate in 1848.

Although McPhee questioned the degree to which the Revolution had succeeded in involving the French in national elections, Eugen Weber argued that the peasants, especially those in the "undeveloped" rural regions of the West, Center, and Southwest were not integrated into the French nation-state until the early years of the Third Republic. The peasants were not involved in "modern" politics, that is, national and ideological politics, before 1870—1914.[4]

Peter Jones, who studied the peasantry of the southern Massif Central, seems to agree with Weber in his conclusion that "modern" politics did not come to that region until the 1880s. On the other hand, Jones disagrees with those historians of the Second Republic who emphasize its role in initiating the politicization of the peasants. He argues, "It is a frequently overlooked fact that the first apprenticeship to manhood suffrage and the institution of republican democracy was served between 1792—1799."[5] Although I agree that historians of the Second Republic tend to overlook the Revolution's role in politicizing the peasants, I have argued that their apprenticeship in citizenship began in 1789—1793.[6]

This chapter discusses participation rates in a series of national and local elections from 1789 to 1799 as *one* measure of the Revolution's success in politicizing France's citizenry. Although it was logical for McPhee to compare two democratic national elections, my research on voter turnout from 1789 to 1799 produces a somewhat different picture than the one he described.[7] Historians have focused excessively on high voter absenteeism, but, in fact, there were instances of high voter turnout, especially in the countryside. The political integration of "undeveloped" regions of rural France in the early years of the Third Republic was only the culmination of a long-term process that had begun in 1789 and had gone far before 1870. Finally, we will offer an alternative to McPhee's explanation for the transformation of French electoral participation and the nationalization of politics.

Any comparision of revolutionary elections to those in 1848 or thereafter is made difficult by the fact that we know very little about elections during the Revolution. There are no national calculations of participation rates for the revolutionary decade. The only truly "national" estimates are for the constitutional plebiscites of 1793, 1795, and 1799. Our task is further complicated by the absence of voter registration lists. Crucial documents sometimes have disappeared. Nonetheless, using the minutes of electoral assemblies and other documents, historians have been able to calculate local and regional voter turnout.

As a result of my own work, that of Malcolm Crook in England, as well as the studies done by a number of French scholars, it is now possible to provide a sketch of the evolution of electoral participation rates in the French Revolution and the Napoleonic era.

Combining the estimates from my article published in 1975, the averages for 1790—1992 from a recently completed doctorate by Patrice

Gueniffey, including corrections based on my research, averages for the plebiscites of 1793 and 1795 by René Baticle and Jean-René Suratteau, estimates for the Directory Period by Martyn Lyons, and averages for the plebiscites of the Napoleonic era by Claude Langlois,[8] we can construct the following table:

Table 1 **Electoral Participation in the Revolutionary-Napoleonic Era**

Election	Percent Participation	Correction
1. Elections to the Estates General in 1789	Median of 40%	
2. Municipal elections of January-March 1790	Median of 65%	Estimated average of 50%
3. Administrative elections of March-August 1790	Average of 31%	Estimated average of 40-50%
4. Legislative and administrative elections of June 1791	Average of 17%	Estimated average of 20-25%
5. Elections to the National Convention in August 1792	Average of 15%	
6. Plebiscite on the Constitution in July 1793	Average of 28%	
7. Plebiscite on the Constitution in September 1795	Average of 14-17%	
8. Legislative elections of the Year V (1797)	Estimated "less than one-third"	
9. Legislative elections of the Year VI (1798)		My estimate of 20-25%
10. Legislative elections of the Year VII (1799)	"Nearly 10%"	

Election	Percent Participation	Correction
11. Plebiscite on the Constitution of 1799	Average of 25-30%	
12. Plebiscite on the Life Consulate in 1802	Average of 47-48% (over 50% with the army's vote)	
13. Plebiscite on the Empire in 1804	Average of 42%	
14. Plebiscite on the Additional Act in 1815	Average of 22%	

The table shows that, although McPhee was correct that participation in August 1792 was under 20 percent, he was in error when he assumed that the 1792 elections merely continued a pattern of low participation. Voter turnout was higher in 1789 and 1790. Agreeing with my earlier conclusion that 1790 was a year of relatively high participation, Gueniffey called it the "golden age" of voting. He also confirmed my earlier conclusion that turnout declined precipitously in 1791 and then fell again in 1792, while rising sharply in 1793. If my estimate for 1791 is valid, it appears that the only times that voter turnout was under 20 percent in national elections was in 1792, 1795, and 1799. Although participation in national elections was low, the average was generally 20 to 30 percent, while voting in plebiscites varied from 22 percent to over 50 percent. But the "national" averages tend to obscure the many instances when participation at the local or regional level was higher than the national average. Unfortunately, the limits of this chapter do not permit me to develop that argument. Nor do I have time to explain the variations in electoral participation.

The Bourbon Restoration did little to advance France's civic education. Although legislative elections were restored, universal male suffrage was eliminated. The suffrage was restricted to about 100,000 adult males. Napoleon's system of appointed officials was retained. Although the July Monarchy doubled the electorate, it never reached 250,000. On the other hand, professors Agulhon, Vigier, and Tudesq have stressed the importance of the law of March 21, 1831, creating elected municipal councils in reawakening the political consciousness of large numbers of Frenchmen. Nearly 3 million men could vote in the municipal elections, or 20 to 25 percent of adult men. The electorate was proportionally greater in the small rural communes than in cities. In 1834 nearly 56 percent of the electorate participated nationally, but the rate was 64 percent in the small communes. Because these elections were held every three years, they prepared the way for the massive turnout in April 1848.[9] The law of June 22, 1833 restoring elections to the general council of the *départements* and *arrondissements* also raised political awareness.

We have seen that participation in local and national elections from 1789 to 1815 sometimes reached relatively high levels. Tilly is correct that the nationalization of politics begun during the Revolution reached fruition during the Second Republic. At the same time, McPhee is correct to insist that 1848 represented a major transformation of electoral participation. High rates of voter participation in national elections became habitual after 1848. As Gordon Wright observed, 1848 was the date when mass politics began to emerge. The short-lived Second Republic had an enduring effect on French political development.[10]

McPhee pointed out that turnout in the first democratic election in April 1848 was 84 percent. Although participation declined in the presidential elections of December 1848 and the legislative elections in May 1849, turnout was still as high as 75 percent and 68 percent. At 81 percent and 83 percent, turnout in the two plebiscites of December 1851 and November 1852 had returned to the level of April 1848.

The nationalization of politics can be seen in the fact that participation was higher in national elections than in local elections. This is unlike the French Revolution, when turnout was higher in the "local" elections of 1790 than in the national elections of 1791 and 1792. The pattern in the Second Republic is more like that of today when the French vote more heavily in national than in local elections. In 1848 voting was heavier in the municipal elections than in the elections for the general councils of the *arrondissements* and *départements*. This too is like contemporary France. In the Isère, whereas 85 percent of registered voters turned out in April 1848 and 80 percent voted in December 1848, only 30 percent voted in July-August 1848 for the general councils.[11]

That Weber was off in his timing of the shift to habitual massive participation in national elections can be seen in the turnout in "undeveloped" rural France after 1848. The Third Republic's high voter participation in national elections, generally 76 to 84 percent, had already been reached in rural France from 1848 to 1870. Between 1852 and 1869, voter turnout in legislative elections was 62 to 78 percent. From 1857 to 1869, electoral participation in the village of Pont-de-Montvert in the Lozère was 75 to 82 percent as compared to an estimated 50 percent or less from 1789 to 1815. Four *départements* in the East-Aquitain, the Ariège, Haute-Garonne, Tarn, and Tarn-et-Garonne had such high voter participation between 1848 and 1870 that André Armengaud called 60 percent a low turnout. In the legislative elections of 1869, participation was 83 percent in Lot-et-Garonne, 75 percent in the Nièvre, 78 percent in the Vendée, and 85 percent in Gers. The plebiscite of May 1870 attracted a turnout of 82 percent.[12]

Let us return to McPhee's crucial question: How do we explain the transition from lower participation in national elections during the Revolution to the sustained high voter participation after 1848? I disagree with McPhee's contention that we must start from a "materialistic basis." He explained the transition by the development of a national market economy. But a national market economy does not explain the high rates of participation in "undeveloped" regions that did not participate fully in the market economy. The Seine, including Paris, had a 69 percent turnout in April 1848, whereas the Sarthe had 85 percent, and the Ille-et-Vilaine had an 87 percent turnout. If the Seine had a 76 percent turnout in December 1851, the Ariège had a 77 percent rate and the Basses-Pyrénées had a 74 percent rate.

I would like to offer an alternative explanation for the transformation of French electoral participation and the nationalization of politics. It is based on political modernization or transformation. Because Napoleon created the centralized bureaucratic "modern" state, it was used throughout the nineteenth century for political mobilization. Various governments and regimes used the state and its officials to mobilize the voters, especially the peasants, for elections. René Rémond pointed to this when he commented that it was the prefects, the administration, that influenced opinion.[13] The July Monarchy had "official" candidates before Napoleon III. In 1848, unlike 1789, the government "organized" the elections. Government agents, starting with the prefects and subprefects, were used to get out the vote. Teachers and priests even mobilized the voters. That the elections of April 1848 were held on Easter Sunday helps explain the 84 percent turnout, but elections during the Revolution took place on Sunday after Mass. Voting in communual groups as described by Alexis de Tocqueville also contributed to the high turnout. Unlike 1789, there were also national electoral organizations in the Second Republic to mobilize the voters. They had at their disposal a much more highly developed press than in 1789—1793. The "organization" of elections as in the nineteenth century, especially for plebiscites, was never really attempted in 1789—1793, even under the Montagnard dictatorship.[14]

Just as important for the nationalization of French politics was the peasants' realization that only the national government could provide the villagers with the roads, schools, post offices, and other public works they wanted. They came to understand that control of the national government was as important, if not more important, than local self-government in solving their problems. Peter Jones seems to have arrived at the same conclusion for the southern Massif Central, but he dates the change from the 1880s. He argues that "the locus of relevant politics shifted" as the peasants learned to use their votes as a bargaining device to get what they wanted from what he calls the "milch cow" state.[15] But the political system of Louis Philippe and especially that of Louis-Napoleon Bonaparte had taught the voters that the central government would trade local favors for votes.[16]

The July Monarchy and the Second Empire abetted the nationalization of politics by developing a market economy, transforming the transportation and communication networks, expanding literacy and schooling, and industrialization. Greater exposure to the printed media played an important role.[17] Maurice Agulhon's *classerelais* contributed to peasant politicization by spreading new ideas to the villagers. A series of changes and outside influences contributed to what Agulhon called "la descente de la politique vers les masses."[18]

Changes in voting procedures might also explain the higher voter participation in the Consulate and the First and Second empires. Whereas voting in the Revolution and the Second Republic was in the capital of the canton (except for municipal elections before 1795), in the Napoleonic regimes, voters voted in their commune. The voting places were multiplied and the registers were kept open for several days or even a week.[19] Voting by assemblies and in the capital of the canton as well as complicated voting procedures reduced participation during the Revolution. Voting in the capital of the canton did not affect participation in the Second Republic, however.

In conclusion, the French Revolution initiated and accelerated France's experience with mass electoral politics, while promoting the nationalization of politics. This experience occurred in the absence of political parties and national candidates, however. The Second Republic and the Second Empire advanced France's civic education considerably. When rural electoral participation in national elections had reached the high levels of the Third Republic, French politics had been nationalized. What had been true for various communes, cantons, districts, or *départements* during the Revolution became a consistent national pattern after 1848. Although the transformation of French, especially rural, electoral participation from low levels to consistently high rates is one of the major developments of the period 1789–1870, it has not received the attention it deserves.[20]

NOTES

1. Franklin Ford, "The Revolutionary-Napoleonic Era: How Much of a Watershed?," *American Historical Review* 69 (1963), 23.

2. Charles Tilly, "Did the Cake of Custom Break?" in John Merriman (ed.), *Consciousness and Class Experience in Nineteenth-Century Europe* (New York, 1979), 19; Charles Tilly, Louise Tilly, and Richard Tilly, *The Rebellious Century, 1830–1930* (Cambridge, Mass., 1975), 26-29.

3. Peter McPhee, "Electoral Democracy and Direct Democracy in France, 1789–1851," *European History Quarterly* 16 (1986), 77.

4. Eugen Weber, *Peasants into Frenchmen: The Modernization of Rural France, 1870–1914* (Stanford, Calif., 1976), Eugen Weber, "The Second Republic, Politics, and the Peasant," *French Historical Review* 11 (1980), 521-550; Eugen Weber, "*Comment la Politique Vint aux Paysans*: A Second Look at Peasant Politicization," *American Historical Review* 87 (1982), 357-389.

5. Peter Jones, *Politics and Rural Society: The Southern Massif Central c. 1750—1850* (Cambridge, 1985), 317.

6. Melvin Edelstein, "L'Apprentissage de la Citoyenneté: Participation électorale des Campagnards et Citadins (1789—1993)," in *Communications présentées lors du Congrès Mondial pour le Bicentenaire de la Révolution. Sorbonne, Paris, 6-12 juillet*, 1989 4 vols. (Oxford, 1989), I, 15-25.

7. Ibid. The author is working on a lengthy article synthesizing the data he has compliled on electoral participation.

8. Melvin Edelstein, "Vers une 'sociologie électorale' de la Révolution Française: La Participation des Citadins et Campagnards (1789—1793)," *Revue d'Histoire Moderne et Contemporaine* 22 (1975), 508-529; Patrice Gueniffey, "La Révolution Française et les élections. Suffrage, participation et élections pendant la période constitutionnelle (1790—1792) (unpublished Ph.D. thesis, l'Ecole des Hautes Etudes en Sciences Sociales, 1989); René Baticle, "Le plébiscite sur la constitution de 1793," *La Révolution Française* 57 (1909), 145-150; Jean-René Suratteau, "Les élections de l'an IV," *Annales Historiques de la Révolution Française* (1952), 52; Martyn Lyons, *France Under the Directory* (Cambridge, 1975), 167; Claude Langlois, "Napoléon Bonaparte Plébiscité?," in *L'Election du Chef de l'Etat en France de Hugues Capet à Nos Jours* (Paris, 1988), 91.

9. Philippe Vigier, "Elections Municipales et Prise de Conscience Politique sous la Monarchie de Juillet," in *La France au XIXe siècle: Mélanges offerts à Charles Pouthas* (Paris, 1973), 276-286; André-Jean Tudesq, "La Vie Municipale dans le Sud-Ouest au Début de la Monarchie de Juillet," in *La France au XIXe siècle: Mélanges offerts à Charles Pouthas* (Paris, 1973), 262-275; André-Jean Tudesq, Institutions Locales et Histoire Sociale: La Loi Municipale de 1831 et ses Premières Applications" in *Annales de la Faculté des Lettres et Sciences Humaines de Nice* 9-10 (1969), 327-363; Maurice Agulhon, *La République au Village* (Paris, 1970), 262-264.

10. Gordon Wright, *France in Modern Times*, 4th ed. (New York, 1987), 129. For the impact of the insurrection against the coup d'état of December 1851, see Ted Margadant, *French Peasants in Revolt: The Insurrection of 1851* (Princeton, N.J., 1979). For the important elections of 1849, see Jacques Bouillon, "Les démocrates-socialistes aux élections de 1849," *Revue Française de Sciences Politiques* 6 (1956), 70-95.

11. Georges Argenton and Philippe Vigier, "Les Elections dans l'Isère sous la Seconde République: Essai géographique" in *Les Elections dans l'Isère sous la Seconde République* (Grenoble, 1949), 26-42; Charles Pouthas, "Une Enquête sur la Réforme Administrative sous la Seconde République," *Revue Historique* 193 (1942—1943), 1-12.

12. See Peter Campbell, *French Electoral Systems and Elections, 1789—1957* (London, 1958), 68-69; Patrice Higonnet, *Pont-de-Montvert: Social Structure and Politics in a French Village, 1700—1914* (Cambridge, Mass., 1971), 122; André Armengaud, *Les Populations de l'Est-Aquitain au Début de l'Epoque Contemporaine: Recherches sur une région moins développée (vers 1845-vers 1871)* (Paris, 1961), 344-467; Jean-Paul Landrevie, "Le Tarnet-Garonne de l'Empire à la République, 1869—1877," *Annales du Midi* (1984), 283-312; Marcel Vigreux, "Des Paysans Républicains à la Fin du Second Empire: Les Elections de 1869 dans le Morvan Nivernais," *Revue d'Histoire Moderne et Contemporaine* 25 (1978), 443-469; Louis Girard, *Les Elections de 1869* (Paris, 1960).

13. See the comments on Claude Langlois's paper by René Rémond in *L'Election du Chef de l'Etat en France* 98.

14. See Alfred Cobban, "The Influence of the Clergy and the '*Instituteurs Primaires*' in the Election of the French Constituent Assembly of 1848," *English Historical Review* (1942), 334-344; Alfred Cobban, "Administrative Pressure in the Election of the French Constituent Assembly of 1848," *Bulletin of the Institute of Historical Research* 25 (1952), 133-159; Theodore Zeldin, "Government Policy in the French General Election of 1849," *English Historical Review* 74 (1959), 240-248; Georges Fasel, "The French Election of April 23, 1848: Suggestions for a Revision," *French Historical Studies* (1968), 285-298; Jacques Bouillon, "Les Démocrates-Socialistes aux élections de 1849," 70-95; Philippe Vigier, *La Seconde République dans la Région Alpine*, 2 vols. (Paris, 1963); Agulhon, *La République au Village*; Alain Corbin, *Archaïsme et Modernité en Limousin au XIXe siécle, 1845—1880*, 2 vols. (Paris, 1975); John Merriman, *The Agony of the Republic: The Repression of the Left in Revolutionary France, 1848—1851* (New Haven, Conn., 1978). For the press, see Claude Bellanger, Jacques Godechot, Pierre Guiral, and Fernand Terrou (eds.), *Histoire Générale de la Presse Française*, 4 vols. (Paris, 1969—1974), II.

15. Jones, *Politics and Rural Society*, 316.

16. Sherman Kent, *Electoral Procedure under Louis-Philippe* (New Haven, Conn., 1937); Theodore Zeldin, *The Political System of Napoleon III* (New York, 1971).

17. See David Pinkney, *Decisive Years in France, 1840—1847* (Princeton, N.J., 1986); Maurice Agulhon, La Vie Sociale en Province Intérieure au Lendemain de la Révolution (Paris, 1970); Agulhon, *La République au Village*, 259-284; Jean Vidalenc, *La Société française de 1815 à 1848: Le Peuple des Campagnes* (Paris, 1969); Peter McPhee, "Historians, Germs, and Culture-Brokers: The Circulation of Ideas in the Nineteenth-Century Countryside," *Australian Journal of French Studies* 23 (1986), 115-130.

18. Agulhon, *La République au Village*, 259-284.

19. Langlois, "Napoléon Bonaparte Plébiscité?," 86.   See Agulhon's comment on page 95.

20. There is no mention of this transformation in the excellent volume by Maurice Agulhon, Gabriel Désert, and Robert Specklin, *Histoire de la France Rurale*, 4 vols. (Paris, 1974—1976), III. Raymond Huard's forthcoming book on the development of universal suffrage will undoubtedly be a major contribution to the study of democracy since 1848.

19

The Impact of the French Revolution on London Reform Societies

Marilyn Morris

With *The Making of the English Working Class* in 1963, E. P. Thompson sparked a long-running debate on the revolutionary potential of Britain in the decade of the French Revolution, the motives of the reform societies, and the reasons for their disintegration. Thompson contended that "the revolutionary impulse was strangled in its infancy" by reactions to events in France. Fear united landowners and manufacturers against reformers. The resultant campaign of repression, together with a growing disenchantment with the direction the Revolution in France was taking, drove the educated, middle-class members from the reform societies. However, he added, a democratic tradition had been established and continued to flourish underground.[1] Subsequent studies of the British reform movement by James Walvin, Albert Goodwin, Malcolm Thomas, Peter Holt, and H. T. Dickinson emphasized its moderation and marginalized the extremist element in its membership. These historians suggested that it was more the internal dissensions within the movement than repression which brought about its demise.[2]

But in the early 1980s, other historians began taking a closer look at the period after 1795 when the reform societies were supposedly in a decline and small, disparate, breakaway groups of extremists were living in a fantasy world of revolutionary conspiracy. J. Ann Hone's investigation of London radicalism from 1796 to 1821 presented the reform movement's diversity in a more positive light and emphasized its members' flexibility, pragmatism, and vitality. She pointed out continuities and collaboration between moderate reform society members, Whig politicians, and those who wished to bring about a revolution in Britain.[3] A contemporaneous study by Marianne Elliott showed the great degree of collaboration between Irish, British, and French revolutionaries to coordinate an Irish rebellion, a French invasion, and an insurrection in London, and gave a palpability to the revolutionary threat.[4] The following year, Roger Wells called Elliott's study myopic for having treated the British underground movement as disparate, loosely organized, and an appendage to that of the Irish. He painted a vivid picture of Britain from 1795 to 1803 as a hotbed of covert militant republicanism, and he dismissed E. P. Thompson's detractors as suffering from the same visual handicap as Elliott.[5]

Meanwhile, yet another set of historians were approaching the questions of the French Revolution's impact on British radicalism from a completely different perspective. They sought to debunk what H. T. Dickinson had pointed out in 1977 to be a generally accepted myth: "that the radicals won the intellectual argument about reform but lost the struggle for power."[6] In a book published in 1983, the same year as Wells', R. R. Dozier argued that Britain was preserved from revolution by the loyalist associations that had been formed to counteract the spread of Jacobinism. Those who joined these organizations, he claimed, were motivated by love of country, by a desire to be part of national life, and by patriotism, "and in this respect, loyalists represented the true nature of Englishmen during these chaotic years."[7] In his Ford Lectures the following year, I. R. Christie also asserted that the ideology of revolution in the 1790s did not fit the British character. Britons realized that the universal suffrage for which the reformers campaigned would lead to the subversion of the British Constitution and the social order. Christie argued that the radical platform was based on a naive perception of the French Revolution and the speculative notion of natural rights. Thus, it lacked the intellectual rationalization capable of attracting leaders from the ranks of the elite, which would have been essential for mobilizing the masses into revolt.[8] In 1985 J.C.D. Clark took this view even further by arguing that studies of these so-called radicals (a term he predicted would be expended from eighteenth-century history books) undertaken since the 1960s had endowed them with undue importance. England in the eighteenth century, he claimed, was still part of the *ancien régime*. Furthermore, it was religious dissent, not republicanism that proved to be the more significant force of social and political change.[9]

So, where does this leave us in our evaluation of the French Revolution's impact on the British reform movement of the 1790s? After considering these different approaches to the problem, we are left with two major questions. First, how doctrinaire were British reformers in their support of the French Revolution? Second, how significant an impact did the repression that grew out of the fear generated by events in France have on reformist argument?

It seems important to recognize that the French Revolution was both an inspirational and a repressive force for British radicalism (if I may be allowed to indulge in this anachronism). The purpose of this chapter is to illustrate the pragmatism and adaptability of British reformers in the face of a continually shifting political situation accompanied by increasing repression. It also seeks to reassert the significance of repression, not only in discouraging the moderate members of the movement and turning the republican ones to militancy, but also in causing tensions between reformers as they responded to it with different degrees of patience and belligerence.

Given the space limitations, I wish to concentrate on the two main reform societies in London, although one historian at least might call this myopic. The Society for Constitutional Information (SCI) was established in 1780 by gentleman-reformers, while the London Corresponding Society (LCS) started out as a small artisan's reading group lead by a shoemaker called Thomas Hardy in January 1792. It will be seen that despite their efforts to accommodate their principles to the realities of the situation in Britain, these reformers were continually having their ideas misrepresented because these were viewed through the smokescreen of revolutionary France.

This is not to say that reformers were never naive and impractical. In fact, they were stupendously so in the manner in which they corresponded with French revolutionaries and supported radical republican writings in the period between the storming of the Bastille and France's declaration of war against Britain in February 1793. The spectacle of fallen tyranny in France enlivened existing English reform societies and inspired the formation of new associations. But as reformers celebrated French liberty and what they saw as a new era of enlightenment, they did not consider carefully the domestic implications of their proclamations. For instance, on July 14, 1791, the SCI held a celebratory dinner during which Dr. Joseph Towers read an address from the Jacobin Society at Nantes, which observed, "at our voice, the nations have raised their degraded fronts; tyrants have turned pale upon their thrones."[10] Whether the man who sat on the throne in Britain fell under this category was not specified in their speeches.

Edmund Burke had already raised the alarm against such celebrations of republican revolution with his *Reflections Upon the Revolution in France*, published the previous November. In March 1791, Thomas Paine published the first part of his *Rights of Man* and took Burke to task, as did other sympathizers of reform. A pamphlet war between reformers and loyalists raged for the next three years.[11] The Church and King riots that occurred when Birmingham reformers tried to hold their own July 14 celebration in 1791 was an early indication of the violence of the loyalist reaction.[12]

Loyalist alarms and accusations made reformers more determined to stand by their principles. They firmly believed that the French Revolution would not have turned violent had it not been for the aggression of Austria and Prussia, Britain's traditional allies. So the SCI and LCS stubbornly held onto their correspondence with France despite the September massacres, the declaration of a republic, and the Decree of Fraternity of November 19 which promised aid to any people who wished to free themselves from oppression. They wanted Britain to avoid entering the war at all costs. At the end of September, the LCS initiated a plan for the reform societies in Britain to unite in voting addresses to the French National Convention.

To Maurice Margarot, who drafted the LCS's address, the object was "an animated but safe declaration" to quiet French jealousies toward Britain, to encourage their struggle for liberty, and to discourage any "underhanded ministerial attempts" to betray British neutrality. But the language of solidarity had insurrectionary implications. The address hailed the French as "fellow citizens of the world" and concluded: "If you succeed as we ardently wish, the triple alliance (not of crowns but) of the people of America, France and Britain, will give freedom to Europe and peace to the whole world."[13] The SCI address also gave the impression that something was being fomented in Britain, prompting the president of the National Convention to observe in his reply: "The moment cannot be distant, when the people of France will offer their congratulations to a national convention in England."[14] At the same time, the LCS was vigorously insisting to its provincial correspondents and in public declarations that it was for liberty and equality but not for kings, nor parliament.[15]

As the political situation became more ominous, it was more difficult to sustain this assertion. Nonetheless, the SCI gamely took on the challenge of proving that the execution of Louis XVI in January 1793 did not constitute a threat to George III. It elected to honorary membership three prominent members of the French National Convention and published their speeches justifying the execution.[16] The SCI and LCS believed that the free discussion of political ideas could only bring about change for the better. They knew that they were not plotting rebellion and thought that only ignorance or self-interest could make their opponents level such an accusation.

On the same principle, the SCI and LSC preferred to focus on the inspiring parts of Paine's *Rights of Man* such as his ideas on the natural rights and duties of men to participate in their government and to ignore his violent denunciation of monarchical tyranny, stupidity, and fraudulence, and his insistence that the British Constitution was a myth.[17] But Paine's republican critique and demystification of the British government and its trappings was the first step toward political enlightenment. In his memoirs, Thomas Hardy described how he had founded the LCS after reading SCI tracts on the state of the representation and realizing that a radical reform of parliament was necessary. He decided that political knowledge had to be disseminated to all classes because the greatest obstacle to change was "that gross ignorance and prejudice of the bulk of the nation."[18]

The government did not appreciate the consciousness--raising qualities of *Rights of Man*, nor did it choose to ignore Paine's antimonarchism. On May 2, 1792, three months after the second part of that work was published, George II issued his first Proclamation for the Prevention of Seditious Meetings and Writings. When Paine informed the SCI that the government intended to prosecute him, both societies responded with public addresses. The SCI proclaimed that the excess of taxes, military buildup, and menacing proclamations during peacetime made it imperative for free inquiry into the principles and measures of government. The LCS took the line that the May 2 Proclamation could not possibly apply to the societies. Both they and the king were working to preserve the Constitution, guard against the subversion of good government, secure peace and prosperity, encourage civil and religious liberties, and repress riot and tumult.[19]

Such arguments could not stem the tide of repression and loyalist reaction. Even some of the older members of the SCI were alarmed by the society's uncritical championing of Paine; a few requested that their names be expunged from the membership books.[20] Maurice Margarot was concerned that the subscription fund that the LCS had opened for Paine's defense would be interpreted as an approbation of the whole of Paine's works.[21] Margarot's protest went unheeded, so when the SCI and LCS leaders were arrested for high treason in May 1794, their support of Paine, as well as their correspondence with France, made up a large part of the case against them. Paine, who had gone to France to take a seat at the National Convention, was tried *in absentia* on December 18, 1792. *Rights of Man* was declared a seditious libel and outlawed. The legal authorities then moved on to printers, publishers, booksellers, and newspaper editors sympathetic to reform. They were often assisted by members of the Association for Preserving Liberty and Property Against Republicans and Levellers, established the previous November, who procured works by Paine from reformers and then testified against them.[22] These events pushed the reform societies into challenging the government in a way they had not intended. The provincial reform societies, antagonized by the disruption of their meetings by local loyalist associations, pressed the LCS to decide on the best method of bringing about parliamentary reform. Republican aspirations were laid aside as members united to seek a more democratic House of Commons through a redistribution of seats, annual elections, and universal suffrage. Yet they could not agree on tactics. Should they petition parliament or the king? Or should they first hold a convention to assert the majesty of the people? This debate would continue until the arrests of the SCI and LCS leaders in 1794.[23]

Scottish reformers had formed a convention of delegates to consider these questions in December 1792. The resultant arrests and convictions for sedition of two of their leaders convinced them that they had to unite with the English reformers.[24] Despite their strong speeches in favor of a convention, most of the English societies were not prepared when summoned to Edinburgh at the end of 1793. In choosing their delegates, the LCS began an activity that would endure as the most suitable to their purposes: the public open-air mass meeting. Although the Edinburgh proceedings were dominated by debates on tactics, the speakers were arrested, Margarot among them. The remaining delegates resolved to form a secret committee to meet in the event of a hostile act of government, such as the suspension of the Habeas Corpus, and declare the convention permanent. These resolutions, on top of their assumption of the title, "The British Convention of the Delegates of the People" were ample proof in the Scottish courts of law that they were proceeding on a French plan and were guilty of sedition.[25]

These latest arrests provoked the LCS and SCI into a more aggressive approach. The LCS held more mass meetings to stir public outcry and were joined by the SCI in issuing addresses that asserted the people's right to resist tryanny. One gets the impression that they used the planning of another convention as an object around which they could call meetings and generate interest while hopefully intimidating the government.[26] Frustration and anger generated by the worsening repression provoked intemperate speeches and audacious satire.

For instance, the infamous "La Guillotine" handbill allegedly circulating at one of the LCS's mass meetings and used as evidence in the trial of Thomas Hardy for treason was undoubtedly an April Fool's Day joke.

It began:

For
The Benefit of John Bull
At the
FEDERATION THEATRE in EQUALITY-SQ.
On Thurs. the 1st of April 4971
will be performed,
A new and entertaining Farce, called
LA GUILLOTINE
or
GEORGE'S HEAD IN THE BASKET!
Dramatis Personae
Numpy, the Third, by Mr. GUELPH

(Being the last time of his appearing in that character)

It featured "Tight Rope Dancing, from the Lamp-post" and the singing of "Ca Ira" and "BOB SHAVE GREAT GEORGE OUR _____!" And

The whole to conclude with
A GRANDECAPITATION
OF
PLACEMEN, PENSIONERS, and GERMAN LEECHES.[27]

The LCS and SCI leaders were acquitted despite the mountains of evidence presented by the prosecution.[28] But the trials left the societies with debts and falling membership. The LCS and many provincial societies were revived by the summer of 1795 when war-weariness and food shortages inspired a renewed interest in reform. Employing the old "evil-ministers misleading the king" theory, the LCS petitioned George III to end the war, dismiss his ministers, and institute universal suffrage and annual parliaments.[29] When this petition was not acknowledged by the autumn, the LCS held a public meeting on October 26, 1795 addressing a remonstrance to George III, reminding him of their rights and his duties. Although reformers considered such a remonstrance the last constitutional means by which the common people could obtain a redress of their grievances, they remained purposefully vague regarding the next step should this too be ignored.[30]

But the LCS's bluff was never called. Three days after this meeting, George III's coach was attacked en route to the opening of Parliament. Loyalist versions of the incident compared the mob that surrounded the carriage to the French rabble that had confronted Louis XVI on his way to St. Cloud.[31] On November 6 and 10, Grenville and Pitt introduced "A bill for the Safety and Preservation of His Majesty's Person and Government Against Treasonable and Seditious Practices and Attempts," and "a bill for the more effectually preventing Seditious Meetings and Assemblies."[32]

The LCS reorganized itself so that it could continue to meet, discuss politics, issue propaganda, and correspond with provincial societies within the terms of the two acts.[33] The society worked toward another remonstrance to the king and tried to hold a legal public meeting on July 31, 1797. This resulted in the arrests of six speakers.[34] The LCS continued to meet and debate on tactics until the authorities raided their committee room on April 19, 1798. Ironically, at the time of the arrests, members were voicing their disillusionment with revolutionary France and debating on the action to be taken in the event of a French invasion. Many argued that they ought to join the volunteers to fend off French military despotism. But there were also others who in 1797 had started to meet in secret and make contact with Irish revolutionaries.[35] Repression starved off the constitutional reform movement and fed the revolutionary zeal of republican extremists.

The French Revolution's message of liberty, equality, and fraternity inspired the disenfranchised citizens of Britain to find their political voice. But it was not mere mimicry. As they applied their new ideals to traditional methods of applying for the redress of grievances, the members of the reform societies developed a species of republicanism separate from that of France or America. Republican ideology not only had an impact on reformist aspirations but also on reformist organization. In reading the minutes of LCS meetings, one is struck with how they had created a small haven of democracy within Britain's hierarchical society.

NOTES

1. E. P. Thompson, *The Making of the English Working Class* (New York: Vintage Books, 1966), 177, 183.

2. Walvin, "English Democratic Societies and Popular Radicalism 1791-1800," Ph.D. thesis (University of York, 1969); A. Goodwin, *The Friends of Liberty* (London, 1979); M. Thomis and P. Holt, *Threats of a Revolution in Britain, 1789-1848* (Hamden, Conn., 1977); H. T. Dickinson, *Liberty and Property* (London, University Paperbacks, 1979).

3. J. A. Hone, *The Cause of Truth, London Radicalism 1796-1821* (Oxford, 1982).

4. M. Elliott, *Partners in Revolution: The United Irishmen and France* (London, 1982).

5. R. Wells, *Insurrection, the British Experience 1795-1803* (Gloucester, 1983).

6. Dickinson, *Liberty and Property*, 271.

7. R. R. Dozier, *For King, Constitution and Country: The English*

Loyalists and The French Revolution (Lexington, Mass., 1983), 180.

8. I. R. Christie, *Stress and Stability in Late Eighteenth-Century Britain* (Oxford, 1984).

9. J.C.D. Clark, *English Society 1688-1832* (Cambridge, 1985).

10. Trial of John Horne Tooke, T. B. and T. J. Howell, eds., *A Complete Collection of State Trials* . . . , 33 vols. (London, 1809-1826) [hereafter *State Trials*], xxv, 115.

11. For analyses of this pamphlet debate, see Dickinson, *Liberty and Property*, 244-262, 272-318; J. T. Boulton, *The Language of Politics in the Age of Wilkes and Burke* (London, 1963).

12. M. H. Smith, "Conflict and Society in Late Eighteenth-Century Birmingham," Ph.D. thesis (Cambridge, 1978), 2-41.

13. Second Report from the Committee of Secrecy of the House of Commons respecting Seditious Practices, presented June 6, 1794, W. Cobbett, ed., *The Parliamentary History of England* . . . 36 vols. (London, 1806-1820) [hereafter Report from the Committee of Secrecy], 768-769.

14. Ibid., 754-755; Trial of Thomas Hardy, *State Trials*, xxiv, 530.

15. See confiscated LCS papers in P[ublic]   R[ecord]   O[ffice] T[reasury]   S[olicitors]   11/965/3510A(2) also printed in Report from the Committee of Secrecy, 795-811; and public declaration printed in trial of Hardy, *State Trials*, xxiv, 767.

16. *Morning Chronicle*, January 25, 1793; Report from the Committee of Secrecy, 713-716.

17. See correspondence regarding Paine printed in Report from the Committee of Secrecy, 752-754.

18. Excerpts from Thomas Hardy's *Account of the Origin of the LCS* (1799) reprinted in M. Thale, *Selections from the Papers of the London Corresponding Society* (Cambridge, 1983), 6-7.

19. Report from the Committee of Secrecy, 751-752, 764-765.

20. See Christopher Wyvill's correspondence with Jeremiah Batley, April 6, 1792, regarding the SCI's support of Paine, printed in C. Wyvill, *Political Papers*, 5 vols. (York, 1804), V, 1-4;   SCI correspondence in P.R.O. TS 11/960/3506 and TS 11/953/3497.

21. Thale, *Selections*, 15-16.

22. The best account of the APLP is still E. C. Black, *The Association* (Cambridge, Mass., 1963), 233-274; for the use of Paine's books in evidence against reformers, see M. A. Morris, "Monarchy as an Issue in English Political Argument During the French Revolutionary Era," Ph.D. thesis (London, 1988), 204-208.

23. See LCS and SCI correspondence with provincial societies printed in Thale, *Selections*, 47-48, 80-81, see also 84n; Report from the Committee of Secrecy, 722-723, 812; *State Trials*, xxiv, 412; Nottingham to SCI and reply, 6, March 22, 1793, P.R.O. TS 11/951/3495; Birmingham SCI's circular letter of March 13, 1793, TS 11/956/3501i; LCS to Norwich, July 25, 1793, TS 11/953/3497.

24. See trials of Thomas Muir and Thomas Fyche Palmer, *State Trials*, xxiii; H. W. Meikle, *Scotland and the French Revolution* (Glasgow, 1972).

25. Trial of William Skirving, *State Trials*, xxiii, 407-410; Report from the Committee of Secrecy, 731; Trial of Joseph Gerrald, *State Trials*, xxiii, 866.
26. See *At a General Meeting of the LCS Held at the Globe Tavern*, January 20, 1794 (London, 1794); A Report from the Committee of Secrecy, 781-785; "The LCS to the Various Patriotic Societies of Great Britain," P.R.O. H[ome] O[ffice] 42/28/148-150; Minutes from the LCS's General Meeting at Chalk Farm, April 14, 1794, printed in Thale, 135-140. T. M. Parssinen has observed that reformers were deliberately imprecise regarding the way in which a convention would achieve their object, wishing to preserve the threat of a formation of an anti-Parliament while evading prosecution and public hostility: "Association, Convention and anti-Parliament in British Radical Politics, 1771-1848," *English Historical Review* 88 (1973), 515.

27. *State Trials*, xxiv, 682-683. Its source was never discovered: see P.R.O. P[rivy] C[ouncil] 1 22 A 37.

28. See the trials of Thomas Hardy and John Horne Tooke, *State Trials*, xxiv-xxv.

29. *Account of the Proceedings of a General Meeting . . . St. George's Fields, on Mon., the 29th of June, 1795* (London, 1795).

30. *Account of a Proceedings . . . Held in a Field near Copenhagen House*, Monday, October 26, 1795 (London, 1795).

31. See J. Gifford, *An Account of the Attack Made on the King* (London, 1809); and newspaper accounts reprinted in Anon., *A History of Two*

Acts (London, 1796), 4-7.

32. *Parliamentary History*, xxxii, 244-245, 272-276.

33. For detailed accounts of the LCS after 1795, see Goodwin, Thale, Hone, and Wells.

34. *A Narrative of the Proceedings at the General Meeting of the LCS, Held on Monday, July 31, 1797, in a Field Near the Veterinary College, St. Pancras*, P.R.O. PC 1 40 A 132; *The Times*, August 1, 1797.

35. Minutes and Correspondence of the LCS, September 15 to November 14, 1797 in papers confiscated from Wych Street, P.R.O. PC 1 41 A 138; R. Hodgson, *Proceedings of the General Committee of the LCS . . . on the 5th, 12 and 19 April 1798* (Newgate, 1798); *The Autobiography of Francis Place*, ed. M. Thale (Cambridge, 1972), 151-155.

20

The French Revolution and Spain

Richard Herr

Economic historians have a near monopoly of so-called counterfactual history. Because they deal in numbers, they feel empowered to calculate whether free labor would have been more profitable than slave labor or how much the GNP of a country would have been at such-and-such a date if railroads had never existed. Although we other historians do not approach our issues with such an impressive term, we are in fact all writing counterfactual history as soon as we describe a cause and effect. If we say an event E was the effect of cause Q, we imply that if you project developments without Q, E would not have occured. Similarly, to analyze the impact of the French Revolution on Spain is to ask what the future history of Spain might have been without the French Revolution.

Before the French Revolution, Spain enjoyed one of its most successful reigns, that of Carlos III (1759-1788), who deserves high rank among the enlightened despots of Europe. It was marked by economic prosperity, especially after the end of the United States War of Independence; an empire expanding into California, the Carribean area, and southern South America; and major legislation aimed at reforming the administration, the Church, the universities, the countryside, and foreign and colonial trade. Some of the king's subjects objected to his reforms, especially in the colonies, but almost no one questioned his authority to decree them.

After 1815 the situation was markedly different. The economy was depressed, the colonies were in revolt, and at home Spaniards had violently opposing views on the just authority of the king and the doctrines and jurisdiction of the Church. Some hoped to restore the liberal Constitution of 1812 enacted by the opponents of Napoleon's occupation, and others approved of the persecution of its authors. A century and more of intermittent civil strife had begun. To what extent can this radical transformation in the climate of Spain be attributed to the French Revolution, whether or not one includes

Napoleon as part of the Revolution?

Let us begin by noting that there is sharp disagreement on the issue, although the question is not usually posed in these terms. A century ago the eloquent defender of Spain's Catholic tradition, Marcelino Menéndez y Pelayo, traced the political and religious conflicts of his time back to the reign of Carlos III and most directly to his expulsion of the Jesuits in 1767. He accused the king's ministers of beginning an attack on the Church that turned Spain into one of the most backward countries of Europe. He included in his gallery of heterodox Spaniards a few who supported the Revolution and others who joined the government of Napoleon's brother, King Joseph Bonaparte, but he had more severe strictures for the members of the Cortes (estates) of Cadiz who enacted the Constitution of 1812 and abolished the Inquisition. For him they were all heirs of the reformers of Carlos III's day.

Carlos III's reputation has come a long way since Menéndez y Pelayo. In 1983 the government of Spain, now in socialist hands, used the bicentennial of his death to glorify his reign and the Spanish Enlightenment. Nevertheless, a minority of voices still sing a different tune. Josep Fontana, an economic historian and long-time student of the period and no disciple of Menéndez y Pelayo, has attributed the major subsequent catastrophes of the Spanish monarchy to the policies of Carlos III. According to Fontana, his reforms were embodied more in words than in deeds; the real Spain remained destitute and its colonies exploited. "What, in sum, did these reformers reform? From their administration the empire came out split asunder and Spain impoverished and reduced to a third rate power. It is hard to imagine that matters could have gone worse without these reforms [counterfactual history again!]¹ By implication, little share of the dismal future of Spain could be attributed to the French Revolution. In sum, Fontana adds a new twist to the long-accepted view of colonial historians that the imperial reforms of Carlos III, by awakening colonial antipathy for the mother country, set the stage for the independence movement.

Against this negative evaluation of the colonial policies of Carlos III can be set the view that serious difficulties began only after 1789. Tulio Halperín Donghi, the leading historian of this period in Latin America, has recently written: "What was going to create a crisis in the colonial order was not the more vigorous affirmation of [royal] authority during a quarter century of reforms [under Carlos III]; it was rather the progressive collapse of this same authority when the defenses these reforms had tried to erect could no longer withstand the military and political crisis of Europe."²

As for the negative view of Carlos III's domestic policies put forward by Menéndez y Pelayo, I attempted to refute it thirty years ago.³ I maintained that, although many Spaniards disliked Carlos III's reforms, until after his death the vast majority of both his educated and illiterate subjects accepted the legitimacy of royal authority in political and economic matters and in the temporal affairs of the Church. The future divisions of Spain, I said then, originated in the decade of the 1790s, and the side effects of the French Revolution had much to do with it. I shall reassess this conclusion in what follows.

The news coming out of France in 1789 and later years was not the sort to leave its neighbors unmoved. Although the royal government and the Inquisition did their best to prohibit the circulation of newspapers, broadsides, and other written materials that mentioned revolutionary events, many Spaniards became aware of developments beyond the Pyrenees. The common response of those who did get information was more curiosity than a desire to emulate. The Constitution of 1791 inspired a few royal counselors to consider the benefits of a written supreme law that would limit royal absolutism. The Civil Constitution of the Clergy, passed in July 1790, produced much more excitement. Its establishment of local authority in temporal matters and its abolition of tithes and confiscation of church properties appealed to the enlightened Spaniards' regalist partisanship against the Jesuits and other ultramontanes.[4]

This was in the early years of the Revolution. When the Terror came, it alienated most of these people, and those whose revolutionary passion still burned were no threat to the government. A small conspiracy headed by one Juan Picornell reached the stage of circulating a manifesto in February 1795. This group was alone, and it was easily crushed.[5]

One has to get to the war against Napoleon to find what appears to be a serious case of revolutionary political influence. After enticing the recently proclaimed King Fernando VII along with his father Carlos IV, who had just abdicated, to Bayonne in May 1808, Napoleon forced the two kings to cede the Spanish crown to him, and Napoleon in turn, gave it to his brother Joseph. At the same time he drew up a constitution for Spain and had a submissive assembly of Spaniards ratify it. A small number of Spaniards became partisans and collaborators of Joseph, the so-called *afrancesados*. They tended to admire in Napoleon the enlightened despot more than the heir of the Revolution.

Most Spaniards adopted a position opposed to the Bonapartist takeover, and they made possible the "War of Independence," the five-year struggle in cooperation with the English and Portuguese armies that produced the defeat of the French forces in the peninsula. The liberators were sharply divided between opponents of the Enlightenment and the reform policies of Carlos III, and the "liberal" partisans of civil rights and popular or "national" sovereignty. These partisans took control of the Cortes that assembled at Cadiz in 1810, and they produced the Constitution of 1812 that embodied a democratic representative monarchy.

The Cortes adopted other legislation in the same vein. A year later it abolished the Inquisition and transferred issues of freedom of expression to civil courts. The Cortes also abolished *señorios*, semifeudal jurisdictions held by aristocrats, and they created elected city councils to eliminate a center of aristocratic political power at the local level. They decreed a uniform political and administrative structure for Spain and its empire in place of the distinct regional rights and practices that had survived from the Middle Ages and Habsburg days.

The conservative opponents of the Liberals of Cadiz accused them, then, of being Frenchmen in Spanish clothing, and historians have since found them to be disciples of the French Revolution. In particular, the Constitution of 1812 is said to have been modeled on the French Constitution of 1791. Both created limited parliamentary monarchies.

The liberals certainly appeared to be presenting Spain with the benefits of the French Revolution. And yet one can find precedents in the reforms of the eighteenth century for almost every measure they enacted, although usually more timid in content. The kings had sought to cut back the prerogatives of señores. The Inquisition had been a bone of contention since the middle of the eighteenth century, when the Jesuits had used it to silence the opponents of their doctrines. And while the Constitution spoke repeatedly of the Nation and the *Patria*, these words had come into use under Carlos III to encourage public participation in service to the monarchy.[6]

Can we then discard the influence of the French Revolution on the Cortes of Cadiz? On the direction they took, yes, on the whole; it originated in earlier domestic developments. Can we then attribute to the French Revolution the radicalization of the policies of their eighteenth-century forebears? Undoubtedly, the fact that France had had written constitutions, as had the United States, and that Napoleon had presented one to Spain, goes a long way to explaining the choice of such a document to embody their reforms. Yet they acted on their own. Joseph Bonaparte had given Spain both a constitution and the abolition of the Inquisition, and most Spaniards had refused them from his hands.

The Revolution may well have had a stronger effect on the opponents of reform than on its partisans. If a minority of Spaniards approved of some features of the Revolution, the much more general response was one of rejection. Very soon nonjuring priests and other opponents of the Revolution began to arrive in Spain. The government sought to silence them as it did pro-revolutionary propaganda, but when it went to war with France in 1793, the émigrés were free to arouse Spaniards against the godless revolutionaries. Conservative clergymen and others could now denounce royal reform policies as imitations of those of the French Revolution, timidly at first, but openly after 1808.

Radicalization was also a response to the discredit into which the Spanish monarchy had fallen under King Carlos IV (1788-1808). Unfortunately for the monarchy, Carlos IV was a very different man from his father and was apparently pushed around by his virago of a queen. His dismissal within a few months in 1792 of two successive first ministers who had been leading figures under Carlos III, the Conde de Floridablanca and the Conde de Aranda, and the replacement of them by Manuel Godoy, a young officer of the guards, shocked many people. Godoy was rumored to owe his extraordinary advancement to his being the queen's lover.

Because the monarchs allowed him to dominate the government for the next sixteen years, the legitimacy of the crown as the sole fount of legislation was tainted. A major cause cited by conservatives for rejecting the right of

Carlos IV and Fernando VII to give the crown of Spain to Bonaparte was that the despotism of a royal favorite had brought on Spain's plight. Liberals later used the same argument to justify the adoption of a constitution. Both parties believed that some means had to be found to prevent the repetition of an incompetent swaggerer in charge of the national destiny.

Another development beyond the control of the government of Carlos IV also contributed to the discredit of the royal entourage. One of the most serious charges that Josep Fontana has directed against Carlos III was that he initiated the fiscal collapse of the monarchy by creating paper notes to finance Spain's participation in the War of American Independence.[7] Although they were discounted during that war, these *vales reales*, as they were called, soon recovered their credit and were quoted at or above par until Spain entered the war against France in 1793. The expenses of that war forced the crown to issue more *vales reales*, and they were again traded at a discount. Confidence in them fell even more after Spain switched sides and declared war on Great Britain in 1796. The British navy all but sealed off trade with Spain's colonial empire, and the *vales reales* fell to as low as one-quarter of their face value against hard currency.

To meet this threat to the monarchy--the king's counselors were well aware that a fiscal collapse had brought on the French troubles--Carlos IV decreed the disentail (that is, the sale) of large portions of ecclesiastical property--the endowments for religious funds and charitable institutions and services--and the use of the proceeds to pay off the *vales reales*.

Again, one cannot but be struck by the similarity to the case of the French revolutionary *assignats*. The *assignats* were created to liquidate the debt of the old regime; they could apply to the purchase of church properties, and they subsequently lost their value. However, the *vales reales* existed before the *assignats*, and the idea of disentail went back to Carlos III and the Enlightenment. The reformers of his day criticized the practice of entailing property--tying it up legally so that it could not be disposed of, a privilege enjoyed by the church and the high nobles. The reformers believed that the practice kept land off the market and out of the hands of industrious private farmers. Before the French Revolution, they had not dared propose openly the sale of church and aristocratic property, but the wars gave them their opportunity.

The sale of church properties was no more successful financially in Spain than in France. The income from the disentail went down the maelstrom of the war against Britain, subsidies for Napoleon, and the relief of natural disasters: famine, earthquakes, and floods. Disentail of church properties made enemies for Godoy of a goodly share of the clergy, who denounced his luxurious living style as the cause of the fiscal crisis, however fantastic such an accusation might be.[8]

The impact of the French Revolution in Spain thus appears to come more from the direct physical impact of the Revolutionary and Napoleonic wars than from the political example it offered. It exacerbated tensions and acted as a catalytic agent, but it did not initiate new directions in Spain. Spain was running on a track parallel to that of France, not one that branched off from it.

There are two grand historical schemes that might account for this pattern. One is that Spain, France, and the Western world in general were passing from a feudal to a capitalist stage, the French Revolution and the end of the Spanish absolute monarchy being different tracks headed to the same destination. The debate in the last generation was over the bourgeois nature of the French Revolution: Cobban versus Lefebvre: Soboul versus Cobban: Furet versus Soboul. The bourgeois revolution thesis for France seems laid to rest, at least in its crude form. Some distinguished Spanish historians have also described the end of the old regime and the long-drawn-out process of creating a constitutional monarchy as a bourgeois revolution.[9] I have put in my oar to counter this thesis.[10] To put it simply, there was no bourgeois class powerful enough for such an achievement. I am not alone, but the thesis will not easily be laid to rest.

The other grand historical scheme deserves more consideration. R. R. Palmer gave it its best known form and applied to it the term "the age of the democratic revolution."[11] Emphasizing political rather than economic conflicts and with a more limited time span than the materialist dialectic, Palmer maintains that the countries of Europe and the United States were involved in a broad conflict between hereditary groups or "aristocracies," who were entrenched in political control through their hold over constituted bodies, and their opponents, who wished to replace their power with a broader form of "democratic" community. The enlightened despots might have satisfied the wishes of the "democrats," but when they failed to tame the aristocracies, the democrats took matters in their own hands and in the process established the people as constituent power. The process first ran its course in the future United States. The French Revolution was the most violent case because unlike the British colonies in America and the states later liberated by the French armies, French democrats got no help from abroad against their aristocracy.

The Spanish world is conspicuously absent from Palmer's story. Prima facie, his pattern does seem to apply to it. Although Spain had no aristocratic constituted bodies, aristocratic control of municipal governments guaranteed them against too ambitious royal reforms. The faith of Spanish "democrats" (if they can so be termed) in the king vanished with Carlos IV, and they too, turned the people into constituent power in 1812. The constitution and the legislation of the Cortes of Cadiz had distinctly anti-aristocratic intentions, as noted above. All this fits the Palmer scheme.

In an essential way, however, Spain offers a deviant case. Spanish democrats received no help from France. They were in fact engaged in a life and death struggle against Napoleon, for those Spaniards who joined Joseph Bonaparte were not democratic in outlook. How could Spanish democrats be at war with the self-proclaimed home of democracy and not be aristocratic in outlook? Palmer has no explanation. Spain does not fit into the "Grande Nation" of European sympathizers united around the French Revolution identified by Jacques Godechot, the other historian whose name is tied to this thesis.[12] The Spanish case suggests that indeed a democratic revolution was in process, but that it proceeded with less reference to the Revolution in France than the accepted francocentric view of the period recognizes.

Does this mean that, without the French Revolution and Napoleon, Spain would somehow have passed from the enlightened despotism of Carlos III to the constitutional monarchy of the late nineteenth century without the trauma of economic collapse and civil conflict? I can imagine that the empire might have remained together if it had been spared the wars of the period and that its prosperity could have continued, although it would have required major political restructuring. What I cannot imagine is that such restructuring at home and in the empire could have been achieved without some form of violence. The absolute monarchy was too well entrenched bureaucratically, institutionally, and morally to give way easily. Some version of the Carlist wars would have occurred, probably broader in geographic scope than those of the 1830s and 1870s. The French Revolution and Napoleon through their wars provided an alternative form of violence, more violence surely than was needed, with more disastrous economic results.

The wars of the French Revolution made Spain a poorer country than it would have been otherwise, especially if we include Napoleon's attempted conquest. The violence of its wars also acted as a catalyst to accelerate and radicalize change. In this, however, it shared credit with Godoy's scandalous reputation. But our experiment in counterfactual history indicates that the French Revolution per se had only minor influence on the direction of Spain's political and institutional development. To borrow from Robert Fogel's conclusion on American railroads, because of the way the French Revolution dominated people's imagination, its impact on the future of Spain looks more impressive than it would appear to have been when one attempts to predict the future without it.

NOTES

1. Josep Fontana, "Presentación: En torno al comercio libre," in J. Fontana and Antonio Miguel Bernal (eds.), El "Comercio Libre" entre España y América (1765-1824) (Madrid: Fundación Banco Exterior, 1987). Not too long ago Stanley J. Stein also disputed the economic achievements of Carlos III (Stanley J. Stein, "Reality in Microcosm: The Debate over Trade with America, 1785-1789") in Historia Ibérica: Economia y sociedad en los siglos XVIII y XIX, 1 (New York: Anaya, Las Américas, 1973) (only number issued).

2. Tulio Halperín Donghi, Reforma y disolución de los imperios ibèricos, 1750-1850, Vol. III of Historia de América Latina, ed. Nicolàs Sànchez Albornoz (Madrid, 1985), 74.

3. Richard Herr, *The Eighteenth-Century Revolution in Spain* (Princeton, N. J., 1958), Part I.

4. Ibid., Part II.

5. Ibid., 325-327.

6. Richard Herr, "La Ilustración española," in Spain, Ministerio de Cultura, *Carlos III y la Ilustración*, Vol. 1 (Madrid, 1988), 37-51.

7. Richard Herr, *Rural Change and Royal Finances in Spain at the End of the Old Regime* (Berkeley, Calif., 1989), Part I.

8. "Good, Evil, and Spain's Rising against Napoleon," in Richard Herr and Harold T. Parker (eds.), *Ideas in History*, Durham, N. C.: Duke University Press, 1965, 157-181.

9. Miguel Artola Gallego, "La España de Fernando VII," in Ramón Menéndez Pidal (ed.), *Historia de España*, Vol. 26 (Madrid: Espasa Calpe, 1968).

10. Richard Herr, "Spain," in David Spring (ed.), *European Landed Elites in the Nineteenth Century* (Baltimore, 1977), 98-126; Herr, *Rural Change*, especially 720-733.

11. R. R. Palmer, *The Age of the Democratic Revolution*, 2 vols. (Princeton, N. J., 1959-1964).

12. Jacques Godechot, *La Grande Nation: l'Expansion révolutionnaire de la France dans le monde de 1789 à 1799* (Paris, 1956).

21

Republican Revolution or Absolutist Reform?

Uffe Østergaard

Enlightened Absolutism as a political regime and a political philosophy in 18th century Denmark and France.[1]

The first links in the long chain of reforms and revolutions, projects and delusions, rebellions and repressions that led in the eighteenth century to the collapse of the old regime are to be sought not in the great capitals of the West, in Paris and London, or in the heartland of Europe, in Vienna and Berlin, but on the margins of the continent, in the unexpected and peripheral places, on the islands and peninsulas of the Mediterranean, among lords and peasants in Poland and Bohemia, and in Denmark and Sweden to the north. There emerged the passions and hopes, and the revolts and protests of the sixties and seventies, which proved in the end to be incompatible with the political and social realities inherited from traditions of the past. The end of the old regime presented itself at first as a peripheral event in the Europe of the Enlightenment. (Venturi 1979: IX)

Thus, Franco Venturi, the unrivaled master of the history of Enlightenment Europe, introduces the English translation of his third volume of *The End of the Old Regime*. In the same spirit, I have embarked on my somewhat more modest rethinking of "enlightened absolutism" as a political regime and philosophy. Seen from today, the very notion of absolutism seems obsolete and doomed. The term "enlightened despotism" was invented by German historians in the nineteenth century primarily as a defense of the Second German Empire of Kaiser Wilhelm and Otto von Bismarck in the scholarly battle between German autocracy and British and French democracy. Germany lost the two world wars, and so did "enlightened despotism" as a political philosophy, even though it held the ground in a rearguard action in the proceedings of the International Committee of Historical Sciences between the wars (see its *Bulletin* 1928, 1930, 1933, and 1937). But despotism is not absolutism, just as absolutism is not totalitarianism. In the light of the present problems for democratic theory and practice as well as the rising doubts of the advantages of revolution over reforms, it might be worthwhile to return to the old questions of the eighteenth century with a fresh mind and a knowledge of other situations than the well-known cases of France, England, and Prussia.

ENLIGHTENED ABSOLUTISM AND THE FRENCH REVOLUTION

Was the *ancien régime* of prerevolutionary France doomed to disappear in a revolution that for good or bad overthrew the existing order? The answer, of course, depends on what is meant by the old order. If, as is often the case, it is taken to mean the political regime of enlightened absolutism, I am not so certain. Historical evidence when taken from a broader and more comparative context, suggests a more ambiguous verdict than is usually pronounced. Denounced by its aristocratic as well by its liberal enemies, absolutism has gone down in history as almost synonymous with unrestrained dictatorship. That never was the truth about this type of political regime. In principle, absolutism designated a system of monarchical rule in which the king was responsible only to the law of God, *Lex Divina*. Apart from that, the monarch was *legibus solutus*; that is, the law was a product of his sovereign will (Poggi 1978). Yet this does not imply that absolutism was unrestricted despotism either in historical reality or in theory. It is very important to distinguish between modern totalitarianism and absolutism.

As a political system, it gradually developed in a number of European states from the middle of the sixteenth to the middle of the eighteenth century. The French historian Roland Mousnier has suggested a development in four phases. In the beginning, power was exercised by the royal council dominated by aristocrats and the king in cooperation, while in the end, after a series of internal changes, bureaucratic rule by a royal cabinet without personal participation of the king became the norm in fully developed absolutist regimes (Mousnier 1982). This later type designated what contemporaries usually understood by enlightened monarchy.

The expression "enlightened despotism" was never used by the contemporaries; as noted earlier, it is an invention of German historians of the nineteenth century (Soboul 1979: 519). Modern historians seem to have agreed on the use of "enlightened absolutism" for the theory and reality of a number of the absolutist regimes of the eighteenth century. In these regimes the monarch derived his powers from the people and not from God. Friedrich II of Prussia was thinking in these terms when in his *Essai sur les formes de gouvernement* (1777) he called the sovereign prince "le premier serviteur de l'Etat." In another context, he expressed it in this way: "It is apparent that the sovereign, far from being the absolute master of the people under his dominion, is himself nothing more than the first servant" (Oeuvres VIII, p. 168, quoted after Holm 1883: 3). This did not imply that the absolute prince was powerless. On the contrary, because of this unity between ruler and ruled, he (or she) ought to be to society "what the head is to the body; he has to look out, think, and act in order to acquire the utmost possible for all of the society." Frederick II, Catherine II of Russia, and a number of other eighteenth century rulers tried to live up to this autocratic ideal of unrestricted monarchy in the service of a greater common good.

Ultimately, the king's power was absolute; it was, however, understood as "legitimate" power exercised within inherent limits, bureaucratically organized, and never personally exercised. According to the German historian, Fritz Hartung, it is highly unlikely that even Louis XIV ever would have uttered the famous sentence: "L'Etat c'est moi" (Hartung 1949). Absolutism came into disrepute mainly as a consequence of the Revolution in France. Enlightenment thinkers in France and Germany from Montesquieu onward dismissed unrestrained absolutism as (Oriental) despotism; but the majority did not criticize absolutism as such. On the contrary, apart from England, the Netherlands, and Switzerland, enlightened absolutism was held in high esteem by Enlightenment thinkers all over Europe. Baron Paul Henri d'Holbach (1723-1789), with help from Denis Diderot (1713-1784), Joseph Louis Lagrange (1736-1813), and other Encyclopedists, formulated a veritable code of enlightened absolutism (Holbach 1770 and 1772). After having done away with the metaphysical bases of morals, politics for him became an art of regulating the passions of man in the interest of society at large, the so-called *bien commun*. The obligations of the social pact on the ruler as well as on the ruled are stressed again and again. The law was conceived as an expression of the *the volonté générale* and was equally binding for sovereign and people (Trenard 1979: 629). To these thinkers, it was not important *who* was the agent of these secular reforms as long as they were carried out. Consequently, they had no problems in subscribing to the *bon mot* often attached to absolutist rulers of the Enlightenment: "Tout pour le peuple, rien par le peuple" (Linvald 1933: 715).

This interpretation is not uncontroversial. The specialist of Enlightenment political philosophy, Maurice Cranston, dismisses such an interpretation in the opening paragraph of his recent book on the political philosophy of the Enlightenment:

It is widely believed that the philosophers of the French Enlightenment were all more or less in agreement in their support of "enlightened despotism" as the form of government that would most readily further their programme of salvation through science. . . . "But very few if any of the philosophes themselves were champions of 'enlightened despotism'". On the contrary, the one thing they all had in common was a sincere attachment to freedom. (Cranston 1986: 1)

This would have been a devastating statement had it not been for the subsequent qualifications. After a brief analysis of the contrasts between two strands of Enlightenment thinking, that of Montesquieu as a repetition with modern arguments of the old *thèse nobiliaire* and that of Voltaire as a repetition of the *thèse royale*, Cranston continues:

"Enlightened despotism" is an unfair name for what Voltaire and his followers had in mind when they called for enlightened absolutism; for they combined with their adherence to the Baconian political design a liberal or Lockian belief in the natural rights of the individual to life, liberty, and property. Montesquieu wrote for the *Encyclopédie*, and he was acknowledged by the younger philosophes as Voltaire's equal as a patriarchal theorist of the Enlightenment; but in the 1750s, when the first volumes of the *Encyclopédie* were published, few of its contributors had any sympathy for the claims of the parliamentary estate which Montesquieu represented. When Louis XV banished the Paris parlement in 1753 to make way for a royal court, the encyclopédistes made no protest. They were more concerned just then to reform the Paris theatre and French music, a revolution in taste being seen as a step towards a revolution in thought. (Cranston 1986: 3).

Cranston is correct in the sense that they did not call for enlightened despotism. But freedom and absolutism did not seem to exclude each other in the way they came to do after the French Revolution. The previous thinking only looks obsolete in the light of the subsequent development of a renewed republican theory inspired by Rousseau and the success of the republican revolution in North America. I therefore suggest a return to the situation before the American and French revolutions in order to gain a real historical understanding of what the concepts meant to contemporaries.

Voltaire (1694-1778) tried to work with Friedrich II and praised the absolutism of Louis XIV in *Le siècle de Louis XIV* (1751) as the best of those four "most perfect periods of human history" Ancient Greece, Imperial Rome of Caesar and Augustus, the fifteenth century of Mahomet II and the Medicis of Florence, and the century of Louis XIV. In fact, it was the most perfect of them all enriched by the discoveries of the others (Voltaire 1751 I: 36). Later on in the book when treating the situation of the sciences, Voltaire characterizes the century of Louis XIV as "Ce siècle heureux, qui vit naître une révolution dans l'esprit humain" (Voltaire 1751, vol. II: 39) ["This fortunate century which witnessed a revolution of human understanding"]. This does not mean that Louis XIV was an enlightened absolutist ruler. He derived his powers from God and exercised "une fonction toute divine" because it was the will of God, not because of some sort of contract with his people. Any talk of his ruling in the service of the people would have produced nothing but incomprehension. This kind of thinking was passed on to his successors with disastrous consequences. As late as 1766, Louis XV publicly stated that

The sovereign power rests exclusively in my person, the judiciary is derived solely from me, I alone give the laws. . . . My people is only united through me. The rights and interests of the nation are necessarily united with mine and rest solely in my hands. [My translation from Holm 1883: 2]

Such thinking, however, was an exception, not a rule, in eighteenth century Europe. Most European countries subscribed to the theory of enlightened absolutism. Comparisons tend to fail when they take as their point of departure the French (and for other reasons the English) experience. This holds true for the otherwise laudable and highly interesting international conference on enlightened absolutism which the late Albert Soboul organized in 1978. In the preface of the proceedings, he concludes in a way that is actually contradicted by the subsequent analyses of the individual cases: "However, in taking an overall assessment of enlightened despotism one has to conclude that, as was true in the case of enlightened reform in France, it ended up finally as a failure." (Soboul 1979: 533) and further: "Enlightened absolutism, progressively oriented as it may have been, could not be divorced from its absolutist character and used, in the name of Enlightenment, to overthrow the foundations and structures of power" (1979: 530).

All right. But the very reason why these reforms from above failed was the outbreak of the French Revolution, that is, a consequence of the very exception he originally had set out to explain. Soboul's premises are found a little earlier: "Tout autre que celle de l'absolutisme éclairé fût, en effet, la voie de la Révolution française" ["Any way other than enlightened absolutism led, in reality, to the French Revolution"] (531). Soboul could only reach this conclusion because he interpreted the successful case of reforms in Denmark-Norway as "a preuve a contrario" (530).

The Danish case has value as example when it is compared with the Prussian reforms and the attempts of Joseph II on one hand, and with the French Revolution on the other; here enlightened absolutism could respond to fundamental social needs by initiating a policy of radical structural change which profoundly affected the position and the interests of the landed aristocracy to the advantage of the peasantry and the urban bourgeoisie. (Soboul 1979: 530)

According to Soboul's analysis of absolutism, it was a political system based fundamentally on a feudal order of society and thus incapable of reforming itself. He expresses it as follows:

The enlightened monarchs could not blame aristocratic privilege and feudal structure, which were the basis of old regime society, without undermining the foundations of their own absolutism. This is proved by the case of Denmark where the destruction of the *ancien régime* was imposed from above and even more by that of France where it came from below. (Soboul 1979: 531)

But how do we know that? Soboul's apparently factual statement reveals itself as a counterfactual statement when investigated somewhat more closely. He and most contemporary historians with him assume that enlightened absolutism was doomed to failure. But that is exactly what should be proven in the comparative analysis. Had it not been for the French Revolution and the subsequent wars of national liberation from Republican and Imperial French rule, there seems to me to be no fundamental reason why enlightened absolutism as a political regime should not have been able to transform itself from within in a peaceful way in France as well as in a number of other European absolutist states. I therefore invite you to join me on a different journey of counterfactual speculation based on an investigation of that most truly enlightened absolutist regime, the Danish. However, before that, it is necessary to investigate somewhat more closely the processes through which the French Revolution was unleashed.

THE FRENCH REVOLUTION: HISTORICAL ACCIDENT OR MANIFEST DESTINY?

All differences in the historiographical interpretations of the causes, development, and effects of the French Revolution aside, the overwhelming majority of historians, even after the revisionisms of the Bicentennial, seem to agree on the inevitability of the Revolution, but for very different reasons. François Furet and his entourage of "revisionist" historians condemn the Revolution because it led to verbal and later physical violence. But he also subscribes to Tocqueville's interpretation of the revolutionary episode as a logical step in the development of a monolithic concept of politics in France beginning under the absolutist rulers and culminating under the republican successor regimes (Furet 1988b). In the opposite camp it seems obvious that, as much as Michel Vovelle and his guardians of the revolutionary heritage disagree with the "Furetistes" over practically everything, they also think of the Revolution as the only possible result. The difference lies in their positive attitude toward it as a step in the direction of the modernization of France.

I am not suggesting that the Revolution never happened, not at all. What I do want to question, however, is the inevitability of the process. Was revolution really the only possible outcome of a series of structural imbalances in the *ancien régime*? Would it not be more historically correct to understand it as a political event, an "accident" in the historian's sense of the word, that is, something that can be explained afterward but that never could have been predicted before the event. Decades of revisionist research point in this direction, as does our recent experiences with the sudden and unexpected democratic revolutions in Eastern Europe.

Admittedly, one of the leading revisionist historians, William Doyle, in his precise and detailed analysis of the origins of the French Revolution, has written: "The revolution that was to sweep away the political institutions of old France, and shake her society to its foundations, did not begin on July 14, 1789. By that time the old order was already in ruins, beyond reconstruction" (Doyle 1980: 43). This statement, however, is to be understood in a much less deterministic sense than structuralistically inclined readers are apt to do, as he continues: "This was the result of a chain of events that can be traced as far back as August 20, 1786" (1980: 43). As far back as August 1786! This hardly qualifies as support of the textbook version of the inevitable coming of the French Revolution. The date August 20, 1786, marked the day when the financial crisis of the state became irreparable. Other historians have chosen the collapse of the reforms of Maupeou in 1774 or those of Turgot in 1776 as their points of no return. Still, measured against the enormity of the traditional verdict pronounced on the old regime, a difference of ten years does not amount to much.

If we choose to follow Doyle's interpretation, a procedure that makes sense as his analysis of the political events leading to the outbreak of revolution is still the most detailed and precisely argued on the market, then what happened on August 20, 1786? On this day the controller-general of the royal finances, Charles Alexandre de Calonne (1734-1802), informed Louis XVI that the state was on the brink of financial collapse. In his own words, the situation was as follows:

I shall easily show that it is impossible to tax further, ruinous to be always borrowing and not enough to confine ourselves to economical reforms and that, with matters as they are, ordinary ways being unable to lead us to our goal, the only effective remedy, the only course left to take, the only means of managing finally to put the finances truly in order, must consist in revivifying the entire State by recasting all that is vicious in its constitution. (Quoted from Doyle 1980: 51).

This analysis prompted Calonne to propose something absolutely unprecedented in the history of the French monarchy namely, a total and comprehensive reform of all its institutions in order to create a rational and uniform organization of the economy, the government, and the society. In the eyes of the king, the proposals might very well have appeared to be a revolution. We know for sure that the proposals were understood as being revolutionary by some of the main benefactors of the *ancien régime*. They were, however, only intended as a reform, albeit a radical reform. Compared with the reforms actually carried out in other absolutist countries, Calonne's proposals appear less novel and certainly not very revolutionary. First came fiscal and administrative reforms designed to remedy once and for all the structural problems besetting the royal finances. Second, Calonne proposed a program of economic stimulation of agrarian production: abolition of the internal customs barriers, substitution of the corvée, that is forced labor for road building, to be replaced by a tax. All this was intended further to increase the tax yield already improved by the administrative reforms. Finally, Calonne proposed to relax governmental controls over the grain trade (Doyle 1980: 96-97).

These proposed reforms failed utterly when in February 1787 Calonne did not succeed in convincing an Assembly of 144 Notables of the impending crisis and his measures to overcome it. Alfred Cobban, more than thirty years ago, blamed the selfishness of the aristocrats in the *parlements* for this result (Cobban 1957). Instead, William Doyle tends to blame the intransigent and autocratic way in which Calonne handled the Assembly of Notables (1980: 98-102). Interestingly, Patrice Higonnet, in his comparative analysis of the American and the French revolutions, reaches the opposite conclusion and blames Calonne's overbearing manner (Higonnet 1988: 220). However, the precise attribution of guilt is of less importance for my argument. What matters is that the necessary administrative and economic reforms were blocked. Calonne was ousted from power in March, and on April 30, 1787, his rival, Cardinal Brienne (1727-1794), was brought in to try to persuade the

Assembly of Notables of the seriousness of the financial situation. He only succeeded in further offending them and in introducing the politically fatal idea of the convening of the Estates General.

Yet, even Brienne might have succeeded had not the finances suddenly collapsed in August 1788. As late as November 1787, the credit of the regime was still sufficient to secure a vast loan from its citizens. But the day-to-day finances did not depend just on public loans. They also depended on "anticipations," that is, short-term credits from bankers and financiers with security in the tax revenues of the subsequent years. Like Calonne, Brienne hoped in the long run to be able to eliminate the need for such anticipations, but the budget for 1788 was still burdened with 240 million livres, due from previous years. And suddenly it proved impossible to borrow short-term money from the usual creditors. Whether it was because they no longer saw any interest in supporting a minister who was planning to dispense with their services or because of a deliberate political plot to bring down an offensive minister, we do not know for sure (Doyle 1980: 113-114).

Brienne tried in vain to fend off the defeat by fixing May 1, 1789, as the precise date for the meeting of the Estates, but it did not help restore confidence in the finances of the state. On August 16, 1788, he had to suspend payments from the royal treasury and resign. The Swiss financial wizard Jacques Necker (1732-1804) was brought in to patch things up. He did nothing and only ran what amounts to a caretaker government which saw its *raison d'être* as supervising things until the convocation of a meeting of the Estates General. To him and many others, the situation seemed hopeless. As the American ambassador in France, the future president Thomas Jefferson (1743-1826), wrote to his friend John Adams (1744-1826) in late 1787: "I think that in the course of three months the royal authority has lost, and the rights of the nation gained, as much ground, by a revolution of public opinion only, as England in all her civil wars under the Stuarts" (quoted from Higonnet 1988: 222).

Still, the course toward a complete overthrow of all existing institutions was not the only possibility. The determining factor was not the very convocation of the Estates General but how it was to meet, its composition, the methods of election, and whether the vote was to be cast en bloc or in separate groups.

The first governmental act calling the Estates General stipulated neither how they were to be elected and constituted nor which voting procedures they were to follow. Immediately before the collapse of the finances in July 1788, Brienne had declared that the government's mind was open on these matters, and he invited all interested parties to present their ideas. Doyle interprets this lack of detail as an attempt to gain time, while dividing the opponents in the privileged orders on one side and the mass of commoners on the other (1980: 140). Brienne implied that the government reserved for itself the right to set up the Estates as it saw fit. The former minister Malesherbes (1721-1794) had argued that because no precedent existed, the king could simply dictate one.

The suspicion that this was the intention of the king's ministers triggered the financial collapse we have just seen.

Because of the financial collapse, the *parlement* of Paris was able to attach the condition that the Estates General had to meet "according to the forms observed in 1614" when on September 25, 1788, it registered the government act convening them on May 1 of the following year. There is no evidence that the magistrates had thought deeply about the implications of this or even that the members of the *parlement* were sure what these "forms observed in 1614" were. They simply copied a formulation produced by the *parlement* in Vizille in Dauphiné three months earlier. Under the leadership of the coming revolutionary leader of the moderate *Feuillants*, the Protestant lawyer Antoine Barnave (1761-1793), they had drawn up the following conditions as to how the Estates should be constituted: all deputies were to be elected rather than sit as of right; they were to vote by head rather than in their separate orders; the Third Estate was to have as many deputies as the clergy and the nobility together; and whatever taxes the Estates might vote should fall with equal weight on all members of society (Doyle 1980: 142).

These propositions from a relatively unimportant provincial assembly were to prove ominous for the old order, although there was nothing new in the individual demands. The novel feature was the combination of all these points in a single program, formulated at a meeting in which all three orders had freely participated. It was largely due to the activities of one political club, later called la Société des Trente, that this program became a widespread demand all over France. "La conspiration d'honnêtes gens" as Marquis de Mirabeau (the younger, 1749-1791) later called it, launched a campaign of pamphleteering and agitation directed at the bourgeoisie that soon developed into a floodtide far beyond anyone's control. Necker, like everybody else, was taken by surprise by the *parlement's* insistence on the "forms of 1614." Like Calonne, he tried to gain time and presented the reconvened Assembly of Notables with a long list of questions. Nobody doubted, however, that the crucial question was the number of Third Estate deputies.

The notables were split on the question, and time dragged on and on. In this situation, petitions calling for double representation began to pour in from provinces, cities, and corporations from all over the country. By December they numbered eight hundred and were still arriving. The Assembly of Notables still had not made up its mind, but Necker had. December 27, 1788, he issued the Result of the King's Council of State which formally decreed that the number of Third Estate deputies in the Estates General should be doubled so as to equal that of the clergy and nobility combined. On the other hand, he did not go all the way and let the estates vote in one body. This bastard solution was to satisy nobody and more than any other single decision was responsible for provoking the chain of events from the opening May 5 to June 27, 1789, when the king accepted the reformed Estates General as a national constituent assembly. The mood, even among the most radical representatives of the Third Estate when they met in Versailles in May 1789, still was that of reforming rather than of destroying the existing institutions

(Doyle 1980: 256). Yet within half a year an assembly composed of the very same men did destroy these institutions.

It was not the old regime as such but the experiences of the months May, June, and July which turned some liberal reformers into democratic revolutionaries and other liberal reformers into reactionaries. Until then, a large variety of different outcomes had been equally possible. The overwhelming majority of informed observers of the day regarded a political modification of the absolutist rule from within leading to some constitutional arrangement or other as by far the most likely outcome. A number of other absolutisms of the day took this route. Patrice Higonnet in his stimulating comparison of the two revolutions in the United States and France does not believe that there were chances for absolutism, not even of a reformed kind. But neither does he subscribe to the inevitability of revolution. According to him, the notables had little sense that the *ancien régime* of which they were part was coming to an end. They spoke fair words but stood their privileged ground. Still, in Higonnet's opinion, some sort of agreement ought to have been possible between the crown and the elite. He concludes: Louis and Necker might have turned the corner had they revived, in a more flexible context, Turgot's economic and social program of possessive individualism and rationalist reform. Louis could not have gone on as an absolutist monarch, but he might have survived as a "patriot king," (Higonnet 1988: 221).

The prime example of such successful reform in an absolutist regime was the double monarchy of Denmark and Norway. There, a liberal set of reforms was carried out without the king compromising his God-given absolute power. I will address myself to this apparently paradoxical case of enlightened absolutism in the following part of this counterfactual analysis.

REFORM FROM ABOVE:
ABSOLUTISM IN DENMARK-NORWAY

On April 14, 1784, the young son of the insane king Christian VII and heir to the throne, Crown Prince Frederick--who in 1808 on the death of his father became King Frederick VI--carried out a peaceful coup d'etat. At the very first meeting of the royal council which he attended after he reached the age of 16, he persuaded Christian to dismiss the prior cabinet and grant to himself the reins of government. The former ministers, caught completely off guard, put up no resistance. The young prince was not educationally well prepared for this task, but he had the good luck of an extremely gifted group of advisers. They were headed by the minister of foreign affairs, Count Andreas Peter Bernstorff (1735-1797) and the minister of finances, Count Ernst Schimmelmann (1747-1831). Both men followed illustrious German-born predecessors bearing the same family names, an uncle and a father, respectively. They were joined by the Danish-born, influential aristocrat Count Christian Ditlev Reventlow (1748-1827) and the Norwegian lawyer Christian Colbiørnsen (1749-1814).

With the exception of Colbiørnsen, these were all noble landowners, among the biggest in the country. Yet they immediately set off to follow up earlier endeavors to reform the agriculture that had been investigated from 1757 onward. From 1786 Andreas Peter Bernstorff, together with Christian Ditlev Reventlow, chaired the Great Land Commission, with Colbiørnsen as secretary. It worked with unprecedented speed and immediately enacted a series of measures that eventually were to grant the middle and larger Danish peasants as much personal freedom as their English counterparts but better protection against economic exploitation. First, in 1786 and 1787, landlords were deprived of their right to impose degrading punishments on their tenants, such as riding the "wooden horse," and tenants were granted the right to economic compensation for improvements they had made if they were evicted from their plots. In 1788 the Danish equivalent of serfdom, the so-called Stavnsbånd, was abolished. Literally, Stavnsbånd means adscription, a peculiar form of servitude enforced by the state on the tenant peasants and brought into existence as late as 1733. Serfdom in the East-Elbian sense had never made it farther north than Holstein. The Stavnsbånd was to be terminated in stages, which would leave all peasants completely free by 1800; but 1788 was from the beginning seen as the point of no return for the agrarian reforms in particular and the whole complex of reforms. Recently, Danish historians have questioned the degree of unfreedom under the Stavnsbånd, and the social reality seems to have been very different from the harsh words of the law and the popular myths established later on. Nevertheless, its abolition took on a symbolic importance that was to have an enormous political impact.

Labor services remained, but landlords were encouraged to define these services in a contract with their tenants, if necessary with the help of state arbitrators, and preferably convert them into cash payments. The landlords were not compelled by law to sell off their lands, nor were the peasants bound to buy the land they cultivated. However, both parties were heavily encouraged to do so. Many landlords found it more profitable to sell their estates and rely exclusively on the demesnes that they worked with hired labor. The plight of these landless laborers or very small smallholders called *husmaend* was the reverse side of the Danish agrarian reforms (Kjaergaard 1979). Their numbers had been rising throughout the eighteenth century, but by the end of the century the reforms were to deprive this rapidly growing class of all hope of entering the middle strata of society for more than a century.

As in most other cases of successful modernization, the poor paid the price by becoming even poorer. Similarly, the reforms never threatened the central economic interests of the manorial class (Kjaergaard 1979). Yet, Soboul's harsh judgment of the incapacity of a feudal system to reform itself (1979: 531) does not hold true. The reforms were meant to create a middle class of entrepreneurial peasant farmers, and that they did. Over the next thirty years, more than half of the tenant peasants bought their own middle-sized farmsteads. Together with other reforms, this process did away with the old system of communal village farming. In less than a generation, the core areas of the Danish state, though still thoroughly absolutist, for all practical purposes had done away with the feudal agricultural structure and laid the foundations of a new agrarian capitalism dominated by a self-conscious class of capitalist peasant farmers. When the feudal system was formally abolished in 1919, it had long since ceased to exist in social reality.

The agrarian reforms of 1784 to 1788 were followed in the years 1793-1796 by a thorough reform of the legal system in the spirit of Beccaria (1764) bearing the unmistakable imprint of Christian Colbiørnsen. Legal processes were rationalized, and prison conditions improved. A regular system of poor relief was instituted, financed by compulsory contributions from the peasants under the supervision of the priests in their capacity as local representatives of the state. [The king had been head of the church in this Lutheran country since the Reformation in 1536.] The system worked relatively well until the middle of the nineteenth century when the peasant farmers, as a result of the democratization, took over local government themselves. The subsequent period from the 1840s to the 1880s represents a nadir in the relations between the poorer and the wealthier strata of Danish agrarian society.

A more liberal tariff abolishing many import prohibitions was introduced in 1797, and the grain trade was liberalized. In 1792 Ernst Schimmelmann took steps to end the slave trade in the Danish West Indies from 1803 as the first country in the world. However, he failed to abolish slavery itself on these islands because of intransigent resistance among the planters and fear of loss of revenue (Degn 1974). He also presided over a commission that in 1789 proposed the introduction of universal free elementary schooling for all children between 7 and 14 years of age, a measure to be enacted in the so-called Great School Law of 1814 in the midst of military defeat and economic catastrophe. Similarly, the Jews were emancipated in 1798 with full rights to marry Christians and enter secondary schools.

The whole reform program was accomplished in an atmosphere of almost unlimited free debate as censorship was banned in the period between 1770 and 1799. On September 4, 1770, the king had declared:

We are deeply convinced that it is as detrimental to the search for truth as it is an obstacle to the discovery of errors and hereditary prejudices for good patriots to hesitate to write freely in accordance with their intelligence and convictions and to attack abuses and unfounded assumptions. (Linvald 1933: 723)

In the wake of the coup of 1784, the freedom had become even more extended, and the abolishment of censorship was put into law in 1790.

The agents of these reforms were some of the most influential nobles in the double monarchy. They did not act on an impulse of pure idealism, although Reventlow for one, like the American republican Thomas Jefferson, left office poorer than he entered. They were sufficiently far-sighted to give up the untenable political prerogatives of their class and gamble on future economic gains. The majority of the owners of large estates were to profit from this policy in the nineteenth century. The initiators were sufficiently well off to be able to risk the gamble. This was not the case for many of the smaller estate holders, especially in the peninsula of Jutland. In the summer of 1790, one hundred and three of the greatest proprietors organized a so-called Address of Confidence to the crown prince on the occasion of his betrothal to a German princess. They protested against the newly proposed civil reforms and drew attention to the rising "insubordination of the peasants encouraged by the French example." The latter was the real meat. The nobles' anxiety over the rising expectations among the liberated peasants triggered a reaction that has gone down in history under the name of the Revolt of the Proprietors of Jutland ("Den jyske Proprietaerfejde," Bjørn 1979a). The outcome, however, would be a complete contrast with the noble protest in France two years earlier.

The reform ministry reacted on the challenge swiftly and with determination. Christian Colbiørnsen, besides serving as secretary of the Great Agrarian Commission in 1788, had also been appointed procurator general and legal Porte-Parole of the regime. In this capacity in October 1790, he published the address and a detailed refutation (Colbiørnsen 1790). He stressed the privileges of the grand holders of estates, and he publicly denounced the signatories and their motives. This offense forced the main instigator of the protest, a German noble by the name of Lüttichau, to sue Colbiørnsen privately in order to protect his honor. Thus, the ministry cleverly succeeded in maneuvering the revolt into the courtroom while mobilizing the predominantly nonnoble "public opinion" of the capital to support its cause. Lüttichau was completely isolated as the signatories in the following months, one by one, withdrew their signatures or even denied that they ever signed. On April 7, 1791, when the verdict in Colbiørnsen's favor was pronounced, Lüttichau was finished, as was the Danish revolt of the nobles. He sold his manors and moved to Brunswick in Germany, while the reform of the Danish absolutist state continued as planned.

It is hard to imagine a more striking contrast to the development in France. The Danish case certainly confirms the opinion of many modern historians that had the French ministers and the king agreed on their policy--or just agreed on any one coherent policy--it would have been impossible to organize a force to oust them from power (Doyle 1980: 113). Little wonder then that Danish reformers of noble descent in their letters and diaries, when commenting on the events in France, somewhat condescending could note: "Finally France is catching up with the rest of enlightened Europe." They kept thinking along these lines until the dethroning of Louis XVI in September 1792 and his subsequent execution in January 1793. Then everything changed. But until 1791-1792, they had been all for the Revolution as the French monarchy, in their eyes, had failed to do its duty toward the society it was supposed to serve.

THE DANISH IDEOLOGY OF ENLIGHTENED ABSOLUTISM

The revolt of the nobles marked the epitome of a very peculiar Danish

ideology of "absolutism guided by public opinion" as it has somewhat paradoxically been termed by a modern Norwegian historian (Seip 1958). A less
clumsy rendering into English could be "absolutism by consent" if consent is
understood as openly expressed opinion. A key thinker in this tradition was
Jens Schelderup Sneedorf (1724-1764). In a book called *Om den borgerlige
Regiering (On Civil Government)*, he combined the notions of "justice" and
"common good" from the tradition of the German-Swedish author Samuel von
Pufendorf (1632-1694; see Tamm 1986) with Montesquieu's concepts of
"honor" and "civic virtue" (Horstbøll 1988: 17). Sneedorf followed Montesquieu in claiming these two sets of "mentalities" to be typical of monarchical
and republican regimes, respectively, but added that "civic virtue which is all
too easily corrupted under the unstable republican form of government" also
could blossom under monarchy if the "exercise of government aimed at the
common weal." According to Horstbøll's analysis, "civic virtue" was expressed in the "patriotism" and "public spirit" of the citizens, while concerns
about the "common weal" originated in the public debate over the proper
"advice" to give to those in power (Horstbøll 1988: 17).

     Apart from the title that is copied from John Locke (1690), this is a
highly original ideological construction developed in the second half of the
eighteenth century by Danish and Norwegian historians and lawyers. As
Sneedorf said in his speech in 1760 at the commemoration of the centennial
of Danish absolutism: "We are the only people who have given ourselves
unrestricted monarchs" (Sneedorf 1760, vol. 7: 504). As they were not of
noble descent, they feared more than anything else the selfishness and egoism
of the aristocracy. The only instrument capable of policing this class and its
excessive and inappropriate privileges was a king with absolute powers. Only
he was able to rule in the interest of the whole people and not just one class.
Thinking of this kind had a long and honorable tradition in Denmark. The
proponents of the theory referred to the circumstances in 1660 when King
Frederick III had assumed absolute power dismissing the aristocratic Council
of the Realm (Rigsrådet) with the support of the Estates General. They called
this a contract between the ruler and the ruled. This was definitely not the
opinion of Frederick III who ordered his prime minister Peder Schumacher
(1635-1699), later ennobled as Griffenfeld and even later condemned to prison
for life for high treason, to render the new absolutist system in writing. This
he did in 1665 in the so-called *Lex Regia* (King's Law), a document heavily
inspired by the writings of Hugo Grotius (1583-1645; see Fabricius 1920: 1-21
and 270 ff., Latin transl. in Jørgensen 1886: 38-67). It confirmed the king's
divine right to rule, relying on the kind of advice he found best. However,
even if this absolutist constitution was not published until 1709, the very
existence of it lent some credibility and legitimacy to the theory of the king's
"absolute rule by law," even if the absolute rulers never openly accepted it
(Horstbøll 1988: 6ff.)

     In absolutist France, after the December 1788 decision to convene the
Estates General and before the proclamation of the "Constituante" in June
1789, the king's absolute power turned out to be absolute only as long as it

was exercised according to "the law" or a constitution. The only problem was that nobody agreed on what was "the law." Here we find the fundamental difference between the apparently so similar absolutisms of Danish and French style. From its very beginning the Danish absolute monarchy had taken on the task of formulating a comprehensive system of coherent laws. Under the names "Danske Lov" and "Norske Lov," respectively, they were finished in 1683 and 1687 (Horstbøll, Løfting, and Østergård 1989). Obviously, these laws did not amount to a bourgeois *Code Napoléon*, but they were much more than a simple codification of feudalism. The relation between these laws and *Lex Regia* was ambiguous (Ekman 1957; Jørgensen 1886) but the Danish absolutist state had a modern, reasonably coherent, and comprehensive set of laws to refer to when it reformed the society from the top down. This is a striking contrast to absolutist France. Louis XIV had never bothered to modernize and rationalize the structure of his state apparatus and thus left his successors without references outside their own persons when their governments ran into economic troubles.

This does not suggest that the alliance between the tenant farmers and their "liberators" could have endured stresses such as those put on the French agrarian society during the Revolution. The fundamental precondition for the success of the reforms was the economic boom of the so-called flourishing epoch of commerce. Under less fortunate circumstances, as Thorkild Kjaergaard has pointed out in a recent article, the alliance of peasants and landlords of the Vendée against revolutionary Paris might easily have been repeated in Denmark. And here the outcome would have been very different (Kjaergaard 1989: 229). The agrarian reforms of Denmark were never seriously challenged and thus had the time to ripen and stabilize so that they became a matter of course.

THE ABSOLUTIST STATUE OF LIBERTY

The concept of the central position of public opinion in the political process was more than mere ideology or wishful thinking on behalf of a few intellectuals. The leading journals and newspapers were widely distributed and read, as demonstrated convincingly by Thorkild Kjaergaard in an analysis of their lists of subscription. The total readership may have amounted to as much as 10 percent of the adult population (Kjaergaard 1989: 224). This figure lends credibility to the assumption of the importance of the written press shared by most contemporaries. A typical example concerning the public attitudes toward the rebellion in North America is found in a private letter from the minister of foreign affairs, Count A. P. Bernstorff, to Ditlev Reventlow (1712-1783) in Holstein, October 22, 1776:

Here the public is extremely supportive of the rebels (in America), not out of any understanding of the situation, but due to the mania for independence which has really contaminated everyone's mind, and because this poison spreads imperceptibly from the works of the philosphes all the way to the village schools. (Friis 1913: 498; cf. Kjaergaard 1989: 227)

The "public opinion" was expressed and believed to be influential by the majority of the contemporaries. The opinions expressed were relatively cautious, for the writers wanted to provoke neither the monarch nor his servants. (The classic analysis of the content of the public opinion is Holm 1883, 1888a, and 1888b). But the necessary prerequisite for the formation of a public opinion was established on September 4, 1770, when all censorship was abolished, as we have already seen (Holm 1885). Restrictions on the press were reintroduced only in 1799 when Russian political pressure forced the Danish government to silence some republican critics. Censorship of the newspapers before printing was reinstated in 1810 because of the pressures of war (Jørgensen 1944; Linvald 1933: 724). The abolition of censorship in the crucial period from 1770 to 1799 did not mean that everything was allowed in print. On the contrary, the authors had to face trial and verdict *after* the publication, but the verdicts had to accommodate to written codes of law. Such verdicts could bankrupt offenders and helped several promising careers. Nevertheless, the whole process was given a legalistic form and thus allowed writers to discuss even matters of the state in a serious way and to disagree openly with the absolutist king and his administration. A good example of that is the debate following the drafting of Reventlow's report on the abolition of servitude 1788 (Kjaergaard 1980).

The ideology of "absolutism by consent" was given physical form during the revolt of the nobles. In order to support the reform ministry and keep the crown prince on the track of reform, a group of influential citizens in Copenhagen decided to raise funds for a monument to commemorate the liberation of the peasants. The explicitly expressed intention was "in clear and unambiguous symbols to depict the regime's official ideology of liberty." Accordingly, it was to be executed in the language of neoclassical iconography. The elaboration of the details was put in the hands of the painter and architect Nikolai Abildgaard (1743-1809), in collaboration with three sculptors Nikolai Dajon (1748-1823), Andreas Weidenhaupt (1738-1803), and Johannes Wiedewelt (1731-1802). Abildgaard had been trained in Rome at the same time as Jacques-Louis David and was an ardent republican. This, however, did not prevent him from being a successful professor at the Royal Academy of Arts, that is, the official artist of the regime. He demonstrated his political opinion in highly sophisticated allegories inaccessible to most spectators or in private satires (Sass 1986).

Abildgaard chose the form of an obelisque for the monument because it was traditionally used to remind spectators of power and eternity. Thus, Abildgaard and the group behind him in the disguise of an unconditional support of his policy hoped to convey to the crown prince the idea that the law was inflexible and equal for all. The artists decided to erect four female statues, one at each corner of the base, embodying fidelity, bravery, labor, and civic virtue. Two base reliefs representing justice balancing the two extremes on a scale, and a female Denmark liberating serfs and slaves alike, respectively, were placed on the base. Officially, the monument was called the Monument in Honor of the Generous Acts of his Majesty toward the Noble

Class of Peasants. However, according to the neoclassical taste of the day, not a single peasant was to be found on the entire column. From today's point of view, the most important expression of ideology are the two inscriptions on the base between the reliefs. They run like an official declaration of the anti-aristocratic ideology of absolutism by consent:

THE KING DECIDED THAT FREEDOM OF THE CITIZENS GUARANTEED BY JUST LAWS PRODUCES PATRIOTISM, COURAGE TO DEFEND THE FATHERLAND, LOVE OF KNOWLEDGE, INDUSTRY, AND PROGRESS (East Side) THE KING ORDERED TO END THE SERVITUDE OF THE PEASANTS, TO ENACT THE AGRICULTURAL LAWS IN ORDER THAT FREE PEASANTS IN HAPPINESS MAY LIVE A DECENT AND INDUSTRIOUS, AN HONEST AND ENLIGHTENED LIFE (West Side)

The fund-raising drive took place in 1791 in an atmosphere full of hope and glory, and the first stone was laid outside the main western entrance to Copenhagen on July 31, 1792, at the wedding of the young Crown Prince Frederick. Nevertheless, when the monument was finally dedicated in 1797, the silence was thundering. What had happened in the meantime? The excesses and the violence of the French Revolution had choked most of the well-intended reformers, and the very notion of republican ideals had become dangerous. Thus was rendered obsolete all thought of republican virtues being defended by an absolutist monarchy. The idea of the differences between people and aristocracy arbitrated by an absolutist king, guided by the reason of the well-educated public opinion, seemed ludicrous after the introduction of the modern political cleavage between left and right.

This, however, should not make us overlook the existence of real alternatives to full-scale revolution in the years before the unleashing of the French Revolution. Until the events in the summer of 1789, everybody even in France was in favor of reforms that would improve the existing institutions of advising the king. What turned benign reformers into radical revolutionaries was not the experience of the deficiencies of the old regime as such, but the revolutionary logic and self-radicalization of the political language in the months of May, June, and July 1789 (Furet 1978; Hunt 1984; Østergård 1985). The events of those months represent one of those unpredicted and unpredictable turns of history, which when it first happens, cannot be undone and subsequently changes all the rules of the game. It would, however, be utterly unhistorical to evaluate all prior experiences and strategies from this vantage point. Had the reformers succeeded in France as they did in other absolutist European countries, history would have taken a somewhat different turn.

THE SOCIAL EFFECTS OF THE FRENCH REVOLUTION

The agrarian reforms of the Danish monarchy would fundamentally revolutionize the countryside over the next couple of generations. A thorough agrarian revolution created a system of middle-sized capitalist peasant farmers who later in the century succeeded in setting up cooperatives to process and market their agricultural products on the world market (for details, see Østergård 1990). What happened to agriculture in France?

According to one of the leading historians of the Annales school, Marc Bloch, nothing. As he put it in his history of rural France:

> The Revolution was to leave the large estate relatively unimpaired. The picture presented by the rural France of our own day--which is not, as it is sometimes said, a land of petty proprietors but rather a land where large and small proprietors co-exist in proportions which vary considerably from province to province--is to be explained by its evolution between the fifteenth and eighteenth centuries. (Bloch 1931/1966: 149)

The much-hailed "abolition of feudalism" on August 4, 1789, was not an agrarian revolution as is so often assumed. The hero of Italian Marxism, Antonio Gramsci for one, coined the phrase "rivoluzione agraria mancata" to denominate the differences between revolutionary capitalist "normal" France and underdeveloped Italy. This interpretation has been repeated so often that it hardly needs any proof. Yet it seems only to be based on a reading of the parliamentary debates. A good example of such orthodoxy is Herbert (1921), but it has recently been repeated by none other than Furet himself. Normally an ardent revisionist, Furet repeats the intentions of the deputies in the Constituante of August 4 and 11, lock, stock, and barrel. He distances himself much less than usually from the proclamations in his subtle analyses of revolutionary rhetorics.

> By suppressing from top to bottom the "feudal" structure of the old society, the decree of August 11, 1789, gave the French Revolution a radical individualist character, which was seen as an indispensable prerequisite of democratic equality. "Feudalism," like aristocracy, became the negative of this new world. . . . By decreeing an end to the principles of organization of the old society, the Revolution, even though it compensated the victims of its bold move with money, added to its banners a victory as radical as the reconquest of sovereignty in June and July--as radical, but easier, quicker, and more durable: for with the inception of popular sovereignty, the French embarked upon a long journey marked by abrupt changes of direction and many setbacks, while on the grave of "feodalité" they laid the foundations of modern, individualistic society for centuries to come. (Furet 1988a: 692-693.

This may hold true at the level of discourse. As to social reality, however, it has become commonplace among agrarian historians to interpret the effects of the revolution as a process of freezing the existing unequal distribution of land among the peasants and substituting non-noble proprietors ("notables") for noble proprietors. They vary somewhat as to whether the subsequent losses of efficiency were compensated by the relative protection of the poorer peasants. Very recently, this debate has been reopened by the historian Peter McPhee (1989). He questions the revisionist orthodoxy of seeing the small peasants protected by the Revolution as necessarily retarding the process of modernization. He draws upon an impressive range of comparative research into agrarian development in different areas of the world. As yet, however, his work only amounts to a program for further research, and I for one, am not at all convinced. His approach contradicts all the major results of comparative historical sociology from Barrington Moore to Immanuel Wallerstein.

The grand old man of the agrarian history of the Revolution, Georges Lefebvre, has formulated the effects of the Revolution as follows: "By increasing the scope of small property and small-scale farming, it probably slowed down the innovations it had legally authorized" (1929: 44). Lefebvre had a positive perspective on the long-term effects of this policy because of his general political inclinations. In his opinion, the Revolution "accentuated the characteristic features of the agrarian physiognomy of France, created a better climate for social equilibrium, and saved some people from the suffering that technological progress brings to the poor" (1929: 44). That may very well be true in the short run, but the majority of specialists of nineteenth-and twentieth-century France have tended to underscore the disastrous results of this protection of the small farmers in terms of contributing to the creation of a "societé bloquée" (Hoffmann 1963, 1976). The prevailing theme of French social and economic history of the period before the 1950s was the society's inability to unleash its inherent energies. The main social basis of Republican France after 1870 was a class of relatively small peasants unable to compete on the world market (Østergård a.o. 1986).

What strikes the modern comparative historian is not that the revolutionaries wanted to carry the agrarian reforms of the old monarchy to a successful conclusion. On the contrary, it is their relative failure that is noteworthy, the radical nature of the revolutionary rhetoric taken into account. Faced with massive popular resistance, the revolutionaries eschewed prescriptive legislation (Jones 1988: XIII). Despite the initial commitment to individualism and to private property, legislation was never issued to abolish communal control over agriculture. The revolutionary government did not suppress the communities' rights to common pasture, and, as a result, the arable land of the villages was still open to the communal herd after the harvest. Even though the revolutionary government recognized that enclosure was a prerequisite of agricultural improvement, legislation to facilitate villagewide enclosures was never issued. Similarly, it was ruled that only debt-free villages were allowed to partition common fields. Because only a few villages were free of all debts, this effectively prevented the majority of villages from partitioning their common lands. A rural code that would abolish gleaning rights or impose mandatory enclosure was not produced. By 1796, the revolutionary government decisively turned its back on agrarian individualism when it annulled the code for partitions. A law of May 21, 1797, divested communities of the right to alienate or exchange their communally owned properties. With this law, the Revolution, just like the monarchy before it, had become the protector of village properties and rights (Root 1989). That is why Georges Lefebvre, in his massive study on the conditions of the peasants in northern France, concludes on a favorable note. "This is the way that the agricultural revolution emerged: not only conservative, but also of moderate impact in spite of appearances, a sort of accommodation between the bourgeoisie and rural democracy" (Lefebvre 1924: 882).

Political evaluations aside, Lefebvre admits that the Revolution halted the great agrarian transformation that it had legally authorized, with the consequence that an "unbridgeable gap between the old France and the new" did not occur (1919: 44). Again, one might be for or against this continuity with the *ancien régime* and relative protection of the weaker; the effects in terms of slowing down the modernization of France seem obvious.

Whether the Revolution accorded the concessions to the peasants because of fear of violence in the countryside, "la Grande Peur" as it was called (Lefebvre 1932) or because of traditional fiscal interests as claimed by some modern scholars (Root 1989) need not concern us here. The important thing is that the concessions were given and that they stifled rural France for more than 150 years. Perhaps, after all, a total political revolution was not the most efficient way to revolutionize society. This is not meant to deny the desirability of democracy, but it has to be admitted that democracy and efficiency are very different things. And that does not always come through in pro-revolutionary and pro-democratic writings.

REPUBLICAN REVOLUTION OR ABSOLUTIST REFORM IN POLITICAL THEORY

The French Revolution was nourished by one powerful idea that foundation comes only from initiation (Ozouf 1988: 809). That meant everything had to be invented all over (again) if it was to have any authority in the brand new revolutionary society. And yet nobody had foreseen this coming of events. According to Doyle, the old monarchy collapsed by itself in 1788. It was not overthrown by opposition to its policies, much less by revolutionaries dedicated to its destruction. It fell because of its inner contradictions (1980: 115). These ideas of invention and revolution as the mother and father of a totally new society brought about by words spoken in a political assembly was as much a surprise for the coming revolutionaries as it was for the representatives of the old order (Østergård 1989: 51-62).

In the light of subsequent events, it is often forgotten that there is no evidence in France of major hostility to the principle of nobility and its pretensions among eighteenth-century thinkers (Doyle 1980: 120-121). Indeed, it is often forgotten that several of the Enlightenment philosophers produced arguments in favor of the nobility. The elder Mirabeau (1715-1789) argued that "noble landowners who tended their estates and resisted the temptation to squander their money in Paris were among the most valuable members of society" (Mirabeau 1756). One, of course, has to keep in mind that he himself was an aristocrat, as was Montesquieu (1689-1755) who expressed equally benign attitudes toward the potentials of this group. In *De l'Esprit des lois* (1748), Montesquieu suggested that, although the honor so beloved of nobles was really nothing more than a prejudice, nobles performed an essential public service in the intermediary bodies that prevented monarchs from becoming despots. Nobility, he declared, "enters in some way into the essence of monarchy, whose fundamental maxim is: no monarch, no nobility; no nobility, no monarch; but there may be a despotic prince." (1748 Book II, Chap. IV).

Montesquieu divided constitutions into republics, monarchies, and despotisms. He defined a republic, whether democratic or aristocratic, as a state where the people or a section of it retains sovereignty, monarchy as a state where a single person governs according to fixed and known laws, and despotism as arbitrary government by a single person. Once he had lost his republican illusions of *Les Lettres persanes* (1721), the difference between a democratic and an aristocratic republic seemed of small importance compared to the difference between despotic and constitutional monarchy, that is between France and England. His main criterion was freedom. Freedom by definition was negated by despotism, whereas a monarchy made constitutional could assure freedom and reconcile it with law.

In Montesquieu's taxonomy of governments, each system has a "principle"; the principle of a republic is virtue, that of a monarchy is honor, that of despotism, fear. He wanted France to recover from its own traditions and its own historical experience with political institutions and instead follow the English example toward constitutional monarchy, and thus reverse the decline of the French monarchy toward despotism. He argued that the predominantly aristocratic "intermediary powers" should be given back their old influence because as he argued in the original version of the manuscript "Intermediary powers constitute the nature of monarchical government" (Cranston 1986: 31). In subsequent editions he softened this formulation but the meaning was well understood by his contemporaries. The four most important of these "intermediary powers" were the landed nobility (*les seigneurs*), the clergy (*le clergé*), the cities (*les villes*), and the legal nobility (*la noblesse de robe*). This latter element turned out to be the most important. He envisaged the legal nobility as an estate and the *parlements* as an institution to balance the powers of the crown.

Montesquieu was an extreme proponent of the legal aristocracy, but his positive attitude toward the nobility was widespread and prevailed until the very outbreak of the Revolution. Not a single one of the sixty thousand *cahiers de doléances* suggested that France might do without a nobility, and everyone agreed to its desirability when taken as an honorary order (Higonnet 1988: 221). This kind of prerevolutionary thinking was precisely what distinguished Danish and Norwegian political thinking from French in the eighteenth century. In France, the nobles were allowed to think of themselves and their institutions such as the *parlements* as carriers of the old liberties. With the growing finanical crisis of the monarchy, they considered a return to aristocratic rule as a progressive step forward and were not impeded in doing so by the Enlightenment thinkers. As we have seen, Montesquieu, who had served as president in the *parlement* in Bordeaux, explicitly assigned a role of intermediary bodies between the ruler and his subjects to the aristocratic courts and the nobility. By their power to resist the king they prevented him from degenerating into a despot. This fear of despotism as arbitrary rule permeated *De l'Esprit des lois* and influenced subsequent opinion in such a way that very few thinkers dared dispute it.

One, however, did dare: the Danish playwright, historian, philosopher, and professor at the university of Copenhagen, Ludvig Holberg (1684—1754). In a book published in French in 1753, he launched a direct attack on Montesquieu's critique of enlightened despotism. He based his refutations of Montesquieu on an earlier treatise on natural jurisprudence (Holberg 1716, cf. Holm 1879 and Tvarnø 1989). Holberg developed a political theory of the so-called double social contract. According to this theory (and here I follow Horstbøll 1988: 13ff), the first social contract that led humankind out of "the historical state of nature," in Denmark, resulted in monarchy. The second social contract determined the delimitations of sovereignty. In Denmark, it took the form of a transfer of absolute power from the Estates General to the king in 1660 and the subsequent limitations of royal sovereignty in the King's Law.

Henrik Tvarnø, in his detailed analysis of Holberg's thinking, does not accept the validity of this position. He accuses Holberg of misreading Montesquieu in a number of crucial areas and points out the basic parallels in their thinking:

Montesquieu did not exclude the possibility of virtue as exemplar under a monarchy, but for him virtue was not the pillar of monarchy, that is to say it was not essential to its existence. In consequence, Holberg's objection does not challenge the basis of Montesquieu's theory when he says that a subject can love both his country and his king. (Tvarnø 1989: 175)

According to his analysis, Holberg accepted the risk of despotism. The greater interest was the existence of a monarchical power strong enough to establish an equilibrium between nobles and bourgeois. This leads Tvarnø to the following comparison:

Again the parallels between the arguments of Holberg and Montesquieu are obvious. The regime should guarantee the domestic tranquility and security of the country. In Denmark [this] internal peace could be assured by the absolute monarchy because it had modified a very important situation: Kings no longer excluded meritorious bourgeois from important posts. . . . (And he concludes): Thus Montesquieu and Holberg agreed in their reliance upon a sovereign, but their expectations were different.• The first wished to establish a balance between the sovereign and the nobility, the second, between the nobility and the bourgeoisie. (Tvarnø 1989: 176)

Be that as it may, Holberg was to influence a whole school of thinkers in Denmark. As they saw it, it was only the uninhibited power of the king that would be able to check the greedy and selfish aristocracy and thus guarantee "justice" for the whole people. The non-noble Holberg and his colleagues could think along these lines because Denmark-Norway at the middle of the eighteenth century, according to the well-informed opinion of a contemporary English writer John Andrews, had recovered from the effects of what, in his eyes, was the "impardonable" monarchical restoration of 1660. John Andrews published *The History of the Revolutions of Denmark*, with an account of the present state of that kingdom and people. This book reflects the tension between republican tradition and the attempts at reform in the absolutist regimes better than any other publication of the time.

Just like his compatriot Robert Molesworth (1656-1725), who in 1694 had published a defamation of the absolutist despotism in Denmark, Andrews detested the apparent lack of liberties. Nevertheless, the country had revived and within "the course of not so many years" had reached a relatively "flourishing state." What were the reasons for such an incredible fact? According to Andrews, the merit had to be attributed to the government. "The wise management of individuals in power" had "counterbalanced the defects of an evil constitution." Grudgingly, he admitted that it might happen even in an absolute monarchy. There were rare cases of good administration in absolutist states. Only "liberty, like an open high road, leads more directly to the term proposed. . . . Despotism is, at best but an oblique path, subject to numberless errors and perplexities" (Andrews 1774: 74ff.) On principle, he did not like the kind of rule he found in a situation where "few of the Danish peasants are free and independent possessors of land" (p. 359). If this problem were resolved, however, "no nation in Europe could boast a better system of internal polity, and Denmark would afford the singular example of a people subject to absolute monarchy enjoying the most equitable laws and living under most moderate government in Christendom" (p. 441ff.)

It was this state of affairs that Danish thinkers, as we have already noticed, tried to develop into an alternative political theory of "absolute rule by law" the same reality modern historians have labeled "absolutism guided by public opinion" (Seip 1958). The physiocratic thinkers and the Encyclopedists in France had advocated an absolutism supplemented by a critical opinion, whereas Rousseau (1712-1778) advocated democracy without public discussion (Habermas 1962: 112). They never succeeded, mainly because the French monarchy was never absolutist or enlightened (Trenard 1979: 632). In Denmark, the somewhat parallel theory of guided absolutism lost out as a political regime mainly because of the political and military repercussions of a more democratic revolution than the aristocratic one it had tried to forestall. Events took place in a country over which the reformers exercised no influence. The Danish social reality, however, did not lose out as the Danish *ancien régime* developed rather smoothly into capitalist modernity, whereas Republican France took a much more cumbersome path. But maybe the *ancien régime* was not so old after all.

That the Danish thinkers did not forecast the events in France was no particular weakness of theirs. Nobody foresaw the Revolution, least of all the coming revolutionaries. The Revolution in France was certainly never planned as would later be the case in Russia. Maximilien Robespierre (1758-1794) for one, was, according to the memoirs of his sister Charlotte, an ordinary provincial lawyer who played cards in the evenings, participated in musical gatherings, and courted his benefactor the archbishop in the provincial town of Arras in the predominantly Flemish region of Artois. He was interested in the ideas of the Enlightenment as were most other young men and some women who had been to school. But he certainly did not sit in secret dark rooms planning the overthrow of the government. Before the events of 1788-1789, neither Robespierre nor the majority of his generation were overtly disaffected from society (Schama 1989). In Robespierre's case there was no recorded crisis of alienation, no outward rebellion before 1788. Later, in revolutionary oratory and journalism, he would talk a lot about himself, but he never revealed details of his life before the Revolution (Furet 1989; Jordan 1985).

It was the coming of the Revolution that released new political possibilities, a new political discourse unimaginable under the *ancien régime*. Just as the English Revolution discovered in Oliver Cromwell, an otherwise obscure and undistinguished landowner and parliamentary backbencher, a political and military genius equal to the great events of his century, so too did the Revolution reveal Robespierre (Jordan 1985: 27-29). Only a tiny minority could envisage any other form of government than monarchy. The idea of republic was synonymous with the direct democracy of antiquity. It was only after the king's flight to Varennes on June 21, 1791, that it became conceivable to think in terms of a republic. As late as in the summer of 1791, Robespierre expressed outrage at the very notion of republicanism: "Accuse me if you will of republicanism. I declare that I abhor any kind of government in which the factious reign" (Nora 1988: 794).

It turns out then, that the ideology of classic republicanism so often invoked by critiques of enlightened despotism as the only guarantee of civic liberty, when it came to social reality, was heavily tinged by aristocratic values. In contrast, the detested absolute monarchy, when it functioned, was more democratic in the modern social and egalitarian sense of the word. This is obvious to the modern observer, but it also came through in some of the theoretical treatises of the time. They have gone into oblivion because a new version of revolutionary republicanism came to dominate the world through the success of the French and the American revolutions. Those who thought in terms of reforms of absolutism from within were the more reasonable and well informed of their day. The problem is, alas, that history rewards not those who are right, but those who triumph.

NOTE

1. Venturi, Franco, *The End of the Old Regime in Europe, 1768-1776*, Cambridge, Mass., 1989, ix.

REFERENCES

Andrews, John. *The History of the Revolutions of Denmark, with an Account of the Present State of That Kingdom and People.* I-II. London, 1774.

Baker, K. M. (ed.) *The French Revolution and the Creation of Modern Political Culture I, The Political Culture of the Old Regime.* London, 1988.

Beccaria, Cesare Marchese Bonesane di. *Dei delitti e delle pene.* Milano, 1764, de. by Franco Venturi, Torino 1965. Danish trans. Copenhagen, 1796-1798.

Bjørn, Claus. "The Peasantry and Agrarian Reform in Denmark." *Scandinavian Economic History Review* 25 (1977), 117-137.

_____. "Den jyske Proprietaerfejde." *Historie* XIII (1979a), 1-70.

_____. "Christian Colbiørnsen." *In Dansk Biografisk Leksikon* 3, Copenhagen, 1979b, 457-462.

Bloch, Marc. *Les caractères originaux de l'histoire rurale française*, 2nd ed., Oslo 1931, Paris, 1955, English trans. French Rural History. Berkeley, 1966.

Cobban, Alfred. *The Myth of the French Revolution.* London, 1955. Reprinted in 1968, 90-111.

_____. *A History of Modern France* I. London, 1957-1961.

_____. *Aspects of the French Revolution.* London, 1968.

Colbiørnsen, Christian. *Betragtninger i Anledning af endeel jydske Jorddrotters Klage til Hs. Kgl. Høihed Kronprindsen over deres Eiendommes Kraenkelse, ved Forordningen om Bondestandens frigivelse fra Stavnsbaandet til Godserne, og de flere udkomne Lovgivelser om Bøndernes Rettigheder og Pligter.* Copenhagen, October 1790.

Cranston, Maurice. *Philosophers and Pamphleteers.* Political Theorists of the Enlightenment. Oxford, 1986.

Degn, Christian. *Die Schimmelmanns im atlantischen Dreieckshandel.* Gewinn und Gewissen, Neumünster, 1974.

Doyle, William. *Origins of the French Revolution.* London, 1980; 2nd ed., 1988.

Ekman, Ernst. "The Danish Royal Law of 1665." *Journal of Modern History* 29 (1957), 102-107.

Fabricus, Knud. *Kongeloven.* Dens tilblivelse og placering i samtidens naturog arveretlige udvikling, Copenhagen, 1920.

Feldbaek, Ole. *Danmarks historie.* Vol. 4. 1730-1814. Copenhagen, 1980.

Friis, Aage. (ed.) *Bernstorffske Papirer: Udvalgte Breve og Optegnelser vedrørende familien Bernstorff i Tiden fra 1732 til 1835.* Vol. 3. Copenhagen, 1913.

Furet, François. *Penser la Révolution française.* Paris, 1978. English trans: *Interpreting the French Revolution,* New York, 1981.

_____. "Feodalité." In Furet and Ozouf (eds.), *Dictionnaire critique de la Révolution française.* Paris 1988; English trans. Cambridge, 1989, 684-693.

252 Uffe Østergaard

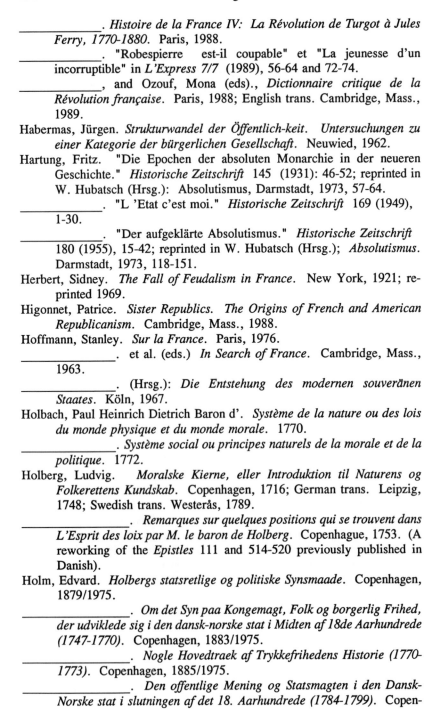

_____. *Histoire de la France IV: La Révolution de Turgot à Jules Ferry, 1770-1880*. Paris, 1988.

_____. "Robespierre est-il coupable" et "La jeunesse d'un incorruptible" in *L'Express* 7/7 (1989), 56-64 and 72-74.

_____, and Ozouf, Mona (eds)., *Dictionnaire critique de la Révolution française*. Paris, 1988; English trans. Cambridge, Mass., 1989.

Habermas, Jürgen. *Strukturwandel der Öffentlich-keit. Untersuchungen zu einer Kategorie der bürgerlichen Gesellschaft*. Neuwied, 1962.

Hartung, Fritz. "Die Epochen der absoluten Monarchie in der neueren Geschichte." *Historische Zeitschrift* 145 (1931): 46-52; reprinted in W. Hubatsch (Hrsg.): Absolutismus, Darmstadt, 1973, 57-64.

_____. "L 'Etat c'est moi." *Historische Zeitschrift* 169 (1949), 1-30.

_____. "Der aufgeklärte Absolutismus." *Historische Zeitschrift* 180 (1955), 15-42; reprinted in W. Hubatsch (Hrsg.); *Absolutismus*. Darmstadt, 1973, 118-151.

Herbert, Sidney. *The Fall of Feudalism in France*. New York, 1921; reprinted 1969.

Higonnet, Patrice. *Sister Republics. The Origins of French and American Republicanism*. Cambridge, Mass., 1988.

Hoffmann, Stanley. *Sur la France*. Paris, 1976.

_____. et al. (eds.) *In Search of France*. Cambridge, Mass., 1963.

_____. (Hrsg.): *Die Entstehung des modernen souveränen Staates*. Köln, 1967.

Holbach, Paul Heinrich Dietrich Baron d'. *Système de la nature ou des lois du monde physique et du monde morale*. 1770.

_____. *Système social ou principes naturels de la morale et de la politique*. 1772.

Holberg, Ludvig. *Moralske Kierne, eller Introduktion til Naturens og Folkerettens Kundskab*. Copenhagen, 1716; German trans. Leipzig, 1748; Swedish trans. Westerås, 1789.

_____. *Remarques sur quelques positions qui se trouvent dans L'Esprit des loix par M. le baron de Holberg*. Copenhague, 1753. (A reworking of the *Epistles* 111 and 514-520 previously published in Danish).

Holm, Edvard. *Holbergs statsretlige og politiske Synsmaade*. Copenhagen, 1879/1975.

_____. *Om det Syn paa Kongemagt, Folk og borgerlig Frihed, der udviklede sig i den dansk-norske stat i Midten af 18de Aarhundrede (1747-1770)*. Copenhagen, 1883/1975.

_____. *Nogle Hovedtraek af Trykkefrihedens Historie (1770-1773)*. Copenhagen, 1885/1975.

_____. *Den offentlige Mening og Statsmagten i den Dansk-Norske stat i slutningen af det 18. Aarhundrede (1784-1799)*. Copenhagen, 1888/1975.

_____. *Kampen om Landboreformerne i Danmark i slutningen af det 18. Aarhundrede (1773-1791)*. Copenhagen, 1888/1974.

Horstbøll, Henrik. "Enevaelde, opinion og opposition." *Historie* 17, no. 1 (1987), 35-53.

_____. *Natural Jurisprudence, Discourses of Improvement, and the Absolutist State*. Århus, 1988.

_____, Løfting, C., and Østergärd, U. "Les effets de la Révolution Française au Danemark." In M. Vovelle (ed.), *L'Image de la Révolution française aujourdhui* I. Oxford, 1989, 621-642.

Hunt, Lynn. *Politics, Culture and Class in the French Révolution*. Berkeley, 1984.

Johansen, H. C. *Dansk okonomisk politik i årene efter 1784*. Vol. I, *Reformår 1784-1788*. *Århus, 1968*. Vol. II, *Krigsfinansieringsproblemer 1789-1793*. Århus, 1980.

Jones, P. M. *The Peasantry in the French Révolution*. Cambridge, 1980.

Jordan, David P. *The Revolutionary Career of Maximilien Robespierre*. Chicago, 1985.

Jørgensen, A. D. *Kongeloven og dens Forhistorie*. Aktstykker, Copenhagen, 1886/1973.

Jørgensen, Harald. *Trykkefrihedssporgsmaalet i Danmark 1799-1848*. Copenhagen, 1944/1978.

Kjaergaard, Th. "Gårdmandslinien i dansk historieskrivning." *Fortid og Nutid* 28, no. 2, (1979), 178-191. English trans. "The Farmer Interpretation of Danish History. *Scandinavian Journal of History* 10 (1985), 97-118.

_____. *Konjunkturer og afgifter*. C. D. Reventlows betaenkning af 11. Februar 1788 om hoveriet. Copenhagen, 1980.

_____. "Christian Ditlev Reventlow." *Dansk Biografisk Leksikon* 12. Copenhagen, 1982, 164-168.

_____. "The Rise of Press and Public Opinion in Eighteenth-century Denmark-Norway." *Scandinavian Journal of History* 14 (1989), 215-230.

Krüger, Kersten. "Der aufgeklärte Absolutismus in Dänemark zur Zeit der Französischen Révolution." In Herzig, Stephan, Winter (Hrsg.) *"Sie, und nicht Wir": Die Französische Révolution und ihre Wirkung auf Norddeutschland*. Vol. I, Hamburg, 289-315.

Ladurie, Emmanuel le Roy, Vovelle, Michel et Doyle, William. "Pouvait-on réformer la monarchie?" *Le nouvel Observateur* 4/5 (1989), 10-11.

Lefebvre, Georges. *Les paysans du nord pendant la Révolution française*. Paris, 1924/1972.

_____. "The Place of the Revolution in the Agrarian History of France". *Annales* 1929, no. 1. English trans. in R. Forster and O. Ranum (eds.) *Rural Society in France*. Baltimore, 1977, 39-49.

_____. *La grande peur de 1789*. Paris, 1932; English trans. London, 1973.

_____. "La Révolution française et les paysans." Reprinted in Lefebvre. *Etudes sur la Révolution française*. Paris, 1954, 246-268.

_____. "Le déspotisme éclair." *Annales historiques de la Révolution française* 21 (1949), 97-115.

L'héritier, M. "Le déspotisme éclairé, de Frédéric II à la Révolution française." *Bulletin of International Committee of Historical Sciences*, 9, no. 35 (1937), 181-225.

Linvald, Axel. "Comment le déspotisme éclairé s'est présenté dans l'histoire du Danemark." *Bulletin of the International Committee of Historical Sciences* 5, no. III (1933). VIIe Congrés international des Sciences historiques en Varsovie, 714-726.

_____. "Andreas Peter Bernstorff." *Dansk Biografisk Leksikon* 2, Copenhagen 1979, 25-32.

Locke, John. *Second Treatise on Civil Government*. London, 1690.

McPhee, Peter. "The French Revolution, Peasants and Capitalism." *American Historical Review* 94, no. 5 (December 1989), 1265-1280.

Medick, Hans. *Naturzustand und Naturgeschichte der bürgerlichen Gesellschaft: Die Ursprünge der bürgerlichen Sozialtheorie bei S. Pufendorf, J. Locke u. A. Smith*. Göttingen, 1973.

Mirabeau, Victor Riqueti Marquis de. *L'Ami des Hommes*. Paris, 1756.

Modéer, Kjell Å. (ed.), *Samuel von Pufendorf 1632-1982*. Lund, 1986.

Molesworth, Robert. *An Account of Denmark as It Was in the Year 1692*. London 1694.

Montesquieu, Charles Louis de Secondat de. *Les Lettres persanes*. Amsterdam, 1721.

_____. *De l'Esprit des lois*. Genève, 1748; English trans. *The Spirit of the Laws*. Cambridge, 1989.

Mousnier, Roland, and Hartung, Fritz. "Quelques problèmes concernant la monarchie absolue." *Comitato internazionale die Scienze storiche, X Congresso di Roma*. Relazioni vol. IV, Firenze, 1955, 1-55.

Mousnier, Roland. *La monarchie absolue en Europe du Ve siècle a nos jours*. Paris, 1982.

Nora, Pierre. République." F. Furet and M. Ozouf (eds.) *Dictionnaire critique de la Révolution française*. Paris, 1988; English trans. Cambridge, Mass., 1989, 792-805.

_____. "Nation et Révolution 1789-1799." *Le Monde de la Révolution Française* no. 9 (1989), 18-19.

Østergård, Uffe. "The Symbolic Nature of French Politics. The French Revolution Reconsidered." *French Politics and Society* 12 (1985), 23-33.

_____. "Politikkens arena." H. Fink (ed.) *Arenaer. Om politik og iscenesaettelse*. Århus, 1989, 23-65.

_____. *Peasants and Danes*. Rutgers University, New Brunswick, N. J., 1990.

_____. "Magtens tomme sted." In *Omverden* 2, 1990.

_____. *Vive la France. Vive la république*. Århus, 1986.

Østerud, Øøjvind "Configurations of Scandinavian Absolutism." In Per

Torsvik (ed.), *Mobilization, centerperiphery structures and nation-building.*. A volume in commemoration of Stein Rokkan, Oslo, 1981, 127-149.

_____. *Det moderne statssystem.* Oslo, 1987.

Ozouf, Mona. "Revolution." In Furet and Ozouf (eds.) *Dictionnaire critique de la Révolution Française.* Paris, 1988; English trans. Cambridge, Mass., 1989, 806-817.

_____. "L'esprit public guidant le peuple." *Le Monde de la Révolution Française*, no. 1 (1989), 20.

Poggi, Gianfranco. *The Development of the Modern State.* London, 1978.

Pufendorf, Samuel von. *De Jure Naturae et Gentium Libri Octo.* Lund 1672/ 1688; reprint Oxford, 1934.

_____. *De Officio Hominis et Civis Juxta Legem Naturalem Libri Duo.* Lund 1673/1682; reprint New York, 1927.

Root, Hilton L. "The Case Against George Lefebvre's Peasant Revolution." *History Workshop Journal* 29 (1989), 88-102 and 106-110.

Sass, Else Kai. *Lykkens tempel.* Et maleri af Nicolai Abildgaard. Copen-hagen, 1986.

Schama, Simon. *Citizens. A Chronicle of the French Revolution.* New York, 1989.

Seip, Jens Arup. "Teorien om det opionsstyrte enevelde." (Norwegian) *Historisk Tidsskrift* 38, 1958, 397-463, repr. in J. A. Seip. *Politiskideologi.* Tre laerestykker. Oslo, 1988, 13-66.

Skrubbeltrang, Fridlev. *Agricultural Development and Rural Reform in Denmark.* Rome:, FAO. 1953.

_____. "Developments in Tenancy in Eighteenth Century Denmark as a Move Towards Peasant Proprietorship." *Scandinavian Economic History Review* (1961).

Sneedorf, J. S. *Om den borgerlige Regiering.* Copenhagen, 1757. German trans. *Über die bürgerliche Regierung.* Vienna, 1780.

_____. "Jubel-Tale til Erindring om den lykkelige Arve-Eenevolds Regiering som for 100 Aar siden blev indført i disse Riger." Soroe Academi 18. October 1760. Reprinted in *Samlede Skrifter*, vol. 7, Copenhagen, 1776, 489-516.

Soboul, Albert. "Sur la fonction historique de l'absolutisme éclairé." *Annales historiques de la Révolution Française* 51 (1979), 517-534.

Sørensen, Øjstein. *Frihet og enevelde.* Jens Schelderup Sneedorfs politiske teori. Oslo, 1983.

Tamm, Ditlev. "Pufendorf und Dänemark. "In Modéer (ed.), *Samuel von Pufendorf,* Lund, 1986, 81-89.

Tocqueville, Alexis de. *L'Ancien Régime et la Révolution.* Paris, 1856/1988.

Trenard, Louis. "L'absolutisme éclairé: le cas français." *Annales historiques de la Révolution Française* 51 (1979), 627-646.

Tvarnø, Henrik. "Ludvig Holberg - Un historien bourgeois au service de l'Absolutisme." *Analecta Romana* XVII-XVIII, 163-179, Copenhagen, 1989.

Tønneson, Kåre. "Problèmes de l'histoire constitutionelle en Scandinavie à l'époque de la Révolution et de l'Empire." *Annales Historiques de la Révolution Française* 167, no. 2 (1967), 221-250.

_____. "Sur la fonction historique de l'absolutisme éclairé." *Annales historiques de Révolution Française* 51 (1979), 611-626.

Venturi, Franco. *Settecento riformatore I. Da Muratori a Beccaria*. Torino, 1969.

_____. *Utopia and Reform in the Enlightenment*. London, 1971.

_____. *Settecento riformatore II. La chiesa e la repubblica dentro i loro limiti, 1758-1774*. Torino, 1976.

_____. *Settecento riformatore III. La prima crisi dell' Antico Regime, 1768-1776*. Torino, 1979, English trans. *The End of the Old Regime in Europe*, 1768-1776. Cambridge, Mass., 1989.

_____. *La caduta dell'Antico Regime, 1776-1789. 1: I grandi stati dell'Occidente; 2:Il patriottismo repubblicano e gli imperi dell'Est*. Torino, 1984.

Voltaire, François-Marie Arouet de. *Le Siècle de Louis XIV,* Paris, 1751/ Flammarion, 1966.

22

The French Revolution of 1789 and its Impact on Spanish-American Independence

Gregory Ludlow

Historians have paid relatively little attention to the impact of the French Revolution on Spanish America.[1] Although this may not seem altogether surprising, given the location of the events, it should nonetheless, be noted that the movements for Spanish-American independence, lasting from 1808 to 1826, followed closely on the events of the French Revolution and its Napoleonic aftermath. Those historians who have attempted to interpret the impact of the French Revolution on the Spanish-American independence movements have come primarily from the English and Spanish-speaking worlds. They are the first to assert, however, that the French Revolution was only one of several external factors to have an impact on Spanish-American independence. Setting aside the internal causes, such as the Bourbon reforms and the Creole-peninsular controversy,[2] the other external factors mentioned include the American Revolution; the crisis of Spanish government during the period 1808–1814; and the growing British commercial penetration of Spanish America.[3]

The various assessments of the impact of the French Revolution on Spanish-American Independence differ according to the importance attached to the Revolution relative to these other external factors, as well as to their own ideological bent. Some historians tend to enhance its importance, whereas others diminish it. In this sense, one may speak of both a positive and a negative impact of the French Revolution on Spanish-American independence.

The first group of writers maintains that Anglo-Saxon ideas, as distinct from Anglo-Saxon action, have never exerted much influence on Latin Americans, in contrast to the French *philosophes* who spoke a language they could understand. In their view, the French Revolution had a far greater effect on the outlook of Latin Americans than any republican theories produced in the United States. In short, Rousseau was a far greater force in the Spanish-American struggle for independence than the Founding Fathers. This school of thought recognizes, however, that it was above all the French Revolution in its Napoleonic expression that constituted the greatest of all the forces that made revolution in Spanish America inevitable.[4]

The second group of authors stresses that political influence was less favorable to revolution than to reform within the established order, and even

at times to enlightened despotism. Indeed, these writers contend that the
general reaction to the French Revolution and its ideas, as inherited from
certain of the Enlightenment philosophers, was not only limited but negative.[5]

Given the importance writers of both groups attach to French Enlightenment thought and its subsequent influence on events in France and in Spanish
America, it would seem appropriate at this point to give a brief review of the
role played by French Enlightenment thought in Spanish America in order to
determine how it shaped the reactions of the leaders of Spanish-American
Independence to the French Revolution and its Napoleonic sequel.

The French *philosophes* most frequently quoted by Spanish-American
leaders were Montesquieu, Voltaire, Diderot, Rousseau, and Raynal. The last
two seemed to have been the most widely read, particularly the *Du Contrat
social* and the *Histoire philosophique et politique des établissements et du
commerce des Européens dans les deux Indes*. The philosophic, moral, and,
above all, political concepts associated with these Enlightenment thinkers left
their mark on the shapers of Spanish-American Independence. In the moral
and philosophical sphere, a faith in reason; the acquisition and application of
practical knowledge to economic and educational matters; freedom as applied
to the emancipation of slaves, a belief in progress; and the adoption of the
general secular viewpoint of the Enlightenment directed the thoughts and
actions of Simón Rodriguez, Francisco Miranda, Andrés Bello, and Simón
Bolívar in Venezuela; Antonio Nariño in Colombia; and Manuel Belgrano and
Mariano Moreno in Argentina. In the more pertinent political realm of ideas,
Spanish Americans were torn between enlightened absolutism, oligarchic
constitutionalism, and the more radical theories of Rousseau's *Du Contrat
social*. Nariño translated the *Déclaration des droits de l'homme* into Spanish
in 1794; Simon Rodriguez, Bolivar's teacher was a devotee of Montesquieu
and Rousseau; and Mariano Moreno, also an enthusiastic admirer of Rousseau,
had edited a Spanish edition of *Du Contrat social* in 1810.[6]

Many of the ideas of the French Enlightenment not only were tempered
by Spanish peninsular sources of the same period, notably those of Feijoo,
Benito Jerónimo, and Gaspar Melchor de Jovellanos, but were also filtered
through such channels as the *Sociedades Económicas de los Amigos del País*
and through the efforts of such Spaniards as Altuna, Rousseau's Spanish friend
in Paris. This is but to say that the ideas of the French *philosophes* were not
accepted indiscriminately and brings us back to the central question concerning
the conflicting assessments of the impact of the French Revolution in its
different stages on Spanish-American Independence.

Generally, the more radical the French Revolution became, the less
attraction it had for most Spanish-American leaders who saw in Jacobinism the
manifestations of extreme democracy and social anarchy. They had already
had a premonition of this in one of their own regions, the Viceroyalty of Peru,
where, in 1780, the Indian social uprising, led by the self-styled Túpac Amaru
II, alias José Gabriel Condorcanqui Noguera, a mestizo who claimed direct
descedancy from the Inca king, Túpac Amaru, caused considerable upheaval
among the Spanish occupation forces. The revolt was ruthlessly supressed and

Túpac Amaru II executed. Those Creoles who had had radical democratic leanings turned to more moderate political stances after the Tupac Amaru rebellion had threatened their privileged position.

A more personal example of this shift from radicalism to a more moderate and even conservative position can be seen in the life of Pablo Olavide, a Peruvian born in Lima in 1725, who had been Aranda's private secretary in the Paris Embassy prior to the Revolution. Having left France, Olavide later returned to Paris, filled with sympathy for the Revolution, only to be imprisoned by a local Committee of Public Safety in Meung during the Terror. He was later released and withdrew to Andalusia where he died in 1804. His autobiographical work, *El Evangelio en triunfo, ó historia de un filósofo desengañado*, written in 1798, reflects his disenchantment with the Revolution and a return to the faith of his early days.

These transformations in political outlook were reinforced by an event that had lasting consequences for Latin America, including the Portuguese Empire in Brazil, namely the invasion of Spain and Portugal by Napoleon in 1807-1808. By the Treaty of Bayonne of May 5, 1808, Charles IV was forced to renounce his right to the Spanish throne. Three days later, Charles IV further ceded to Napoleon sovereignty over the Spanish dominions, and on May 10, 1808, Ferdinand VII, prince of Asturias, was forced to follow his father's example by renouncing his rights as heir to the crown of Spain and the Indies. An Assembly of Notables was convoked at Bayonne on May 19, 1808, consisting of one hundred and fifty Spaniards and six Spanish-American members representing the viceroyalties of New Spain, New Granada, Peru, and the Rio de la Plata. A month later, Napoleon proclaimed his brother, Joseph, king of Spain.

The net result of these events dramatically affected the social and political structure of the Spanish-American dominions. The Constitution adopted by the Assembly of Notables at Bayonne declared that Spain's colonies were to have the same rights as its provinces in the Peninsula. In the words of William Spence Robertson, "For the first time in history, Spanish America was viewed as a distinct political entity."[7] The Spanish monarchy had been severely shaken, and its grip on its colonies weakened. This loosening of the ties that bound Spanish Americans to Spain was encouraged by Napoleon and Joseph, and their agents who attempted to foment discontent in the colonies by stressing the advantages that would ensue from independence. This was met with stubborn resistance by Spanish colonial officials who, fearing the consequences of such actions on the part of Napoleon, followed in the footsteps of the *juntas* in the major cities of Spain by swearing allegiance to Ferdinand VII. Their view was that Napoleon stood for French imperialism and not their national interests.

Bonapartist policy toward the first phase of the Spanish-American independence movement was to encourage the independence of the Spanish colonies, provided that no alliances were formed with England. Material aid was given in the form of arms shipments and the dispatching of French agents to the various Spanish colonies in mid-1810. During the same year, five major revolts broke out in Venezuela, Colombia, Buenos Aires, Chile, and Mexico, encouraged by Spain's weakened position and Napoleon's support. On July 5, 1811, the United Provinces of Venezuela became the first Spanish colony to formally declare itself independent of the motherland. Negotiations even took place between France and Venezuela to seek protection for Venezuelan independence, but the counterrevolution in Venezuela in March-July 1812 prevailed and put an end to such negotiations. Bolívar escaped and Miranda surrendered. The precarious military situation in Europe prevented Napoleon from rendering any effective aid to the Spanish-American insurgents at this juncture. Napoleon's later downfall occurred at a time when the situation of the Spanish colonists was also in jeopardy. In May 1814, Ferdinand was reinstated as king in Spain and announced the restoration of royal absolutism. By the end of 1816, all the Spanish-American independence movements, with the exception of the one at Buenos Aires, had been suppressed. Within a year, however, the independence movements regained momentum and would eventually meet with success.[8]

Napoleon's usurpation of the Spanish throne had effectively humiliated the Spanish monarchy and cut off its ties with the colonies. Despite negative accusations on the part of royalists in the colonies against what was considered French imperialism, the Spanish-American leaders, encouraged by Napoleon's largely moral aid, made their first bid to free themselves from colonialism under a weakened Spanish monarchy. Although they were not successful in their first attempts, military and political lessons had been learned which were to prove vital to the second phase of the independence movement. Unlike the first phase of the movement in Spanish America, the colonists could no longer count on French help after the fall of Bonaparte in 1815. On the contrary, Louis XVIII and his ministers wished to promote the reunion of the insurgent Spanish colonies with Spain and rehabilitate the Bourbon Family Compact. France felt endangered by the establishment of republics in the New World which might constitute a threat to herself and the rest of monarchical Europe. Indeed, France, encouraged by other members of the Holy Alliance, threatened indirectly the independence movement in Spanish America by invading Spain in 1823 to deal with the Spanish liberal revolution. Notwithstanding this threat, the independence movement followed its course, aided, in part, by the promulgation of the Monroe Doctine and by the commercial interests of Britain, supported by its navy.[9]

By the mid-1820s, owing largely to the combined efforts of Bolívar in the north and San Martín in the south, what is today Argentina, Bolivia, Chile, Colombia, Ecuador, Peru, and Venezuela had become independent. The United States was the first country to officially recognize the independence of the Spanish-American nations, followed by Britain in 1825. France, prompted by its official acknowledgment of Haitian independence in 1825, some twenty years after the fact, and of Brazilian independence in 1827, finally recognized the majority of the Spanish-American republics in 1830 after the downfall of Charles X. The Bourbon Family Compact between France and Spain was finally rescinded.[10]

Once independence was achieved, what were the effects of the French Revolution and its prolongation under Napoleon on the new Spanish-American republics?   It would be fair to state that, in general, the principles of the French Revolution as manifested in the Constitutional Monarchy of 1789-1792 and in the Napoleonic period, exerted the most influence on the thought and actions of the Spanish-American leaders, both before and after the struggle for independence, while the principles of the first French Republic were uppermost in their minds during the struggle for independence. Or, to put it another way, in the words of one critic, "Spanish-American bourgeois society was classically liberal in the Lockean mold prior to independence, and, after justifying its steps toward independence with Rousseau and Suárez, it fast became Lockean liberal again."[11]

Certain of these effects are manifest in the Constitutions framed by the Spanish-American leaders, both before and after independence. At the Congress of Angostura, called in 1819 by Bolívar to draft a constitution for Venezuela, the delegates opted for a constitution that resembled others of a later period by its emphasis on the protection of private property and restrictions on voting rights. The latter divided the citizenry into active and passive categories based on the possession of property and the ability to read and write.   It promulgated a presidential form of government, with the president serving a four-year term and the senators life terms, a modification of Bolívar's desire to see a hereditary senate. Congress rejected Bolívar's wish to institute a fourth branch of government, formed of censors to act as a moral power.

Bolívar, however, realized this wish in the Constitution of Bolivia, which he himself had framed in 1826. In addition to a tricameral legislature consisting of tribunes, senators, and censors, Bolívar now favored a lifetime term for the presidency, as opposed to the four-year term he had advocated at Angostura.   Again, a strong emphasis was placed on property and voting rights qualifications. Administratively, following the Napoleonic example but using a slightly different nomenclature, the Bolivian Constitution divided the country into departments under the jurisdiction of a prefect, with the departments, in turn, being divided into provinces administered by governors and the provinces into *cantons* under the control of *corregidores*.   The Peruvian Constitution was also closely modeled on that of Bolivia. These constitutions bear a certain resemblance to the French constitutions of 1791, 1795, and 1799, though little to that of 1793, particularly in the areas of property and voting rights.

Another example of Napoleonic administrative influence on Spanish-American postindependence events was the promulgation of the Civil Code in Chile by Andrés Bello, based on the *Code Napoléon*. A less auspicious Napoleonic influence took place in Mexico, where Augustín de Iturbide, modeling himself on Bonaparte, had himself proclaimed Emperor Agustín I in 1821. This is as far as the comparison with Napoleon goes. Iturbide's reign lasted only ten months.[12]

Perhaps the most notable example of Napoleonic influence on a Spanish-American leader can be found in the thought and actions of Simón Bolívar, generally hailed, like Napoleon, as the Great Liberator. Bolívar had lived in Paris during the height of Napoleon's fame and had studied the Emperor's military strategy. From a political point of view, Bolívar believed, like Napoleon, in a powerful executive, within a strong centralized government. This was in opposition to many of his contemporaries, like Santander, who, fearful of arbitrary actions on the part of the state, believed in a weak central government, with the power of the executive being curtailed and that of state and local government enhanced. Bolívar, cognizant of the lack of racial, social and geographical homogeneity in Spanish America, had believed in a strong centralized power to avoid social anarchy. In the words of Charles C. Griffin writing of Bolívar, "The enthusiastic Jacobin of 1810 and 1811 gave way rapidly to the more cautious and hardheaded author of the Cartagena Manifesto and to his still liberal but less democratic principles communicated to the Congress of Angostura in 1819."[13] One could also add to this Bolívar's creation of the Bolivian Constitution of 1826.

This more conservative shift in the political thought of Bolívar reflected the general trend in Spanish America of the postindependence period. For the Spanish-American leaders, in the aftermath of the independence movements, it was the masses that now posed a threat to society. Once victory had been achieved, the Creoles in Spanish America sought to consolidate their social and economic predominance. For the black slaves, the peons, and the Indian population, to quote John Lynch, "the fruits of revolution were not all sweet and not all shared."[14]

This is not surprising since the ideological underpinnings of the movements for Spanish-American independence came, like its leadership and financial support, from the Creole population, which was hardly representative of the society at large. Although oppressed by the Spanish peninsulars, their oppression was relatively benign compared to that experienced by other classes of society. The achievement of independence did little to change the existing social order, the most significant change coming at the upper echelons of society, where power was transferred from the peninsulars to the Creoles. At the other end of the social scale, the lower classes still generally remained in a subservient state, despite the abolition in certain localities of the Indian tribute and black slavery. Although the various Spanish-American leaders in the different declarations of independence and the new constitutions wrote in favor of the French Enlightenment's and Revolution's principles of freedom of speech, freedom of religion and association, constitutional rule, in short of liberty, fraternity, and equality, little effort was made to implement these principles in the face of privileged groups and the forces of traditionalism. Such high-blown rhetoric rang false to those still oppressed by tributes, debt labor, and slavery.[15] To quote John Lynch once again, "Independence swept away the lines of attachment to Spain and the fabric of colonial government, but left intact the deeply-rooted bases of colonial society."[16]

In conclusion, the French Revolution and its Napoleonic sequel, when viewed as the culmination of the ideals of the Enlightenment, was a factor, albeit not the only one, in shaping events leading to Spanish-American independence. The thoughts and actions of the major Spanish-American leader and thinker, Bolívar, reflected, at different times and under different circumstances, the various liberal, radical, and Napoleonic phases of the Revolution, before settling for a moderate position of oligarchic constitutionalism, tinged with Bonapartism. In this regard, these triple strains of liberalism, radicalism, and *caudillismo* found in the French Revolution and its Napoleonic sequel still persist in Spanish America today and, as in the early nineteenth century, are still found to be in conflict with one another. In this sense, the legacy of the French Revolution in Spanish America is still alive. It is in the twentieth century that the struggle for social, political, and economic justice, rooted in the colonial past, has taken on more radical dimensions.

NOTES

1. Jacques Godechot, *Regards sur l'époque révolutionnaire* (Toulouse: Privat, 1980), 205, 246. Georges Lefebvre, *Etudes sur la Révolution Française* (Paris: Presses Universitaires de France, 1963), 431-443.

2. Jay Kinsbruner, *The Spanish-American Independence Movement* (Huntington: Krieger, 1976), 18.

3. Jorge Basadre, "Conciencia de sí," The Origins of Latin American Revolutions 1808-1826 in R. A. Humphreys and John Lynch (eds.), (New York: Alfred A. Knopf, 1966), 298-299.

4. Sir Charles Kingsley Webster, "British, French, and American Influences," in Humphreys and Lynch (eds.), *The Origins of the Latin American Revolutions*, 75-83.

5. Francisco A. Encina, "The Limited Influence of the French Revolution," in Humphreys and Lynch (eds.), *The Origins of the Latin American Revolutions* 106-110. Charles C. Griffin, "The Enlightenment and Latin American Independence," in Arthur P. Whittaker (ed.), *Latin America and the Enlightenment*, (Ithaca, N. Y.: Cornell, 1961), 119-141. John Lynch, *The Spanish American Revolutions 1808-1826* (New York: W. W. Norton, 1973), 28.

6. Such francophilia was not just restricted to Spanish-American thinkers and political leaders. José Joaquin Fernández de Lizardi of Mexico, considered the first Spanish-American novelist, was well acquainted with the French *philosophes* of the eighteenth century, as his satirical picaresque novel,

El Periquillo Sarniento, published in 1816, amply demonstrates through its lengthy, digressively didactic sections on education and social justice.

7. William Spence Robertson, *France and Latin-American Independence* (Baltimore: Johns Hopkins University Press, 1939), 39.

8. Kinsbruner, *The Spanish-American Independence Movement*, 48-59. Robertson, *France*, 72-104.

9. Kinsbruner, *The Spanish-American Independence Movement*, 67.

10. Robertson, *The Spanish-American Independence Movement, France*, 523-559.

11. Kinsbruner, *The Spanish-American Independence Movement*, 25.

12. Germán Arciniegas, *Latin America: A Cultural History*, trans. Joan MacLean (New York: Alfred A. Knopf, 1967), 330, 338-339.

13. Griffin, "The Enlightenment" 138. The opposition between Bolívar and Santander is also treated in Gabriel García Márquez's historical novel on Bolívar, *El General en su laberinto*, published in 1989.

14. Lynch, *Spanish-American Revolutions*, 342.

15. Charles Gibson, *Spain in America* (New York: Harper and Row, 1967), 207.

16. Lynch, *Spanish-American Revolutions*, 347.

23

Waves Breaking on a Distant Shore: Puerto Rico in the Era of the French Revolution

Julia Ortiz Griffin

Puerto Rico and revolutionary France — at first impression, few places could be more remote from one another in space and spirit. But first impressions are often superficial, and a better acquaintance with Puerto Rico's history reveals the profound impact that the shock waves sent out by the French Revolution had on the shores of this distant island. In their response to the challenges of the revolutionary era, the inhabitants, overlords and neighbors of Puerto Rico effected its transition from a primitive colonial outpost to a modern society imbued with a distinct identity. This chapter examines some of the stages in the process of transition.

After a promising start as one of the first settlements in the Spanish conquest of America, Puerto Rico had been drained of its inhabitants by the lure of gold in Mexico and Peru. During the seventeenth century, English and Dutch raids, constant harassment by pirates and a series of natural disasters had reduced its population and commerce still further. It was not until the defeats sustained in the Seven Years' War awakened the Spanish regime to the need for a reassessment of its whole American policy that Puerto Rico began to receive any serious attention from the mother country. In 1765 Carlos III received a shocking report from his special emissary, General Alejandro O'Reilly, on the inadequacy of the island's military resources and the stagnation of its economy. Puerto Rico, O'Reilly reported, produced virtually nothing of value to Spain, and its people repaid that country's long neglect of their well-being by ignoring its laws, evading its taxes, and subsisting on goods smuggled in from the colonies of her rivals. The king's inspector-general recommended that Puerto Rico be taken seriously and that its problems be taken in hand lest it be lost to Spain.[1]

During the next two decades, Puerto Rico benefited from a measure of those "Bourbon Reforms" associated with the enlightened despotism of Carlos III. Its seat of government, San Juan, was heavily fortified, its administration was made more efficient, and its population was increased by subsidies offered to immigrants. New capital and new energies resulted in an increase in cultivated land and the promotion of sugar and tobacco industries. Even Spain's policy of commercial exclusivism was modified by the opening of trade with a wider range of European ports. By 1790 Puerto Rico's population had tripled, its prosperity had increased dramatically, and a more varied and vigorous society had emerged. There was an acute consciousness of the possibilities resulting from change and of the restraints that still remained firmly in place.[2]

Although Carlos IV, who succeeded his father in 1788, was scarcely the most sophisticated of monarchs, even he was able to grasp the dangerous implications of the events in France that had followed so swiftly upon his accession. Not only were the censors quick to exclude printed discussions of the French Revolution from Spain, but the overseas territories were also seen to be at risk. In Puerto Rico, the government became obsessed with the potentially subversive influence of foreigners. Danes, Dutchmen, Germans and Frenchmen had intermingled with the large number of Spaniards who had been encouraged to settle in the island during recent years. Irish Catholic exiles were particularly numerous and somewhat ironically were counted as British subjects and therefore suspect in the face of possible hostilities with Britain. As Spain shifted from neutrality to war against revolutionary France to alliance with France against Britain, the status of these resident foreigners changed repeatedly, and there was a bewildering succession of arrests, banishments and recalls. Because these aliens were among the most important members of the newly developed business community, the fluctuations merely served to disrupt the economy without markedly increasing security. Strictly military preparations had better practical results. For the first time Puerto Ricans were inducted into regular army units stationed in the island, and the militia was increased in numbers and training. A flotilla of some thirty light vessels for coastal defense was stationed in the vicinity of San Juan, and the city's harbor was accurately charted for the first time. During 1796, when it became obvious that Spain's desperate shifts in alliance would bring Puerto Rico into direct confrontation with Britain in the Caribbean, hasty repairs and improvements were made to the already formidable line of walls and forts that encircled the capital.[3]

The long-anticipated crisis arrived in April 1797, when an English fleet disembarked an invading army a short distance up the coast from San Juan. The siege that followed lasted only a few weeks before an outbreak of disease among his troops and rumors of Spanish reinforcements impelled the British commander to withdraw. But the sturdiness of San Juan's walls and the loyal combativeness of its citizens had done much to dispel the Spanish government's fears about the stability of its control over the island. Despite the twenty-odd years of attention given to Puerto Rico during the previous reign, Spain still really knew little about this colonial outpost and its inhabitants. The king was, therefore, relieved and grateful to have this demonstration of reliability and to receive a report from the bishop of Puerto Rico that his islanders were all "very loyal and faithful to the Spanish Crown." They were, the prelate assured him, patriotic and ready to sacrifice their lives and property for their sovereign. Moreover, they were "inclined to war, navigation and every bold enterprise", qualities that called for "high resolve, courage and daring." They were not perfect, to be sure, having an addiction to "gambling and sensuality." These were not vices that the crown felt inclined to condemn. Indeed, San Juan was rewarded for its "heroic defense" by the abolition of an unpopular excise tax and by its designation as the "most noble and most loyal city." Furthermore, all the inhabitants of the island were declared to be "Faithful and Loyal Subjects," and relieved of certain sales taxes.[4]

Although the threat of a British invasion now receded, the reminders of the French Revolution's ongoing impact were everywhere. Survivers of the overthrow of the monarchy, some of them titled nobles or former officials of the Versailles Court, were joined in San Juan by other refugees fleeing from the slave revolt in Saint Domingue. An ongoing struggle for control of that neighboring island involved black rebels, successive French regimes, and Spanish-speaking residents who refused to accept the transfer of their territory from Spanish to French rule. The prospect of these tumults spilling over into Puerto Rico was a source of constant anxiety, and the accounts of atrocities related by escaped planters stirred apprehension among Puerto Rican slave owners. Mexico, too, had already begun to experience political convulsions and military revolts that would culminate in its declaration of independence, and these could not help but affect the situation in Puerto Rico. A large part of the island's income was derived from the annual subsidy, or *situado*, sent from Mexico to pay for the maintenance of the garison. This silver shipment did not arrive in 1799, nor was it delivered for the next seventeen years. As a result, the Puerto Rican authorities were forced to issue a paper currency. Although the island's businesses made do with this arrangement for the time being, unapproved currencies from other parts of the Caribbean began to circulate once again. Trade with the United States grudgingly accepted by the Spanish authorities became an increasingly important, yet also potentially disruptive factor in Puerto Rico's affairs during these years.[5]

As the Spanish regime drew up its balance sheet at the end of the eighteenth century, however, it could come to positive conclusions about Puerto Rico. The census of 1800 showed a population of over 150,000 (about one-tenth of them slaves) whose loyalty and stability seemed secure. If the rising prosperity that had been interrupted by the onset of the French Revolution had not yet been fully reestablished, then at least, the island seemed to be holding its own.[6]

Whether from complacency or preoccupation with European affairs, the Madrid government had little attention to spare for Puerto Rico during the early years of the new century. Construction projects were limited to the building of a naval arsenal, and only modest efforts were made to improve such services as education and health care. (Vaccination for small pox was introduced in 1803.) The first book printed in Puerto Rico made its appearance in 1806, as the result of private initiative. Although it contained nothing more sinister than romantic poetry, the government was aware of the printed word's potential for trouble making. In 1807 the crown set up the island's first full-fledged printing plant and began turning out an official weekly gazette to propagandize the islanders. That their loyalty was still taken for granted, however, is demonstrated by the use of Puerto Rican troops and

ships under the command of the Puerto Rican naval officer Ramón Power to
aid in the recapture of Eastern Hispanola.[7]

Nevertheless, even the most self-confident administrators could not
delude themselves that Puerto Rico had remained entirely exempt from what
some were calling "the spirit of the age." The demands for radical reform and
even national fulfillment generated by the great events in France had already
penetrated to the Spanish-American colonies. They were given further stimulus in 1808 when Napoleon's army invaded Spain, set up a puppet government
and forced the Spanish colonies to decide whether they would support Joseph
Bonaparte, adhere to the loyalist *junta* at Cadiz, or seek their own destiny.
By the beginning of the nineteenth century, Puerto Ricans, like the inhabitants
of other Spanish-American colonies, had developed a sense of their own
distinctive identity. Customs, speech patterns, life-style, geographical setting,
all made them something other than mere Spaniards oversees. Whether this
consciousness would be translated into full-fledged nationalism would depend
as much on the vigilance of the mother country as on the still tentative
political instincts of the Puerto Rican population.[8]

Clear signs of a potentially dangerous situation emerged in 1809 when
the *junta* that had undertaken to rule Spain and its colonies in the name of the
captive Fernando VII called for colonial delegates to meet with them in Cadiz.
Ramón Power was chosen to represent Puerto Rico. At an emotional cere-
mony in which the first representative Puerto Rico had ever sent to the
Spanish legislature was officially charged with his mission, Bishop Arizmendi,
the first native Puerto Rican ever to hold the episcopate, presented his ring to
Power "as a sure pledge that will sustain you in the memory of your resolution
to protect and maintain the rights of our fellow countrymen, as I myself am
resolved to die for my beloved flock." These words were considered defiant
and subversive by the government and may have inspired the seizure in 1810
of all ecclesiastical stipends and benefices by the royal treasury.[9]

In the meantime, Power had received an even blunter charge from the
municipal council of San Germán, the island's second largest municipality.
He was instructed to demand a reform of the "despotic, arbitrary and
tyranical" government that Spain maintained in Puerto Rico. In the event that
Napoleon's troops overran Spain, the council added, then Puerto Rico should
consider itself "independent and free to choose the best method for the
preservation and subsistence of its inhabitants in peace and the Christian
religion."[10]

Power, on reaching Spain, played an active role in the creation of the
Cortes that produced the liberal Constitution of 1812, and secured a number of
practical benefits for Puerto Rico. Back in the island, however, those fearful
of "subversion" had already taken action. On December 23, 1811, a squadron
of ships acting under the orders of the governor of Puerto Rico landed four
thousand troops on the west coast and occupied San Germán and several
nearby communities. The government declared that an incipient rebellion had
been crushed. The alleged ring leaders of this conspiracy, including the
mayor of San Germán, were transported to San Juan for trial. It was alleged

in official documents that a plan had been hatched in conjunction with Venezuelan rebels. The latter were to provide arms for a revolt in Puerto Rico that would secure its independence, and at the same time prevent it from being used as a staging area for Spanish forces sent to put down the Venezuelans. The crown prosecutor (specially imported from Quito to head the investigation) reported that it would be harmful to go ahead with the process because "many persons of high quality are involved," and a formal prosecution "would touch off hatred among the families, most of the inhabitants of this island would be put into contention, and far from creating justice, would be a fountainhead of irreparable damage." Although the matter was referred to Spain, it was subsequently allowed to lapse without any punishment being authorized."[11]

Whether or not the rhetoric of this period represented a truly revolutionary spirit among Puerto Ricans, the proclamation of the new Constitution in 1812 seems to have satisfied most of the island's demands for redress of grievance. Under its provisions, Puerto Ricans received full Spanish citizenship and such basic rights as suffrage, inviolability of domicile, person and property, freedom of thought, freedom to work, and the right to submit petitions. A civil intendent was appointed, taking over the nonmilitary functions previously exercised by the governor. A supply of silver was shipped to the island and replaced the paper currency. A mercantile court was established to regulate and adjudicate trade. In accordance with Puerto Rico's new status as a province of Spain, a Provincial Council was created. The Inquisition (more a nuisance than a menace in Puerto Rico) was abolished and steps (still rather modest) were taken to encourage education.[12]

While offering these carrots, the Regency in Spain also wielded the stick by imprisoning the captured Venezuelan rebel chief, General Francisco Miranda, in San Juan. This veteran of the French revolutionary armies who had dedicated himself to the liberation of his own colony from Spanish rule, was held in Puerto Rico for some four months before being shipped to Spain. His fate was intended as a warning to potential dissidents in the island. Moreover, troops inducted from the Puerto Rican population were sent to aid in crushing the Venezuelan revolt, thus reinforcing the image of the island as a stronghold of Spanish power.[13]

Faithful adherents of the monarchy hailed the restoration of Fernando VII and were rewarded in 1815 with a shower of titles and decorations. San Juan received such evidences of the royal favor as improved pavements, the installation of oil lamps to illuminate its streets, and the city's first public clock. Of more general benefits were decrees authorizing free trade with the United States and the colonies of European nations in the New World, as well as authorization to construct ships in Puerto Rico. The king also authorized lower taxes and eased regulations on immigration and naturalization of foreigners. But Puerto Ricans, who had begun to accustom themselves to the personal freedoms and the voice in public affairs guaranteed by the Constitution of 1812, were chagrined to learn that it had been abolished. With it went their Provincial Council and voice in the Cortes. In short, Fernando

VII, was continuing the game of intensifying control over the island, while offering material bribes for good behavior. As the struggle to reestablish Spanish authority in America grew steadily more bitter, the need to preserve Puerto Rico as a launching pad for counterrevolutionary expeditions became even more acute. The attempt to combine an iron hand with acts of generosity involved great risks, for exasperation was clearly growing among certain elements of the Puerto Rican population. Rumors of conspiracies and contact with the Venezuelan rebels abounded, and several landings were attempted by Bolívar's forces, who fully appreciated the strategic significance of the island.[14]

Puerto Ricans, who detested the oppressiveness of the crown but feared the perils of revolution, welcomed the news of the Liberal coup in Madrid that reached them late in 1820. The Constitution of 1812 was reinstated, corporal punishment abolished, and the island's first civil governor appointed. A resurgence of political discussion centered on the newly founded *Sociedad de Liberales Amantes de la Patria*. Its members proclaimed their support of the liberties set forth in the 1812 Constitution and in their periodical *El Investigador* explored the implications for Puerto Rico of the new freedom. In 1821 Puerto Rico's first daily newspaper, bearing the significant title *Diario Liberal y de Variedades de Puerto Rico*, made its appearance. Their towns were now free to elect their own mayors, instead of having them appointed by the crown, and the Puerto Ricans could once again send a delegate to the Cortes at Madrid. They chose Demetrio O'Daly, who, like his late predecessor Ramón Power, was a member of the influential Irish community and an ardent Liberal.[15]

Those Puerto Ricans who hailed the changes in Spain as offering them new options for their political future were soon to be disappointed. The Liberal regime was overthrown in 1823, its prominent supporters, like O'Daly, were driven into exile, and Fernando VII resumed his represssive policies. The island was deprived of such institutions of local government as had lately emerged, political organizations and the independent newspaper were eliminated, and even the Inquisition reappeared. Although the king was forced to accept the loss of his last footholds on the American Continent in 1825, Puerto Rico was more firmly than ever in his grasp. Along with Cuba it would remain under Spanish rule for the rest of the century.[16]

In the space of a single generation, between 1790 and 1825, Puerto Rico had been propelled into the modern age. It had scarcely emerged from the stagnant isolation that had characterized most of its colonial history when the pace of change was drastically accelerated by the military and political shock-waves emanating from Europe. Its strategic location made it a focal point for the movement of fleets and armies vying for domination of the Caribbean region. Furthermore, the spread of revolutionary ideology into the Spanish dependencies created a climate in which liberal reforms were demanded. When Spain was thrown into chaos by the Napoleonic invasion, nationalist sentiments rapidly revealed themselves in the colonies. In the midst of these developments, Puerto Rico, small in size and population, remained unsure of its role. Successive Spanish regimes, whether liberal or reactionary, combined coercion with concession in order to retain their grip on this bastion of empire.

By 1825 the opportunity for Puerto Rico to gain its independence had passed: it was not simply a bastion but virtually the *last* bastion. It is doubtful, however, whether a desire for independence, as distinguished from autonomy, had much of a following in Puerto Rico during the period when the other colonies were breaking away. There seems to have been little response to rhetorical exhortation or offers of "fraternal assistance" from Bolívar and his associates. Nor would it have been easy to liberate his heavily garrisoned island.

But if independence does not appear to have been a serious prospect for Puerto Rico during the revolutionary era, the Puerto Ricans had come to think of themselves in nationalist terms: they spoke of their country, their people. Moreover, they had learned to relish the liberties that had been conferred and then rapidly revoked. The rising generation would demand full civil liberties and full self-government, and Spain's prolonged refusal to meet these demands would generate an authentic independence movement.

To the achievement of this self-awareness and political consciousness must be added the modernization of Puerto Rican society brought about by the material innovations introduced by the Spanish government and the opening of the island to a wider range of commerce and ideas. On this distant island, as in countries far closer to its center, the explosive force of the French Revolution had precipitated changes that shaped the history of the next two centuries.

NOTES

1. "Memoria de D. Alexandro O'Reilly sobre la Isla de Puerto Rico, Año 1765," in Eugenio Fernández Méndez (ed.), *Crónicas de Puerto Rico* (Rio Piedras: Editorial Universitaria, 1969), 268-269.

2. Iñigo Abbad y Lasierra, *Historia de Puerto Rico*, in Isabel Gutierrez del Arroyo (ed.), (Rio Piedras: Editorial U.P.C., 1979), XIX-XXXII; "Relación del Viaje a la Isla de Puerto Rico," in Fernández Méndez, 327-331.

3. Bibiano Torres Ramírez, *La Isla de Puerto Rico (1765–1800)* (San Juan): Instituto de Cultura Puertorriqueña, 1968), 156-170.

4. Arturo Morales Carrión, *Puerto Rico: A Political and Cultural History* (New York: W. W. Norton, 1983), 51-53.

5. Arturo Morales Carrión, *Puerto Rico and the Non-Hispanic Caribbean. A Study in the Decline of Spanish Exclusivism* (Rio Piedras: University of Puerto Rico Press, 1971), 118-121.

6. Torres Ramírez, *La Isla*, 172.

7. "Informe de D. Pedro Irizarri, alcalde ordinario de San Juan . . .," in Fernández Méndez, 345-350.

8. Morales Carrión, *Puerto Rico*, 56-57.

9. Germán Delgado Pasapera, "Orígenes del independentismo puertorriqueño," *Revista de Historia* I, No. 1 (1987), 58-61.

10. Aurelio Tio, "La Conspiración de San Germán del Año 1809," *Revista del Instituto de Cultura Puertorriqueña*, No. 19 (April-June 1983), 8.

11. Francisco Lluch Mora, *La Rebelión de San Germán* Mayagüez: Editorial Isla, 1981), 21-26.

12. Alejandro Tapia y Rivera, *Noticia Histórica de Ramón Power* (San Juan: Imprenta Venezuela, 1946), 72-76.

13. H. J. Liden, *History of the Puerto Rican Independence Movement*, Vol. 1 (Hato Rey: Master, 1981), 12.

14. Luis E. González, *Alejandro Ramírez y su Tiempo* (Rio Piedras: Editorial Universitaria, 1978), 10-15.

15. "Memoria de todos los ramos de la administración de la isla de Puerto Rico, 1838, por D. Pedro Tomás de Córdova," in Fernández Méndez, 373-375.

16. Morales Carrión, *Puerto Rico: A Political and Cultural History*, 82-83.

24

The Influence of the French Revolution on Lenin's Conception of the Russian Revolution

George Jackson

The French Revolution was a beacon to all modern revolutions, lighting the way from the past to the future, providing inspiration and structure for frustrated radical politicians who needed to give form and historical legitimacy to their strategies for bringing about radical political change. It also became in some ways a warning light, closing off, through historical analogy some alternatives by flashing signs that they were traps or pitfalls.

The most striking degree of continuity is between the French Revolution of 1789 and the Russian Revolutions of the twentieth century, perhaps because the Russian revolutionary leaders were so acutely aware of the course of the great revolution that came before. Crane Brinton, in his well-known *Anatomy of Revolution*, which relies heavily on the writings of Leon Trotsky while recognizing the important differences between the two, makes much of the close analogies. He suggests that there is a common pattern, not only between the French and the Russian revolutions, but also between those two and the American Revolution of 1776 and the English Revolution of 1689.[1]

John Keep in a recent article goes a step further, calling his analysis "The Tyranny of Paris over Petrograd" arguing that Russia's conception of the French Revolution permeated all of educated Russian society.[2]

Not that the imitation of France or French culture was a new phenomenon in Russia. Educated Russians viewed France as their cultural model throughout the eighteenth century; French was the preferred language of the Russian aristocracy and the members of the "intelligentsia who were their heirs."[3] The French Revolution had its initial impact on Russian contemporaries who suffered for their interest in and sympathy for the ideals of the revolutionaries.[4]

In 1917 the belief that Russia was following in the great tradition of the French Revolution was evident everywhere, and the terminology of the French Revolution was abundant in all of the speeches of revolutionary leaders of every persuasion.[5] It was especially evident in the thoughts and actions of Vladimir Lenin who brought the Bolsheviks to victory in the struggle for power in 1917.[6] After the Bolshevik victory in Russia, Lenin would tell a conference on adult education:

Let us take the Great French Revolution. It is with good reason that it is called great. For the class which made it, for the bourgeoisie, it accomplished so much that it left its imprint on the whole nineteenth century, that century which gave civilization and culture to all humanity. Its influence reached every corner of the planet, bringing into being those forces which had created the great French revolutionary bourgeoisie, whose interests it served, even though it was not the last word on liberty, equality and fraternity.[7]

How did it influence Lenin's conception of the Russian Revolution? As Alfred Meyer points out in his *Leninism,* for Lenin the October Revolution of 1917 was quite clearly to be Russia's 1789, but unlike other Russian Marxists, who in 1917 believed that Russia had to go through its bourgeois-democratic 1789 before it could move on to a genuine proletarian revolution, Lenin by that time argued that Russia would combine or "telescope" the achievements of both.[8]

On the fourth anniversary of the Bolshevik Revolution in 1921, Lenin contended that he had managed to combine the achievements of the great French Revolution with the immediate goals of the socialist revolution:

The direct and immediate task of the revolution in Russia was a bourgeois-democratic one, namely to destroy the survival of medievalism and sweep them away completely, to purge Russia of this barbarism, of this shame and to remove this immense obstacle to all culture and progress in the country.

And we can justifiably pride ourselves on having carried out that purge with much more determined speed, more rapidly, more boldly and more successfully, and from the point of view of its effect on the masses, much more widely and deeply, than the French Revolution over one hundred and twenty-five years ago. . . .

A hundred and fifty and two hundred and fifty years ago the progressive leaders of that revolution (or of those revolutions, if we consider each national variety of one general type) promised to free mankind of medieval privileges, of sex inequality, of state privileges for this or that religion (or *religious ideas,* or religion in general) and of national inequality. They promised, but did not keep their promises, for they were hampered by their "respect" for the "sacred right of private property." Our proletarian revolution was not afflicted with this medievalism and for the "sacred right of private property". . . .

. . . We solved the problems of the bourgeois-democratic revolution in passing, as a "by-product" of our main and genuinely proletarian-revolutionary, socialist activities.[9]

But that, of course was after the fact. What is important about the speech was that it presupposed continuity. There was, of course, no reason for Lenin to believe either that these stages of developments were inevitable, or even possible, or necessary stages, except that these notions had been distilled from Marx's own writings on the French Revolution. Some have argued that Lenin's interest in the French Revolution, and his knowledge of it, apart from the writings of Marx and Engels were rather limited. Keep, for example, says that "A check of his *Collected Works* gives the impression that his knowledge of the French Revolution was derived wholly from the writings of Marx, Engels and other classic authorities."[10] Contrasting Lenin and Trotsky, Keep argued that Lenin does not seem to have read French or historians who wrote in French, that he referred to the Revolution infrequently and then only to buttress arguments about three political issues of current concern to him.[11] Those interests were the "need for an alliance between proletariat and peasantry," the dangers inherent in the decentralization of any new state structure, and the need for the use of terror against all oppressors. He describes Lenin's approach as "coldly utilarian and instrumental."[12] I would like to take issue with many of these judgments. Even if it were true that Lenin's views of the French Revolution were shaped primarily by Marx and Engels, it was in any case, the vocabulary, models, and conceptions evoked by that event that provided the parameters of his own thought on the issue of revolution. Even if it were true that the French Revolution only influenced Lenin's views on the three issues identified, that in itself would be an extraordinary influence. But neither of these assumptions is completely accurate.

Keep's comments raise more questions than they answer. In what form does one great historical event influence another? In my opinion, the assumption that there was little or no influence on Lenin is an unhistorical evasion of the problem. It is true that those individuals who are affected by the past rarely possess a scholar's balance and objectivity. Historical actors are more likely to be influenced by popular--sometimes mistaken--conceptions of the past. In judging the influence of the French Revolution on the Russian, we need to be more concerned about the popular image of the prior event than its reality. Perhaps it would be more accurate to say that we are exploring Lenin's image of the French Revolution as it affected his judgment about the proper course for the Russian Revolution, and he was keenly aware that the historical circumstances were often strikingly different in his own country. Moreover, Lenin's opinions about the French Revolution, like Marx's, were not fixed in concrete. They changed at various times in his career.

In any case, Keep's assumptions are not true or, at most, are only partially true. Lenin did indeed see the French Revolution of 1789 through the Marxist prism, frequently describing the whole period from 1789 to 1871 as the French Bourgeois Revolution. But at the same time, he was well read in the history of that period from early youth, and he frequently departed from Marx in his judgments of that event. His background in history was fairly sound through his reading of various historical works at home and through his years at the gymnasium where he also studied French, along with German, Latin, and Greek.[13] Although there is no doubt that he was steeped in the writings of Marx and Engles on the French Revolution, he read some of the works of such "bourgeois" historians as F. A. Mignet, Charles Seignobos, and Jules Michelet.[14]

The notebooks he used between 1912 and 1916 in preparing for his famous brochure on imperialism show a dazzling array of sources in English, French,

German, and Russian, including a carefully annotated series of notes on the
French Revoluton from a political history of Europe between 1500 and 1815
written by a German historian, Edmund Ulbricht.[15]
    Lenin did not, of course, suddenly show an interest in the French
Revolution in 1921 after he had accomplished his own versions of it. As early
as 1905, he defined the goals of the Russian revolutionary movement in terms
of the French experience, expressing the conviction that European (and
Russian liberals) lost their revolutionary zeal after the French Revolutions of
1789 — 1799 and could no longer be trusted to respond to the revolutionary
activity of the masses. In an answer to an article by the Russian liberal
history professor, Paul Vinogradov, who warned Russians away from the
model of France in 1789, Lenin wrote:

In Russia the people and the intelligentsia have a completely worthless political
education. . . .
    . . . That is what the Russian bourgeoisie is thinking of most of all; the
tremendous dangers of the "road" of 1789! The bourgeois has no objections to the
path taken by Germany in 1848, but he will exert "every effort" to avoid the path
taken by France. An instructive pronouncement, one which provides much food for
thought.
    What is the radical difference between the two roads. It is that the
bourgeois-democratic revolution carried out by France in 1789 and Germany in 1848,
was brought to its consummation in the first case, but not in the second. The first
ended in a republic and complete liberty, whereas the second stopped short without
smashing the monarchy and the reaction. The second proceeded under the
leadership mainly of the liberal bourgeoisie, which took an insufficiently mature
working class in tow, whereas the first was carried out, at least to a certain extent,
by the revolutionarily active masses of the people, the workers and peasants, who
for a time at least, pushed the respectable and moderate bourgeoisie aside. The
second led rapidly to the "pacification of the country", i.e. the suppression of the
revolutionary people and the triumph of the "Cossack sergeant and the village
constable" whereas for a certain period he first placed power in the hands of
revolutionary people which crushed the Cossack sergeants and the village
constables."[16]

But Lenin did not believe that Russian "backwardness" would make the
Russian Revolution less able to reach its objectives, for Russian
revolutionaries, despite the "backwardness" of their country would be armed
with a more "advanced" program, and they would be able to combine the
revolutionary forces of 1789 with those of the modern social revolution through
an alliance between the peasants and the workers. In recommending the route
of 1789, Lenin asked his party to become the Jacobins of the Russian
Revolution, cautioning,

This, of course, does not mean that we are compelled to imitate the Jacobins of
1793, and to borrow their views, programs, slogans and strategies. Our program is
not an old one but a new one — the minimum program of the Russian Social
Democratic Workers' Party. We have a new slogan: the revolutionary-democratic

dictatorship of the proletariat and the peasants. If we live to see the real victory of the revolution, we shall also have new methods of action in keeping with the nature and aims of the working-class party that is striving for a complete socialist revolution."[17]

In some respects, the question of whether or not Lenin was a Jacobin is an academic one. Western studies frequently refer to an earlier period in his life and question whether or not he adhered to the Russian populist movement in his youth. The usual implication is that he was an elitist putschist who really had no serious interest in anything other than the seizure of power. This use of the word "Jacobin" has been the source of endless and often unfruitful scholarly controversy.[18] Trying to pinpoint Lenin's own meaning when he describes his party as Jacobin is also an attempt to hit a moving target, not only because Lenin frequently changed his own definition of the concept, but also because Marx and professional historians shift their ground from book to book, decade to decade, on the precise meaning of the word. Even in historical studies of French politics the word "Jacobin" is used for a wide variety of political figures from 1789 through 1871. In the period 1789 to 1799, "Jacobin" was more of a generic term than a coherent political movement. At the beginning of the nineteenth century, it was frequently used as an epithet, apparently borrowing more from Taine than Marx, as a synonym for political opportunism, personal aggrandizement, and the relentless pursuit of dictatorial power by demagogic slogans designed to recruit support for middle-class revolutionary leaders.[18] Some American historians have used the Jacobin label for Lenin in a quite different sense, implying that Lenin borrowed his ideas from the terrorist populist movement, as manifest in his early dismissal of an alliance with bourgeois liberals, and that he merely disguised those goals with Marxist terminology.[19] As Neil Harding has pointed out, this involves a misreading of Lenin and a rather eccentric definition of Jacobinism.[20] Yet, "Jacobinism" in all of these incarnations remained one of the major charges against Lenin by his Menshevik opponents in the years that followed.

When Lenin himself first mentioned the term in his *What Is To Be Done* in 1902, he turned the tables on his opponents by proudly accepting the label and branding his fraction (soon to be called the Bolsheviks) the Mountain, and the opposition (soon to be called the Mensheviks) the Gironde.[21] This gave Lenin, who always had an unerring instinct for an effective political label, the opportunity to portray his faction as the heirs to the major revolutionary traditions of the Great French Revolution and to portray his opponents as indecisive moderates.

During the 1905 revolution Lenin gleefully returned to these metaphors at the Third Congress of the Russian Social Democratic Workers' party, using the label "Mountain" or "Jacobin" to reinforce the impression that only the Bolsheviks were the "keepers of the flame," the group that would not relinquish the minimum program of the RSDWP in the face of adverse circumstances. He insisted that those goals be pursued under the leadership of a small elite that would guide the insurgent masses through revolution and, if necessary, terror.[22] Despite his elitism and the emphasis on the need for force and violence, Lenin at the same time never underestimated, as many of his American critics argue, the need for responding to the radicalism of the industrial working class and the poor peasantry.[23] Bolshevik leaders should heed the radical strivings of the masses and time their own actions in response to them, but the party would shape and focus that revolutionary consciousness. Lenin differed from the Jacobins whom he professed to admire in his belief that none of the other political parties, even if allied to the Bolsheviks, could follow through to conduct the socialist revolutions. None of the political groups, he thought, created spontaneously by the masses could be trusted to create their own destiny without Bolshevik tutelage. By 1917, his distrust would reach a point where he began to move toward Trotsky's notion of "telescoping," the bourgeois and socialist stage of revolution and move beyond his belief in the need for a separate Russian 1789 in order to reach a socialist state.

In June 1917, for example, he cited favorably the Jacobin use of terror in response to an article by a liberal historian (probably Miliukov). Lenin made it clear that the use of terror was a virtue and a necessity and that he did not fear it. Once again he proudly adopted the Jacobin label for the Bolsheviks, but this time he indicated that the Bolsheviks would do the original Jacobins one better because they would not suffer the same historical limitations. The Russian Jacobins would benefit by the fact that they were surrounded by more advanced capitalist countries that were ripe for proletarian revolution: "The Jacobins were not destined to win complete victory, chiefly because eighteenth century France was surrounded on the continent by much too backward countries, and because France herself lacked the material basis for socialism, there being no banks, no capitalist syndicates, no machine industry, and no railways."[24]

Keep is correct, not only about Lenin's praise for the terror--which placed Lenin in opposition to Marx[25]--but also about Lenin's emphasis on the need for the new revolutionary state to be highly centralized and about the need for a strong alliance with the peasantry. In the first case, he used the results of the first wave of revolutionary activity in 1789 as proof of the need to create a more centralized government. In the second, he used the success of the Jacobins (in reality, a different set of Jacobins) in 1789 as proof of the need for the revolutionary party to establish an alliance with the peasantry (though in the French case it is difficult to see the analogy except through the famous decisions of 1789 abolishing feudal distinctions and the subsequent recognition of peasant land seizures).

After the 1905 Revolution, Lenin argued that unless the Russian Revolution completely eliminated the old ruling classes, self-government would be a disaster. Citing the French Revolution of 1789, he argued, "Would the municipal self-government in France in 1789 have been possible if on July 14 the people of Paris, who had risen in arms, had not defeated the royal troops, taken the Bastille and completely smashed the resistance of the auto-cracy?"[26] On the peasantry, Lenin would attribute the victory of the Revolution of 1789 to the alliance with the peasantry (presumably meaning its acceptance of the peasant seizures of land in the same manner as Lenin): "In the France of 1789 it was a question of overthrowing absolutism and the nobility. At the then prevalent level of economic and political development, the bourgeoisie believed in a 'harmony of interests'. It had no fears about the stability of its rule and was prepared to enter into an alliance with the peasantry. That alliance secured the complete victory of the revolution."[27] He goes on to argue that the failure to support the demands of the peasantry in 1848 led to the failure of that revolution in France, a conclusion which has some historical accuracy if one takes into account the elections in France in that year.

Although Lenin did indeed pounce on the French Revolution of 1789 – 1794 as proof of the need for the above revolutionary strategies, there are other areas of influence that have escaped the attention of most Western historians. For example, Lenin also saw in that event a blueprint for every modern revolution including his own. Marx had expressed some skepticism about the wisdom and perspicacity of the French Jacobins and "denounced the terror unequivocally," along with the Jacobin dictatorship and the idea that it served as a model for a future communist revolution.[28] Marx saw it as a tragic consequence of their inability "to realize a political order still lacking its socio-economic preconditions." Lenin, though carefully noting such passages in 1895 while reading "The Holy Family,"[29] took an opposing view, seeing the Jacobins as the incarnation of the revolutionary spirit and the period of terror between 1793 and 1794 as the consummation of that process.

In June 1917 he chided George Plekhanov for criticizing the Terror during the French Revolution, and credited the Jacobins (not the Mountain) for its success.

The Jacobins of 1793 belonged to the most revolutionary class of the eighteenth century, the town and country poor. It was against this class, which had in fact (and not just in words) done away with its monarch, landowners and its moderate bourgeoisie by the most revolutionary measures, including the guillotine-against this truly revolutionary class of the eighteenth century-that the monarchs of Europe combined to make war.[30]

This was perhaps good propaganda but very bad history.

More accurate perhaps was Lenin's conception of 1794 – 1801, the Thermidor and the Napoleonic era, both of which seemed to have been ignored by his Western critics. Having identified the weaknesses of the French bourgeois revolution as the lack of leaders with full revolutionary consciousness and decisiveness, the consequent failure to establish a strongly centralized revolutionary state and the failure to maintain a strong revolutionary alliance with the peasantry and the working poor in general, Lenin went on to argue that those shortcomings lead to "Bonapartism," a phenomenon that he saw repeated in the career, first of Peter Stolypin and then of Alexander Kerensky. Bonapartism was, he argued a coup d'état engineered by a political opportunist that offered to the poorer classes those rewards denied them by their revolutionary leaders. In July 1917, for example, he offered an article on the Kerensky cabinet called "The Beginning of Bonapartism."

We see the chief historical symptom of Bonapartism: the maneuvering of state power, which leans on the military clique (on the worst elements of the army) for support. Between two hostile classes and forces which more or less balance each other out.
    The class struggle between the bourgeoisie and the proletariat had reached its limit on April 20 and 21, as well as on July 3-5, the country was within a hair's breadth of civil war. This socio-economic condition certainly forms the classical basis for Bonapartism. . . .
    The landowners and peasants, too, live as on the eve of civil war, the peasants demand land and freedom, they can be kept in check, if at all, only by a Bonapartist government capable of making the most unscrupulous promises to all classes without keeping any of them.[31]

Finally, Western observers have given very little attention to Lenin's views on the French Revolution as a model for defining the character and goals of revolutionary war. In 1914 Lenin cited the example of the French Revolution to denounce the participation of the Russians in World War I and to justify revolutionary war against all capitalist states.

The Great French Revolution ushered in a new epoch in the history of mankind. From that time down to the Paris Commune i.e. between 1789 and 1871, one type of war was of a bourgeois-progressive character waged for national liberation. In other words, the overthrow of absolutism and feudalism, the undermining of those institutions and the overthrow of alien oppression, formed the chief content, the historical significance of such wars. These were, therefore, progressive wars. During such wars, all honest and revolutionary democrats as well as socialists, always wished success to that country (i.e. that bourgeoisie) which had helped to overthrow or undermine the most baneful foundations of feudalism, absolutism and oppression. For example, the revolutionary wars waged by France contained an element of plunder and conquest of foreign territory by the French, but this does not in the least alter the fundamental historical significance of those wars which destroyed and shattered feudalism and absolutism in the whole of the old serf-owning Europe.[32]

After the Treaty of Brest-Litovsk, Lenin would again allude to war in the Napoleonic era, using, however, the analogy between the defeat of the Soviet state and the defeat of nationalist movements against Napoleon, arguing that even in defeat all such movements had achieved something through their struggle. Revolutionary wars, so the message went, were always supportable, even if they were only struggles for national independence and even if they were not at first successful. War, like class struggle, always served a useful purpose in mobilizing people's sentiments.[33]
    I don't propose to explore the role of the French Revolution in Lenin's conception of the new socialist state, except for the comments already made about the need for terror and a strong centralized state; that is a subject worthy

of further investigation.

The French Revolution, or, at the very least, Lenin's perception of it, had a powerful influence on his conception of his own revolution. It provided an historical justification for his taxonomy of the political forces at work, appropriate revolutionary strategies and the pitfalls to be avoided. Although not always agreeing with Marx and Engels' insights on those events, and in some respects pointing to the significant differences between Russia in the twentieth century and France in the eighteenth, Lenin found in the French Revolution a source of inspiration and guidance. Does that mean his view of the French Revolution, or his use of it to support his own policy decisions was merely utilitarian? That is a question for which there is no clear answer. People tend to be taken in by their own magic, however. Even if Lenin were picking and choosing the most convenient and useful interpretations of the history of the French Revolution, those conceptions in turn were shaping and conditioning his own views of the proper course of action in attempting to seize and maintain power in Russia.

NOTES

1. Crane Brinton, *The Anatomy of Revolution* (New York: Vingage Books, 1952).

2. J.L.H. Keep, "1917: The Tyranny of Paris over Petrograd," *Slavonic and East European Review*, No. 1 (1968), 22.

3. See, for example, J. H. Billington, *The Icon and the Axe: An Interpretive History of Russian Culture* (New York: Alfred A. Knopf, 1966), Chap. 4. Russian scholars have devoted a great deal of attention to this question. See, for example, M. Balabanov, *Rossiaa i evropeiskie revoliutsii v proshlom*. Vyp I. *Rossii i Velikaia frantsuzskaia revoliutsiia*, Izd. 2 (Kiev, 1924); T. Bogoslovskii, "Rossii i Frantsiia v 1789—1792 gg.," *Literaturnaia nasledstvo*, Tom 33/34 (1939), 25-48; P. K. Alefirenko, "Pravitel'stvo Ekateriny II i frantsuzskaia burzhuaznaia revoliutsii," *Istoricheskie zapiski*, No. 22 (1947), 206-251; A. Kaganova, Frantsuzskaia burzhuaznaia revoliutsii kontsa XVIII i sovremennaia ei russkaia pressa," *Voprosy istorii*, No. 7 (1947), 87-94; A. G. Brikner, "Ekaterina II i frantsuzskaia revoliutsiia," *Istoricheskii vestnik*, No. 8 (1985), 411-420; and most recently, B. S. Itenberg, *Rossiia i velikaia frantsuzskaia revoliutsiia* (Moscow, 1988).

4. This was especially true of those, like Alexander Radishev, who was more of a devotee of the Enlightenment than of the Revolution. But there is little doubt that he was arrested and exiled in 1790 for the publication of his *Journey from St. Petersburg to Moscow* because of events in France. In her comments on the book, Catherine the Great refers directly to the relationship between Radishchev's comments and the events in France. See *The First Russian Radical: Alexander Radischev 1749—1802* (London, 1950), 188-189.

5. Keep, "1917," 22-35.

6. Neil Harding, *Lenin's Political Thought*, Vol. 1 (New York: St. Martin's Press, 1977), 214-215; Alfred Meyer, *Leninism* (Boulder, Colo.: Westview Press, 1986), 262-263.

7. V. I. Lenin, "Pervoi vserosiiskii s'ezd po vneshkol' nomu obrazovaniiu," *Polnoe sobranie sochinenii* (henceforth referred to as PSS), 38, 367. In English, V. I. Lenin, *Collected Works* (henceforth referred to as CW), 29, 371-372.

8. Ibid., 263.

9. V. I. Lenin, "K chereterykhletnei godovshchine oktiabr'skoi revoliutsii," PSS, 44, 144-148; in English, V. I. Lenin, "The Fourth Anniversary of the Russian Revolution," CW 33, 52-53.

10. Keep, "1917," 30.

11. Ibid., 31-32.

12. Ibid., 31. Soviet historians go to the opposite extreme and argue that Lenin provided a masterly analysis of the history of the French Revolution. See, for example, V. G. Revunenkov, "Novoe i izucheniia Velikoi frantsuzskii revoliutsii i vzgliadoy V.I. Lenina," in *V. I. Lenin i istoricheskaia nauka* (Leningrad: 1969), 117-149; Galkin, *V. I. Lenin i razvitie sovetskoi istoriografiii novoi i noveishei istorii stran Evropy i Ameriki* (Moscow, 1970), and Itenberg, *Rossia*, Chaps. 8 and 9.

13. Lenin's curriculum in the gymnasium and his grades are available in *Lenin i Simbirsk: dokumenty, materialy, vospominaniia.* 3rd ed. (Saratov, 1967).

14. The reference to Seignobos appears in Lenin, PSS, 55, 60; and CW, 37, 137. The latest biography of Lenin informs us that Lenin read Michelet's account of the Terror during the French Revolution while living in the apartment of Finnish socialist Kustaa Rovio in August 1917. Ronald W. Clark, *Lenin: A Biography* (New York: Harper and Row, 1988), 245. Clark does not, however, give the source of his information. Lenin's family had a copy of F.A.O. Mignet's *History of the French Revolution* in the family library at Simbirsk. See *Lenin i Simbirsk*, 433.

15. Lenin, "Tetrady po imperializma," PSS, 28, 583; in English in CW, 38, 66.

16. Lenin, "chego khotit i chego botitsia nasho liberal'nye burshua?"

PSS; in English in "What Our Liberal Bourgeois Want," CW 9, 240-241.

17. Lenin, "Dve taktiki sotsial'demokratii v demokraticheskoi revoliutsii," PSS 11, in English in CW, 38, 59-60.

18. Neil Harding, who does not share this point of view, has suggested the following qualities attached to the Jacobin label, when it is applied by Western scholars to Russian revolutionary leaders as an epithet or criticism: "we can understand his precocious description of Russia as already capitalist in 1893, his rejection of the democratic revolution as the immediate objective, his call for a party of professionals to make the revolution as a proxy for the proletariat, his engineering of a socialist revolution in a backward uncongenial environment--all of this can be comprehended as a persistent pattern of imposing the imperial will of the dedicated disciplined group upon a racalcitrant historical process.   It is, in short, the classical Jacobin formulation." Harding, *Lenin's Political Thought*, 2.

19.   Some of the leading Western scholars who have followed the Menshevik critique of Lenin in one form or another, arguing that Lenin was a Jacobin as opposed to being a Marxist, are: R. Pipes, "The Origins of Bolshevism, the Intellectual Evolution of the Young Lenin," in R. Pipes (ed.), *Revolutionary Russia* (London, 1968; A. B. Ulam, *Lenin and the Bolsheviks* (London, 1969); L. B. Schapiro, *The Communist Party of the Soviet Union* (London, 1970); V. Utechin, *Russian Political Thought* (London, 1964); R.H.W. Theen, *V. I. Lenin: The Genesis and Development of a Revolutionary* (London, 1974, 38-42.

20. Harding, *Lenin's Political Thought*, 4.

21. Lenin, "Chto delat'," PPS, VI, 10. Lenin attributes the use of the word "Jacobin" and the labels "Mountain" and "Gironde" to his mentor, George Plekhanov. Lenin is correct. Plekhanov first used the word "Jacobin" in the 1880s to criticize the peasant political movement; see T. Dan, *The Origins of Bolshevism* (New York: 1974. By 1900, however, he began to think of himself as a Jacobin and indicated this in a letter to Jonathan Frankel Aksel'rod, *Vladimer Akimov on the Dilemmas of Russian Marxism 1895–1903* (Cambridge; 1969) and S. Baron, *Plekhanov, the Father of Russian Marxism* (Stanford, Calif., 1963), 129.

22.   Three Western studies emphasize the balancing act that Lenin conducted between his desire to act through a team of professional revolutionaries and the need to wait for the necessary objective conditions for revolution, including the spontaneous movement of the masses in that direction. See Meyer, *Leninism* 29-30; Harding, *Lenin's Political Thought*, 4; and Robert Service, *Lenin: A Political Life* (Bloomington, Ind., 1985).

23. Harding, *Lenin's Political Thought*, 51.

24. Lenin, "Mozhno li zapugat' rabochii klass iakobinstvom?," PSS, 32, 374. In English, "Can Jacobinism Frighten the Working Class," CW, 25, 121.

25. Marx's views on the Terror in the French Revolution, according to Shlomo Avineri, clearly state that "This Jacobin attempt to force the state on socio-economic conditions and thus direct them according to its political will grow out of the Jacobin incomprehension of economic circumstances." In 1847 Marx would put it in his own words, "If the proletariat brings down the domination of the bourgeoisie, its victory will be merely ephemeral, only a moment in the service of the bourgeoisie (just like *anno* 1794, so long as within the process of history, within its 'movement', those material conditions have not been created that make necessary the abolition of the bourgeois mode of protection and, therefore, also the definitive fall of political bourgeois domination." Avineri, Shlomo, *The Social and Political Thought of Carl Marx* (New York: Cambridge University Press, 1971), 189-191.

26. Lenin, "V khvoste u monarkhicheskoi burshuazii ili vo glave revoliutsionnogo proletariata i krest'ianstvo," PSS, 11, 205. In English, CW, 9, 221.

27. Lenin, "O dvukh liniiakh revoliutsii," 27, 76-81. In English, "On two lines on Revolution," *Collected Works*, 21, 416.

28. Avineri, Shlomo, 187-189.

29. Lenin, "Kinspekt knigi Marksa i Engel'sa sviatoe semeistvo," 29, 27-28. In English, "Conspectus on the Holy Family," CW, 38, 40.

30. Lenin, "O vragakh nardoda," PSS 38, 39. In English, "The Enemies of the Peoples," CW, 25, 37.

31. Lenin, "Nachalo Bonapartizma," PSS, 34, 49. In English, "The Beginning of Bonapartism," in CW, 25, 220.

32. Lenin, "Printsipy sotsializma i voina 1914-15 gg." PSS, 26, 311. In English, "The Principles of Socialism and War," CW, 27, 51.

33. Lenin "Neschastnyi mir," PSS, 35, 382. In English, "An Unfortunate Peace," 27, 51; or even earlier and more fully in "O broshure Iunusa," PSS, 30, 12-13. In English, "The Junius Pamphlet," CW, 22, 309.

25

Uses of the Past: Bolshevism and the French Revolutionary Tradition

Gabriel Schoenfeld

Some months after the October Revolution, when the fate of the Revolution still hung in the balance, the new Soviet government turned its attention to the important matter of renaming the streets of Petrograd. A street in St. Petersburg — Petrograd as it was called at the time — that bore the name of two tsars, Nicholas the First and Nicholas the Second, was renamed after Marat. An embankment along the Neva was renamed after Robespierre.[1]

One day after the Soviet government moved from Petrograd to Moscow in March 1918, Lenin, together with his wife Krupskaia, and his comrades Sverdlov and Bonch-Bruevich, took a tour of historical monuments in and around the Kremlin.[2] For several days before this walking tour, Lenin had been discussing the idea of "propaganda through monuments" with the Soviet government's Commissar of Enlightenment, A. V. Lunacharskii. As Lenin and Lunacharskii conceived of it, this type of propaganda would involve, on the one hand, the dismantling and removal of statues and other monuments to the now deposed tsarist rulers and other objectionable historical personages, and on the other hand, the erection of statues commemorating leading scholars, writers, and artists and great revolutionaries, including the outstanding figures of the French and Russian Revolutions.[3]

On April 12, the Council of People's Commissars, the principal ruling body at the time, issued an ukase entitled "Decree on Statues of the Republic." Signed by Lenin, Stalin, and Lunacharskii, it initiated a program of "monument propaganda." Monuments that were deemed undesirable, according to the decree issued by the Kremlin, were to be removed from public view and "consigned to warehouses" or used for "utilitarian purposes," the latter category presumably including melting the metal of the statues for reuse in some other form. A special commission was established to decide which statues to remove as well as to "mobilize artistic forces" and to organize an extensive competition for the creation of sketches of the new statues that would take the place of the monuments left by the tsarist regime.

In late July after considerable delay that greatly agitated Lenin, the historian Mikhail N. Pokrovsky presented a report to the Council of People's Commissars with a tentative list of the names of fifty great men who were to be honored with statues. On July 30 the Council of People's Commissars

ratified the list, and Lenin signed it.[4]   Along with Karl Marx and Frederick
Engels, among the revolutionaries who were deemed worthy of inclusion on
the list of honor were Babeuf, Danton, Marat, and Robespierre.[5]

A statue of Danton was completed by winter. Although it was given
a place of honor in a public square a moment's walk from the Kremlin, in the
rush to execute Lenin's wishes the statue fell short of fulfilling the
aesthetic indicators of the plan. *Pravda* reported that the statue of Danton
"unfortunately . . . must be recognized as unsuccessful. It is too small for the
large space of the square, and the artistic approach of presenting just
a head — which was acceptable for Karl Marx — turned out to be unsuitable."[6]
This "unsuccessful" rendition of Danton was removed from public view some
years later. Statues of Babeuf and Marat were never completed.

The commission did manage to have a sculpture of Robespierre
prepared by early November 1918, just in time to be unveiled at the commemoration of the first anniversary of the Bolshevik seizure of power.[7] The
statue to the "hero of the French Revolution," the first anywhere in the world
of Robespierre, was given a prominent location in the center of Moscow and
unveiled before a large crowd that was addressed by leading Bolsheviks,
including Lev Kamenev. Lenin, who saw the statue frequently during his
walks in the vicinity of the Kremlin, greatly admired it for the way it
depicted Robespierre's "decisiveness," and he praised it as "our" kind of statue
in contrast to some recently erected cubist sculptures that he described as
"decadent, . . . disgusting" and "impermissible" for proletarian streets.[8]

Unlike the statue of Danton, the statue of Robespierre was an artistic
success. But Lenin's persistent importuning had evidently led its designer to
take various construction shortcuts in an effort to pacify the impatient leader.
Not only had it been buillt too rapidly, but it had been cast out of an
inferior type of concrete. After a series of rainy days, followed by a severe
cold spell, fissures appeared in it one evening, and by morning the sculpture
of Robespierre had entirely disintegrated into a pile of rubble.[9] No attempts
were ever again made in the USSR to erect another statue of Robespierre.

Although the ignominious collapse of the statue of Robespierre cannot
be taken as a metaphor that illustrates anything beyond the perennial
difficulties plaguing the Soviet concrete and building industry since its
earliest days, its fate as well as that of the other statues commemorating the
French Revolution does call attention to the Bolshevik fascination with French
revolutionary history.

Political scientists such as Richard Neustadt, Ernest May, and Robert
Jervis have inquired into how historical analogies, and the "lessons of the
past" have been used by political leaders in formulating policy.[10] May and
Neustadt have attempted to use the study of historical analogies at Harvard's
Kennedy School of Government as a didactic device to sharpen the sensivities
of policymakers to the pitfalls and perils of drawing lessons from the past.
Although their effort has been mocked by some as "History Appreciation 101
for Bureaucrats," the subject of historical analogies and "lessons of the past"
is nevertheless not without importance, and there is a growing political

science literature devoted to this topic.

Unfortunately, most of this literature is devoted to the study of how foreign policy decision makers have used political analogies. Although this has limited the usefulness of these studies for the purpose of the present inquiry, reference has been made to the existing political science literature when appropriate. It should be stated at the outset that the conclusions of the present study are in agreement with the central and common-sensical conclusion of most of the political science literature on historical analogies: the lessons of the past do influence political behavior.

Inquiry into the Bolsheviks' use of the lessons of the past yields interesting results for a comparative study of Soviet and American decision making. Although such a comparative inquiry has yet to be systematically undertaken, judging by the findings of most treatments of the American case, it can be safely noted that American policymakers tend to have a rather casual interest in the lessons of the past, drawing on them sporadically and only rarely choosing historical examples from periods through which they have not lived.[11] For the Bolsheviks, on the other hand, the lessons of the past have a rather different character and occupy a far more important place in their thinking.

In inquiring into how the Bolshevik leaders used history, one need not search far to find a set of historical analogies that they consistently utilized. As anyone remotely familiar with the historical literature would know, the early Bolsheviks were obsessed with the French Revolution and its aftermath. As Bertram Wolfe put it, "Almost every figure on the Russian political state wore a costume tailored in Paris. . . .

As the French revolutionaries had donned imaginary togas and fancied themselves ancient Romans, so Russian revolutionaries sought to reenact the scenes and roles of revolutionary France.[12] Although virtually every author who has written on the Russian Revolution has been struck by the extent of the Bolshevik immersion in French revolutionary history, no sustained attempts have been made to explain this phenomenon or to think about its implications.

In the course of this inquiry, three aspects of this problem will be considered. The first is an account of why the Bolsheviks used history and in particular, French revolutionary history. The second is to offer a classification of the various uses they made of history. Using this classification, a range of examples drawn from early Soviet history will be presented. Third, we will conclude with some reflections on the implications of the early Bolshevik use of history for contemporary Soviet politics. We shall first consider the origins of the Bolshevik absorption in the French revolutionary precedent.

The French Revolution had a profound effect on the thinking part of Russia's population throughout the nineteenth century. In 1802, for example, Count Rostopchin, the former minister of foreign affairs under Paul the First, wrote a letter to Prince Vorontsov in which he said: "I am infernally afraid of the society of Petersburg youth. If you returned to Petersburg, you, who so much hate all that shakes the social order, would be stunned by the spectacle of hundreds of young people who would like nothing more than the honor of becoming the foster sons of Robespierre and Danton."[13]

In the course of the nineteenth century, the French Revolution generated two very powerful currents in Russia both of which fed into the Bolshevik outlook.

On the one hand, there was a tradition that the Bolsheviks inherited of so-called Russian Jacobinism, a whole series of nineteenth-century Russian revolutionaries who had been in part inspired by the French Revolution. The Russian Jacobin, Zaichnevsky, for example, in his famous manifesto "Young Russia," looked back to the method of the guillotine as an example to be emulated: "We are not frightened," he said, "if we see that for the overthrow of the existing order it will be necessary to spill three times as much blood as was spilled by the Jacobins in the 1790s."[14] The influence on the Bolsheviks of these Russian Jacobins has undoubtedly been great — and this is a subject that has been extensively explored in a number of fine studies. It has also been the subject of considerable debate among Soviet historians.[15]

Although the inheritance left by the Russian Jacobins is one strand of thought that tended to place the French Revolution in the forefront of Bolshevik political consciousness, the second, and even more important strand, is Marxism. Many Russian intellectuals looked to the West and especially to France as a way of gauging Russia's progress or lack thereof in its social, political and economic development. When turmoil engulfed Russia as it did in 1905 and again in 1917, the memory of the French Revolution loomed large in the minds of supporters and detractors of the autocracy alike. But for Russian Marxists, and in particular the Bolsheviks, the tendency to see Russian history in the mirror of the French Revolution was especially pronounced.

Marxism for the Bolsheviks was taken as a science of history and revolution, and French revolutionary history was seen as the great laboratory of that science. The laws of history that derived from this science, the Russian Marxists were convinced, applied universally. Engels believed that Marx had discovered the "great law of motion of history." "This law," he said, "has the same significance for history, as the law of the transformation of energy has for natural science."[16] Plekhanov, the father of Russian Marxism and one of the great influences on Lenin, drew the connection to the Russian case when he argued that "the general philosophical-historical viewpoint of Marx has exactly the same relationship to contemporary Western Europe, as to Greece and Rome, India and Egypt and can be inapplicable to Russia only in the event of its general unsoundness."[17]

Even though Great Britain was more economically developed, it was France that had experienced the most thoroughgoing modern revolution, a revolution that as Engels put it, "established the unalloyed rule of the bourgeoisie in a classical purity unequalled by any other land."[18] Marx's position that class conflict was the driving force that both divided society and propelled it forward is formulated almost entirely in his writings on French revolutionary history.[19] Both Marx and Engels themselves engaged in the practice of comparing Russia to France and thought the parallel an apt one. Engels, for example, once declared that "Russia is France of this century,"[20] and in a letter to Vera Zasulich he wrote: "What I know or believe about the situation in Russia impels me to the opinion that the Russians are approaching their 1787."[21] It was only natural that the Bolsheviks, given this background, continually looked to the history of France for an understanding of the factors at work in shaping Russia's historical destiny.

If we have an explanation of why the Bolsheviks looked to French history for an understanding of Russia, we can now ask, What did they see and what were the principal ways in which the French revolutionary precedent was put to service in Russian politics?

Numerous uses of the past of various sorts and types can be identified that can be classified for the purpose of illustrating the extent and diversity of the ways that the Bolsheviks employed history. Of the existing schemes that political science has created for classifying the uses of history, none is entirely adequate for my purposes. Although I have made use of the most satisfactory of these classificatory structures, that of Yaacov Vertzberger, I have altered it to suit the broader purposes of my study.

Vertzberger has divided the various ways that history can be used into those that "define the situation," those that "circumscribe the role of the actor," those that "determine strategy," and those that "justify strategy."[22] Because the scope of the present inquiry aims at an understanding of the uses of the past that is broader than Vertzberger's concern with international security problems, it has been necessary to add a fifth category, which is the use of history to "characterize the environment."

"Characterizing the environment" can be defined as using historical analogies and lessons of the past to gain an understanding of the basic nature of the historical/political process. To illustrate this category, consider how Plekhanov used history in the application of a fundamental theoretical problem in Marxism to Russian circumstances. A question that greatly preoccupied Plekhanov is the role of great men in the historical process. This was not a sterile philosophical question but an issue that lay at the heart of Russian Marxism's quarrel with the Populist strategy of individual terror.

If it could be convincingly argued that individuals play an insignificant role in shaping the course of historical events, the strategy of assassinating tsars and tsarist officials as practiced by the Populists and by their successors, the Socialist Revolutionaries, would be exposed as philosophically bankrupt in addition to being politically inexpedient. The evidence that Plekhanov adduced to support his proposition that great men are in reality unimportant, while not very convincing, was drawn from French history. Plekhanov maintained:

If a bullet struck Bonaparte, say in the battle of Arcola, what he did in Italy and other campaigns, would have been done by some other generals. They surely would not have displayed such talents as he did, and not won such brilliant battles. But the French republic would nevertheless have emerged victorious from the wars of those times because its soldiers were incomparably better than all of the other European soldiers.[23]

Other examples of the use of history to define the political environment include Lenin's assertion in *What Is To Be Done* that the "working class, exclusively by its own effort, is able to develop only trade-union consciousness."[24] Lenin explicitly says that this is what the history of all countries shows.

Let us turn now to Vertzberger's category of the use of history to "define the situation." By "defining the situation" Vertzberger means that the political actor uses history in "the search for structuring and interpretation of information with the purpose of constructing a consistent, valid and meaningful body of knowledge" about the nature of the environment.[25] This category is fully applicable to the Bolshevik case, and examples abound of uses of history that can be characterized as "defining the situation."

Lenin's writings and speeches, for example, are replete with attempts to locate the position of Russian development along the West European revolutionary time scale. An instance of this is Lenin's summing up of the accomplishments of the Bolshevik Revolution in the spring of 1918 by declaring that "if we measure our revolution by the scale of West European revolutions, we shall find that at the present moment we are approximately at the level reached in 1793 and 1871."[26] A more extreme example of this type of thinking in time is Lenin's declaration during the turmoil of 1905 Revolution, that an uprising is necessary to ensure that the present revolution will not end in a mere March 18, 1848, that we shall have not only a July 14, 1789, but also an August 10, 1792."[27] It is worth noting that Lenin's public evidently understood the significance of these dates without needing an explanation.

If one believes, as the Bolsheviks did, that history develops according to certain ascertainable and universal laws, then the possibility of gaining a navigational fix on Russia's present position would lead one to believe that charting its future course is also possible. Although the Bolsheviks did believe that drawing parallels to the past would help them foresee the future, this aspect of the argument should not be overstated. Neither Lenin nor any of the other Bolsheviks believed that Russia was destined to mimic the West European course of development in all of its particulars, and they looked to previous revolutions in part to avoid repeating their shortcomings. They also were fully conscious that Russia might be different. Lenin warned, for example, that "in no event must we send to oblivion the peculiarities of Russia."[28] But the overall direction and pace of Russia's development would, he believed, repeat the Western model. "The comparison of the political and economic development of different countries," Lenin held, "has enormous significance, for without a doubt, just as there is a general capitalist character of modern states, there is also a general law of their development."[29]

We shall now consider Vertzberger's category regarding the use of history in circumscribing the role of the political actor. This he defines as the use of history for "the recognition of the roles and status appropriate for the actor."[30]

Perhaps the most stunning example of the use of history in this kind of circumscribing role involves the circumstances of Trotsky's dismissal as Commissar of War in 1924. In 1923 a whispering campaign had started, alleging that Trotsky had Bonapartist ambitions. According to one first-hand account, "a rumor into which one ran everywhere indicated a well-prepared maneuver. . . . Trotsky imagines himself a Bonaparte, it was said, or "Trotsky wants to act a Bonaparte."[31]

Trotsky's decision not to resist his dismissal as War Commissar—and Trotsky made no attempt to appeal to the military forces at his disposal to act against his enemies—was not based on the calculation that in open conflict with his rivals he would lose. Rather, Trotsky failed to use a mailed fist in part because he did not want to play the role of a Bonapartist gravedigger of the Revolution by striking with the army against the Party. He saw the Party as "the only historic instrument that the working class possessed for the solution of its historic tasks," while the army was a potentially counter-revolutionary force.[32] Of course, alternative explanations must be considered. Trotsky's Hamlet-like behavior throughout the 1920s may also explain his failure to move against his enemies. At the very least, however, the historical analogy played a contributing, if not the major, role in Trotsky's casting himself in the part of a Hamlet rather than the part of a Bonaparte.

We now come to what Vertzberger calls the use of history for determining strategy. This category is fairly self-evident. As Vertzberger defines it, the decision-maker draws upon history "in the search for ideas and orientations about the most effective range of policies for coping with acute problems facing the actor and the choice among these policy alternatives."[33] This category is of primary importance because it raises most explicitly the question of the link between the use of historical analogies and actual political behavior. In other words, it poses the question of causality. Several examples of this type from the Bolshevik case can be cited. For example, the Bolshevik financial policy of closing the budget deficit in the period of War Communism did not resemble the Gramm-Rudman Act. In a direct imitation of their Jacobin forebears, the Bolsheviks melted church bells for coinage to balance their budget. But the major example that should be considered revolves around the question of Jacobin terror.

The application of terror in creating and consolidating a revolution was a central problem that had preoccupied Russian Marxism since its inception. In its struggle with and emergence from populism, the Russian Marxists developed a clear position regarding the ill-advised nature of a strategy of individual terror. Assassination of political opponents was rejected for sound doctrinal reasons connected to the Bolshevik understanding of the historical process.

Mass terror of the French type involving the execution of thousands of people, however, was a different matter. Incidentally, in Russian revolutionary jargon, individual terror was called "March First terror," referring to the date of the assassination of the Tsar Alexander II, and mass terror was known as "1793 terror."[34] Russian Marxism's fundamental attitude toward these two types of terrorism; individual and mass terror, can be summed up by Plekhanov's pithy assertion that in combating Russian despotism "dynamite is not a bad means, but the guillotine is still better."[35] Plekhanov asserted that "every Social-Democrat must be a terrorist à la Robespierre." Unlike the Socialist-Revolutionaries, he added, "we will not . . . try to shoot the tsar and members of his entourage," but "after our victory, we will erect a guillotine for them on Kazan square."[36]

Regarding individual and mass terror, Lenin was very much in the tradition that Plekhanov had set. He spelled out his view quite clearly in his remarks on the assassination of the King of Portugal in February 1908. The assassination causes "regret," he said, because an "element of conspiratorial, that is, impotent terror" is visible. This kind of terror "fails to achieve its purpose and falls short of that genuine, popular, truly regenerative terror for which the Great French Revolution became famous."[37]

After the October Revolution, and especially during the Red Terror of the War Communism period, the lessons offered by the Jacobin dictatorship became of direct use. The same problems that beset the Jacobins, it seemed to Lenin, were now facing him. It was clear to Lenin from French history that in prior revolutions terror had not been firmly enough applied: "The misfortune of previous revolutions" he said, "was that the revolutionary enthusiasm of the people, which gave them the strength to suppress ruthlessly the elements of disintegration, did not last long." Only in a proletarian revolution, because it contains the "majority of the working and exploited people," can terror be applied so as to "suppress completely all the exploiters, as well as all the elements of disintegration."[38] Thus, Lenin saw the Jacobins as insufficiently resolute in applying terror, a failing that, following Marx, he also ascribed to the ill-fated Paris Commune. A proletarian revolution led by the Bolsheviks would not suffer from this shortcoming. As Stanley Hoffmann has put it: "The lesson that Lenin . . . drew from the failure of the French revolution is that terror has to be deliberate, has to be planned, and has to last as long as necessary."[39]

Lenin's associates were of a similar persuasion. Trotsky, for example, at a session of the Central Executive Committee in December 1917 warned that "in not more than a month's time, terror will assume very violent form after the example of the great French Revolution. The guillotine and not merely the jail will be ready for our enemies."[40] Dzherzhinsky, the first head of the Cheka, the earliest version of what was to become the KGB, was repeatedly compared to the public prosecutor of the French Revolutionary Tribunal, Fouquier-Tinville. As one of Lenin's closest colleagues recalls:

The stern and fiery manner of this unparalleled warrior of the French Revolution was well known to all of us. We well knew the dimensions of the terror of this great struggle. We since long ago were all prepared for the arrival of the era when the conquests of the dictatorship of the proletariat would have to be defended not only with arms in our hands, but also by applying one of the most radical and forceful means of our revolutionary struggle — Red Terror. . .

And a Fouquier-Tinville of the Russian proletarian revolution did appear. It
was our hardened fighter and close comrade, Felix Edmundovich Dzherzhinsky.[41]

Not only did the French revolutionary past indicate mass terror as the
policy option of choice, but it even provided more specific instruction as to the
application of the terror. In his discussion of the Paris Commune, Marx had
lent his approval to the French Communards' seizure and execution of
innocent hostages, of whom he said: their "lives have been forfeited over and
over again by the continued shooting of prisoners" by the Versailles
government.[42] It is reasonable to assume that when the practice of seizing
random members of the bourgeoisie as hostages and executing them was
resurrected during the Bolshevik Red Terror, this was a direct inspiration from
the Paris Commune.[43] The French revolutionary practice of sinking barges
with full cargoes of prisoners, "vertical deportations" as they were known in
contrast to the horizontal guillotining, was also adopted in the USSR as early
as 1918, with pristine Lake Baikal one of the receptacles for the hostages
"deported" in this fashion.[44]

In thinking about the link between the lessons of the past and actual
political behavior, it is useful to ask the question: "Without the historical
analogy to the French Revolution, would Bolshevik political behavior have
been any different?" Another way of putting this question is: "Can an
additional factor or variable explain the behavior?" In the case of terror,
the answer must be yes. With or without the precedents offered by the French
revolutionary past, terror would have been exercised in the course of a
Russian revolution. In making a revolution, the Bolsheviks did have real
enemies to dispose of, and as the Russian proverb has it, you can't chop wood
without the chips flying. In conceding that terror would have been exercised
with or without the lessons of the past, I am not arguing that the historical
analogies are irrelevant or insignificant rhetorical devices. Although the
precedent set by the Jacobin dictatorship and the lessons offered by the Paris
Commune were not the decisive factors impelling the Bolsheviks to a policy
of revolutionary terror, these did shape the form of the terror as the examples
of hostage taking shows. More importantly, the Bolshevik glorification of
French revolutionary terror had tangible implications of another sort. It led
them to glorify the application of terror and elevate it into a virtual cult in a
fashion that had dire consequences for the entire course of the revolution.
Terror became the basic technique of revolutionary rule.[45]

Vertzberger defines the use of history for justifying strategy as using
history in "the process of convincing other relevant participants domestic or
foreign, that a particular policy is the most logical, practical and normatively
acceptable."[46] From the Bolshevik experience numerous examples can be cited
that fit into this category.

The names of the villains and heroes of French history came to be
used by the Bolsheviks as weapons with which they castigated their enemies.
The split of Russian Social-Democracy into two wings was accompanied by
a debate in which the Bolsheviks branded the Mensheviks as Girondist
opportunists. The Mensheviks, in turn, replied that the Bolsheviks were

Blanquist conspirators. Over the course of a decade Lenin applied the label "Bonapartist" to many of his opponents, including Stolypin and Kerensky. Trotsky on one occasion compared Lenin to Robespierre, calling him a "Maximilian Lenin," whose "malicious and morally repulsive suspiciousness is a flat caricature of the tragic Jacobin intolerance."[47] It was not uncommon for the Bolsheviks to tar their enemies and each other with uncomplimentary comparisons to Danton and Cavaignac. If one judges by the frequency with which the *dramatis personae* of French history entered onto the Russian stage, this evidently was an effective form of argumentation.

It would be a mistaken impression to assume in this case as well that this use of history had a purely rhetorical function. Some of these terms of abuse, Bonapartism most prominently among them, have a definite and elaborate theoretical content. To call someone a Bonapartist in Marxist discourse is not merely to pin an unpleasant label on him. It is a label that contains an elaborate conception of how one expects the would-be Bonaparte to behave.[48]

Having illustrated a variety of uses of the past in the early Soviet period, it is time to reflect on the implications of the Bolshevik fascination with the French revolutionary past for contemporary Soviet politics. In the Siberian city of Irkutsk, and in innumerable other cities across the Soviet Union, there are streets and parks named after Marat, Robespierre and other figures drawn from French revolutionary history. In Moscow the Marat Chocolate Factory continues in production, despite a severe sugar shortage. A skeptic might be tempted to suggest that these place names are the only legacy of the tremendous role that French revolutionary history played in the early Soviet period. This is what Ferenc Fehér argues in *The Frozen Revolution:*

Lenin's, Trotsky's and Luxemburg's generation still knew by heart what had happened in Paris in those distant days. The troglodytes who came after them could not care less about it. This passing into oblivion of a once powerful story could, so it seems, have been accounted for by the perfection of its appropriation. Apparently, everything there was to learn has been learned. The faults of the original blueprint have been corrected, no Thermidor has ever come, the edifice has not only been erected but also preserved intact in storms the like of which History has never seen.[49]

There is little to disagree with in Fehér's assessment. Clearly, the post-Stalin Soviet leadership is very different from the founding fathers of the Russian Revolution. It is hard to imagine that someone like Mr. Brezhnev or Mr. Chernenko would have had more than a vague notion, if even that, of who Danton or Saint-Just were. On the other hand, if the French Revolution is far from being the decisive event that stamped the outlook of Soviet political and intellectual leaders in the 1970s and 1980s, the mark it left remained visible on the Russian body politic. Thus, the well-known economist Nikolai Shmelev was haunted by the economic crisis and "snowballing" inflation that provoked the French Revolution. "What is in store for us?" asked Shmelev in *Pravda*, "the script for this train of events was written two-hundred years ago at the time of the French Revolution. . . . We are faced with the prospect of a universal rationing system, a drastic depreciation of the ruble, the wild rampage of the black market and the shadow economy, the collapse of the consumer market."[50]

The economists are not alone in invoking the French past. Long after the Ninth of Thermidor put an end to Robespierre's Reign of Terror, the iron blade of the guillotine was reforged into the barbed wire of the Gulag. And in the Aesopian language of Soviet political discourse, reflections on the Russian Revolution, are still sometimes couched in references to the Jacobin dictatorship. For decades Soviet historians engaged in heated discussion about Lenin's assessment of the Jacobin Reign of Terror, a controversy that explored in proxy form the historical necessity (or lack thereof) of Stalin's mass terror and Lenin's Red Terror.[51] As the dialectic of glasnost progressed, this debate emerged from under its veil of cryptic references.[52] As 1989 unfolded, a flood of new and revealing Soviet publications was unleashed in connection with the bicentennial of the French Revolution. These are a fertile source for understanding the reevaluation of Soviet history that is now proceeding apace in the former USSR.[53]

Thus, in 1988 at a conference devoted to French revolutionary historiography in which most of the leading Soviet historians of France participated, one scholar, Professor A. V. Ado of Moscow State University, characterized the Jacobin terror "as the older brother of Stalinist terror."[54] And Professor Ado complained of the unbalanced and "uncritical" writings of Soviet historians of the 1920s and 1930s which "frequently approached an idealization" of the Jacobin Terror.[55] This tendency, said Ado, finds its roots in the events of 1918 and is connected with a desire to find a historical justification for the Red Terror.

Several Soviet historians argued that the Marxian categories tradi-tionally employed in the Soviet school of French history were woefully inadequate. "In order to understand the essence of Jacobinism," noted the summary of the 1988 conference, "it is necessary to reject the standard and habitual conception that the factional struggle within the Convention and the Jacobin 'party,' was a reflection of contradictions between social groups." New approaches are needed which take into account Jacobinism's "political and ideological autonomy" and do not consider it strictly as a social phenomenon. Furthermore, the "diseased reaction" of Soviet historians to the work of non-Marxist historians of the French Revolution frequently exhibited "a purely ideological criticism" that made no contribution to Soviet social science.[56] The historian G. V. Revunenkov, reviewing Soviet historiography of the French Revolution, notes that it has proceeded down a "great and complicated" path of development:

On that path were definite achievements, and undoubtedly failures and mistakes. It is not a secret that in the period of the Stalin cult of the personality and in the "years of stagnation" primarily the works of those authors were published who strove for a canonization of the Jacobin dictatorship, who strove to suppress its internal contradictions, who idealized Jacobin terror, and to a certain degree justified Stalin's repression.[57]

One attempt to rectify these deficiencies has been undertaken by Vladislav P. Smirnov, a professor of history at Moscow University. His study, like many others now undertaken by Russian historians of France, is animated by a desire to apply the "new thinking" not only to the past but also to the current dilemmas of the former Soviet Union. Smirnov thus calls for a fresh look at the tendency of Marxist historians to contemptuously dismiss the "principles of 1789," the rights of man, as "bourgeois democratic freedoms, which only are of use to the property owning minority of the population."[58] Smirnov laments that the rights of man that were heralded by the French revolutionaries were for a "long time not observed in the Soviet Union," as Stalin eliminated freedom and resorted to mass repression. But today, he says, we better understand the "universal historical significance" of the principles that were the great contribution of the French Revolution. It has been said that the revolution devours its children, but in the new states which sprang from the USSR, it is the children who are now devouring the revolution. A thoroughgoing revision is now underway, not only of the French Revolution, but also of the traditional categories and modes of thought that characterized Soviet historical inquiry for so many decades.

It can be readily conceded that at the very summit of Soviet politics, the USSR's political leaders were no longer in the grip of the "lessons" of the French Revolution. They were certainly not debating contemporary issues with reference to the French Revolution with anything resembling the passions of their forebears. But the events of 1789 had not yet made their final departure from center stage.

On the eve of the seventieth anniversary of the October Revolution, Mikhail Gorbachev resurrected the French ghost from a long period of dormancy (at least at the highest levels) when he declared that the French Revolution was "a vast contribution to the history of mankind,"[59] and "if we were to seek the roots of our perestroika, we should turn to the French Revolution and then to the Paris Commune. . . .

We . . . are proud of the French Revolution. It was an enormous contribution to the history of the French people."[60] Gorbachev returned to this theme once again in December 1988 when, before the assembled United Nations, he referred to the French Revolution as one of the two great historical episodes that shaped the modern world.[61] One might conclude from these platitudinous remarks that the fire ignited by the French Revolution in the minds of Russian revolutionaries has finally dwindled to a flicker. But this is not entirely the case.

Bonaparte may have been the gravedigger of the revolution, but in the former Soviet Union a grave had not yet been dug for the contempt of Bonapartism, although the theoretical trappings of the term had been largely stripped away. Some months before Boris Yeltsin was removed from his Politburo post in November 1987, he was already being accused of Bonapartism. At a meeting in which Yeltsin addressed midlevel Moscow party workers, one of the apparatchiki present accused him in the following terms: "You have Napoleonic plans; what do you think you're up to? Go back to Sverdlovsk before it's too late."[62]   When Yeltsin was finally dismissed, the same accusation was repeated at the Moscow Communist Party meeting where Mr. Yeltsin was given his pink slip. *Pravda* reported that an obscure Moscow communist, Mr. Fedor F. Kozyrev-Dal, was given the floor and denounced Mr. Yeltsin in the following terms: "He needed authority at any cost. . . . And I would qualify this as nothing but political adventurism. . . . He intensified a bureaucratic style of work. . . . Comrade Yeltsin usurped the city party leadership and elements of Bonapartism began to appear, totally deforming personnel policy."[63]

The fear of a military man riding in on a white horse has also surfaced over the years in connection with the rise and fall of various Soviet military leaders, Marshal Zhukov being the most prominent among them. In the aftermath of his dismissal in 1957, Zhukov was publicly accused of "having Bonapartist aspirations toward a personal seizure of power," Khrushchev, in his memoirs, held that Zhukov had been "voicing Bonapartist aspirations in his conversations with military commanders."[64]

The charge of Bonapartism was even made against Gorbachev. At the first meeting of the Congress of People's Deputies, one delegate, a truck driver from Kharkov, motor transport enterprise No. 16301, attacked Mr. Gorbachev and his wife Raisa in the following terms:

I compare you not to Lenin and Stalin but rather to the great Napoleon, who, fearing neither bullets nor death, led the people to victories. But, thanks to yes-men and to his wife, he went from a republic to an empire. Evidently, even you cannot avoid flattery and the influence of your wife. It has never yet happened in history that the rich and the poor sat at the same table. Some ate chicken, while others licked their fingers clean and simultaneously made the same old speeches. The majority of the people will not go for such perestroika.[65]

Even if the current Russian leadership does not have a fixation on the French past that is in any way comparable to that of their forerunners, a new set of historical episodes have clearly come to preoccupy them. To mention just a few, these include the lessons of NEP, collectivization, Stalinism, and World War II. The list could go on. The intensity of the debate in the former USSR over Soviet history, and the premier part this debate played in Gorbachev's policy of glasnost, might lead one to conclude that Karl Marx was right when he said that the "tradition of all the dead generations weighs like a nightmare on the brain of the living." The lessons of the past continue to remain one of the keys to the political future across the new states that have arisen from the old Soviet Union.

NOTES

1. A. E. Manfred, *Tri portreta epokhi Velikoi frantsuzskoi revoliutsii* (Moscow, 1978), 411-412.

2. *Kulturnaia zhizn' v SSSR. Chronika 1917—1927* (Moscow: Nauka, 1975), 41.

3. Lenin, *Polnoe Sobranie Sochinenii*, Vol. 36, 684.

4. *Chronika*, 67-69.

5. *Izvestiia*, August 2, 1918, 3.

6. *Pravda*, February 4, 1919, 3.

7. See V. M. Dalin, *Istoriki Frantsii xix-xx vekov* (Moscow: Nauka, 1981), 72.

8. B. D. Bonch-Bruevich, *Izbrannye Sochineniia*, Vol. III, "Vospominaniia o V.I. Lenine 1917—1924" (Moscow: Izdatelstvo Akademii Nauk SSSR, 1963), 365-366.

9. Ibid.

10. The most important studies are Robert Jervis, "How Decision-Makers Learn From History," Chapter 6 in *Perception and Misperception in International Politics* (Princeton, N. J.: Princeton University, 1976); Ernest May, *"Lessons" of the Past: The Use and Misuse of History in American Foreign Policy* (New York: Oxford University Press, 1973); Richard E. Neustadt and Ernest R. May, *Thinking in Time: The Uses of History for Decision-Makers* (New York: Free Press, 1986); Yaacov Y.I. Vertzberger, "Foreign Policy Decision-Makers as Practical-Intuitive Historians: Applied history and Its Shortcomings," *International Studies Quarterly* 30 (1986), 223-247.

11. Jervis, for example, stresses the importance of firsthand experience as one of the "events from which people learn most." The extent to which the Bolsheviks drew on French revolutionary history for lessons offers a case in which secondhand experiences seem to play at least as great a role as firsthand experience. See Jervis, "How Decision Makers Learn," 239.

12. A larger portion of the quotation is worth reproducing:

Almost every figure on the Russian political stage wore a costume tailored in Paris. Tsarism was the ancien régime. Vyshnegradskii, Witte, and Stolypin were the Turgot, Calonne, and Necker. Lenin was a Jacobin--his opponents said this to denounce him, and he repeated it after them with pride. He was a Russian Robespierre--on this, too, both he and his opponents agreed. And he was as well a Russian Blanqui. In a gentler mood, he called his rivals Girondins or the Swamp; when harsher, Cavaignacs. Trotsky dramatized himself as the Marat of the Revolution, later as its Carnot. . . . Trotsky and Stalin in their debates hurled at each other the epithet "Bonapartist."

Trotsky branded Stalin's regime as "Thermidor." Bertram Wolfe, *An Ideology in Power: Reflections on the Russian Revolution* (New York: Stein and Day, 1969), 8.

13. Dalin, *Istoriki Frantsii*, 65.

14. S. Mitskevich, "*Russkie iakobintsy*," *Proletarskaia revoliutsiia*, No. 6-7 (18-19), 1923, 6.

15. See Volodymr Varlamov, "Bakunin and the Russian Jacobins and Blanquists," in Cyril Black (ed.), *Rewriting Soviet History* (New York: Random House, 1962).

16. Frederick Engels, *Preface to the Third German Edition* (1883) *of The Eighteenth Brumaire* by Karl Marx, New York: (International Publishers n.d.) 10.

17. Plekhanov, *Sochineniia*, Vol. II, 46.

18. Engels, *Preface*, 10.

19. These are *The Communist Manifesto, The Class Struggles in France, Eighteenth Brumaire of Louis Bonaparte, and The Civil War in France*.

20. Cited in Walter Laqueur, *The Age of Terrorism* (Boston: Little, Brown and Co., 1987), 60.

21. Cited in Fishman, *The Insurrectionists*, 160.

22. Vertzberger, "Foreign Policy Decision-Makers," 225.

23. Plekhanov, *Sochineniia*, Vol. VIII x K voprosu roli lichnosti v istorii, 297-298.

24. V. I. Lenin, *What Is to Be Done?* (New York: International Publishers, 1929), 32-33.

25. Vertzberger, "Foreign Policy Decision-Makers," 225.

26. Lenin, *Polnoe Sobranie Sochinenii*, Vol. 30, 266. "Otkrytoe pis'mo Boris Suvarinu" (December 1916).

27. Lenin, *Polnoe Sobranie Sochinenii*, Vol. 11, 245. "Vstrecha druzei" (September 26, 1905).

28. Lenin, *Polnoe Sobranie Sochinenii*, Vol. 4, 220. "Proekt programmy nashei partii."

29. Lenin, *Polnoe Sobranie Sochinenii*, Vol. 25. 268. "O prave natsii na samoopredelenie."

30. Vertzberger, "Foreign Policy Decision-Makers," 225.

31. See Isaac Deutscher, *The Prophet Unarmed, Trotsky 1921—1929*, (New York: Vintage, 1959), 95, 160-163. For a contemporary account of this whispering campaign, see Max Eastman, *Since Lenin Died* (London: Labour Publishing Co., 1925) and Alfred Rosmer, *Lenin's Moscow* (London: Pluto Press, 1971), 207.

32. Deutscher, *The Prophet Unarmed*, 161.

33. Vertzberger, "Foreign Policy Decision-Makers," 225.

34. V. Rumii, "Plekhanov i terror," *Pod Znamenem Marksizma*, No. 6-7, June-July 1923, 24.

35. Ibid.

36. Ibid., 32.

37. Lenin, *Polnoe Sobranie Sochinenii*, Vol. 16, 441. "O proisshestvii s korolem portugal'skim" (February 19, 1908).

38. Lenin, *Polnoe Sobranie Sochinenii*, Vol. 36, 195. "Ocherednye zadachni sovestskoi vlasti" (April 28, 1918).

39. Stanley Hoffmann has argued that the major difference between the Jacobins and the Bolsheviks regarding terror "is that the Jacobins stumbled into undeliberate, unplanned terror. . . . They were forced into terror by a combination of the beliefs that were so deep in them, and the hectic and heated circumstances in which France almost died in 1793; the lesson that Lenin, in particular, drew from its failure is that terror has to be deliberate, has to be planned, and has to last as long as necessary" (155). "The French Revolution and the Language of Violence," *Daedelus, Proceedings of the American Academy of Arts and Sciences* 116, No. 2 (Spring 1987).

40. Trotsy, *Lenin*, 133.

41. V. D. Bonch-Bruevich, *Izbrannie Sochineniia*, Vol. 3, 114.

42. Marx, *The Civil War in France*, 78.

43. It should be noted that in the period leading up to the Red Terror Lenin displayed a greater interest in the lessons of the Paris Commune than during any other moment in his life. His *State and Revolution*, which devotes a chapter to an account of the Commune, was written during August-September 1917. The Red Terror was initiated following the assassination attempt on Lenin and the assassination of Uritsky, chairman of the Petrograd Cheka, on August 30, 1918.

44. See Simon Schama, *Citizens, A Chronicle of the French Revolution* (New York: Alfred A. Knopf, 1989), 789, and Aleksandr Solzhenitsyn, *The Gulag Archipelago*, Vols. I-II (New York: Harper and Row, 1973), 435.

45. Adam Ulam has written on this point: "It would have been better for the future of Communism and their country had the Bolsheviks regarded the whole subject of terror in an entirely cynical way: as a necessary but distasteful business to be handled by sadists and thugs who in any case infiltrated the security apparatus from the very beginning. Instead terror was extolled, the Cheka was presented as the sword of the Revolution, its first head, Felix Dzerzhinsky, is still and even in the most anti-Stalin literature described as a veritable Communist saint, a 'knight without fear or blemish.'" Adam Ulam, *Stalin, The Man and His Era* (New York: Viking Press, 1973), 175.

46. Vertzberger, "Foreign Policy Decision-Makers," 225.

47. Cited in Baruch Knei-Paz, *The Social and Political Thought of Leon Trotsky* (New York: Oxford University Press, 1978), 203.

48. According to the 1950 *Great Soviet Encyclopedia*, for example, Bonapartism "is one of the forms of the counterrevolutionary dictatorship of the big bourgeoisie, resting on the militarists. It maneuvers in the conditions of an unstable equilibrium of class forces. Bonapartism appears in circumstances when class struggle is sharpened to its limits, during which the basic contending classes seemingly balance each other off: the bourgeoisie is unable to cope with the revolutionary movement, and the proletariat is still weak and cannot win in the struggle."

49. Ferenc Fehér. *The Frozen Revolution* (Cambridge: Cambridge University Press, 1987), 153.

50. *Pravda*, June 9, 1989, 2. Soviet economists had a tradition of looking at the French experience of hyperinflation for policy lessons applicable to Russia. See, for example, A. M. Smirnov, *Krizis denezhnoi sistemy frantsuzskoi revoliutsii* (Petersburg, Pravo, 1921; S. A. Falkner, *Bumazhnye den'gi frantsuzskoki revoliutsii* (1789 — 1797) (Moscow, 1919. For a treatment of how early Soviet economists attempted to learn from the French Revolution,

see Laure Després, "Des Assignats aux Sovznaks: la théorie de l'économie d'émission de S. A. Fal'kner," paper presented at the colloquium "La Pensée Economique pendant la Révolution," Paris, 1989.

51. Some of the key documents in this controversy are. I. Tokin, *Lenin o Velikoi frantsuzskoi revoliutsii*, 1932; B. P. Volgin, "Lenin i revoliutsionnye traditsii frantsuzskogo naroda," in *Frantsuzskii ezhegodnik*, 1958; N.M. Lukin, "Lenin i problema iakobinskoi diktatury," *Istorik Marksist*, 1934, Vol. l; "Lenin i istoricheskoe nasledie iakobinskoi diktatury, B.G. Veber in *Frantsuzskii ezhegodnik*, 1970; V.S. Alekseev-Popov and Iu. Baskin, "Problemy istorii iakobinskoi diktautury v svete trudov V.I. Lenina," in *Iz istorii iakobinskoi diktatury* (Odessa, 1962).

52. Thus, the Leningrad historian V. G. Revunenkov has come under strong criticism for his view that Marx and Engels abandoned their positive evaluation of Jacobin terror after 1848, but Lenin remained under the influence of their original view. The historian V. M. Dalin notes that Revunenkov has "rejected the Leninist appraisal of the class basis of the Jacobin Convention" and that his position "has not found support among Soviet specialists on the history of the Revolution" (*Istoriki_Frantsii*, 81). A special symposium of the Institute of Universal History of the USSR Academy of Sciences was devoted to condemning Revunenkov's work for its negative appraisal of the Jacobin dictatorship. The key documents in this controversy are V. G. Revunenkov, *Marksizm i problema iakobinskoi diktatury* (Leningrad: Leningrad University, 1966); V. G. Revunenkov, "V.I. Lenin o iakobinskom terrore," *Vestnik Leningrad-skogo universiteta*, No. 2, 1970; V. G. Revunenkov, "Problemy iakobinskoi diktatury v noveishikh rabotakh sovetskikh istorikov," in *Problemy vseobshchei istorii*, 1967; and V. G. Revunenkov, "Marat i melkoburzhuaznaia revoliutsionnost," in *Problemy otechesvennoi i vseobshchei istorii*, 1969. For a discussion of this symposium, see V. M. Dalin, *Istoriki Frantsii XIX-XX vekov* (Moscow: 1981), 81, and *Frantsuzskii ezhegodnik*, 1970.

53. See, for example: V. Smirnov, "Velikaia frantsuzshaia revoliutsiia i sovremennost" *Mirovaia Ekonomika i mezhdunarodnye otnosheniia*, No. 7, 1989; Iu. N. Afanas'ev, S. F. Blumenau, "Sovremennye spory vo frantsii vokrug velikoi revoliutsii, voprosy Istorii, No. 3, 1989; N. Molchanov, "Revoliutsiia na gil'otine," *Literaturnaai Gazeta*, July 9, 1986; Alexander Sogomonov, "The Bicentenary of the French Revolution," *New Times*, No. 28, 1989; E.B. Cherniak, "1794-i god. Nekotory aktual'nye problemy issledovaniia Velikoi frantsuz-skoi revoliutsii," *Novaia i noveishaia istoriia*, 1989, No. 1.

54. The conference met on September 19-20, 1988. A summary of the proceedings has been published in A. V. Chudinov, "Nazrevshie problemy izucheniia istorii Velikoi frantsuzskoi revoliutsii (po materialam obsuzhdeniia

v Institute vseob-shchei isktorii AN SSSR)," *Novaia i Noveishaia Istoriia*, No. 2 (March-April 1989), 66.

55. Ibid., 67.

56. Ibid., 68.

57. V. G. Revunenkov, "Velikaia frantsuzskaia revoliutsiia: traditsii izucheniia i novye podkhody," *Voprosy Istorii*, No. 5, May 1989, 108-109.

58. Vladislav Pavlovich Smirnov, "Velikaia frantsuzskaia revoliutsiia i sovremennost'," *Mirovaia Ekonomika i Mezhdunarodnye Otnosheniia*, No. 7, 1989, 59.

59. *Foreign Broadcast Information Service*, September 30, 1987, Moscow Television Service.

60. *Pravda*, September 30, 1987.

61. "Vystuplenie M. S. Gorbacheva v Organizatsii Ob' edinennyx Natsii," *Pravda*, December 8, 1988.

62. "Can Moscow Believe in Yeltsin?," *Detente* (Autumn 1986), 2.

63. *Pravda*, November 13, 1987.

64. For an account of the Bonapartism charge in the Zhukov affair from which both of these quotations are drawn, see Timothy Colton, *Commissars, Commanders and Civilian Authority: The Structure of Soviet Military Politics*, (Cambridge, Mass.: Harvard University Press, 1979) 178-184.

65. *Foreign Broadcast Information Service*, June 13, 1989, 25.

26

Marianne Revisited:
Anti-Republican Political
Caricature, 1880–1900

Willa Z. Silverman

The republican iconography generated by the French Revolution forms a rich visual tradition, now two centuries old. The tricolor flag, pike and sheaf of fasces are familiar symbols in works evoking revolutionary and republican themes. But the best known (and most controversial) icon from the revolutionary era is Marianne. Over a two-hundred-year period, this female allegorical figure has come to represent the separate or combined values of Liberty, the Revolution, the Republic and France itself.

Since the Revolution, Marianne's image has adorned postage stamps, currency, war monuments and contemporary busts of the Republic resembling Brigitte Bardot, Catherine Deneuve, and now Chanel model Inès de la Fressange. All these representations glorify this tutelar deity of the Republic.

The sanctification of Marianne was especially visible during the early decades of the Third Republic. For republicans the new regime fulfilled the messianic revolutionary promise of *liberté, égalité, fraternité*. The political class explicitly proclaimed itself the inheritor of the revolutionary legacy and sought to legitimize this claim by promoting a secular cult of republican civic virtue. This cult sought to strengthen its authority through the proliferation of traditional republican images, including that of Marianne.

Yet Marianne's image has served not only the champions but also the enemies of the revolutionary and republican heritage. Among these adversaries were the Third Republic's opponents on both the Right and the Left, who viewed the regime as ineffectual at best, corrupt, perverse and exploitative at worst. They expressed their opposition not only through political agitation and writing, but again also through visual symbols. From 1880 to 1900, during the so-called Opportunist Republic, gifted caricature artists exploited generic republican symbols, most notably that of Marianne. Yet they infused them with new meaning in order to accentuate their anti-republican stance.

Revisiting Marianne at the end of the nineteenth century, then, means witnessing the visual profanation of an icon. The nature of this profanation may indeed reveal something about the status of the republican idea at that time in a nation where political conflict is often expresesed symbolically.

A brief history of the visual representations of Marianne reveals the different iconographic elements available to late nineteenth-century caricaturists. As Maurice Agulhon has noted in his typological study, *Marianne au combat*,[1] a female allegory of Liberty, reminiscent of the Roman prototype, existed before a female allegory of the Republic. Almost always identified by such symbolic attributes as the pike, fasces and Phrygian cap, revolutionary allegories of Liberty are nevertheless of two types. One, as depicted in a 1792 painting for the Jacobin Club, **Figure 1** is a calm figure, often seated, and fully dressed in classical robes; the Phrygian cap is sometimes absent.

Figure 1

Nanine Vallain, *Liberty* **(1792)**

The other, illustrated in Gros' painting, **Figure 2** is a more youthful figure with legs and breast bared, often standing or even on the march. Serene power or dynamic, popular power: these two images of Liberty would be evoked and satirized in the late nineteenth century.

Figure 2

Gros, allegorical figure of the Republic

It was not until the proclamation of the first Republic in September 1792 that the female allegory of Liberty, whom some counterrevolutionaries derisively labeled Marianne,[2] became the official symbol of the Republic. Displayed in town squares, meeting halls, festivals and on the first seal of the Republic, **Figure 3**, Marianne's image--of the serene variety-- became associated in popular imagination with a fusion of the principles of Liberty, the Republic and the *patrie*.

Figure 3

The first seal of the Republic.

The first seal of the Republic

During the Empire and Restoration, republican imagery disappeared from public view, replaced by that of Napoleon and the Bourbon monarchs. This policy changed again under the July Monarchy, a liberal and secular regime intent on cultivating civic spirit. Marianne made a timid return, but her meaning was carefully circumscribed. Because the regime in power was indeed a monarchy, Marianne could no longer, at least in official imagery, represent the Republic. With her Phrygian bonnet often replaced by the *coq gaulois* and her chest discreetly covered, this allegory of Liberty reflected the same ambiguity toward revolutionary principles that characterized the regime itself. Bolder visions of Liberty were proscribed; Delacroix's 1831 *Liberté guidant le peuple*, **Figure 4**, evoking the poet Auguste Barbier's description of Liberty as "a strong woman with powerful breasts" ("une forte femme aux puissantes mamelles"),[3] was relegated to the Louvre's basement.

Figure 4

Delacroix, *La Liberté guidant le peuple* (1831)

Yet, Delacroix's painting served as a precursor for other dynamic, popular images of Marianne, especially abundant in 1848. As in the years 1789 to 1792, the early months of 1848 had "a revolutionary effect upon symbolism."[4] In 1848, as during the Revolution, two female allegories, reflecting two conceptions of the Republic, vied for attention. Proponents of a liberal bourgeois Republic admired the Marianne depicted on the seal of the Second Republic, **Figure 5**, a serene, immobile figure with orderly hair and bosom covered.

Figure 5

The second seal of the Republic

The second seal of the Republic

The Phrygian cap, symbol of popular agitation, is absent, compensated by many other symbolic and didactic attributes. This woman is a maternal figure, sharing even with Daumier's unorthodox painting of the Republic, **Figure 6** also from 1848, an aura of abundant and equitable generosity.

Figure 6

Daumier, *La République française* **(1848)**

Confronting this moderate vision of "Liberty triumphant" is an aggressive image of popular revolt, inspired by socialism--"a bloody woman coiffed
in red" ("une femme sanglante à la rouge coiffure"),[5] in the words of the
mystic poet and painter Louis Janot. Unlike the calm matrons seen previously,
these youthful Mariannes stand or march, their hair flowing, their breasts
exposed, and their full red bonnets pointing resolutely forward. The tranquil
mother has become an alluring and energetic mistress.

For the next two decades, the emblem of the "Red Republic" associated
with Louis Blanc and Auguste Blanqui would again be forced underground,
as the conservative Second Republic favored depoliticized, derepublicanized
allegory. Marianne's bonnet was again removed and her hem lengthened.
And she nearly disappeared under the Second Empire, when her image was
systematically replaced by that of the emperor or of a more acceptable
goddess: the Virgin Mary. Yet it was during this period as well that the
name Marianne, once a term of contempt, became the password of Republican
secret societies awaiting the return of their favored regime.

The Commune marked the comeback of a popular, leftist version of the
Republic. In an 1871 lithograph, **Figure 7**, for instance, a muscular, semi-
nude Marianne, draped in red, asks an allegorical figure of France if she has
"finished" with Monsieur Thiers, head of the provisional government.

Figure 7

"La dernière étape?" Lithograph (1871)

This suggestion of illicit activity would in the next decades be turned against the Republic. An 1872 caricature from the monarchist newspaper *Le Grelot* **Figure 8** pits the two Mariannes against one another: the tricolored matron on the left, incarnating Thiers' conservative bourgeois Republic, inherited from 1789, confronts the bloody Fury descended from 1793 and 1848, representing a popular social republic. By depicting both Mariannes (and the social ideals they represented) as equally grotesque, the caricaturist (Alfred Le Petit in this case) summarily dismisses both political options.

Figure 8

Alfred Le Petit, "Les deux Républiques," *Le Grelot* (1872)

The first decades of the Third Republic mark a watershed in the history of the representation of Marianne. The new regime, a republic almost by default, sought legitimacy by stressing its affiliation with the early phases of the 1789 Revolution. "La Marseillaise" was declared the national anthem in 1879, and the following year Bastille Day became the national holiday. The Revolution's centennial was celebrated with much pomp, and the Sorbonne established an official chair in French revolutionary history.

This grounding of the Third Republic in the First was also expressed iconographically. Marianne became the regime's goddess in a civic cult meant to rival Catholicism. Busts of Marianne now graced France's 36,000 *mairies*, while monumental statues of the republican divinity, such as Clésinger's contribution to the 1878 Paris World's Fair, **Figure 9,** dominated town squares.

Figure 9

Clésinger, *La Republique* (1878)

In popular imagery, too, Marianne flourished (**Figure 10**); an 1880 calendar distributed by republican propagandists and a poster created for the 1889 inauguration of Dalou's triumphal statue of the Republic (**Figure 11**) brought Marianne into thousands of Republican homes.

Figure 10

Calendar distributed by Republican propagandists (1880)

Figure 11

Poster for the inauguration of Dalou's statue of the Republic (1889)

The early Third Republic's official image of Marianne thus accentuates her serenity and motherliness. This Marianne personifies a moderate regime and a France of Republican banquets and colonial conquests.

The republican fervor of the political class, however, was matched by the passionate anti-republicanism of its opponents, whose numbers included both right-wing nationalists and left-wing anarchists. This antagonism became particularly apparent during a series of scandals that rocked the Republic from 1880 to 1900 and threatened the regime's recent stability. The Wilson and Panama scandals and the "Affairs" associated with Boulanger and Dreyfus whipped up not only antiparliamentary feeling but also its often attendant ideology of anti-Semitism. Significantly, republican enemies often directed their attacks against the regime's most powerful symbol, Marianne; to the poet Paul Verlaine, a former Communard, Marianne was no longer a mother, wife or mistress, but had become a frightful shrew, "rambling, hairless and tooth-less" ("radoteuse, au poil rare et sans dents").[6] To others, her corruption had turned her into "la gueuse," the slut.

Verbal assaults on Marianne had their pictorial equivalents. Between 1880 and 1900, caricature was the privileged and highly effective visual means of anti-republican expression. New techniques of photomechanical reproduction, often in color, greatly facilitated the dissemination of caricatures, while the 1881 law reestablishing freedom of the press allowed artists to create in a climate of security. The artists in question were among the most talented and original of their time; this was truly a Golden Age of French caricature. And their subject matter--the scandals and foibles of the Third Republic--seems perfectly adapted to an artistic genre defined by satire and exaggeration.

How did anti-republican caricaturists differ from their pro-republican counterparts, both stylistically and thematically, in depicting Marianne? A special 1896 issue of *Le Rire*, entitled "Histoire de la Troisième République," is revealing here. The author and illustrator of this special issue, known by the cryptic pseudonyms of "Gyp" and "Bob," was in fact the Countess Sybille-Gabrielle Marie-Antoinette de Riquetti de Mirabeau, great-grand-niece of the revolutionary orator. The fervent Bonapartism of this widely read novelist had led her to crusade for General Boulanger and to declare herself a "pro-fessional" anti-Semite during the Dreyfus Affair. None of her contemporaries doubted her anti-republicanism.

In the first "chapter" of this revisionist history *par excellence* **Figure 12**, a lithe, virginal Marianne is shown floating in an idyllic landscape above the outstretched arms of bourgeois, workers, and France itself; all greet the new regime in good faith. But "Bob" inserts an ominous visual warning; behind Marianne looms a bat with a stereotypically "Jewish" head and body — a Jewish "vampire." We next see the Republic "opening her arms" to Algerian Jews, naturalized by the 1871 Crémieux Decree **Figure 13.** Here, Bob depicts the Jews as a swarm of hideous insects with spindly tentacles, which lunge toward a plumper, alluring Marianne; the tableau suggests an unhealthy eroticism.

Figure 12

Le Rire

Figure 13

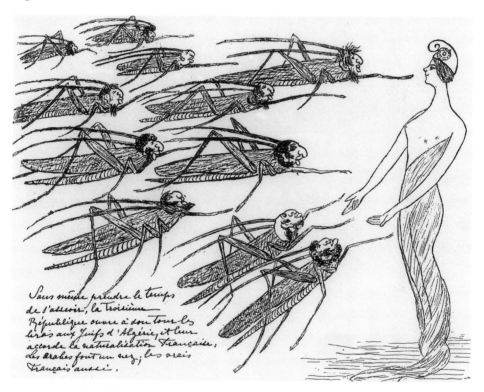

Sans même prendre le temps
de s'asseoir, la troisième
République ouvre à son tour les
bras aux Juifs d'Algérie, et leur
accorde la naturalisation Française:
Les arabes font un nez; les vrais
Français aussi.

Gyp, "Histoire de la Troisième République," *Le Rire* (1896)

Marianne grows fatter as she flirts with Thiers, "her little assassin of a President" ("son petit assassin de Président") **Figure 14**, and rejects a potential lover, Gambetta.

Figure 14

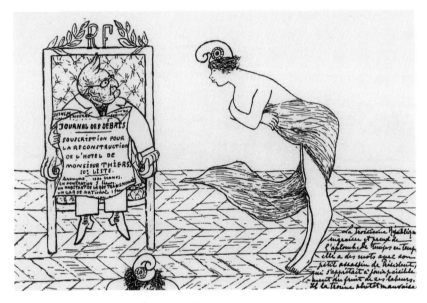

Gyp, "Histoire de la Troisième République," *Le Rire* **(1896)**

She hurls stones at a priest and nun (a reference to the Republic's anticlerical legislation) and hides her face in shame when "a bizarre rain of crosses[7] beats down on Paris" ("une bizarre pluie de croix s'abat sur Paris") during the Wilson scandal. Marianne "thinks her final hour has come" ("croit la dernière heure venue") in 1889 with the Boulangist episode, **Figure 15**; the general straddles a gigantic, red carnation as if it were a horse while a fat, wild-haired Marianne writhes on the ground.

Figure 15

Gyp, "Histoire de la Troisième République," *Le Rire* (1896)

An attempted monarchist comeback in 1890 adds to her worries, and the
Panama Scandal "puts her in a wretched state. Her friends think for a moment
she is done for." ("[la] met dans un fichu état. Ses amis la croient un instant
perdue"). In the next drawing, **Figure 16**, a corpulent Marianne has left her
sickbed and slumbers in a chair while "Jewish" rats, "her beloved little rats,
whom she adores" ("ses petits rats chéris, qu'elle adore") nibble into bags of
gold and tease her dress. A huge cat with Edouard Drumont's face waits to
pounce.

Figure 16

Gyp, "Histoire de la Troisième République," *Le Rire* **(1896)**

In the final drawing, **Figure 17**, the rural setting is the same as in the first, but the trees are barren and brittle.

Figure 17

Gyp, "Histoire de la Troisième République," *Le Rire* (1896)

A now obese Marianne with enormous, flabby breasts "has become power-ful. She only trembles before the friend to whom she can refuse nothing" ("est devenue puissante. Elle ne tremble que devant l'ami auquel elle ne sait rien refuser"). This, of course, is the Jew, here shown pouring coins from a sack labeled "French Money Article for Export" ("Bonne Galette de France-- Article d'Exportation"). In the background, the skeletal figure of France sits on a tree branch, head in hands. The Republican regime, Gyp suggests, has literally sucked the life blood from the French nation, consummating the rupture between the two.[8]

Gyp's crudely drawn, shocking representations of Marianne in "Histoire de la Troisième République" evoke the work of many other anti-republican caricaturists. Clearly, Gyp has modeled her Marianne on the popular, comba-tive figure of Gros and Delacroix, but the result is quite different. This Marianne is no longer the sexually desirable and firm-breasted young woman who symbolized both popular energy and the nourishment of *l'Etat Provi-dence*, but a debauched "Madam," both physically and morally corrupt. This obscene woman dominates Aristide Delannoy's cover for the extreme left-wing *l'Assiette au beurre* **Figure 18**; an amorphous Marianne, grown fat at the expense of the needy, nevertheless taunts them with sausages at Christmas.

Figure 18

Delannoy, "Les petits noëls de Marianne,"
L'assiette au beurre, **December 24, 1904**

Similarly, in Jean Veber's caricature (also in *l'Assiette au beurre*); **Figure 19**, a slovenly Marianne wearing gaudy jewelry (symbol of her bourgeois status) crushes the poor with her weight; Veber protests the regime's repression of strikes and anarchist agitation.

Figure 19

Jean Veber, *L'assiette au beurre*

Another drawing of Veber, entitled "L'effroi" ("The Great Fear");
Figure 20, condemns the Republic's anticlerical legislation, including the
abolition of various religious orders. The naked body of a giant Marianne
wreaks havoc on a village, as priests and nuns scatter. The insistence on the
destructive quality of female sexuality in these three drawings is, of course,
a recurrent *fin-de-siècle* motif. Yet these fat Mariannes, battling the fertile,
benevolent icons of the Republic, also form a countertradition to the one that
dates from the Revolution.

Figure 20

Jean Veber, "L'effroi"

Some anti-republican caricatures of the late nineteenth century portray Marianne not as a sexual deviant but in fact as completely asexual. She has become an ogress, whose vital energies, like those of the Republic, have been sapped.   In J. Blass' 1881 caricature in the monarchist newspaper, *Le Triboulet*, **Figure 21**, a jester sarcastically suggests to Zola that the woman best suited to play the role of the courtesan Nana in an upcoming production is the shrewish Marianne.

Figure 21

J. Blass, *Le Triboulet*, February 6, 1881

In an 1893 caricature in the right-wing *Le Pilori*, Alfred Le Petit offers a grotesque version of the matronly, moderate Republic. This personification of the Opportunist Republic is reduced to bodily functions; tightly reined in by President Sadi Carnot, Marianne ingests the flesh and sweat of the people, while she defecates coins, hastily caught up by her prime ministers. The scatalogical images become the metaphor for the Republic's corrupt exploitation. Marianne the exploiter reappears in a caricature in *l'Assiette au beurre*, **Figure 22**, as a bloated monster, who orders a little boy to "freely" choose between a life of misery in her factories or the oppression of the Church.

Figure 22

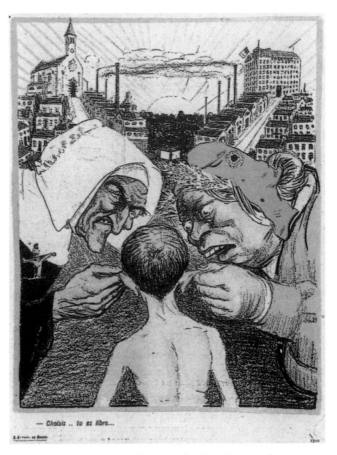

— *Choisis .. tu es libre...*

"Choisis . . . tu es libre . . ," *L'assiette au beurre*,
March 19, 1904

Not all anti-republican caricaturists, however, chose to portray Marianne as the "radoteuse au poil rare" described by Verlaine. Some artists felt that the Republic's selling of favors could best be incarnated by a tantalizing young woman, in fact, a prostitute. In Pepin's 1888 drawing for *Le Grelot*, **Figure 23**, a seductive Marianne mocks her potential suitor Boulanger.

Figure 23

Pepin, *Le Grelot*, July 1, 1888

Little does she know that the general intends to "poser un lapin"; he will "stand the Republic up" and become a hero for those disillusioned with the regime. Adolphe Willette shows an erotic figure of Marianne snuggling with the Russian bear, **Figure 24**, in a caricature of the preliminaries to the 1894 Franco-Russian defensive alliance.

Figure 24

Alfred Willette, "Marianne et l'ours du nord" (1892)

And in an 1899 issue of the anarchist review, *Le père peinard*, a scantily clad Marianne seduces German emperor William II while her "pimp," French President Félix Faure, provides "service"; the caricaturist condems the pro-German orientation marking French foreign policy through 1898. By depicting Marianne as a whore, a hag, or a prostitute, then, anti-republican caricaturists could aim their attacks against what they considered the most reprehensible qualities of the regime: its social oppression yet also its weakness, its excesses and corruption.

A final and novel feature of anti-republican caricature between 1880 and 1900 is its association of Marianne with anti-Semitic themes. Anti-republicanism and anti-Semitism shaded into one another at the end of the century; right-wing nationalists argued that the complicity between Jews and the Republic dated from the First Republic, under which the Jews had been granted citizenship. The Third Republic had compounded this "evil" by bestowing the same right on Algerian Jews. The Panama Scandal, which revealed the guilt of Jewish middlemen, and the Dreyfus Affair provoked more simultaneous attacks on Republic and Jew.

It is thus perhaps not entirely surprising, although shocking, to discover an 1899 extreme right-wing caricature of "Marianne la Youpine," **Figure 25**, with her semiticized features and indecently erect bonnet.

Figure 25

"Marianne la youpine" (1892)

Similarly, Adolphe Willette's drawing of a fat and aging Marianne, **Figure 26**, trudging toward the Chamber of Deputies is clearly anti-Semitic.

Figure 26

Alfred Willette, caricature of the Republic

Willette, a talented artist associated with the Montmartre cabaret scene, ran for election in 1889 on an anti-Semitic platform.

The illicit sexual relations between the Jew and Marianne is the subject of Forain's 1898 drawing in *Psst*, the newspaper that this master caricaturist founded during the Dreyfus Affair. Marianne, in her dressing gown, here refuses to listen to her Jewish lover's complaints, when, as she tells him, he should have contented himself with his *tripotages*, a double entendre meaning either corrupt schemes or masturbation. In "Histoire de la Troisième République," as has been suggested, Gyp is also preoccupied with the sexual collusion between the Jew and Marianne. She implies that Jewish sexuality, perhaps a symbol to her of Jewish avarice, has transformed the Republic from a virgin into a whore; hypersexuality and greed, she argues, are equally dangerous, for they produce nothing tangible.

A final caricature (not shown) is again reminiscent of Gyp and is chillingly prescient of future Jewish history; it shows Marianne ridding France of Jewish "vermin" with a strong pesticide. This group of jointly anti-Semitic and anti-republican caricatures, then belongs not only to the history of representations of Marianne but also to that of a mythic "Jewish Republic."

The republican idea, born of the Revolution, remained a potent yet highly contested concept through the nineteenth century--contested not only by anti-republicans but also among partisans of either a moderate bourgeois or a popular social Republic. At no time were these tensions felt more urgently than during the formative decades of the Third Republic. The new generation of republicans pursued the task of rooting the regime with almost religious conviction; education, colonialism, historiography, and civic culture all became means of spreading the republican gospel. Their opponents, however, riled by republican corruption, launched an equally impassioned counterattack.

These competing visions of the Republic, and indeed of France, found expression in the figure of a woman, Marianne. One wonders if the female allegory was the only one capable of inspiring such a range of powerful emotions, from passionate hatred to filial love to erotic attachment. Marianne still reflects French collective psychology, but as the Republic is now an object of almost universal consensus in France, the range of representations of this figure has grown more limited. Extreme right-wing publications today still feature unflattering visions of Marianne which recall their late nineteenth-century predecessors. Yet the dominant contemporary image of Marianne, as in 1789, reveals a pretty young woman in a Phrygian bonnet and a provocative décolleté.

ILLUSTRATIONS

1. Nanine Vallain, *Liberté* (decoration for the meeting hall of the Club des Jacobins (Agulhon, 17).

2. Gros, *Figure allégorique de la République* (Garrigues, 43).

3. First seal of the Republic (Agulhon, 19).

4. Eugène Delacroix, *Liberté guidant le peuple* (1831) (Garrigues, 52-53).

5. Second seal of the Republic (Agulhon, 90).

6. Honoré Daumier, *La République française* (1848) (Garrigues, 65).

7. "La dernière étape?" (Lithograph, 1871) (Garrigues, 74).

8. Alfred Le Petit, "Les deux Républiques," *Le Grelot* January 1, 1872 (Garrigues, 75).

9. Clésinger, *La République* (Paris World's Fair, 1878) (Agulhon, 175).

10. Poster-calendar by Republican propagandists (1880).

11. Poster for inauguration of Dalou's statue of the Republic, Place de la Nation, Paris, for the 1889 centenary.

12-17. Gyp/Bob, "Histoiré de la Troisième République," *Le Rire*, November 14, 1896.

18. Delannoy, "Les petits noëls de Marianne," *L'assiette au beurre*, December 24, 1904 (Garrigues, 110).

19. Jean Veber, *L'Assiette au beurre*, n.d. (Trouillas, 238).

20. Jean Veber, "L'effroi," 1904 (Fuchs, *Die Frau in der Karikatur*, 37).

21. J. Blass, "Nana as Marianne," *Le Triboulet*, February 6, 1881 (Grand-Carteret, 120).

22. "Choisis . . . tu es libre . . . ," *L'assiette au beurre*, March 19 1904 (Garrigues, 110).

23. Pepin, "La République narguant Boulanger," *Le Grelot*, July 1, 1888 (Trouillas, 235).

24. Alfred Willette, "Marianne et l'ours du nord," 1892 (Fuchs, *Die Karikatur des europaischen Volker*, 360).

25. "Marianne la youpine," in *Les mémoires de l'Europe* (1972)

(Trouillas, 234).

26. Alfred Willette, caricature of the Republic (Fuchs, *Die Karikatur des europaischen Volker*, 359).

NOTES

1. Maurice Agulhon, *Marianne into Battle: Republican Imagery and Symbolism in France 1789—1880*, trans. Janet Lloyd (Cambridge, Eng., 1981), 11-14.

2. Maurice Agulhon's recent study and pendant to his first volume, *Marianne au pouvoir: L'imagerie et la symbolique républicaines de 1880 à 1914* (Paris: Flammarion, 1989), reveals new information about the origins of "Marianne." According to Agulhon, the first reference to Marianne (in this case, the symbol of the revolutionary *patrie* and not necessarily of the Republic) was in a patriotic Occitan song written in late 1792, called "La Garisou de Marianno" ("The Healing of Marianne"). Marianne was a popular girl's name at the time of the song's writing. Agulhon, *Marianne au pouvoir*, 11-14.

3. Auguste Barbier, "La curée," quoted in Agulhon, *Marianne into Battle*, 40. All translations except that of note 4 are the author's.

4. Agulhon, *Marianne into Battle*, 62.

5. Louis Janot, "Liberté," quoted in Agulhon, *Marianne into Battle*, 56.

6. Paul Verlaine, "A Bust for the Town Halls," quoted in Agulhon, *Marianne into Battle*, 179.

7. This is a reference to the sale of military decorations by Daniel Wilson, son-in-law of President Jules Grévy, who was forced to resign due to the scandal.

8. Maurice Agulhon has noted two types of doublings in late-nineteenth-century depictions of Marianne: the opposition between the "two Republics," one bourgeois and conservative, the other working-class and revolutionary (as seen in Le Petit's caricature), and the opposition between the French regime and the French nation, the *pays légal v.* the *pays réel* (as seen in Bob's drawings). The firm rooting of the republican regime, writes Agulhon, "could not help but influence the representation of France." Agulhon, *Marianne au pouvoir*, 285.

REFERENCES

Agulhon, Maurice. *Marianne au pouvoir: L'imagerie et la symbolique
      républicaines de 1880 à 1914*. Paris: Flammarion, 1989.
_____. *Marianne into Battle: Republican Imagery and Symbo-
      lism in France 1789—1880*.   Trans. Janet Lloyd.   Cambridge:
      Cambridge University Press, 1981.
Birnbaum, Pierre. *Un myth politique - la "République juive:" de Léon Blum
      à Pierre Mendès France*. Paris: Fayard, 1988.
Cate, Phillip Denis. "The Paris Cry: Graphic Artists and the Dreyfus Affair."
      In Norman L. Kleeblatt (ed.), *The Dreyfus Affair: Art, Truth, and
      Justice*. Berkeley: University of California Press, 1987.
Fuchs, Eduard. *Die Frau in der Karikatur*. Munich: A. Langen, 1907.
_____. *Die Karikatur des europaischen Volker*. Munich: A.
      Langen, [1921].
Garrigues, Jean (ed.). *Images de la Révolution: L'imagerie répblicaine de
      1789 à nos jours*. Paris: Editions du May, 1988.
Lethève, Jacques. *La caricature sous la IIIe République*. Paris: Armand
      Colin, 1986.
Trouillas, Paul. *Le complexe de Marianne*. Paris: Seuil, 1988.

27

The Lost Legacy of the French Revolution and the Persecution of French Jewry in Vichy France

Sondra M. Rubenstein

The French Revolution had a profound effect on France's forty thousand Jews. It resulted in their legal emancipation and soon enabled them to claim that they had become the most successfully assimilated and most stable Jewish community in Western Europe.[1] They became linguistically and culturally French. By all appearances they were French, fully integrated and rooted in French tradition. Yet, while individual French Jews gained acceptance and recognition for their accomplishments, an underlying, dormant prejudice remained, an ugly undercurrent of anti-Semitism that surfaced from time to time. Native French Jews, traditionally silent, politically neutral, and non-protesting, tended to disassociate themselves from the periodic anti-Semitic outbursts. They clung to their belief that the attacks were not directed against "French" Jews but only against those "foreign" Jews whose blatant refusal to assimilate had resulted in their merely calling attention to themselves and to their "differences" with French society.

Even with the Nazi invasion of France in May 1940, most native Jews held fast to the myth that their French citizenship and their "Frenchness" would protect them. They had long ago failed to recognize the danger signs and to rally to the call of their co-religionists. Now, they too would fall victim to Vichy-supported, and often instigated, Nazi persecution. With the fall of the Third Republic and the institutionalization of anti-Semitic laws by the Vichy government in the autumn of 1940, French Jewry was brought to the brutal realization: They, too, were collectively Jews and as disposable as the immigrant Jews many of them despised.

This chapter briefly traces the history of the Revolution's "legacy" to French Jewry: emancipation. Then, with references to Marcel Ophuls' *The Sorrow and the Pity*, the chapter focuses on the destruction of that long-held legacy.

A Mixed Legacy

Prerevolutionary French anti-Semitism was part of a general Western tradition fed, in part, by Christian denunciation of "the perfidious Jews." Considered forever alien to Christian tradition, Europe's Jewry was forbidden by law to move about freely or own land in most societies. They generally adjusted to the hostile climate by undertaking tasks deemed necessary but reprehensible (such as money-lending) and by reinforcing and cultivating their separateness.   From a Christian theological perspective, their debased existence served as a reminder that they had chosen to reject the true faith.

Jews settled in France as far back as two thousand years ago. A Paris City Ordinance of 614 C.E. barring Jews from public office was the first recorded official anti-Semitic act.   During the twelfth and thirteenth centuries, French crusaders journeying to the Holy Land to rid it of infidels, frequently attacked and massacred Jews along the way. King Louis IX, later canonized by the Church, convened a council of scholars and churchmen in 1240 to "confound Judaism for ever."[2]

During the eighteenth century, secularization brought many Jews into mainstream European society, but it was the French Revolution that *theoretically* made the Jews part of the European family.   Yet, full legal emancipation for Jews in France was not guaranteed in August 1789 by the National Assembly's adoption of the Declaration of the Rights of Man. Although "community" as a legal entity was abolished, French Jews had to continue to pay "community debts" and were forced to struggle separately (i.e., individually) for their full legal and social rights. With its statutes of 1790 and 1791, however, France did lead the way as the first European society to emancipate its Jews "legally."

Still, there were many interruptions on the road to full emancipation, and it would be incorrect to believe that from the French Revolution to the fall of 1940, every Jewish resident was a full-fledged citizen--both legally and socially--of the French Republic. Legal emancipation exacted a high price, in that Jews, emancipated as individuals and not as a "people," were expected to give up any concept of Jewish national identity they may have held.   The Revolution's solution to the Jewish question was, of course, merely part of an attempt to resolve larger social questions dealing with the unification and cohesion of French society. Because the French Revolution established a political and social order that did not recognize national, cultural, or linguistic pluralism, the Republic sought to solve its "Jewish question" by narrowly redefining Judaism as a religion, similar to Catholicism or Protestantism.

Also disturbed by the staying power of Jewish particularism and the internal cohesiveness of French Jewry, Napoleon I became determined to integrate Jews into French life. By his "Infamous Decree" of 1808, he established his version of the "Sanhedrin," which was the Rabbinic governing court of ancient Israel. Napoleon's decree was an attempt to undermine traditional Jewish community structures. In many ways, he was assisted by

Jewish leaders who aspired to full integration. These leaders turned to the French Protestant Consistorial Administration as their model and accepted Napoleon's design for a similar hierarchical structure for the Jews. As part of the Ministry of Interior, the Central Consistory (Consistoire Central des Israélites de France) and its regional consistories supervised ritual and religious affairs and the appointment of rabbis. Most importantly, it was entrusted with the task of educating Jews to be loyal French citizens, to introduce the true "French Spirit" into their lives, thereby blurring those elements that set them apart from their fellow non-Jews. From time to time, small groups of Jews were offended by the decidedly French orientation of the Consistory's approach to Jewish interests and affairs, but by and large it reflected the consensus of the community.

As French revolutionary influence spread, Jews within Western and Central Europe were granted more rights, but statutory intervention did not eliminate the centuries-old prejudice. Rather, such prejudices took new forms during the nineteenth century as inventive theorists provided new secular justifications for denying the newly acquired rights; ancient notions of Jewish perfidy were kept alive by writers and artisans as well as by ignorant peasants.

In contrast to the significant progress Jews made in Protestant Holland and Catholic Italy where emancipation proceeded smoothly, in agrarian Central and Eastern Europe, in Tsarist Russia, in Protestant Germany, and in German-speaking areas (for instance, in Alsace), Jewish life was plagued by violent and brutal pogroms, such as occurred during the revolutions of 1848. These anti-Semitic outbursts were part of radical protests against the French Revolution's legacy of liberalism, rationalism, bourgeois society, and emancipation.

Within France, Christian groups, believing they were fighting for the "soul" of France, tried to restore the primacy of religion and to nullify the principles of the French Revolution which conflicted with their beliefs. They called for a reappraisal of Jewish rights, demanding that Jews abandon their particularistic character and rituals. Socialists, even before the Revolution of 1848, pointed to the Rothschild family as parasites who had built a fortune by turning workers into "slaves." French Jewry was therefore guilty of promoting capitalism and exploitation.

These renewed expressions of anti-Semitism led most Jews in France, guided by their Central Consistory, to follow a policy of silence and political neutrality. They believed that Jews could prove themselves an integral part of France by accepting French ways rather than by opposing this new anti-Semitism. "Even the Alliance Israélite universelle, established in 1860 in part as a response to anti-Semitism in Europe, saw as its main task the improvement of the civic status of Jews in North Africa and the Levant and refrained from countering anti-Semitism in France proper."[3]

New laws in the latter part of the century prohibited trade unionism. There was, in many respects, no tolerance for the individual's right to organize on a social basis. This can be seen as a reaction to the influx of

Alsatian and East European Jews, who were fleeing pogroms during the early 1880s. They and later immigrants brought with them labor movement ideologies that had been acquired through involvement with the Jewish labor movement, which had its origins in Eastern Europe during this period.[4] Immigrant, working-class Jews tended to settle in Paris. They often became involved in trade unionism, demanding workers' rights as part of the civic rights French Jews had gained through the Revolution. For them, the French Revolution represented merely a first phase, an incomplete revolution.

There were continued attacks from the political extremes of the left and the right against European liberalism which had permitted the rise of Jewish political, social and economic consciousness. In France as in Germany, racism permeated the thinking of the common man. Somehow, it was said, lower racial elements had infiltrated their society and were subverting it. Among the inferior groups were the Jews who had been set free and encouraged by the Revolution. Social failures, including economic insecurity and the debasement of worthwhile values, were blamed on the bankruptcy of revolutionary liberalism. Because it appeared that the Jews had benefited so much from the Revolution, it followed that they were seen as its principal supporters and were therefore held responsible for its major failures.

In 1881 Justice Minister Paul Marchandeau sponsored a press law outlawing press attacks directed against "a group of persons who belong by origin to a particular race or religion when it is intended to arouse hatred among citizens or residents."[5] This "Marchandeau Law" would be repealed by the Vichy government, as part of the dismantling of the Revolution's legacy to French Jewry.

By the mid-1880s, Paris was "the spiritual capital of the European right," which preached anti-Semitism.[6] Although Edouard Drumont's *La France Juive* (1886) viciously attacked Jews on racial grounds, journalist Henri Rochefort and, particularly nationalist writer Maurice Barrès, were more "subtle." They recognized the political potential of anti-Semitism to unite the masses in order to create a national ethos. Barrès realized that two major conflicting factions could be brought together by emphasizing bourgeois concern over the social ruin of France and by supporting the virtues, concerns, and interests of the working class. Thus, French politicians found anti-Semitism a useful tool for attracting votes from the newly enfranchised. A hundred years after the emancipation, one-third of the French Chamber of Deputies demanded that the Jews be deprived of their civil rights, and many anti-republican political cartoons caricatured Marianne, symbol of the French Revolution, in a blatantly anti-Semitic manner (see Chapter 26).

The anti-Semitic attacks that characterized the Dreyfus Affair in the last year of the nineteenth century provided damning explanations for the French defeat in the Franco-Prussian War (1870—1871) and the deterioration of life in French society, including the debilitating economic stagnation. The arrival of Alsatian and Eastern European Jews, though their numbers were small, caused consternation. The Jewish conquest of France became the theme of these attacks, spread by the bulk of France's popular newspapers. Charles

Maurras, among the most enduring, articulate, anti-Semitic, antidemocratic, antiparliamentary forces in France, attacked Dreyfus and the Third Republic which had permitted Jews to rise to positions of power. Maurras believed that it was "Jewish" values that had been imposed on the French nation and perpetuated by the Republicans. He would later write: "The ancestors of the Revolution spring from the Jewish spirit."[7]

Captain Alfred Dreyfus, convicted of espionage in 1894, spent years in the Devil's Island penal colony. Throughout his long ordeal, French Jewish leaders hesitated to get involved in his defense. Viewed through the looking glass of emancipation, Dreyfus was seen as an individual Jew being tried for treason. The Jewish community, they felt, was uninvolved. The Consistory approach was thereby preserved. Dreyfus was finally vindicated years later when a group of anti-Semitic fellow officers confessed to staging the frameup. Ignoring the ugly anti-Jewish atmosphere that surrounded the entire Dreyfus Affair, French Jewry viewed the captain's vindication as proof that the revolutionary spirit of emancipation endured.

At the close of the century, French Jewry numbered about eighty thousand. This excluded those Jews in the Alsace-Lorraine province, which was then under German control as a result of the Franco-Prussian War. Approximately two-thirds of France's Jews resided in Paris. The first wave of immigrants from Eastern Europe prior to 1900 brought some eight thousand Jews.[8] They mostly tended to settle in specific Parisian districts, maintaining their traditional religious life-style and Yiddish-speaking culture. It was during this period, in 1898, that Charles Maurras founded *Action Française*, an anti-republican organization that, more than any other group, served as an inspiration for the extreme right. Ten years later he founded a daily newspaper, the organ of *Action Française*, and used it to spread the poison of anti-Semitism.

The growing workers' movement continued to attract many Jewish immigrants and encouraged them to strike for better conditions, even against Jewish employers. These activities alienated the Jewish immigrant community from the established French Jewry. Baron Edmond de Rothschild, speaking on May 25, 1913, at the Paris Consistory's General Assembly, bemoaned the behavior of the immigrants: "These new arrivals do not understand French customs. . . . [T]hey remain among themselves, retain their primitive language, speak and write in jargon."[9] Writing in *Der Nayer zhournal* on October 31, 1913, Nathan Frank, an immigrant journalist, explained the lack of understanding between the two Jewish communities: "We consider them to be fools, and they consider us to lack honor."[10]

The First World War and the spirit of the common front (*union sacrée*) brought the two Jewish communities closer. By that time, 40 percent of the Jews in France had come from Eastern Europe:[11]

The widespread participation of immigrant Jews in the war effort was positively viewed by native leaders and mitigated their former antagonism. Emerging from the war with a strengthened feeling of national pride, native leaders were now more willing to help draw the immigrants closer to France and into the ambience of native

Jewish life.[12]

    The temporary brotherhood of the common front also seemed to draw off the energy of many on the far right and cause them to temporarily rechannel their anti-Jewish hostilities: "Even Maurice Barrès, the sharpest tongue of the far right, had mellowed to the point of admitting that Jews were one of the 'spiritual families' of France."

    In the following decade, as the United States and England closed their doors to refugees fleeing the effects of the Russian Revolution and the civil war that followed, France became the promised land. Among the millions of refugees and immigrants flocking to France were tens of thousands of Jews from Russia, Poland, Lithuania, and Romania. Many, though not all, chose to settle. They, too, brought with them ideological baggage consisting of anarchistic and Bundist (labor movement) tendencies. Many were also Zionists who still hoped to settle in Palestine, despite the change in British policy limiting immigration.

    This second wave of immigrants followed the pattern of the first wave, settling in distinct areas, joining radical workers' movements and pursuing their own Yiddish-based culture. Again, French Jewry perceived immigration as a threat. Despite their attempts to integrate the immigrants, they met with little success. Their anger and frustration stemmed from their inability to accept Jews who lived by any other ethos than the one which they, and the non-Jews in France, had more or less accepted as part of "Jewish behavior" since the emancipation at the time of the Revolution.

    During the 1920s occasional anti-Semitic incidents flared up in France, such as the publication in 1924 of the *Protocols of the Elders of Zion*, which purported to prove the existence of a Jewish conspiracy to dominate the world. Again, the native Jewish community directed its criticisms not at the anti-Semites, but at the immigrants. In 1925 Jules Meyer, a prominent Jewish leader, warned: "The walls of Paris must no longer be covered with Hebrew characters. Paris must cease being flooded with Yiddish newspapers, books, films, and plays."[14]

    But a year later, Pope Pius XI put the blame where it belonged. He condemned *Action Française*; and in 1928, he condemned anti-Semitism, influencing parish priests to cancel their subscriptions to the Maurras journal. Still, anti-Semitism lay dormant, seeming to follow the ups and downs of the French economy and governmental instability. By the late 1920s the French economy had stabilized, unemployment had decreased, and France's international position seemed secure.

    In 1931, the French began to feel the effects of the United States financial collapse. The downturn in the economy soon led to renewed political instability and to a rejuvenation of anti-Semitism. For example, when a play about the Dreyfus Affair opened that year, some right-wing toughs disturbed the first performance. Economic conditions turned nastier the following year when French industrial production fell 27 percent. Official figures downplayed unemployment with a published figure of over 250,000, which "officially" grew to 400,000 by the end of 1934.[15] Italian and Polish workers, originally recruited by French government agencies (anxious to replace war losses amounting to 1.4 million young men), were soon leaving. Although France was affected by the Depression somewhat later than other countries, it continued to feel the effects longer. By 1936, approximately 500,000 of the 3 million or so foreign workers included in government figures for 1931 had returned to their native lands.[16]

The influx of refugees from Eastern and Central Europe, mentioned earlier, soon offset this decline and served to arouse traditional French xenophobia among native Jews, as well as among non-Jews. By the mid-1930s, the immigrant Jewish population was demanding reasonable representation within Jewish institutions run by the now greatly outnumbered native Jews. Antagonism between the two groups increased as the leaders, hoping to speed integration into French society, pressured the immigrants to limit their political and cultural activities while continuing to ignore their needs and demands. Again, the immigrant journalist Nathan Frank, after some twenty years' experience with native Jewry and now writing for *Parizer haynt*, tried to explain their differences:

Even while adapting we remain ourselves, and it is precisely that which troubles [them]. . . . We want to adapt in a manner in which that adaptation will harm neither our national interests nor our cultural aspirations. We know that that is possible. But the leaders of French Judaism want to assimilate us while leaving us only a bit of Jewish religion.[17]

History seemed to repeat itself in May 1935 when the Paris Consistory's president, Baron Robert de Rothschild, Edmond Rothschild's nephew, made a provocative speech intended to warn the immigrants. He said that their political activity had resulted in increased anti-Semitism and that if they did not learn how to behave and to limit their unbridled criticism of the French government, perhaps they should leave France.[18]

One estimate places the number of refugees in France by the summer of 1938 at 180,000. By that time, France, with its 515 immigrants for every 100,000 inhabitants (compared to the United States, with its 42 per 100,000), had become the major country for immigration.[19] The refugee presence and its economic and cultural implications became a major public question, with most attention focused on Jewish refugees, whose numbers tended to be exaggerated. Citing French census figures for foreign residents in France, Paula Hyman states: "The 175,000-200,000 Jewish newcomers in the years 1906 to 1939 were a small fraction--15 percent--of the total number of immigrants who flocked to France. . . . [Those years] witnessed the immigration of some 990,000 foreigners, primarily Italians, Poles and Spaniards."[20]

As a point of fact, from 1933 to 1945 France admitted approximately 55,000 Jews of all nationalities. Compare this to the presence of over 720,000 Italians living in France in 1936, of whom many thousands had recently fled Mussolini's fascist regime, settling in southern France.[21]

Whereas the Jews had previously been condemned primarily as capitalist exploiters, they were now feared as competitors for scarce jobs and as disseminators of an inferior mass culture. There was talk of the Yiddish sound of radio, Jewish control of the movie industry, the prevalence of kinky hair and curved noses and so on. Typically, and reminiscent of the wave of anti-Semitism at the turn of the century, Jews were blamed for all the ills and instability of parliamentarianism, liberal democracy, capitalism, and life in France at that time.

Amid these circumstances in June 1936, Léon Blum became the first Jewish prime minister of France and the voice of the Jewish refugees. As his undersecretary of state for finance, he chose Pierre Mendès-France, a Jew who would later be wrongly accused of desertion, tried, and sentenced to six years in prison. Yet, in *The Sorrow and the Pity*, Pierre Mendès-France[22] tells his story not with bitterness, but with sorrow.[23] Blum's election unleashed a torrent of anti-Semitic opposition to his Popular Front government. Responding to the silence of the native Jews, he remarked in 1937:

The rich Jews, the Jews of the middle bourgeoisie, the Jewish functionaries feared the struggle undertaken for Dreyfus exactly as they fear today the struggle undertaken against facism. . . . They imagined that the anti-Semitic passion would be turned aside by their cowardly neutrality. . . . They understood no better [then] than they understand today that no precaution . . . would delude the adversary and that they remained the victims offered to triumphant anti-Dreyfusism or fascism.[24]

The outbreak of the Spanish Civil War in July 1936 led to an influx of pro-Republican refugees and raised additional concerns that France could become embroiled in an international conflict. Initially, it seemed that the Blum government would aid the Spanish Republic; but once the British had chosen a position of neutrality, Blum hesitated to go it alone. Without the Radical-Socialists and the right wing of his own Socialist party--neither of whom supported such aid--Blum knew he would lose his majority in Parliament. He therefore feared the collapse of his own government. Thus, France made its decision to stand idly by, while Franco's Nazi-and fascist-backed forces triumphed.

In June 1937, Blum stepped down, and the Popular Front government began its process of dissolution. A new wave of refugees came to France in March 1938 as a result of Hitler's Anschluss with Austria. Blum's short-lived comeback as prime minister from March 13 to April 8 focused government attention on the "Jewish question." He was followed by his former defense minister and nemesis Edouard Daladier who, within weeks of taking office, gave the border-control officials authority to refuse entry to refugees and instituted resettlement, internment, and repatriation as ways of resolving the growing immigrant problem.

In September and October 1938 there were street demonstrations and attacks against Jews in Paris and elsewhere in France. Unlike the native Jews, the immigrant Jews reacted to the rise in anti-Semitism by staging mass demonstrations and protest meetings and by organizing self-defense groups against anti-Semitic gangs in Jewish neighborhoods. They had learned their lessons in the pogroms common in their native lands.

On the other hand, the rise in anti-Semitic outbursts led the grand rabbi of Paris to fall back on the traditional French Jewish way of dealing with anti-Semitism--silence in public. Privately, he issued warnings to the congregants not to appear in groups outside their synagogues, as this might be seen as a provocation. The native Jews did not recognize the changing nature of the anti-Semitic attacks:

> Once it was accepted that Jews were a "problem," the way was open for other elements of the anti-semitic world view to slip quietly into the consciousness of moderates. It is striking how widely fragments of the anti-semitic position permeated moderate political vocabulary after the mid-1930s. Anti-Jewish expressions acquired new kinds of legitimacy. The old taboos against anti-Jewish language, widespread since the vindication of Dreyfus, were clearly softening.[25]

By the late 1930s modest proposals, couched in Republican or liberal language and aimed at curbing foreigners, were set forth. For instance, in July 1938, the Confederation of French Medical Associations called for the use and enforcement of quotas established earlier to exclude foreigners from practicing medicine, and suggested that "any pretext whatsoever" be used to justify their exclusion.[26] This was a precursor to what would happen under the Vichy regime. In *The Sorrow and the Pity*, Dr. Claude Lévy, active in the "Franc-Tireur" group within the Resistance movement, states that of the 137 denunciations by Frenchmen later discovered in the files of the Vichy Office for Jewish Affairs, half of them were doctors denouncing other doctors because of the competition. Businessmen also feared the refugees, and in 1938, the Paris Chambers of Commerce began to study ways of limiting their participation in business.

Anti-Semitic forces in France reacted to Hitler's brutal Kristallnacht, November 8-9, 1938, with anti-Semitic attacks of their own, accusing Léon Blum of having launched a "Jewish revolution" that would inevitably involve France in a war of revenge against the Germans. That November, the French communists, in an attempt to weaken the Daladier government, called a general strike. The Socialists refused to participate, the government promptly suppressed the demonstration, and the major result of the strike was to reveal the vulnerability of the French left. Hitler's invasion of Czechoslovakia in March 1939 sent more frantic Jews fleeing to France.

We turn now to an examination of Marcel Ophuls' *The Sorrow and the Pity*, a chronicle of the collapse of the Third Republic, the Nazi occupation of France and, I believe, the total debasement of what remained of the French Revolution's legacy of "liberté, égalité, fraternité."

The Legacy Destroyed

The Sorrow and the Pity, directed by Marcel Ophuls, examines the behavior of Frenchmen during the darkest hour of their nation's history. France was divided into two zones, one occupied by the Germans and the other, initially a "free" zone, controlled by the French leaders based in Vichy. It should be noted that Marshal Philippe Pétain, head of Vichy France, and his supporters used the language and symbols of the French Revolution to attract mass support. For its part, the extreme right sought to undermine and destroy the very essence of the Revolution's legacy, which had included legal emancipation and full citizenship for French Jews.

The film gives us an understanding that, while the Vichy government claimed to protect France and its rich culture, the leaders made moral choices regarding the life and death struggle of segments of its population. These were decisions and choices, Ophuls believes, that no government should be willing to make. His film depicts the ways in which the Vichy government crossed the line separating compliance from collaboration, showing how it willingly subordinated and directed its police, judicial apparatus and penal system and controlled the media to comply with German ideological and political aims.[27] Ophuls denounces Vichy complicity in anti-Semitic acts and the government's willingness to decide which hostages were to be shot and which Jews were to be turned over to the Germans. Communists were selected to be shot, while foreign Jews were handed over to the Germans for deportation to concentration camps. The film also dispels a number of long-held myths about wartime France and exposes the divisions and disunity that existed among Frenchmen, even within the Resistance movement itself. In part, it does so by juxtaposing scenes from the Vichy era with contemporary interviews of past participants: German, French and British.

Marcel Ophuls was a child when he and his parents fled Nazi Germany and settled in France. Max Ophüls, the famous film director of *Liebelei, la Ronde*, and *Lola Montes*, was Marcel's father. They became French citizens, and Max served in the French Army when the war began. In 1941, not long after the Vichy government issued its discriminatory laws against Jews in various professions and launched its anti-Semitic campaign against naturalized Jewish refugees, the family went to the United States. In 1950, they returned to France where Max Ophüls successfully pursued his film career, and Marcel also became a film director.

It should be noted that *The Sorrow and the Pity* was made for Swiss and West German television companies. While it was seen in many other countries, as far as I know, the film was first shown on French television only in the late 1980s. Until then ORTF, the French state monopoly, had refused to show *The Sorrow and the Pity*. As a result, it was first released as a movie, reaching hundreds of thousands of Frenchmen when, instead, it could have reached millions of home television viewers.

Considering how pro-Resistance and anti-Vichy the film is, the question arises as to why Ophuls was, for so long, denied access to the French television audience. Two reasons come to mind: the political climate at the time the film was released and the desire of those in power to perpetuate the myth of mass support for the French Resistance.

With regard to the first reason, one year before the film was made, in May 1968, France was racked by a massive student rebellion. Tens of thousands of students, joined by thousands of workers, demonstrated their loss of confidence in the policies of the French government.[28] Ophuls and his associates participated in a crippling strike of ORTF's employees. They were opposed to government control, particularly regarding interference in the production of news programs and the coverage of the demonstrations. When the strike ended, Ophuls and his associates were dismissed. Subsequent liberalization in the post-Gaullist period did not change the attitude of ORTF's politically sensitive management toward the Ophuls group, who were still viewed as troublemakers.

On the second reason pertaining to the myth of massive support for the French Resistance;[29] in the film, the message comes through clearly that the Resistance movement was sadly divided and that some French people viewed Resistance fighters as "traitors."

Emile Coulaudon, formerly called Colonel Gaspar while serving as the head of the Auvergne maquis group of the Resistance, states:

The thing which amazes me most when I talk to people who I know very well supported Pétain is . . . they all tell me how they did their share for the Resistance. . . . Sometimes it's quite incredible: "Well if you only knew, Monsieur Gaspar, if I told you what I did. . . ." And so I say: out with it, come on, tell me, tell me all about it. . . . So I have to listen to these fairy tales without wincing. Sometimes they've got tears in their eyes when they tell you: "See this drawer here?"

And then he calls his wife out: "Come here, is it true or isn't it that I kept a gun right here?" And his wife says: "Oh yes, it used to frighten me a lot you know. But as my husband used to say: 'It'll be there when they come, when they come we'll do what has to be done.'" Only they never did what had to be done.[30]

We now turn to the work of Marcel Ophuls, in order to explore with him the tragedy of Jewish life in Vichy France.

The Film Presentation

The first film clip from *The Sorrow and the Pity* contained parts of French newsreels, comments about Vichy anti-Semitism, the propaganda effort directed against Jews, and excerpts from *The Jew Süss*, one of the most blatantly anti-Semitic films made during that period. Mendès-France then comments on the "poisonous arguments" of the Vichy government:

The very excess of propaganda, and the fact that the government's policy led blatantly to collaboration with the enemy, gradually opened people's eyes. But that propaganda still did some damage, since you know as well as I do that anti-semitism and Anglophobia are two things that can always be easily revived in France. Even if such impulses are momentarily dim or dormant, it only takes an event, an incident, an international circumstance, a Dreyfus affair or whatever, to bring them to life again, to suddenly bring springing back things you thought were dead but which were in fact merely inactive.

A French newsreel shows the home of Edouard Drumont, considered to be the first man in France to discuss the "Jewish problem." Monsieur Laville, representing the Institute for Jewish Affairs, comments that

Ninety percent of those Frenchmen of old French stock are true white men, free of any racial mixture. This is not true of Jews. The Jew is the product of the cross-breeding between Aryans, Mongols, and Negroes which took place milleniums ago. The Jew has therefore a face, a body, attitudes and gestures which are peculiar to him [caricatures are displayed]. It is encouraging to see that the public is keenly interested in the study of their characteristics which are presented in the morphological section of the exhibition, "The Jew and France."

In the courtyard of the Lycée Pascal in Clermont, two retired teachers are asked whether there were any Jewish teachers in their school. When they explain that there had been one who was dismissed, they are asked, "Ultimately you could have offered a collective resignation from the Lycée, couldn't you?" With an uncomfortable laugh, one responds that it was out of the question. "You don't have any understanding of teachers . . . collective resignation, come on!"

There follows a scene in a Clermont shop with shopkeeper Marius Klein who had placed an ad in *Le Moniteur* when the anti-Jewish laws first appeared. The shopkeeper tries to explain that his name, Klein, sounds Jewish, but that he is a Catholic and that he was worried. People, he said, bothered him about it, and he told them that he had four brothers who were veterans and that "for goodness sake, I was a Frenchman!" When the narrator comments that a great many Jews also had brothers killed during the First World War, Klein protests that he had never been a racist and that "When a man has done his duty, I consider him to be Frenchman like me, like all the others."

A French newsreel discusses past Jewish domination of the French cinema, and Mendès-France talks about films made during the Occupation. He explains that "films of the period were not presented as German-made films . . . but . . . were presented by French authorities as French-made." About the film, *The Jew Süss*, Mendès-France notes that this particular film created a good deal of revulsion even on the part of those who did not support the Resistance and who had become accustomed to seeing German-produced propaganda films.

We see an eighteenth-century Würtemberg courtroom where the fate of Süss, the Jew, is sealed: "If ever a Jew should commit an act of the flesh with a Christian woman, then he shall be publicly hanged from the town gallows . . . so that his death be a warning to others." A groveling Süss is then hanged at the gallows. The scene closes with the judge reading a proclamation banishing all Jews, "this accursed race," from the entire country.

In the final film clip, we meet three interesting men. The first, Helmut Tausend, was a Wehrmacht captain stationed in Clermont-Ferrand from 1942 to 1944. Proudly wearing the medals awarded him by the Third Reich, Tausend was interviewed on the occasion of his daughter's wedding. The second,

Comte René de Chambrun, is the son-in-law of Pierre Laval, and the third, Dr. Claude Lévy, is a writer and biologist once active in the "Franc-Tireur" group within the Resistance movement. The only thing the three have in common is that they were all there at the same time.

Asked whether he had seen or heard mention of persecutions, Tausend claims that he neither saw nor heard about such things. When asked how that was possible, "You don't deny that persecution of Jews--die Juden in German--took place?" Tausend asks, "You mean jugend, "young people," or Juden, "the Jews"? "Die Juden. Jews," the interviewer responds. Tausend: "Well, as far as Jews were concerned, we really could not know to what extent they had been able to infiltrate the partisan resistance groups. In any case it wasn't up to us, the army, to deal with the Jews."

In another scene, Comte René De Chambrun, son-in-law of Pierre Laval, claims that

In all countries occupied by Germany, except for France, the number of Jews arrested and deported--the number of Jews who never came back--is terrifying. In 1946 only 5.8 percent had survived. But if you take the statistics for French Jews alone, a statistic which no one disputes, it shows that only 5 percent *did not* come back.

The narrator, interrupting, states that he is familiar with that statistic and that it refers only to those French Jews who had not been denaturalized:

It so happens that, of those Jews without citizenship--that is, foreign Jews, or Jews whose citizenship had been stripped away by the Vichy government--that indeed only 5 percent came back: in effect, the same percentage as in other countries. So let me ask you this question: does a statesman, even one who is trying to salvage for better or worse as well as he can, does any statesman have the right to choose in this way between two groups of human beings?

De Chambrun: The situation is a tragic and dramatic one where one has to save the greatest number of human lives possible.

Finally, we meet Dr. Claude Lévy who had considered himself a secular Jew. He tells of his feelings of rejection by his "national community" which he had come to love through his reading of French history. With his sense of rejection, however, came an interest in the Jewish people. In response to De Chambrun's claims, Dr. Lévy states:

[Q]uibbling over figures is . . . a way of trying to balance the accounts in an area where this kind of thing cannot be allowed. The fact that a French government agreed to surrender French nationals and even refugees who sought its protection-- thus denying the traditional right to asylum in France--proves that it was not a government worthy of being labelled French or worthy of what is loved about this country, about France. France collaborated. It is the only country in Europe which collaborated. Others signed armistices, capitulated in the field and so on, but France is the only country in Europe which had a government which collaborated, a government which introduced laws on the racist level that went even further than the Nüremberg Laws--French racial criteria were even more demanding than German racial criteria--so it's not a very pretty chapter of French history. Perhaps it is to be expected therefore that school books would present only the more glorious side of the story. But historically, it is certainly false.

Dr. Lévy talks about the roundup of children on July 16, 1942. The Parisian police were praised for their zeal when they went ahead on their own and arrested 4,051 children whose parents had earlier been sent to concentration camps located throughout France. The children--all under 16--were taken to the Vélodrome d'Hiver, "crying and dirtying their pants, posing serious problems to the social workers, who were mostly Quakers or Protestant women." He continues:

Since it hadn't been planned to deport these children at all--the Germans hadn't planned to anyway--and since the parents had already been deported to camps at Pithiviers and Beaune-la-Rolande, thus separating the children from their parents while a decision was patiently awaited . . . Rothke, who was Eichmann's representative in France, sent a telegram to Berlin to ask what should be done with these children. And while they were waiting, Laval is reputed to have said: "The children will have to be deported too," This is reported in a telegram by Danneker, who was a security officer in France . . . it's in the archives. The telegram is authenticated . . . by the conversation between Pastor Beugner and Laval. Pastor Beugner, who had gone to see Laval to plead for the children, reports: "When I spoke of the children, in particular of the possibility of having them evacuated, perhaps to America, Laval replied: "It does not matter, it is of no importance, I am carrying out the prophylaxis."

Asked whether any of the children came back, Lévy states that it is believed that none returned. He made inquiries and learned that the children had been shot on their arrival at the camp.

Conclusion

This chapter has dealt with one legacy of the French Revolution: Jewish emancipation. Although the Jewish community suffered a tragic reversal under the Vichy-Nazi regime, the surviving Jewish community in France reclaimed its legacy. Its members rebuilt their lives and helped to rebuild France.

In 1954, however, when the Israeli ambassador to France, Ya'akov Tzur, arrived in Paris, René Mayer, a Jewish member of the Radical party and a former prime minister, took him aside and said: "Make no mistake about it, though at present every Frenchman claims to have saved at least ten Jews during the . . . Resistance, there is an endemic phenomenon of antisemitism. In ten or twenty years time, when the occupation has been forgotten, it will surface again."[31]

On November 5, 1984, Zeev Sternhell, speaking in the home of the president of Israel, addressed a small group of distinguished guests on the subject of anti-Semitism in France. He identified French anti-Semitism as a recurring motif: "[A]ntisemitism is an integral component of that attempt to offer an overall alternative to the political culture that originated in the French Revolution. . . . No one doubts that French society is one and indivisible. Nobody harbors any doubts that it is a Christian society." But then he seemed to temper his remarks by adding: "The whole question is whether the ideo-logical struggle, the struggle for cultural hegemony, will be translated into political power. Certainly, that will occur only under conditions of grave national crisis, like the crises that swept Italy, Germany and France in the 1930s."[32]

I agree. I will add that while France is a liberal, open, and democratic society, the legacy of Jewish emancipation dating back to the French Revolu-tion remains fragile.

NOTES

1. Paula Hyman, *From Dreyfus to Vichy: The Remaking of French Jewry, 1906—1939* (New York: Columbia University Press, 1979), 3.

2. Harry Dunphy, "VIEW: In France, a Rebirth of Anti-Semitism," *The Daily News* (New York, October 12, 1980).

3. Richard I. Cohen, *The Burden of Conscience: French Jewry's Response to the Holocaust* (Indianapolis: Indiana University Press, 1987), 3-4.

4. Sondra M. Rubenstein, *The Communist Movement in Palestine and Israel, 1919—1984* (Boulder, Colo.: Westview Press, 1985), 7-19.

5. Michael R. Marrus and Robert O. Paxton, *Vichy France and the Jews* (New York: Schocken Books, 1983), 3.

6. Ibid., 29, citing Zeev Sternhell, *La Droite Révolutionnaire, 1885 —1914: The Origines Françaises du Fascisme* (Paris, 1978), 23-24.

7. S. McClelland (ed.), *The French Right from de Maistre to Maurras* (New York: Harper, 1970), 241, and see Alexander Werth, *France: 1940—1955* (New York: Henry Holt and Co. 1956), Chapter 4, "Maurras: The 'Pure' Doctrine of Vichy," which provides a description of a Maurras-Pétain conversation at a dinner party the marshal gave in honor of Maurras. The chapter includes a description of the statement Maurras, at age 78, made at his trial in January 1945, recounting a lifetime of frantic anti-republican and anti-Semitic activity.

8. Cohen, *The Burden of Conscience*, 4-5.

9. Hyman, *From Dreyfus to Vichy*, 118, citing the *Minutes of the General Assembly* of the Paris Consistory, May 25, 1913.

10. Ibid., 119.

11. Hyman states: "In the years 1881 — 1914, when 1,974,000 Jews arrived in the United States and some 120,000 in Great Britain, France attracted only an estimated 30,000." Ibid., 63-64.

12. Cohen, *The Burden of Conscience*, 5-6, and see Zeev Sternhell, *Antisemitism and the Right in France* (Jerusalem: Hebrew University, 1988).

13. Marrus and Paxton, *Vichy France*, 31.

14. Hyman, *From Dreyfus to Vichy*, 118.

15. Marrus and Paxton, *From Dreyfus to Vichy*, 34-37.

16. Ibid.

17. Hyman, *From Dreyfus to Vichy*, 119.

18. Cohen, *The Burden of Conscience*, 9.

19. Marrus and Paxton, *Vichy France*.

20. Hyman, *From Dreyfus to Vichy*, 68.

21. Marrus and Paxton, *Vichy France*, 36-37.

22. He would later serve as de Gaulle's secretary of finance and as prime minister from 1954 to 1955, successfully negotiating an end to French involvement in the war in Indochina.

23. See Jean Lacouture, *Pierre Mendès-France* (London: Holmes and Meier, 1984).

24. Hyman, From Dreyfus to Vichy, 227.

25. Marrus and Paxton, *Vichy France*, 49.

26. Ibid., 50.

27. For further discussion on France during the war years, see: Robert Aron, *The Vichy Regime: 1940— 1944* (Philadelphia: Dufour Editions, 1966); Bertram M. Gordon, *Collaborationism in France During the Second*

World War (Ithaca, N.Y.: Cornell University Press, 1980); Herbert R. Lottman, *Pétain-Hero or Traitor: The Untold Story* (New York: Wm. Morrow and Co. 1985); Paul Farmer, *Vichy: Political Dilemma* (New York: Columbia University Press, 1955); and Alexander Werth, *France: 1940—1955* (New York: Henry Holt and Co. 1956).

28. See Jean Jacques Servan-Schreiber, *The Spirit of May* (New York.: McGraw-Hill Book Co., 1969), for a description of the events of May 1968.

29. See Anny Latour, *The Jewish Resistance in France: 1940—1944* (New York: The Holocaust Library, 1970), for a discussion on the Jewish Resistance in France.

30. Marcel Ophuls, *The Sorrow and the Pity, a Film Script* (New York: Outerbridge and Lazard, 1972).

31. Sternhell, *Antisemitism*, 1988, 33.

32. Ibid., 42-43.

REFERENCES

American Jewish Committee, Anti-Semitism in France. *Background to a Report*. New York: AJC, Foreign Affairs Department.

Aron, Robert. *The Vichy Regime: 1940—1944*. Philadelphia: Dufour Editions, 1966.

Cohen, Richard I. *The Burden of Conscience: French Jewry's Response to the Holocaust*. Indianapolis: Indiana University Press, 1987.

Dunphy, Harry. "VIEW: In France, A Rebirth of anti-Semitism." *The Daily News*. New York City: October 12, 1980.

Farmer, Paul. *Vichy: Political Dilemma*. New York: Columbia University Press, 1955.

Gordon, Bertram M. *Collaborationism in France During the Second World War*. Ithaca, N.Y.: Cornell University Press, 1980.

Hoffman, Stanley. *Decline or Renewal? France Since the 1930s*. New York: Viking Press, 1974.

Hyman, Paula. *From Dreyfus to Vichy: The Remaking of French Jewry, 1906—1939*. New York: Columbia University Press, 1979.

Lacouture, Jean. *Pierre Mendès-France*. London: Holmes and Meier, 1984.

Latour, Anny. *The Jewish Resistance in France: 1940—1944*. New York: The Holocaust Library, 1970.

Lottman, Herbert R. *Pétain--Hero or Traitor: The Untold Story*. New York: William Morrow and Co., 1985.

Marrus, Michael R., and Robert O. Paxton. *Vichy France and the Jews*. New York: Schocken Books, 1983.

McClelland, S. (ed.). *The French Right from de Maistre to Maurras*. New York: Harper, 1970.

Ophuls, Marcel. *The Sorrow and the Pity, a Film Script*. New York: Outerbridge and Lazard, 1972.

Priaulx, Allan, and Sanford J. Ungar. *The Almost Revolution: France--1968*. New York: Dell Books, 1969.

Reader, Keith A. *Intellectuals and the Left in France Since 1968*. New York: St. Martin's Press, 1987.

Rubenstein, Sondra M. *The Communist Movement in Palestine and Israel, 1919—1984*. Boulder, Colo.: Westview Press, 1985.

Schnapp, Alain, and Pierre Vidal-Naquet. *The French Student Uprising--November 1967—June 1968: An Analytical Record*. Boston: Beacon Press, 1971.

Servan-Schreiber, Jean Jacques. *The Spirit of May*. New York: McGraw-Hill Book Co., 1969.

Sternhell, Zeev. *La Droite Révolutionnaire, 1885—1914: Les Origines Françaises du Fascisme*. Paris, 1978.

——————————. *Antisemitism and the Right in France*. Hebrew University of Jerusalem, 1988.

Tiersky, Ronald. *French Communism: 1920—1972* New York: Columbia University Press, 1974.

Touraine, Alain. *The May Movement: Revolt and Reform*. New York: Random House, 1971.

Werth, Alexander. *France: 1940—1955*. New York: Henry Holt and Co., 1956.

Index

About the Editors and Contributors

TOM CONNER, is Assistant Professor of French at St. Norbert College, and the author of a book on Chateaubriand, *Chateau-briand's Mémoires d'outre-tombe: A Portrait of the Artist in Exile*. He has also edited a book entitled *Dreams and Literature*, and written numerous reviews and articles in Swedish and French, as well as in English, on a broad range of contemporary cultural topics.

BARBARA T. COOPER, is Associate Professor of French at the University of New Hampshire where she served a six-year term as chair of the Department of French and Italian. She is the author of over two dozen articles on early nineteenth-century French theater, and the co-author of *Modernity and Revolution in Late Nineteenth Century France*.

MALCOLM CROOK, is a Senior Lecturer in History at Keele University in the United Kingdom where he has taught since 1972. He specializes in the French Revolution and has contributed a good deal on the subject, most notably *Journées révolutionnaires à Toulon* and *Toulon in War* and *Revolution from the Ancien Régime to the Restoration, 1750—1820*. He is currently completing a study of elections and electoral behavior during the French Revolution, *Apprenticeship in Democracy*, to be published by Cambridge University Press in 1994.

JOHN DUNNE, is Senior Lecturer in History at the School of Humanities of Thames Polytechnic in London. He is engaged in research on the transfer of wealth in France during the Revolutionary and Napoleonic eras.

MELVIN EDELSTEIN, is a Professor of History at William Paterson College of New Jersey. He received his Ph.D. from Princeton where he wrote his dissertation under the direction of R. R. Palmer. His scholarly interests are the revolutionary press, revolutionary elections and the diffusion of the Revolution to the villagers. He has published a book: *La Feuille Villageoise: Communication et Modernisation dans les Régions Rurales pendant la Révolution*. He is currently working on a book entitled *France's Apprenticeship in Citizenship: The Origins of Mass Electoral Politics During the French Revolution*.

JEANNE FUCHS, is Associate Professor of Comparative Literature and Languages at Hofstra University. She has been Associate Dean of Hofstra College of Liberal Arts and Sciences, and Director of the International Student Program at Hofstra. Dr. Fuchs has published on Alfred de Musset and on George Sand, and her monograph on Rousseau's *La Nouvelle Héloïse* will appear in 1993.

EVLYN GOULD, is Associate Professor of French at the University of Oregon. She is the author of *Virtual Theater from Diderot to Mallarmé*, and of various articles on literature and performance. The essay included in this collection represents part of a book project tentatively entitled *Bohemian Narrative*.

MARIO HAMLET-METZ, is Professor of French and Comparative Literature at James Madison University. He has published widely in the fields of nineteenth-century French literature and theater.

RICHARD HERR, is Professor Emeritus of History at the Berkely campus of the University of California where he has taught since 1960. He received his AB from Harvard and his Ph.D from the University of Chicago and also studied at the Sorbonne. He is a corresponding member of the Royal Academy of History of Madrid and has lectured at the College de France. His works include T*he Eighteenth-Century Revolution in Spain, Tocqueville and the Old Regime* and *Rural Change and Royal Finances in Spain at End of the Old Regime*.

CLAUDINE HUNTING, is Associate Professor of Modern and Classical Languages at Texas A & M University. Her publications include two books and many articles on eighteenth-century French literature, and she is currently working on editing a collection, *Women's Experience and Militancy Under the Reign of Terror in France* as well as a book on Jacques Cazotte.

GEORGE JACKSON, who took his Ph.D at Columbia's Russian Institute is Chairperson of the History Department at Hofstra University. A specialist in 20th century Soviet History, his most important publications are *Comintern and Peasant in East Europe 1919—1930* and *Dictionary of the Russian Revolution* published by Greenwood Press in 1989. He has written numerous articles and papers especially on Lenin and is currently researching a longer work on this subject.

JOHN R. JEANNENEY, received his Ph.D from Columbia University and is Associate Professor of History at Hofstra University. His research interests and publications are focused on the history of European public policies of natural resource management.

GREGORY LUDLOW, is an Associate Professor of French at George Washington University where he teaches courses on the Age of Enlightenment. He has published on such 18th century writers as Voltaire, Sébastien Mercier and Pigault-Lebrun and has presented papers at both national and international conferences on Franco-Ibero-American relations and other topics.

ERICA JOY MANNUCCI, studies the culture of the French Revolution and the relations between religious heterodoxy and esoterism, and politics in the eighteenth century. Her most recent book is *Dai cieli la ragione: Gli Illuminati dal Seicente alla Restaurazione*. She has held post-graduate seminars at the Instituto Italiano per gli Studi Filosofici of Naples, at the Labortorio Barnave in Macerata, and at the University of Haifa.

JEFFREY MEHLMAN, is Professor of French Literature at Boston University. His most recent books are *Legacies: Of Anti-Semitism in France* and *Walter Benjamin for Children: An Essay on His Radio Years*.

CATHERINE R. MONTFORT, is Associate Professor of French and Women's Studies at Santa Clara University. Her publications include books and articles in the fields of French literature and women's studies. She is the author of *Les Fortunes de Mme de Sévigné au XVIIième et au XVIIIième siècles*, and the editor of *Literate Women and the French Revolution of 1789*, forthcoming from Summa Publications.

MARILYN MORRIS, received her Ph.D from the University of London in 1988 and worked as an Assistant Editor on *The Papers of Benjamin Franklin* at the Yale University Library. Currently she is Assistant Professor of History at the University of North Texas. She is currently working on a book to be entitled *This Metaphor Called a Crown: The British Monarchy and the French Revolution*.

JULIA ORTIZ GRIFFIN, is a member of the Department of Foreign Languages at York College, the City University of New York. A native of Puerto Rico and educated there and in Spain, she received her Ph.D from New York University. Her published work includes a critical biography, (*Drama y sociedad en la obra de Benevente*), studies of Puerto Rican literature and history, and several volumes of short stories. (*Cuentos de Aqui, de Allá y de Más Allá* and *Mujeres Transplantadas*). In addition, she is an editor of the journal *Letters*, and pursues a commitment to Spanish musical drama as president of Amigos de la Zarzuela.

UFFE ØSTERGAARD, is Director of the European Studies Program at the Centre for Cultural Research at the University of Aarhus, Denmark. He has taught at the Center for European Studies, Harvard University 1984—1985; the European University Institute, Florence 1988—1990; and the Center for Historical Analysis, Rutgers University, 1990. He has published numerous articles and several books in Danish on national identity, national political cultures and nation states in Europe (*Europas ansigter*, 1992).

SONDRA M. RUBENSTEIN, holds a Ph.D in political science from Columbia University and is an Associate Professor of Communication Arts at Hofstra University. She has written *The Communist Movement in Palestine and Israel: 1919—1984*, articles for the *British Journalism Review* including "Message or Massage--The Electronic Illusion," "The Flow and Ebb of U.S. Libel Law," and "The Centrality of Opinion Polls in U.S. Politics." Her recently completed book is scheduled for publication by Wadsworth in 1994.

GABRIEL SCHOENFELD, is a Senior Fellow at the Center for Strategic and International Studies in Washington, D.C. where he is editor of the research bulletin, *Post-Soviet Prospects*. Schoenfeld has written on Russian affairs for a number of major national and foreign newspapers and magazines. In 1985, Schoenfeld was an IREX exchange scholar at Moscow University, and he has also served as a temporary foreign service officer with the USIA in an assignment that took him to Siberia, Central Asia and the Caucasus. He received his Ph.D in political science from Harvard University in 1989 and was awarded a Bradley Foundation post-doctoral Fellowship at Harvard University's Russian Research Center in 1990.

GAIL M. SCHWAB, is Associate Professor of French at Hofstra University. She has published on Flaubert and is the co-editor of the *French Revolution of 1789 and Its Impact*. Her current work is in French feminist theory and she has published on the work of French feminist philosopher Luce Irigaray.

GISLINDE SEYBERT, is Professor of French and Comparative Literature at the University of Hanover in Germany.

WILLA Z. SILVERMAN, is Assistant Professor of French at Penn State University where she teaches courses in modern French culture, society and politics. Her research focuses on the cultural and intellectual history of the Belle Epoque, and specifically, the Dreyfus Affair. Her book, *Gyp: Right-wing Anarchist at the fin du siècle* is forthcoming with Oxford University Press in 1994.

SUSAN TENENBAUM, is Assistant Professor of Political Science at Baruch College and has written numerous articles in the fields of public policy and French intellectual history. She is currently working on a book, *The Political Thought of Germaine De Staël*.

CHARLES TILLY, is Professor and Director of the Center for Studies of Social Change at the New School for Social Research. He has published extensively on social change and revolution in Europe. The long list of his books include *The Vendée, The Rebellious Century, 1830—1930* and *The Contentious French.*

MARY TROUILLE, is currently teaching French at the University of Chicago and is a specialist in eighteenth-century French literature and women's studies. She has published articles on Staël, Wollstonecraft, d'Epinay, Genlis, Diderot and Rousseau and is working on a book entitled *Sexual Politics and the Cult of Sensibility: Eighteenth-Century Women Writers Respond to Rousseau.*

PATRICIA A. WARD, is Professor of French and Chair of the Department of French and Italian at Vanderbilt University. She has also served as Dean of Arts and Sciences at Wheaton College in Illinois. Dr. Ward is the author of several books, including the *Medievalism of Victor Hugo* and *Joseph Joubert and the Critical Tradition.*

ISBN 0-313-29339-2

90000>

EAN

9 780313 293399